Security in a World of Change

Readings and Notes on International Relations

Wadsworth Series in World Politics

General Editor:
Fred Greene
Williams College

Political Modernization: A Reader in Comparative Political Change
Edited by Claude E. Welch, Jr.
State University of New York at Buffalo

On Government: A Comparative Introduction
D. George Kousoulas
Howard University

Security in a World of Change: Readings and Notes on International Relations
Edited by Lee W. Farnsworth, Brigham Young University, and Richard B. Gray, Florida State University

International Politics of Asia
Edited by George P. Jan
The University of Toledo

Security in a World of Change

Readings and Notes on International Relations

Edited by
Lee W. Farnsworth
Brigham Young University

and Richard B. Gray
Florida State University

Wadsworth Publishing Company, Inc.,
Belmont, California

L. C. Cat. Card No.: 76–80723
Printed in the United States of America

Preface

Security in a World of Change is a book of supplementary readings for the introductory course. These materials come from a variety of sources and include the work of statesmen, political leaders, scholars, and journalists. We have attempted to select articles that are readable, lively, and pertinent to an understanding of the basic concepts and conditions of international relations. The authors of these articles often speak with a bias based on their own values, interests, and stereotypes, and the student should be forewarned of this. However, if the student and the teacher will create a dialogue with these articles, using their own values and experience, we believe that they will bring forth a new feeling toward and a better understanding of the complexities of a world in change.

Two themes run through the book—change and security; nation-states invariably seek security, and just as invariably, the conditions under which they act are constantly in flux. Hopefully, these two concepts will help create an understanding of the total picture of international politics.

Most of the articles have been edited to create a blending of ideas and experiences without redundancy, superfluity, or choppiness. Footnotes have been deleted from the materials for uniformity; the original material should be consulted for further information. The bibliography at the end of the book contains recommended sources for further exploration of the themes of each chapter.

The authors worked together in preparing the material, but there was a basic division of labor: Lee Farnsworth had primary responsibility for the selection of materials and for the preparation of the introductory notes; Richard Gray served as chief editor and critic.

We are grateful to many people. The authors and publishers of the selections have been gracious in granting the necessary permissions. Fred Greene and David K. Marvin both reviewed the manuscript several times and made very helpful comments. The help of our graduate assistants and secretaries and the critical comments of our colleagues are very much appreciated. Finally, we acknowledge the assistance and guidance of the editors of Wadsworth Publishing Company, particularly Bob Gormley and Jim Sheppard. We, however, retain full responsibility for the final selections and for the editing and notes.

LWF
RBG

Contents

To Laura L. Gray and Gale Farnsworth, the two ladies who brighten our lives and lighten our cares.

Introduction

In 1945 there were fewer than half the number of nations there are today; the United States alone possessed nuclear weapons; the Soviet Union was an American ally; and the world looked forward to an era of peace and security. On V-J Day one newspaper carried a full page advertisement showing two preschool children gazing at the sunrise. The caption read: "It's all right, kids; there's a bright new world ahead."

But the world of 1969 is different from the world of 1945. The optimist can point to a few bright spots: the success of the Marshall Plan in rebuilding Europe, including vanquished Germany; the economic resurgence of a peaceful Japan; the creation and expansion of such international economic organizations for world development as the International Monetary Fund, the Common Market, and the Inter-American Development Bank; and the success of the world community in combatting disease. All these changes, however, though they have promoted both national and international security, have taken place in the midst of the cold war. The mutual hostility of the world's two great powers has left in its wake mistrust and fear and has led occasionally to hot wars—in Korea and Vietnam, on the Indian subcontinent, in the deserts of the Middle East, and on an island in the Mediterranean.

Even as they profess peace and cooperation to be the basic goals of their foreign policies, nations wage wars. Inevitably, peace and cooperation become secondary goals whenever a nation thinks that it perceives a threat to its vital interests—particularly its security, whether territorial, economic, or ideological. No matter how sincere a nation's pursuit of peace and cooperation, its foreign policy will be far more profoundly shaped by whatever it conceives to be its vital national interests; the first concern of any nation is its own survival.

Complicating the efforts of nations to protect their interests is the pace of change in the modern world. New interests and, more importantly, new possible threats are constantly arising out of changes in the international scheme of things. Many of these changes are qualitative—new nations, new leaders, new forms and bases of power. But many of the most dangerous changes are quantitative—more people, more ideologies, more weapons. Change of both kinds is one of the major themes of this book and of Chapter One of the book in particular. In that chapter the basic concepts of international relations—the basic vital interests of nations—are explored in the context of change.

Chapter Two investigates foreign policies built on the basic concepts of international relations. Again it is important to keep in mind the context—change. In the face of change, both the statement and the practice of foreign policy often lack resilience. Indeed, sadly, it frequently seems that the ability to recognize and accommodate to change is accounted a sign of national weakness.

In the midst of change, nations seek security, the first and most important of national interests. Security, however, may be sought in two ways—through national power or through international order. Historical precedents indicate that the desire for security through international order evolves only in the face of a common power threat. Thus, the individual interests of the separate states have generally driven them to seek security alone, a fact evidenced by the collapse of the Holy Alliance in nineteenth century Europe and by the failures of both the League of Nations and the United Nations in the twentieth century. The balance of power system replaced the Holy Alliance, and the loose bipolar power system has replaced contemporary world organization but has failed so far in bringing security to the twentieth century world.

The struggle for power, the subject of Chapter Three, threatens the security of other nations and, therefore, has led to a continuous series of wars and armaments races. For over twenty years the United States and the Soviet Union have been locked in what Dean Rusk calls "eyeball to eyeball" conflict, waiting for "the other fellow to blink." The rationale behind the creation and continuation of this "war," as for other wars, has been the security of the nations involved.

The tools of the cold war have been the steady and deadly rise in the quantity and quality of weaponry and its strategic placement in the world as well as the torrent of vituperations and charges that have filled the record books in the United Nations. The war that has been prepared for is not, ironically, the war that is being fought, and the power amassed for greater wars is unsuited for fighting lesser ones.

The cold and hot wars of our time have caused increasing numbers of people to question the purposes of war and the inevitability of another world war. Forms of international order, discussed in Chapter Four, seem to create greater possibilities than do wars for world security and have been gradually gaining in impetus and support. The establishment of governments based upon law succeeded in bringing security on the nation-state level. Similarly, men are asking for creation of international security through world government based on world law. The world has been trying for more than twenty years to utilize international organizations (rather than national government) to promote mutual security. The United Nations has promoted cooperation and refereed disputes. In the sphere of cooperation, it has had the most success, but that has been most often outside the area of national security.

Regional organization for the purpose of regional security has been found superior in many ways to world organization. On this level changes seem to be away from military defense organizations such as NATO toward establishment of economic ties of the Common Market type. The entire structure of international organization remains unsettled, however, and the realization of this intermediate goal of regional security requires considerably more diplomatic effort.

The accelerating pace of international trade and investment is evidence of the continuing drive for security through bilateral and multilateral national efforts. Adjustment and adaptation to these steps are often necessary in the face of the fear that they will endanger the economic or military security of the state. The uneven acceptance by the American leaders and people of both general tariff reductions and trade expansion into Eastern Europe is evidence of this caution, as is the hesitancy with which cooperation in the development of the sea (and shortly of space) is undertaken.

Foreign aid has been one of the most confusing attempts to promote order. The Marshall Plan achieved greater American security by increasing European economic stability. This program was undertaken under optimum conditions for assistance—skills available, motivation, steady level of population, and stable government—and could be expected to achieve optimum results. Aid has not been given or received under optimum conditions since that time. Donors have been less convinced that their security was directly involved, and recipients have very often had fewer skills, lower motivation, rapid population growth, and unstable governments. These facts have led to changes in the quantity and quality of aid. The wars of this half of the century are occurring predominantly in the less developed areas of the world and pose a threat to security and stability everywhere. The cost of seeking security in these regions through aid may ultimately be lower than the cost through war.

Chapter Five asks whether peace will come only through joint exercise of the overwhelming power of the United States and the Soviet Union or whether it will come through a recognition of the universal brotherhood of man. Many years ago a British statesman returned from Munich to proclaim "peace in our time." We have still not lived to see it. Pope John XXIII stirred the consciences and hopes of men in 1963 with his *Pacem in Terris* (Peace on Earth) encyclical. But did this affect the behavior of nation-states? The United Nations has proved itself even more ineffective in either preserving or effecting peace since that time. The two great powers have not achieved noticeable conciliation. And refugees of Vietnam and Jerusalem pay moot tribute to the continuing failure of nations to take into account the "human factor." John F. Kennedy's "watchmen on the walls of world freedom" still watch in vain for "the ancient vision of peace on earth, goodwill toward men."

Chapter One

Change and the basic concepts

Security is essentially a condition of not fearing for one's life or property, presently or in the future. National security is much the same as personal security—fearing for neither the life of the nation's people nor its territorial possessions. Security lies at the root of most nation-state behavior. A nation's primary purpose is to "provide for the common defense" of its people, and its second purpose, "to promote the general welfare," is also one of security—economic security. The ferment of the youth of most Western and even many Communist nations is evidence that the kind of security that brings confidence and tranquillity is still a distant dream.

An understanding of the drive for security is based on an understanding of certain basic concepts of international relations. Those this chapter will deal with are nationalism, sovereignty, power, national interests, ideology, imperialism, and change. In the drive for security, individuals and communities have formally established themselves into nation-states, and nationalism has been established in an effort to place the security of the state above all other values. Nationalism appears in many forms and intensities, but it always includes the characteristics of placing the interests of the nation-state above all other interests and demanding the individual's highest loyalty.

In Europe, the birthplace of modern nationalism, the changing security environment is causing reconsiderations about traditional nationalism. In both the economic and the military sphere, Europe feels threatened by the overwhelming power of both the United States and the Soviet Union. In reaction to this common threat, six nations of Western Europe have taken several steps toward the creation of a supranational entity—the European Coal and Steel Community, the European Atomic Energy Commission, and the European Economic Community.

In the area which George Lensen has termed "the world beyond Europe," nationalism is emerging in its more traditional form in a vibrant (and in some instances violent) rebirth after years or centuries of dormancy. The nation-states of Asia, Africa, and Latin America are laboratories of nationalism in flux. Fanned by the flames of anticolonialism but now increasingly focusing on the nation's military and economic security, these nations are experiencing a strong drive toward national identity and integrity. The selections by Ways and Scalapino are directed toward the understanding of nationalism in flux in Europe and Asia.

Among the other concepts which influence the nation-state in the drive for security are sovereignty, power, ideology, and national interests. Of these, sovereignty is the most difficult to define. The traditional definition of sovereignty as a condition of independence from any higher authority and of ability to enter freely into international agreements is increasingly questioned. It is now fashionable to speak of degrees of sovereignty. Thus, the United States and the Soviet Union, possessors of the veto in the U.N. Security Council and wielders of great national power, are more sovereign than are Nigeria and Afghanistan, which have neither veto privileges nor great power. The ability to make decisions in international matters and to execute them is the sliding measure that is currently applied to sovereignty among nations. There is also a current effort to transfer the locus of sovereignty from the national to a higher, supranational level, such as the Common Market. Both the definition and the locus of sovereignty are discussed in the selections by Melville and Cousins. A Soviet view of sovereignty is presented by Piradov.

Whereas sovereignty confers the right to act, power is the ability to act, and whereas sovereignty is something to be secured, power is the means by which security can be achieved. Power and sovereignty are referred to by Professor Fred Warner Neal as the dual cornerstones of the nation-state system. Power, the ability to influence others to think or act in ways beneficial to one's own state, can only be understood and measured in relation to the power of other nations or groups of nations. This ability to influence emanates not from a single source, such as military strength, but from a variety of sources, including material wealth, natural resources, geographical location, demographic resources, and scientific and technological advancement.

The sources of national power and the utilization of this power seem to be undergoing a change in contemporary international relations. For example, the United States, with its great military power, is experiencing great difficulty in Vietnam—a difficulty that is explored in the article by Halle. Seaborg, in his article, suggests that the power of scientific and technological advancement is the power of the future and that this power, properly controlled, will create an interdependence of nations and help to establish new international relationships. Power in this sense will be used by and for all mankind to bring security through joint human progress and peaceful cooperation.

In the present world, however, power is still normally used to achieve national interests, another of the concepts basic to an understanding of the drive for security. Security of territory and national independence are the most basic of national interests, for no others are so critical or so directly related to national security. It is customary for a nation to utilize its full military, economic, technological, and social bases of power to repel aggression against its territory, but it would be surprising to see a nation fully mobilize in like manner to obtain trading concessions or special overseas privileges for its citizens. These secondary national interests are generally negotiable and not rational causes for drastic measures.

National interests not only vary in intensity but also fluctuate over time. If America has interests in Korea and Vietnam that are defensible by war, they were not visibly extant in the late 1940s. Similarly, Great Britain's former interests in colonial power and naval superiority, interests which were linked to her security, no longer exist in their vital form because of the changing world power structure. They have become secondary in what Austin, in his article, calls an "upside down" commonwealth. For a number of years, a debate has been raging over the degree of U.S. interest in Panama. Senators Fulbright and Thurmond give differing views of this dispute. Their debate makes clear that most national interests and their degree of importance are self-determined and limited only by the power available to achieve them.

National interests are not always enlightened interests, rationally based upon the changed conditions. Although military security might at times decree otherwise, not only enlightened interests but also a clear statement of those interests and of their relative degrees of importance might eliminate international misunderstandings which lead to wars and economic conflicts.

Ideology, the systematic rationale for national policies and aims, is another concept that influences international behavior and the drive for national security. The world's many ideologies—fascism, communism, socialism, democracy, and so on—have names and tenable organizational and theoretical characteristics, but these characteristics are not immune to change. There are inevitably several types and versions of all ideologies. For example, the Sino-Soviet feud, at least on the surface, is one largely based on differences in communist ideology. In fact, most policy statements of the Communist nations are reiterations of each one's ideological point of view (see the Soviet and Chinese views in Chapter Two, for instance). Under the surface of this ideological dispute, there is evidence of more practical conflicts over power and sovereignty and over the problem of security on the Sino-Soviet border, the world's longest.

There are similar disputes over forms of democratic ideology. The thesis of the Manglapus article is that the friends of the United States in the developing world have differences in interests, hopes, and cultural backgrounds that require a slightly different road to democracy from that taken by America. The article is a plea for U.S. support rather than control, for an understanding by the United States that the developing nations must be allowed to travel independently through the adolescence of nationhood.

Imperialism is another important concept influencing the security of nation-states. A brief definition of imperialism is the control of the sovereignty of one nation by another through the application of superior power by the latter—regardless of the will of the former. Ironically, nationalism has formed the roots of imperialism. In the Age of Imperialism, the European nationalistic drive for wealth and power led to colonial expansion. In the mid-twentieth century, the process has seemed to reverse itself; the new nationalism of the Asian and African peoples has been built on the largely negative root of anti-imperialism.

Imperialism in its most recent form, called neocolonialism, is a more subtle and less discernible form of international meddling and manipulation than the traditional imperialism of military occupation and colonial government. There are other ways to influence the behavior of another nation besides direct political and military control. The Soviet Union has been accused of imperialistic control and exploitation of the Eastern European nations through the devices of the Communist party and ideology. The Soviet resort to military imperialism in Czechoslovakia in 1968 was due to a failure of political imperialism to achieve its goals. The United States has been accused of control of the policies of the Latin American states through massive economic and military aid. A resume of a United Nations debate, presented in Section 6 of this chapter, illustrates the nature of these charges and the continuing confusion over the extent of modern imperialism. Imperialism is dealt with less directly in several articles in each of the succeeding chapters, which should be consulted for enrichment. See especially the articles by the various communist contributors; *imperialism* is a key word in their vocabulary.

The drive for national security and all the other basic concepts must, of course, be examined in the context of change—how they themselves change and how they adapt to change. One of the few certainties of international relations—a certainty too often ignored in crucial national decisions—is that change occurs. Today's diplomats, most often products of the experience and education of a former era, must constantly strive for flexibility to keep up with changes in both the concepts and the conditions of contemporary international relations.

Changes of remarkable depth have occurred in the past decade. In technology alone there has been more change in this short period than in the entire prior history of the field. Communications satellites are now capable of broadcasting television and radio signals to the entire world, a development that has irrevocably altered the meaning of borders as inviolable barriers. Such events as the funerals of Martin Luther King, Jr., and Senator Robert F. Kennedy are now viewed internationally. The Olympics, too, now has an international audience and immediate international implications in terms of prestige and honor for the nations and athletes involved. As a result of this revolution in communications, diplomats are now in constant touch with decision-makers in their own nations, and all the resources of their governments are at their disposal in negotiations. The computer has introduced a revolution single-handedly. Decisions are made faster and more accurately, and space vehicles are tracked and controlled. These are only two of the myriads of recent peaceful technical advances.

In the armaments field technical changes have made the world an unimaginably more dangerous place to live in. Intercontinental ballistic missiles and satellite launching pads have become the new military reality, so that natural barriers of seas or mountains or conventionally trained and armed military forces have suddenly lost meaning as effective security devices. The entire field of "power politics" has been turned topsy-turvy as the Viet Cong successfully resist the United States and Czechoslovakia stubbornly attempts to move toward reform despite the wishes of the Soviet Union.

Many states continue to behave as if nuclear arms did not exist. Often too little consideration is given to the potential power of satellite communication on world opinion. A nation's policy-making apparatus does not realistically incorporate the changing power positions of other states. These changes have only inconsistently altered international relations. Brzezinski's article is an example of how one scholar-statesman has taken the real and potential changes in international politics and sought an understanding of their implications. In the concluding selection Baker, a columnist known for his humorous commentary on contemporary events, has used a "man in a time-machine" to portray the changes in both the world situation and human attitudes.

Section 1

Nationalism in flux

Europe's new nationalism

Max Ways

What effects have the Common Market, NATO, De Gaulle, and the new liberalism of international communism had on European nationalism? Mr. Ways analyzes the effects and suggests that nationalism is dynamic and adjusts to and accompanies economic, social, and political progress.

Whatever Charles de Gaulle is restlessly seeking cannot be the gratitude of the U.S. Yet the American public in the long run may have good reasons to thank him for his recent disruptions. This year he put Europe back into U.S. headlines—where it belongs. Though the war is in Vietnam, though the Communist opportunity, diminished but still great, lies mainly in the under-developed continents, Europe remains an area of critical importance. If Europe falters or if its relations with the U.S. become seriously diseased, then deterioration everywhere may overtake the effort to build a peaceful and progressive international order.

No deep-seated, inexorable rot affects the North Atlantic Alliance. It remains the strongest, closest, most successful peacetime association ever formed among free nations. In a fast-moving world, however, success has special perils. Without a De Gaulle in center stage, there was danger that public opinion would assume U.S.-European relations to have been "settled." The Europe to which the U.S. public eye now returns is different from the Europe of the years when the Alliance was formed. The health of the Alliance requires a sharper U.S. understanding of the actual Europe of 1966.

De Gaulle's abrupt decision to withdraw French forces from NATO's integrated command and to eject Allied troops from France—unwise and wrongheaded as it is in the NATO military context—was made in the name of France's sacred national sovereignty. The bizarre tactics he employs are products of his complex personality; but his dramatic action calls attention to the impersonal fact that nationalism, in a new sense, is an important and rising element in the Europe—East and West—of 1966. . . .

De Gaulle's antique rhetoric

When nationalism raises its voice in Western Europe, particularly in De Gaulle's antique rhetoric, Americans tend to hear it as the atavistic call of Europe's disordered past. At the same time, Americans quite accurately recognize the growing nationalism of *Eastern* European countries as a progressive movement that gives their peoples a significant measure of national freedom from Communist "integration." Obviously, the North Atlantic Treaty and the Warsaw Pact are not similar instruments. The inhibitions that treaties of cooperation impose on freely contracting governments of free peoples are politically and morally different from the denials of national freedom imposed on Eastern Europe by the Red Army and maintained by Communist police states. Yet U.S. policy appears awkwardly inconsistent when it deplores nationalism in Western Europe while applauding it in Eastern Europe.

Communists, Gaullists, and other U.S.–baiters cynically attribute this inconsistency to a selfish American desire to keep Western Europe weak. Americans can let 20 years of successful U.S. contribution to the reinvigoration of Western Europe answer that charge. But the U.S. does need to look anew at how its postwar policy objectives for Europe came to be so firmly pinned to a particular kind of European integration, which now seems in conflict with European nationalism.

The vision of an integrated Europe that took shape after the war was heavily influenced by the belief that the nation-state had been permanently disabled from becoming again the main framework of Europe's political life.

Instead, the European peoples would federate under some supranational governmental organs. Ideas about the kind and degree of integration differed, but, significantly, the phrase "the United States of Europe" was often used—and is still used—in referring to this "grand design."

Things have not worked out that way. Europe's nationalism revived strongly enough to reject a series of U.S.-sponsored schemes for military integration from EDC (the European Defense Community) to MLF (the Multilateral Force). Moves toward explicitly supranational political organs such as a European parliament have ground to a halt. Western Europe's governments have displayed considerable competence in dealing with an enlarged range of affairs now considered national in scope. Whether or not they deserve it, these governments get a large measure of credit from their citizens for Europe's rapid economic and social progress. Perhaps more significant, national governments are regarded as giving a measure of cohesion to countries in the throes of bewildering social change. Revived confidence in "the nation" has been a factor in the precipitous decline of an extranational ideology, Communism, in Western Europe.

Limits sovereignty

In these circumstances one might expect to find the cause of integration completely stultified. But such is far from the case. In some respects, the leveling of Western Europe's national economic barriers has moved further and faster than the fondest hopes of the late forties thought possible. The European Economic Community (the Common Market) operates by legal arrangements that seriously limit the scope of national sovereignty in the six member nations. The Common Market has strong popular support; De Gaulle's seven-month "strike" against it almost cost him the 1965 elections. Few in Europe today believe that the integrationist trend represented by EEC and EFTA, the looser European Free Trade Association, will be reversed. In purely political affairs, too, rivalry between Western European nations has abated. Though NATO is now in crisis, it has achieved a degree of peacetime political and military cooperation unknown in Europe's past.

In short, Western Europe refused to choose between nationalism and integration. It chose both.

This could not have happened if today's nationalism in Europe was a recurrence of the divisive, absolutist brand of prewar nationalism. In fact, the "new" nationalism has many different qualities from the "old." They have in common the tendency to look upon the nation-state as the main theatre of political action, and to identify it with the character and destiny of "the people." But the two kinds of nationalism are separated by the enormous gulf that divides the economic, social, and psychological conditions of postwar Europe from those of prewar Europe. . . .

Europe, in opting for both nationalism and integration, is not consciously imitating the U.S. and the U.S. is not "leading" Europe along this path. Nevertheless, trends in the internal politics of European nations begin to show characteristics similar to those of internal U.S. politics. Within nearly all European countries regional differences are diminishing. Even more striking is the decline of class struggle, ideological conflict, and religious rivalry. For example, the Socialist Party in West Germany a few years ago formally renounced Marxism as its official philosophy. Since then, the party seems to be attracting more white-collar people who do not think of themselves as working class and who do not like class-structured politics. Meanwhile, as Marxism declines, the "Christian" parties of Germany, Italy, and France are shedding their original character as shields against Marxism. Europeans, who have been bewildered for decades by the low ideological content of U.S. parties, are themselves moving toward similar broad political groupings, which attempt through "consensus politics" to deal with national problems created by economic and social change.

National choice

The new opportunities for individual and social progress that now open before the advanced nations gives them a sense that they must make choices. In all of the Western nations most choices are being made by individuals and nongovernmental organizations operating through markets. But national governments everywhere are expected to have important roles in these conscious choices of what kind of society a nation wants to be. In the U.S., President Johnson has responded by urging the nation to aspire toward "the Great Society." West Germany's Premier Erhard has suggested that Germans give thought to "the shaped society." France has "Le Plan," which sustains national morale by giving the French people the sense that they have some collective influence over economic change. These levers of choice are all aspects of the "new" nationalism.

The growing sense of national choice militates against the possibility that the scope and prestige of national governments, in Europe or elsewhere, will wither away. But while it precludes transference of power to political organs *above* the nations, it does not prevent the development of strong ties of cooperative action *among* the nations. The latter is precisely what has been developing in the Atlantic Community. The U.S., if it understands the new nationalism, will cease to suspect Europe of trying to turn back the clock. Europe, in turn, may eventually stop suspecting the U.S. of nationalist and imperialist self-seeking. If we exorcised these ghosts from the past that now trouble North Atlantic relations we would be better able to deal with certain serious causes of friction that arise from the new situation. Because technology and its management are now seen by the advanced Western nations as the keys to progress, the huge U.S. lead in both these fields gives rise not only to emulation but to jealousy among its European competitor-partners. Much of the latent anti-Americanism in Western Europe, which De Gaulle expresses, arises from the feeling that the U.S. presence looms so large that it thwarts the desire of European countries to feel that they are in control of their own future.

The nuclear dilemma

Certain fundamental facts causing imbalance within the Atlantic Alliance cannot be radically changed. Western nuclear power, necessary to protect Western Europe, resides preponderantly in the U.S. There is no practical possibility that Western Europe could "catch up" in nuclear power even if it wished to do so. No wholly satisfactory plan for redistributing political control of nuclear power on an "equal" basis among the Allies has ever been put forward—and none may be possible. Meanwhile, pretenses of equality, such as the Multilateral Force proposal, do more harm than good.

The existing framework of NATO cooperation has not failed—and should not be allowed to disintegrate. Most Western Europeans prefer it to any other system now in sight. The policy task is to preserve the essentials of the present NATO system while taking the utmost pains to minimize the damage to European national sensitivity and morale that arises from the ineradicable imbalance of power. U.S. spokesmen sometimes disregard this special need for keeping the American preponderance as unobtrusive as possible. Robert S. McNamara, respected among knowledgeable Europeans, is frequently cited by the same Europeans as an irritant. He once announced a change in NATO strategic concepts in a University of Michigan speech not seen in advance by members of Allied governments. This summer he *publicly* twisted the arm of the West German Government on behalf of increased weapons purchase from the U.S. to offset balance-of-payments problems created by American troops in Germany. The objective was valid, but the method tends to hurt German national pride and—more pointedly—to damage the prestige of German politicians in the eyes of their own people. . . .

Light limited in the East

The new nationalism can be seen in Eastern Europe, too. Viewed from the West, its virtues there are obvious because it represents a setback for Communist ideology and Russian imperialism. Such national independence as the Eastern European "former satellites" have achieved is limited and, perhaps, ephemeral. Nevertheless, this independence, which offers opportunities to

Western policy, could not have developed unless there had been a relaxation in the "integration" of the Western bloc.

Rising national independence in the West and in the East restores the possibility of national initiative and maneuver underneath the nuclear umbrella. Bilateral trade deals and cultural exchange agreements between nations have been worked out, whereas a formal agreement between the two blocs would have proved impossible. The Iron Curtain has become a grillwork, open at a hundred points. Considering Western vigor and progress and Eastern Europe's relative stagnation, expanding East-West contact must surely offer more political advantage to the West.

In retrospect we can see the significance of the fact that Tito, though a thoroughgoing Communist, broke with Stalin's Kremlin on grounds of protecting Yugoslavia's national dignity and independence. After the Poznan riots in Poland and the Hungarian rebellion, Khrushchev pursued a line much more respectful to Eastern European nationalism. This more tolerant policy has not prevented a stubborn refusal by the Rumanian Communist Government to submit to too much "integration." Rumania's exports (mainly oil) were earning hard currency, which the central economic planners of the satellite bloc (COMECON) thought might be more efficiently used to help Rumania's Communist neighbors. It did not seem so to Rumania's rulers. Although dedicated Communists, they saw this issue in national terms; they decided to defy COMECON—and Moscow. Subsequently, the Rumanian Government extended its noncooperation from economics to other fields. It has embarrassed its Warsaw Pact allies by reducing its period of military conscription from 24 to 16 months; it has refused to participate in joint Warsaw Pact training maneuvers. Rumania's new nationalism is, in fact, distinctly unmilitarist. . . .

The Soviet Union, of course, can squash the Rumanian national defiance any time it wishes—but it can do so only by the use of military force. The Rumanian Communists calculate that, in view of the USSR's conflict with Red China, in view of its recent wooing of the errant Tito, in view of the generally unhappy state of Communist Eastern Europe, Moscow will continue to refrain from this step. Rumanian brinkmanship is played cautiously. And from time to time, Rumania's leaders express a ritual solidarity with the Communist world.

Will liberalization work?

In other Eastern European countries there is a restless striving for policies that vary from the standard Communist package. Hungarian and Czech Communist leaders have adopted (on paper) programs of economic liberalization. Not even on the editorial pages of the *Wall Street Journal* can one find more bitter denunciation of central economic planning than those now current among Czech and Hungarian Communist intellectuals. They point out specific mistakes of planners: overconcentration on heavy industry, shoddy products, lack of technological advance, worker inefficiency. Agriculture, as is usual in Communist countries, is in the worst mess.

The reformers hope that competition through markets will bring cost cutting, product improvement, better worker discipline, and a spirit of innovation. They associate their reforms with the hope of increased trade with the West. If their liberalized economies become more efficient they could, they believe, export competitively to Western markets; meanwhile, these countries seek credits for capital goods. . . .

An economic system of markets without private capitalism must still depend on central planning to close the link between consumption and investment. If the consumer market beckons a factory manager in one direction and the planners, who control resources, move him in another, the manager may be more helpless, more confused, and less innovative than he was under complete central planning. But should the economic reforms in the Communist world fall short, this would pose no hard problems for Western political policy. Whether liberalization works or not, the experiment will almost certainly stimulate a gradual weakening of tight Communist control.

Communism has failed

The overriding fact about the present condition of the "former satellites" is that Communism has conspicuously failed to fulfill the aspirations of the peoples for national progress. All over the world this fact dampens the effectiveness of the Communist appeal. Zbigniew Brzezinski, a former Columbia professor now serving the U.S. State Department as a member of the Policy Planning Council, has summed it up: "Europe is where the dream of Communist internationalism lies buried."

Although Communism has lost momentum it has not lost the power to defend the positions it holds when they are directly assaulted. In recent years the West has recognized that the direct pressure exercised by the NATO Alliance was unlikely to force the USSR to agree to a reunification of Germany. Partition of Germany remains the most serious specific issue between the USSR and the West—an issue dangerous to Europe's future health.

The growing importance of nationalism and the corresponding decline of tight "bloc strategy"—East and West—offers a new kind of hope for solution of "the German problem." As the USSR recognizes the claims of nationalism in Eastern Europe it should find greater and greater difficulty in denying the German right to national unity.

To sum up, Europe's new nationalism offers more advantage than danger for the true goals of U.S. policy. Future relations between the U.S. and its European Allies—and the relations of the Allies to one another—are probably going to be much more troubled than they were in the fifties. Certain simplicities of the Cold War period will remain—and the essential Western alliance will need to stay intact to deal with any possible reactivation of the Soviet threat to Europe. But in a more complex way Europe's basic economic and social trends are creating a kind of political framework that can also work for the West.

Everywhere in the world rising nationalism is linked to the demands of peoples for progress and with the need to deal politically with the problems created by progress. Viewed in this way, the new nationalism offers opportunity for a whole new range of U.S. policies—including both the reinforcement of the political and economic integration that comes naturally, and support for prideful sovereignties that seek to adjust to progress in their own way.

Nationalism in Asia: Reality and myth

Robert A. Scalapino

Nationalism in Asia is as vibrant and "new" as is European nationalism. It remains personalistic and elitist in nature, not yet reaching into and assimilating all ethnic and racial minorities. Nationalism is truly in flux in Asia, as it is in most developing societies.

Orbis, *Winter 1967. Reprinted by permission of* Orbis, *a quarterly journal of world affairs published by the Foreign Policy Research Institute of the University of Pennsylvania;* *Mr. Scalapino is a professor of political science at the University of California, Berkeley, and the author of numerous articles and books on Asian international and national politics.*

Nationalism is the strongest single political force currently operative in Asia. For most Asian communities, this is an era of nation-building, in which the primary objectives are far from being attained. Thus, it is only natural that nationalist symbols have been given high priority. This is true, moreover, across a broad ideological and institutional spectrum. Communist states, indeed, have been among the most powerfully affected.

Having made these points, one can assert with equal validity that the influence of nationalism in the contemporary Far East is frequently exaggerated, and its true character often misunderstood. What is the content of Asian nationalism at this point? The negative elements remain formidable, possibly commanding. Understandably, the Asian nationalist movement emerged largely as a reaction to the threat or reality of Western domination. It represented another instance of borrowing a Western concept to fight against Western control. The anti-Western element has not vanished. It is to be found at many levels within the complex social structure of Asian states. . . .

The peasant—still the foremost representative of the Asian common man—can undoubtedly be mobilized against "the West" under some circumstances. He probably has had no personal contact with the foreigner. (Even in Japan, at the close of the Occupation era, a survey indicated that less than 10 per cent of the Japanese had ever come in contact with an American, despite the fact that for several years more than a million Americans had been resident in the country.) . . .

Peasant disturbances throughout the colonial era were primarily the result of economic or social issues concerning the immediate community, and they rarely generated bona fide political movements of any duration. Politics, more than ever, became an urban—essentially capital city—phenomenon, progressively involving a new literate, Westernized elite fundamentally separated from the countryside in every respect. By the end of the colonial period, the political gap between city and rural areas had grown much wider.

A few nationalist movements sought to bridge that gap. The Chinese communists built a politico-military revolution on the concept of "surrounding the cities" by using a peasant-based organization, albeit one tightly controlled by "proletarianized" intellectuals who were themselves the products of an urbanized higher education. In India, Gandhi also utilized the technique of "surrounding the cities," appealing in more genuine (and less realistic) fashion to the traditional mores of the peasants via such concepts as cottage industries. It is debatable, however, whether the peasant was effectively molded into a "nationalist" by either of these movements.

In truth, the *institutionalization* of nationalism is still unaccomplished throughout most of Asia. Japan is a notable exception. Elsewhere, nationalism rests upon highly personalized grounds, and most new political institutions of a national type remain weak. Unquestionably, at the mass level at least, the most successful method of advancing national consciousness at this stage remains the cult of personality. To millions of Indian peasants, Nehru *was* India. For vast numbers of rural and urban Indonesians, Sukarno alone made the concept of Indonesia meaningful. Chairman Mao's picture has replaced ancient family idols in millions of Chinese peasant homes, and the cult of Maoism has been raised to absurd heights. In the absence of a modern socio-economic infrastructure and in the midst of new political experimentation, is there a more promising route?

It is for this reason that the monarchical institution, when it can be successfully wedded to the nation-building process, has still proven extremely useful, even in the twentieth century. The cases of Japan, Thailand, Cambodia, Nepal, Sikkim and Bhutan are examples. . . . In a period of bewildering change, the peasant clings to traditional symbols of authority, or acceptable substitutions for these. The transferral of loyalty to a new set of impersonal institutions and procedures—to a new political culture—is obviously a vastly more complex undertaking, one requiring not decades but generations. . . .

At the mass level, therefore, Asian nationalism depends strongly on personalization in most emerging states. Hence, the movement is politically fragile. Premature death (Aung San of Burma comes to mind) or massive failure (the deep troubles of Mao and Sukarno) may drastically transform the political environment, with instability resulting no matter how extensive the organizational undergirding. The first-generation political elite is usually highly politicized, strongly ideological, and its top leader possesses striking charismatic qualities. A second- or third-generation elite is frequently more administrative than political, more pragmatic than ideological, and more trained in and committed to tasks of social and economic engineering. Only with this latter group does the institutionalization of nationalism truly begin.

Thus, at this point in Asian development—irrespective of the precise institutional forms—the primary political principle in operation is one of tutelage, and the political style of the elite . . . determines the character of the polity. The range of guidance possible, through the use of modern techniques of persuasion and coercion, may be wide but it is not limitless. For example, few if any new states have been able to prevent serious internal disturbances connected with economic and socio-political problems. To understand the nature of these disturbances, especially the latter type, we must explore in further detail some aspects of current Asian nationalism.

Spontaneous or near-spontaneous racial disturbances are commonplace throughout Asia, but these incidents are almost never directed against the white man. Overwhelmingly, they involve Asian against Asian—providing one illustration of the fragile nature of the area's political communities. Many incidents in Southeast Asia involve "indigenous" people against the overseas Chinese—notably in Indonesia and Malaysia, although there have been frequent manifestations also in the Philippines, Viet Nam and Thailand. As is well known, the roots of this problem are both economic and cultural, since the Chinese dominate the commerce and many other economic functions of the society, and also maintain their cultural identity with remarkable tenacity. . . .

A profound separation creating many crises and a deep sense of hostility also exists between ethnic majorities and "the hills people" who still occupy vast areas of Asia. Discrimination, major cultural differences and the struggle for authority all prevail. . . .

Apart from ethnic or racial divisions, strong regional attachments constitute a powerful force affecting the political behavior of the Asian "common man." . . . Local authority, moreover, be it traditional or modern, secular or religious, continues to play the dominant role in a significant number of cases.

In truth, nationalism, if defined as a sense of and prior commitment to the nation-state, is largely confined to the urban, better educated classes. At this stage, it is a goal not a reality. . . .

The phenomenon of national communism in Asia deserves special attention. It is unquestionably true that statism has penetrated more deeply in societies like those of Mainland China, North Korea, and—to a lesser extent—North Viet Nam, where organization and ideology have been directed toward controlling every citizen. While certain events in these societies suggest that we may have overestimated the effectiveness of communist organizational techniques, these peoples are without doubt more conscious of the state and its purposes than many other Asians. Once again, however, the primary impact of nationalism has been upon the political elite, causing a profound shift in policies and even in ideology.

While the average Chinese citizen may have a sense of the nation and its goals, his local and regional commitments remain stronger and the nation to him is likely to be personalized via Mao Tse-tung. It is the political elite that have truly grasped the vision of nationalism. As a result, while professing Marxism-Leninism, they have adopted both the vocabulary and the policies of nineteenth-century Europe. Words like sovereignty, patriotism, Fatherland, autonomy and self-sufficiency have become dominant in the writings of Asian communist leaders, especially those in power. These leaders, moreover, have begun to develop economic and political programs in line with such concepts. On the domestic front, the cult of personality is combined with a patriotic literature no different in its primary thrust from that pioneered by the Western nationalists. Economic programs are structured in highly nationalist terms, self-sufficiency being the primary objective. . . .

In internal politics, nationalism has tended to push post-independence leaders in the direction of asserting both political and cultural positions in the name of the ethnic majority. In this phase of the nation-building experiment, minority interests are generally being given scant attention—except as these can be protected by corruption, inefficiency or the remoteness of the minorities involved. At the same time, however, most first-generation independence leaders in Asia have been "Westernized," as a result of foreign or foreign-supervised higher education, to the extent that they are separated from their people, including the dominant ethnic group of which they are a part. Consequently, they face a unique problem of identity.

In no small measure, this accounts for the fierce love-hate attitude displayed by many of the elite toward the West. On the one hand, they cherish a number of Western values, political and otherwise. On the other hand, jealousy, frustration and, above all, an ultrasensitivity to questions of acceptance and prestige create in them emotions of bitterness, suspicion and anger. . . .

Nevertheless, it is important to make a basic distinction between these attitudes and the simple, primitive xenophobia, the embers of which still burn at mass levels. These two emotional forces can be united for political purposes on occasion, but a meaningful, continuous relationship is not possible.

This is all the more true because most political elites view Western aid as highly desirable. In this connection, another extensive area of ambivalence is revealed. The expression of elitist nationalism in foreign policy frequently takes the form of nonalignment, or, as an alternative, willingness to accept exceedingly limited responsibility for the world scene. . . .

However, the period when Asian nationalism was called upon for limited commitments and little accountability is drawing to a close. A much more hardheaded attitude on the part of the West—probably including the Soviet-East European bloc—lies ahead. It is conceivable that this will exacerbate elitist mass relations in Asia rather than solidifying them. Certainly, it will force a number of unpleasant decisions upon the political elite throughout the area. None of this is to suggest that the age of Western aid or Western-Asian cooperation is over. On the contrary, it is entirely possible that the trends indicated may make such activities far more worthwhile and vital than in the past. A new psychological-political foundation will have to be built—one harmonizing the attitudes and policies of both sides.

In summary, we can assert that Asian nationalism, despite certain projections into the mass level, remains essentially an elitist phenomenon. With the exception of Japan, the nation-building process is incomplete everywhere, and in some societies it has scarcely begun. Grass-roots political activity, therefore, can be mounted at the national level only by aggregating local and regional commitments, playing upon traditional sentiments, and keeping the national spotlight on a Father-figure. . . .

The political elite, themselves somewhat ambivalent bearers of the nationalist banner, are well aware of these facts. In a variety of ways, they are seeking to cultivate the nationalist myth and thereby strengthen the foundations of the embryonic states now struggling to survive. Only occasionally do traditional institutions such as a monarchy exist to provide aid. More often, while new political institutions slowly fight for legitimacy, the nationalist myth can be sustained only by an extensive personalization of the polity, with emphasis on the Father-Founder figure. Under these circumstances, it is very easy to overemphasize both the stability and the pervasiveness of the nationalist creed —and the Asian nation-state as an entity. . . .

The great problems confronting the nationalist movements of Asia can be defined succinctly in the form of a few questions. Can ethnic and racial minorities be assimilated and/or incorporated into the nationalist myth, or will policies of coercion, indifference and lawlessness continue to prevail in this highly critical area? Can the excesses that accompanied the maturation of European nationalism be controlled, if not avoided? Is it possible to supplement nationalism by a simultaneous commitment to regional and global responsibilities—or will political behavior in these areas be adversely affected by the rising nationalist tide? Can Western-Asian relations move away from superior-inferior or benefactor-client relationships, and correspondingly, can the responsibility gap characterizing the current foreign policy of many emerging states be narrowed? The answers to these questions, or, more accurately, the trends governing them, should be of commanding interest to the scholar and policy-maker alike.

Section 2

Sovereignty: An unchanging concept?

The constancy of sovereignty

J. Keith Melville

Is sovereignty to be the servant or the tyrant of men and nations? Professor Melville holds that sovereignty is the vital element in the existence of a genuine state and that its basis is enforceable law. As such, it is a "potion" bound to be missing on the international level, which requires the existence of "angelic" statesmen if international anarchy is to be avoided.

Mr. Melville is an associate professor of political science at Brigham Young University.

Contrary to common belief, the American Revolution did not give birth to a new nation; it brought forth a whole litter of self-interested states. The Second Continental Congress was the central governing body during the war, and the Articles of Confederation were accepted and Congress established to serve the American people in futurity; but the bare fact of its inability to govern, to enforce compliance with its will, stands as a cold reminder that the Congress was never clothed with sovereignty.

The Congress established by the Articles of Confederation had some power to act governmentally, but so do a variety of other institutions in society. There is a qualitative difference between power in a general sense and sovereignty, which connotes a particular and exclusive exercise of power reserved to the state. A sovereign state holds a monopoly of legalized coercion or sets the limits for the legitimate use of force within its jurisdiction. Sovereignty, whether or not it is constitutionally assigned, psychologically accepted, arbitrarily imposed, or fraudulently usurped, becomes significant in its magic utility in the existence of a political system. There are many potions in the political brew which give life to the state, but the one which cannot be left out is sovereignty.

It was Jefferson and Madison, Hamilton and Washington, and others of differing political persuasions who lifted their voices and pens to point out the weaknesses of the Congress of the (mislabeled) United States. The traditionally ascribed problems of the Congress during those critical years all become secondary to the lack of sovereignty, the hallmark of the state. Different proposals of change were raised, but at bottom they all rested on a transfer of the locus of sovereignty from the states to the central government.

The nationalists among the Founding Fathers of the Constitution of the United States were realists. They recognized the vices as well as the virtues of men. They seemed to have less faith in men than in a political constitution to control them. They may have had good reasons for their attitudes, for they had observed life in the marketplace and elsewhere. They concluded that men, alas, were not angels and that angels were not going to assume the governmental responsibilities of mankind. With these concepts etched indelibly in their minds, they set forth to structure a constitutional system which would serve the internal and external needs of the American society, a system which could command respect abroad and observance of its laws at home. In short, their intent was to create one sovereign entity out of thirteen.

The Constitutional Convention, meeting in Philadelphia during the summer of 1787, hammered out a new framework of government. Opposition to the nationalist proposals soon arose, and the proponents of the new nation were forced to compromise. They dropped the labels because they knew that the substance of power was more important, but they never wavered in their basic objective of creating a national government. The final result was a delicately "balanced government." Governmental authority and individual rights, federal and state governments, propertied and propertyless classes, branches of government, and so on were all brought into a sort of "balance." Federalism, separation of powers, bicameralism, and civilian supremacy were some of the "auxiliary precautions" included within the document to assure its acceptance. Close examination of the results, however, reveals that the fundamental objective of the nationalists was achieved. The ingredients of a sovereign state were located finally in the political system as a whole, with the national government at its apex and the final judge of conflict within the system. Evidence of this came in the challenge, and failure, of the Civil War.

The political system structured in Philadelphia, though constantly changing, has lasted for 180 years. The Constitution is the oldest written document in effect today. Yet it is constantly being renewed to meet the ever changing needs of a dynamic society. The constant which runs throughout this period is that component called sovereignty. Can its service to the American people be seriously challenged?

State sovereignty, useful as it may be internally, raises some serious questions concerning its utility on the international level. The international society is a political system which operates within a framework of procedures and custom which is generously given the name of "international law." This law, however, is not the same as the law within the nation-state. Its observance is voluntary, not compulsory. Any international body, such as the United Nations, is just that—an international body. It is not a world state. Both international law and the world community are based on the principle of sovereignty and the existence of sovereign states.

The states which make up the international community are not bound to obey a superior authority. They make the rules by which they live and comply with these rules on the international level when doing so serves their national interests. The compulsion toward conformity which the magic of notions of legality and sovereignty induces internally is not found on the international level. Conflict of interests must be worked out in a new dimension. The observance of the "rules of the game" takes on a new significance in this voluntary arrangement. National self-interest remains as the basic motivation of whether international commitments are honored or not; yet in the push and pull of sovereign states to promote their interests, it is surprising how much responsibility emerges in the world community today.

Those who yearn to root out the problems which yet remain in the world community offer a variety of solutions. Some maintain that the creation of a world state would resolve the problems. Would it? Or would it simply internalize them? Innumerable questions turning on what form it would take, how it could be accomplished, the utility of it if structured, and so on require answers before this can be seriously considered.

The proposal to create "semi-sovereign" states on the international level is to misunderstand sovereignty and indulge in wishful fantasy. On the other hand, to demand the honoring of the sovereign rights of some states while these same states violate the sovereignty of others offers nothing to commend it. Similarly, it is foolhardy to refuse to recognize the realities of our world of sovereign states and assume they do not exist.

The resolution of the problems as they continually arise on the international level demands statesmen who understand the realities of the world community of sovereign states and demands that the internal utility of sovereignty will perpetuate the system indefinitely into the future. Sovereignty may have obviated the necessity of angels governing in the affairs of men within the states, but it demands statesmen with angelic qualities on the international level.

The Soviet principle of non-interference

A. Piradov

Piradov here takes a legalistic, if not propagandistic, view of sovereignty and non-interference, basing his argument principally on the United Nations Charter. Despite his statement that this Soviet principle extends "not only to sovereign states, but also to peoples and nations fighting for the exercise of their right to self-determination," *the Soviet Union has shown by its support of the Viet Cong and its invasion of Hungary and Czechoslovakia that it is a "principle" to be applied only to those nations herein termed "the imperialist Powers."*

International Affairs (*Moscow*), *January 1966.*

In our day, the struggle for the establishment and observance of the basic principles of international law, which are supported by the Socialist states, acquires great importance. One of these principles is that of non-interference, which has been revived and given a new and truly democratic content through the efforts of the Soviet Union, the world's first Socialist state. It is the cornerstone of the system of international law and is in dialectical interconnection with the basic prescriptions of that law. Without its faithful and consistent observance there can be no peaceful co-existence of states with different social systems, no disarmament, no assurance of nonaggression, no practice of the principle of self-determination, no respect for, or consolidation of, territorial integrity and sovereignty of nations.

The imperialist Powers have been sabotaging the international measures required for the strengthening of peace and international security, mainly by their interventionist policies. To justify this criminal political course, bourgeois jurists, sociologists and historians have been attacking the principle of non-interference, distorting or rejecting it altogether.

This kind of approach to the principle of non-interference justifies the tripartite aggression against Egypt in 1956, the collective intervention by the Western Powers in the Congo under the U.N. flag, the U.S. war against the people of South and North Viet-Nam, the aggressive U.S. actions against the Dominican Republic and the Western attempts to smuggle spies into the Soviet Union under the pretext of disarmament control.

Lenin repeatedly stressed that a policy of exporting revolution "would be completely at variance with Marxism, for Marxism has always been opposed to 'pushing' revolutions, which develop with the growing acuteness of the class antagonisms that engender revolutions." In reply to an American correspondent's question whether the Soviet Government was prepared to guarantee absolute non-interference in the domestic affairs of foreign states, Lenin said, in October 1919: "We are prepared to guarantee it." . . .

The principle of non-interference has invariably been a key element of Soviet foreign policy, and it continues to be so today. It is owing to this policy, and despite the wishes of the imperialist Powers, that peace has been preserved and that the Socialist system has been growing, strengthening and developing into the decisive factor of world progress.

The fruitful activity of the Soviet Union and the other Socialist countries in foreign policy and international law, aimed at observing and safeguarding the principle of non-interference, helps to strengthen the independence and the sovereign rights of states and nations. That is why the Soviet Union's opposition to all attacks on the principle of non-interference has the support of all countries freed from imperialist oppression, of the many small capitalist states suffering from imperialist interference, and of all freedom-loving democratic forces in the world. . . .

Non-interference is a most important condition for peace and the peaceful co-existence of states belonging to the two systems. The inadmissibility of interference by one state in the domestic affairs of another flows directly from the principle of the sovereign equality of states and peoples, and is one of the key principles of modern international law.

The emergence of the world's first Socialist state in 1917, the victory of Socialism in a number of countries of Europe, Asia and Latin America after the Second World War and the formation of the world Socialist community on that basis, signified a further consolidation of the principle of non-interference. The Socialist countries have not only practised it in their relations with each other and with other states, but have also vigorously opposed any attempts to violate it by anyone, above all the imperialist countries.

The history of the principle of non-interference shows that it has tended to expand in content. This has been especially noticeable in recent times, when two important events took place in international law: aggressive wars were declared illegal, and the principle of the self-determination of nations and peoples was established.

The qualitative content of the principle in question has undergone a change as well. In the past, the violation of the principle of non-interference did not entail any sanctions; today, provision is made for sanctions against its grossest violations. It is therefore of considerable theoretical interest and great practical significance to define the changing content of the principle.

The principle of non-interference can be defined by the sum total of the acts it prohibits. According to the degree of danger these acts fall into two large groups, namely, acts of aggression and ordinary interference. Acts of aggression create an immediate threat to world peace, whereas acts of ordinary interference do not, but they do tend to worsen relations between states and aggravate international tensions. Acts of aggression entail sanctions under the U.N. Charter, but simple interference does not.

In 1953, the Soviet Union proposed a detailed definition of the concept of aggression which can serve as a good basis for analysing the content of aggressive violations of the principle of non-interference. Under the Soviet definition, the aggressor in an international conflict will be deemed to be the state which first commits any of the following acts:

a) declares war on another state;

b) invades the territory of another state with its armed forces even without a declaration of war;

c) subjects the territory of another state to bombardment by its land, naval or air forces, or deliberately attacks its ships or planes;

d) lands or sends in air, sea or land forces within the boundaries of another state without the permission of the latter's Government or violates the terms of such permission, particularly in respect of the duration or extension of the area of their stay;

e) imposes a naval blockade of the coasts or ports of another state;

f) gives support to armed bands which, being formed on its territory, invade the territory of another state, or refuses, despite the demand of the state subjected to invasion, to take on its own territory all possible measures to deprive these bands of any support.

The fact that the acts specified in b, c, d, e, and f are qualified as acts of aggression makes it impossible for the aggressor to evade responsibility for its acts on the plea that they are not formal acts of war. It would make impossible any recurrence of the situation, frequently occurring in the past, in which acts of armed violence were not condemned by international bodies whose duty it was to do so (e.g., Japan's attack on China or Germany's Austrian Anschluss were not qualified by the League of Nations as acts of aggression).

Moreover, a clear-cut enumeration of the possible violations of the principle of non-interference through the use of armed force would make it possible to provide a clear definition of "armed attack," in the face of which the state, in virtue of Article 51 of the U.N. Charter, is entitled to resort to individual or collective self-defence. Finally, the Soviet proposal to define as an aggressor the state which attacks first provides the only possible solution to this fundamental problem in the rocket and nuclear age, when retaliation will be mounted literally a few minutes after the act of aggression.

All the acts violating peace listed above are gross violations of the principle of non-interference, and also of the principle outlawing aggressive war stated in the Declaration Concerning Wars of Aggression, adopted by the League of Nations on September 24, 1927, the Briand-Kellogg Pact, and the U.N. Charter [Article 2 (4)]. Thus, the two principles are partially identical.

However, the principle of non-interference is considerably wider than the principle prohibiting aggressive wars. According to the U.N. Charter, aggression is not confined to "armed attack," which is the subject of Article 51. "Armed attack" is only a specific instance of aggression. But the Security Council is empowered to take steps against any "breach of the peace, or act of aggression" (Article 39). When the definition of aggression was being discussed at the 12th General Assembly, many delegations were justified in saying that in our day some types of economic or ideological interference could well cause a breach of the peace and should therefore be regarded as acts tantamount to depriving a state of its resources or jeopardising its trade, that is, as acts of aggression.

The Soviet definition of aggression, apart from armed attack, lists the following types of interference: indirect, economic and ideological. The need to qualify such types of interference as acts of aggression springs from the fact that the principle of non-interference does not provide for any types of sanctions against those who violate it. This would be righted by qualifying the grossest violations of this principle as acts of aggression.

Under the Soviet definition, a state is deemed to have committed *indirect aggression*, when it: a) encourages the subversive activity of another state by organising terroristic acts, sabotage, etc.; b) helps to fan civil war in another state; and c) helps to stage a *coup d'état* in another state or to alter its policy to the advantage of the aggressor.

Subversive and espionage activity has always been a grave threat to states against which it was aimed; but it is doubly dangerous in our time. It is therefore quite right to qualify this type of interference as aggression. The fanning of war in another state should be regarded as an act of aggression because it creates an immediate threat to world peace. Indirect interference is frequently a prelude to direct armed intervention, as can be seen from the acts of Nazi Germany and fascist Italy in Spain in 1936–1938, and the United States in Korea, Cuba, South Viet-Nam and the Dominican Republic.

The promotion of a *coup d'état,* that is, the forcible overthrow of a government, or chief of state, or alteration of the social and economic system of a state, should also be regarded as a highly dangerous type of interference. The promotion of *coups d'état* is, from the standpoint of modern international law, an act violating the principle of non-interference, and is therefore absolutely impermissible.

There is more to the concept of indirect aggression, but the types of interference listed above give a general idea of this type of aggression. Its distinctive feature is that force is not used by the intervening country directly but obliquely, through front men, or vicariously. Because the concept of indirect aggression helps to expose the most secret and refined forms of interference, the Soviet definition is a substantial contribution to checking violations of the principle of non-interference. Adoption of this definition would make it possible to restrain the interventionist policy pursued by a number of imperialist Powers.

The second group of violations of the principle of non-interference are acts qualified in the Soviet definition of aggression as *economic aggression.* Among them are: a) adoption of measures of economic pressure violating the sovereignty of another state and its economic independence and jeopardising the basis of its economic life; b) adoption of measures in respect of another state to prevent the exploitation of its natural resources or the nationalisation of those resources; and c) economic blockade of another state. . . . Prohibition of the types of interferences qualified as economic aggression is the logical and inevitable result of the assertion in international law of such principles as the sovereign equality of states and the self-determination of nations. . . .

That is how the absolute majority of states interpret the right to self-determination. Article 1 (3) of the draft International Covenants on Human Rights, worked out by the 8th Session of the Commission on Human Rights, says: "The right of the peoples to self-determination shall also include permanent sovereignty over their natural wealth and resources. In no case may a people be deprived of its own means of subsistence on the grounds of any rights that may be claimed by other states." . . .

In order to remove any possible misinterpretations of the matter, the 7th U.N. General Assembly adopted a special resolution stressing that "the right of peoples freely to use and exploit their natural wealth and resources is inherent in their sovereignty and is in accordance with the Purposes and Principles of the Charter of the United Nations."

This proposition was subsequently confirmed in a number of other authoritative international documents, including the historic U.N. Declaration on the Granting of Independence to Colonial Countries and Peoples of December

14, 1960. This does not sanction the abrogation of all international treaties, but only of unjust and unequal ones.

The U.N. General Assembly resolution mentioned above invited member states to "refrain from acts, direct or indirect, designed to impede the exercise of the sovereignty of any State over its natural resources."

Thus, interference under the pretext that a state is violating international treaties or the rights of other states or citizens, under the pretext of a desire to exploit natural resources on the territory of that state, or under similar pretexts, is considered by contemporary international law as illegal and as a threat to peace, and should therefore be qualified as an act of aggression.

Economic blockade is interference in a state's foreign economic activity designed to undermine its economy by isolating it. Today, when trade between states has assumed such exceptional proportions, this type of interference leads to very grave consequences for some states, and should therefore be qualified as an act of aggression.

But economic blockade is not always an act of aggression. By analogy with the definition of other types of aggression stated in the Soviet draft, economic blockade resorted to by a victim of aggression in self-defence (Article 51 of the U.N. Charter), as also a blockade mounted by states under a Security Council decision (Articles 39 and 41), is a legitimate act (on the part of the victim of aggression and the states supporting it) in the struggle against aggression.

The content of the principle of non-interference also extends to those acts which the Soviet definition qualifies as *ideological aggression*. According to this definition, a state commits an act of ideological aggression if it: a) encourages the propaganda of war; b) encourages the propaganda of the use of atomic, bacteriological, chemical and other types of mass destruction weapons; or c) promotes the propaganda of Nazi and fascist views, racial and national exclusiveness, or hatred and disdain for other nations.

Ideological aggression is preparation for armed aggression and is therefore rightly qualified by the Soviet definition as an international crime. This view is shared by many countries and by progressive world opinion, as will be seen from the U.N resolution condemning the propaganda of war. It says: "The General Assembly condemns all forms of propaganda, in whatsoever country conducted, which is either designed or likely to provoke or encourage any threat to the peace, breach of the peace, or act of aggression."

There is yet another type of violation of the principle of non-interference which is widely practised by the imperialist Powers. It is intervention arising from the unequal treaties on military aid, and establishment of aggressive military blocs.

The imperialist Powers resort to diplomatic and economic pressure, play up the class interests of the ruling clique and use other criminal means to impose on other states agreements for the formation of military blocs. Subsequently, these agreements are used as a screen for a policy of gross interference in the domestic affairs of those states. The "right" to some types of interference is explicitly stated in these agreements.

But most of the time the sponsors of military blocs interfere in the internal affairs of other countries without having even that tenuous "right." They send a host of advisers, specialists, military missions, etc., to those countries to secure complete control over their political, economic and cultural life. Nominally sovereign, these states find themselves practically in the status of semi-colonies. This applies to South Korea, South Viet-Nam and certain other states.

The siting of military bases by imperialist Powers on the territory of other countries, too, is interference in the domestic affairs of states. The agreement on the siting of U.S. military bases actually revives the regime of capitulations. The laws of the country where the base is sited do not apply to the territory of the foreign military base. At the same time, the bases are bridgeheads for interference in internal affairs. Finally, bases are a means of drawing the host states on whose territory they are sited into war against the will of their Government and parliament. . . .

Like the other basic principles of international law, that of non-interference extends primarily to all sovereign states, a conclusion inevitably flowing from the principle of the sovereign equality of states, which is proclaimed in Article 2 (1) of the U.N. Charter. There is nothing, whether economic or political backwardness, the real or imaginary flaws in their social or state system, or the strategic considerations of other states, to justify excluding any state from enjoying the principle of non-interference. This specific feature of the principle is stated in a number of international documents.

The U.N. Charter also proceeds from the fact that the principle of non-interference applies to all states when it proclaims that the Organisation shall not interfere in the internal affairs of its members. All of this goes to show that the principle of non-interference is universal.

The principles of Socialist internationalism, which some politicians and scholars in the West try to present as evidence of "subversive Communist activity," do not in any way clash with the fundamentals of modern international law. These principles express the common aims and views of the working people of all countries in their struggle against imperialism. This community of purpose is determined by the class interests and consciousness of the working people of all countries, and not by any "secret" activity. It existed long before the first Socialist state arose, and it is therefore ridiculous to blame the Socialist states for the fact that the working class of the capitalist countries is fighting for its rights and for the unity of the working people of the world.

V. I. Lenin and the Communist Party, the guiding force of the Soviet state, have always resolutely opposed the anti-Marxist idea of exporting revolution. Lenin said: "Revolutions are not made to order, they cannot be timed for any particular moment; they mature in a process of historical development and break out at a moment determined by a whole complex of internal and external causes." That is the view Soviet leaders have always taken. The principle of non-interference continues to be a key element of Soviet foreign policy.

The Soviet state strictly adheres to a policy of non-interference, but, at the same time, abides by the principles of proletarian internationalism. It has always proceeded from the assumption that the all-round strengthening of the Socialist state, the achievement of fresh advances in Communist construction, and the consolidation of world peace provide the most effective assistance to the working class in the capitalist countries. History has fully borne out this policy.

With the transformation of Socialism into a world system the principle of non-interference became one of the fundamental elements in relations not only between Socialist and capitalist countries, but also between Socialist states. The new type of international relations which have taken shape in the process of co-operation between the Socialist countries is convincing evidence that it is possible to harmonise the principles of proletarian internationalism and the principles of complete equality, respect for territorial integrity, state independence and sovereignty and non-interference in each other's internal affairs.

To prevent the principle of the self-determination of nations from becoming an empty phrase, no state must interfere in the affairs of peoples exercising self-determination. This is an obligation undertaken by the signatories of the U.N. Charter, which proclaims the principle of self-determination [Article 1 (2) and Article 55]. In addition, they must refrain from interference in accordance with the historic U.N. Declaration on the Granting of Independence to Colonial Countries and Peoples. Point 2 of the Declaration says: "All peoples have the right to self-determination; by virtue of that right they freely determine their political status and freely pursue their economic, social and cultural development," while Point 7 says that "all states shall observe faithfully and strictly the provisions of the Charter of the United Nations, the Universal Declaration of Human Rights and the present Declaration on the basis of equality, non-interference in the internal affairs of all states and respect for the sovereign right of all peoples and their territorial integrity." It should therefore be accepted that the principle of non-interference extends not only to sovereign states, but also to *peoples and nations fighting for the exercise of their right to self-determination.*

Hindering nations in the exercise of their right to self-determination, regardless of the motives, is a gross violation of the principle of non-interference and international law. If force is used, the interference in the affairs of a nation exercising self-determination is qualified, under modern international law, as an act of aggression, that is, a grave international crime.

The refusal of the colonial Powers to satisfy the urge of the peoples and nations for self-determination is a violation of the principle of non-interference in respect of those peoples and nations; it leads to aggravation of international tensions and creates a threat to peace. That is why the United Nations, which is responsible for the maintenance of universal peace, must raise the issue of the self-determination of the people or nation concerned. The attempts on the part of the colonial Powers to declare such U.N acts interference in domestic affairs are groundless, because, under the U.N. Declaration on the Granting of Independence to Colonial Countries and Peoples, denial of self-determination or the creation of obstacles to the attainment of independence creates a "serious threat to world peace."

The tragic flaw in absolute sovereignty

Norman Cousins

"Codes of morality laboriously built up over centuries for moderating and governing the behavior of men are set aside precisely where they are most needed—the point of confrontation between nations." Mr. Cousins thus indicates where he feels the flaw of national sovereignty lies—it is a barrier rather than a means toward inter-nation communication and understanding.

"The Tragic Flaw," Saturday Review, *February 12, 1966. © 1966. Reprinted by permission. Mr. Cousins is editor of the* Saturday Review.

A misconception is haunting the world. It is the idea that the main danger of war today is represented by the differences dividing the nations. These differences are serious enough, but they are not nearly so serious as the similarities.

What the nations have in common are ways of dealing with foreign affairs that are inconsistent with the requirements of peace. Their habits are conditioned by long centuries of acting and reacting in the arena of absolute sovereignty. These habits have invariably led to violence in the past and are producing violence today. The habits are readily identifiable. The absolutely sovereign nation arrogates to itself the right of decision, whether or not this impinges on the decisions of others. It has no desire to be governed or limited in its ability to propose or dispose. The aggregate of such desires is combustible and potentially catastrophic. Equally dangerous is the absence of objectivity by one nation in appraising the intentions or actions of others.

The tragic flaw in human society is the inability to apply the yardsticks or requirements of logic or decency that exist inside the nations to the national units in their relations with one another. Codes of morality laboriously built up over centuries for moderating and governing the behavior of men are set aside at precisely the point where they are most needed—the point of confrontation between nations. Up to that point, there are all sorts of restraints and procedures and devices for establishing the facts of a case, for clarifying meaning, for measuring action alongside intent.

Inside the nation, an individual cannot draw up his own rules of evidence or invoke the right to make summary judgments where serious disputes with other individuals are concerned. But then, suddenly, all these elaborate safeguards and civilized procedures cease to have meaning or viability at the national summits. Everything goes into reverse at that point. The distinction between defending the national interests and pursuing them becomes almost impossible to define. Judgments can be arbitrary. The men at the top cannot function outside their context; their defined responsibility is to the nation, not to the human grouping as a whole.

War is not merely the result of a sudden breakdown in communication in the affairs of nations; it is the culmination of it. The communication failure is inherent in the way nations try to communicate and in the exemptions from objective reasoning that nations grant themselves. That is why wars grind on to exhaustion; total subjectivity destroys alternatives and options more thoroughly than bombs destroy cities and villages.

All the world's institutions of learning, no matter how hallowed and ivied, remain monuments to the collective ignorance of man in the techniques for maintaining and nurturing civilization itself. All the efforts of religions to make men aware of their ethical obligations and their spiritual resources are largely wasted and marginal unless they have some bearing on the ideas and actions of the national societies in their intercourse with one another.

Meanwhile, too, all the turnings and churnings of men and groups inside the nations—the quest for individual growth and gain, the thrust for even higher levels of prosperity—all these can only be regarded as distractions so long as the world lacks a rational or workable method for preserving peace.

At the core of man's evolutionary struggle is the attempt to create the circumstances under which individuals are more rather than less likely to be decent and rational. Students of human behavior don't exhaust themselves trying to determine whether man is inherently good or evil; they concentrate on the conditions that make it possible for the good to emerge and the evil to be arrested. Absolute national sovereignty sets the stage for the least salutary manifestations of human behavior.

It is difficult to say where the new realizations and energies will come from. Most certainly it would be unreasonable and unrealistic to expect the men who are the highest representatives of the absolute sovereignties, and therefore their prime victims, to lead the way. They need—and many of them would welcome—the full involvement of all those who understand the requirements of objectivity, whose values begin with an awareness of the uniqueness of human life, and who know how to see the connections between cause and effect.

Section 3

The changing bases of power

Overestimating the power of power

Louis J. Halle

Would you use a hand grenade to kill a mosquito in your living room? When does the use of power find itself in a "downward spiral of consequences" of diminishing reward? Professor Halle approaches the questions relative to the American obligation to meet "aggression" wherever it occurs.

 Mr. Halle is a professor at the Graduate Institute of International Studies in Geneva.

The greater one's power or wealth becomes, the more insufficient it is likely to seem, simply because the claims upon it, increasing as it does, tend always to outstrip it. Today the Ford Foundation, while by far the richest of American foundations, is undoubtedly the most inadequately endowed in terms of the expectations it is called on to meet. And today the most powerful country in the world is also, in fundamental respects, the most frustrated, because it finds its power so inadequate to the demands that have grown with it.

One consequence of this paradox is that the more power a nation has the greater the need it feels to use its power in order to increase its power still further. This may lead it, at last, into an open-ended and self-perpetuating process such as has caused great empires of the past to end in overextension and collapse. The problem is a bit like that of a man who, feeling the need to protect some little patch of property, buys the immediately surrounding land, only to find that the protection of his consequently enlarged holdings requires him to buy still more—thus allowing himself to be drawn step-by-step into a process that, unchecked, will end in his bankruptcy.

In 1898 we opened an anti-imperialistic war with Spain for the liberation of Cuba. In the course of the ensuing military operations we struck at and destroyed the Spanish power in the faraway Philippines, thereby creating a power-vacuum that some power was bound to fill. The last thing we had contemplated was that we might acquire an empire on the far side of the Pacific. But we could not hand the Philippines back to the Spanish tyranny, and they were in no condition to govern themselves or encompass their own defense. If we simply got out and came home we would leave chaos behind, and a German naval squadron lay ready in Manila Bay to resolve that chaos in the name of the Kaiser's expanding German empire. Waiting in line behind the Germans, moreover, were the Japanese, who had just taken the island of Taiwan for their own expanding empire, and who appeared ready to go on to the next islands in their path, the Philippines.

Under these circumstances, an unhappy President McKinley concluded that the United States, having inadvertently become responsible for the Philippines, had no alternative to assuming, itself, the obligation of governing and defending what consequently became the first item of an American overseas empire.

Again in 1945, not appreciating what was implied by our objective of permanently destroying Japan's military power, we found that the responsibility for its defense had fallen to us as the successor power. So our military power had to be permanently mounted in the Japanese islands, as in the Philippines, to prevent their falling under the expanding power of Soviet Russia or Communist China.

Also in 1945, when American forces liberated the southern half of Korea from the Japanese, as they had once liberated the Philippines from the Spaniards, there was no thought of keeping them there. On this occasion, in fact, we made the mistake of withdrawing them, whereupon Moscow's puppet state of North Korea moved to fill the vacuum we had left. So we had to come back in, accepting the fact that circumstances had added South Korea to the lengthening list of American protectorates on the rim of Asia.

In the same period, for strategic reasons bearing on the defense of Japan, we brought the island chain of the Ryukyus under our power and government.

Our commitment to the defense of the state that has become identified with the island of Taiwan, like our acquisition of the Philippines, was the unforeseen consequence of military action to meet an emergency, the emergency caused by the surprise attack on South Korea. Because our response to this attack required us to commit all the forces we had in Japan for its defense, our military leaders insisted on the consequent necessity of posing a deterrent threat on the flank of a China that had just fallen under the hostile sway of Mao Tse-tung. We did this by interposing our Seventh Fleet between his victorious forces on the mainland and Taiwan, where Chiang Kai-shek's defeated forces had taken refuge. In thus intervening at the last moment on the losing side in the Chinese civil war we believed and we announced that our action was temporary only, to meet the emergency of the day. President Truman told Congress that our intervention was "without prejudice to the political questions affecting that island." Nevertheless, 17 years later our continuing commitment to that island appears likely to limit for an indefinite future, still, the possibilities open to our diplomacy in the Far East.

Indochina, and specifically Vietnam, was like Korea another vacuum left by the surrender of Japanese power. The victorious allies had not, however, as in the case of Korea, committed themselves to the independence of Vietnam after its liberation. Consequently, a contest to fill the vacuum began between a native independence movement—itself non-communist although under the leadership of the communist Ho Chi Minh—and French forces trying to reestablish France's prewar empire in Indochina.

Without the American intervention that got started in 1950, the French and the client state they had set up in South Vietnam would have been defeated, leaving the native forces commanded by Ho to fill the vacuum. Our intervention in support of the French, which would soon lead to our replacement of them, was again preemptive. Announcing it, Secretary of State Acheson gave its purpose as that of holding back "Soviet imperialism."

In those days we believed that Mao Tse-tung was a simple agent of Moscow who had conquered China only to hand it over to the Russian empire, which consequently extended, now, to the frontier of Vietnam. Our intervention was prompted by the further belief that, without it, Moscow would next proceed, through its agent Ho, to swallow up Vietnam, then the whole of Indochina, and then an ever-widening range of lands around the rim of Asia.

Today, when our intervention in Vietnam has grown to such formidable proportions, we no longer identify the Soviet empire as the antagonist we are holding back in Vietnam. Now we sometimes say it is China—although it has been hard to make the case that the Vietnamese liberation movement is, in fact, a front for Chinese imperialism—or we suggest that it is something we call "the world communist conspiracy," a notional abstraction that retains some hold on our minds long after the fragmentation of world communism.

More explicitly, but more embarrassingly as well, we have held that our purpose is to prevent "national liberation movements" from succeeding, presumably on the grounds that they might be accompanied by a spread of Chinese or of Russian influence. But there is an essential contrast, moral and political, between the former containment of the Soviet Union along the line of the Iron Curtain, in cooperation with the forces that represented national independence, and commitment to oppose "national liberation movements" wherever they may occur.

Finally, we have said that we are in Vietnam simply to discharge a national obligation to meet "aggression" wherever it may occur in the world—as Vice President Humphrey is reported to have told a group of British parliamentarians on April 4, 1967. This immediately poses the problem of identifying "aggression," in each case, to the satisfaction of others as well as ourselves. The nature of this problem, as it presents itself in Vietnam today, may be appreciated if we imagine a Vietnamese army fighting us Americans inside our own country. In that case, could the Vietnamese expect the world to believe them if they said it was we Americans who were committing aggression?

The claims that we have a mission to oppose "national liberation movements" anywhere and to oppose "aggression" anywhere are what raise most acutely the problem of establishing limits to the continuing extension of our military power and the accompanying obligations upon it. Wherever we successfully frustrate a "national liberation movement" or what we identify as "aggression," our success is likely to be accompanied, whether we wish it or not, by the permanent establishment of still another piece of American empire upheld by American armed force. This appears to be already the case in Vietnam, where the state originally set up by the French may, in its dependence on us, become more than our ward, our satellite or puppet.

This continuing expansion of our *de facto* empire could lead only to an increasing and irreversible over-extension of our military power, with sinister implications for our own future.

Is it too early, then, for us to be on our guard against the possibility that a day might come when the rest of the world, driven by fear and hatred, combined for the containment of an expanding American empire?

The admiration and trust that Athens had inspired throughout the Greek world had brought it the support of allies who looked to it for leadership in the common defense of Greek freedom against the expanding Persian empire. So it was that, by the time the Persian threat had been contained and dispelled, Athens found itself possessed of a power that it did not, then, prevent itself from using thoughtlessly in a succession of individual decisions by which, at last, it reduced its allies to the status of satellites. When this unpondered course of action had finally, step-by-step, gone past the point of no return, an unhappy Pericles told his fellow Athenians: "What you hold is, to speak frankly, a despotism; perhaps it was wrong to take it, but to let it go is unsafe." In the end, the other states of the Greek world, driven by mounting fear of an Athens that threatened them all, combined to bring about the downfall of its empire and the permanent destruction of its power.

In August 1943, Sir John Anderson, head of the Scientific Research Committee of the British War Cabinet, told Canadian Prime Minister Mackenzie King that the country which first succeeded in producing atomic bombs would have control of the world. Beginning two years later, our experience of being the first country to produce atomic bombs proved that Sir John had overestimated what could be done with them. They could no more be used for realizing the normal range of our national objectives than, as one of my colleagues used to put it, a hand grenade can be used for killing mosquitoes in one's living-room. The use of nuclear weapons in Vietnam today, or in China or Russia, would surely unleash chaos. It would have a train of immediate political consequences that would lead to the breakdown of the world order on which we, no less than others, depend for the maintenance of our traditional institutions and way of life. Our living-room would be wrecked beyond repair.

The political cost of using any kind of military force, except directly in self-defense, has steadily increased in the 20th century, and especially since the nuclear age began, with the consequence that its use in action has to be avoided except in the direst emergencies, and even then it has to be kept stringently limited. If our escalating military effort in Vietnam has failed to produce decisive results, while seriously darkening our reputation throughout the world, that is surely because our frustrated leaders overestimated the political effectiveness of such means so employed.

Any great nation's influence beyond its borders depends on a delicate combination of force in reserve and the willing consent of others to the pursuit of its interests and the realization of its objectives. Force used with discrimination and careful consideration of others can increase the element of consent. Used indiscriminately and arrogantly, it dissipates consent and thereby may set off a downward spiral of consequences whereby the loss of consent increases the requirements for a use of force that still further dissipates consent—until, like Athens, the doomed nation, which may once have enjoyed the consent of its world, comes to depend entirely on the force that, by itself, cannot save it.

The danger to us, no less than to the rest of the world, resides in our vast and spreading power, which no longer appears quite as beneficent in the world as it did when it was clearly being used for the defense of liberty and civility against the expanding empires of other powers, rather than against native movements of national liberation in faraway lands.

If we are to avert the danger, it will be because we have seen in time that the ideal applicable to a nation in our position is that of the gentle knight, who can afford to act with restraint precisely because he is strong, rather than that of the swaggering frontiersman who bases his standing in the community on demonstrations of his readiness with a six-shooter.

Science in a world of widening horizons

Glenn T. Seaborg

Power now involves less military might and political control and more ability in the production and utilization of new technologies. Mr. Seaborg here investigates the nature of the scientific and technological revolution for "world civilization." He argues that cooperation in the use of this new and expanding power is imperative for world security.

Department of State Bulletin, *February 21, 1967. Mr. Seaborg is chairman of the U.S. Atomic Energy Commission.*

I hope to present several different ideas, but summed up they might lead to the following conclusion: that man may well have reached that point in his history, that stage of his development, where he has not only been made master of his fate, but where his technology and his morality have come face to face, where he can scarcely treat fact and value separately, and where he may see principles as diverse as the second law of thermodynamics and the Golden Rule being considered side by side in the making of decisions which determine his future. For I believe . . . that the major forces that have shaped our lives in the last 20 years . . . are not only widening our horizons but forcing us to shape up for a rigorous journey toward those horizons. We are headed for some new undiscovered shores, and after a million years of headway—of struggle and growth, of conquest and accomplishment—during which time we believed we were all sailing separately, I think we have reached the point where we now realize we are essentially all in the same boat together. I think it is science which has made this so. And it is the power derived from science and how we use or misuse it which will determine our future. . . .

Endowed with an intellect that allows him to reason, and to remember, record, and transmit his ideas, man has been responsible to a large degree for his own creative evolution. In speed and scope it far exceeds his own natural evolution. Physically we are not that much different today than our forebears of the stone age. We exist on a pinpoint of time, temperature, and chemical balance, individually weak and ineffectual, and our only contact with the real world is through our five meager senses. But through the highly organized intelligence we call "science" and the highly organized group we call "society," we have been able to extend our senses and amplify our energy to an incredible degree. We have been able to learn much about ourselves and our environment, and we have developed ways to adapt ourselves to environments not only unsuited to man but to those where no other life has ever existed. . . .

Fortunately we have created new senses as well as extended the range of our natural senses. We have no natural sense organs designed to detect magnetic fields, or the greater range of radiation—that not in the limited areas of the spectrum which produce light, sound, or heat—yet we can detect almost all forms of radiation in the smallest amounts, whether in the confines of a laboratory or in orbit around the earth or sun.

But miraculous as these extensions of our natural senses may be, they would all be for naught if man were not endowed with the ability to remember, to record and transmit these impressions and the ideas he develops from them. It is only through memory and communication that the collective intelligence of mankind grows and that he is able to make any use of the impressions gathered by his senses. It is, therefore, most fortunate for us that the same scientific revolution which has magnified our knowledge-gathering ability has given us the electronic tools to handle this great new accumulation of data, to sort it, store it, recall it when we need it, to solve problems with it, and to some extent put the answers to work for us. If it were not for these tools, how would we begin to handle the incredible input of our information explosion, one which in science alone sees the publishing of 100,000 journals a year in more than 60 languages, a figure doubling every 15 years?

If the past 20 years have seen a modification of man through a vast technological extension of his senses and collective intellect, certainly they have also seen an important, though perhaps less spectacular, modification of man himself. The understanding we have gained of the life processes and of the many biological forces at work in ourselves and our environment has extended our life-span, has allowed us to reduce disease and suffering and to enjoy longer, healthier lives. But this progress, important as it may be and as grateful as we are for it, may soon seem insignificant compared to that which appears to be just ahead of us. The possibilities of new and rather dramatic changes in man loom large, some of them in the not too distant future. They may stem from advances in a number of diverse fields—from newfound knowledge of the body's chemistry, of the electrochemical nature of the brain and nervous system, of our genetic makeup, and from advances by the chemical engineer, the surgeon, the electronics expert, and the biochemist. . . .

Paralleling our growing understanding of the biochemical basis of life has been a growing interest in, and knowledge of, the basic mechanism of the brain and nervous system. . . .

The electrical nature of the brain's activity and its comparison with the computer has become the basis of the relatively new science of cybernetics. Cybernetics, together with another new discipline known as bionics, give us cause to speculate on how far man can go in combining his naturally endowed self with the mechanical products of his creative evolution. Those involved in these new fields suggest that some day in the future it may be possible to "program" information directly into the human brain, or develop cybernetic control systems through which a man's thoughts alone can remotely control a machine. Work in this area of so intimately combining man and machine has already led to the coining of a new word—"cyborg"—standing for cybernetic organism. And to a great extent "Man, the Cyborg" is with us today and making valuable contributions to our programs in space, nuclear energy, and oceanography—in those areas where man must operate in a hostile, hazardous environment.

In a literal and figurative sense man's horizons have been widened most by his ability to venture into, adapt to, and work in new environments. No discernible amount of natural evolution has allowed him to do this, but his creative evolution, through science and technology, has allowed him in recent years to take giant strides in this direction. . . .

When we enter an environment we could not normally survive in, we take the necessities of our own environment with us. These might take the form of an aqualung for limited underwater work, or some type of submarine vehicle should we need warmth, light, oxygen, greater mobility, and protection from great pressures. The fact that we have been able to descend almost to the bottom of the deepest trench in the oceans—a depth of over 35,000 feet—seems remarkable, and yet we are just beginning major efforts to explore this environment of "inner space."

There is no need to go into detail on the efforts we are making to explore our horizons of outer space or the progress we are making in this endeavor. In recent years a good part of the world's attention has been focused on our entrance into this new environment. Here again man is bringing his own environment with him on his journey, and he will have to bring a great deal of it great distances if he is to go far or accomplish much in the incredibly vast areas he hopes to explore and possibly inhabit.

What is perhaps most remarkable about our space program, and perhaps not realized by many, is that the fulfillment of this desire on the part of man to leave his mother planet requires an effort involving almost every one of the scientific disciplines known to man. There is scarcely an area of human knowledge or technology that will not come into play in putting a man on the moon and eventually on the planets.

No review of how science and technology has widened our horizons would be complete without some discussion of the role of energy. For it is man's extraction, conversion, and control of energy which has made all that I have mentioned to this point possible. And it is our relationship to energy—how we use it and what we do with it—which offers us both our greatest promises and our greatest challenges.

[Some twenty years ago it was revealed] . . . that man could release the enormous energy of nuclear fission. With this discovery came the realization that it would be only a matter of time—a relatively short time—before we would have at our disposal enough energy, and the technologies for using it, either to completely destroy our civilization or to lift it to great new standards.

But the energy of the atom is remarkable not only because of its total power. The range and usefulness of nuclear energy, from the standpoint of both fission and radiation, opens to us whole new energy horizons. With our nuclear science and technologies, we will be able to convert, through the man-made element plutonium and a man-made isotope of uranium, almost all of the energy bound up in the natural elements uranium and thorium into a nearly inexhaustible supply of power. And we will be able to do this just at a time when the demands of our high-energy civilization are growing so fast that a new energy source to supplement our fossil fuels will soon be needed. Through our nuclear science and technologies we will also be able to produce enough compact power to make possible our forthcoming adventures in space—to take us, and the equipment we will need, to the planets. This will be possible through nuclear-powered rockets and systems for nuclear auxiliary power, all of which are under development and some of which have already been used successfully in various ways. . . .

The energy revolution of the past few decades has been more than one of a growth of sheer power. It has been one of tremendous refinement in the production and control of power, and of heat, light, and various forms of radiation. It has been one of incredible speed, bringing into almost common use in some fields such previously unused divisions of time as the nanosecond (a billionth of a second). And it has been one inseparable from our revolutions in transportation, communication, and the growth of human knowledge.

Review of the widening of our horizons over the past 20 years may leave us very impressed with our collective accomplishments. And such a review with some contemplation of what the future holds is in many respects overwhelming; to some, it seems almost frightening. But the facts and figures alone do not tell the most important part of the story. Our scientific progress must not be considered apart from our social progress, nor our technology talked of in terms not relating to human values.

Wherever we are headed on our new wide horizons, we are traveling there as the family of man. As such, what has this journey done for us? And what future does it hold? . . .

Certainly, while science has widened our horizons, it has brought us physically closer together. I believe it has done the same in spirit—in engendering broader human cooperation and understanding. Science comes to us from an international heritage, and it promotes a growing internationality. In spite of the scientific ascendancy of some countries, no nation has a monopoly on scientific talents. One does not have to go far back in history to see an outstanding example of the contributions of scientists of many national backgrounds to a single scientific field. Within the past three decades, the nuclear age was born of the labor of such an international group of scientists as Hahn, Fermi, the Joliot-Curies, Rutherford, Bohr, Einstein, Szilard, Lawrence, Compton, Oppenheimer, De Hevesy, and a host of many other multinational names too numerous to mention at this time.

Today the sharing of scientific brainpower is an important inducement toward international cooperation. In this regard, it is interesting to note that last year representatives of the United States attended about 600 international, intergovernmental conferences, mostly on technical subjects. We belong to 53 international organizations, again mostly scientific and technical. These are organizations which exist because they are needed, because they serve the purposes of many nations and many people. It is a fact of 20th-century life that, while nations may stress national sovereignties and avow national purposes, science has created a functional international society. It exists, and it works, in spite of all who doubt it. . . .

Aside from the benefits which science itself gains from cooperation, the social applications and implications of science demand international cooperation. The consequences of decisions in scientific matters and the benefits of scientific progress are inexorably connected to the well-being of all men. They affect life itself—birth, health, and death; they affect living conditions—food, shelter, and environment; they affect human contact—communications and transportation; and they affect the general state of the world—war or peace. In this regard—because of the consequences of science—we have a vital stake in what is being done abroad and an obligation to disseminate the beneficial knowledge we gain here.

In many ways the physical scope of scientific investigation today transcends national boundaries. Global science demands global cooperation. The fields of meteorology and climatology, oceanography and geology, astronomy and space exploration need as their laboratories all the earth's oceans, its lands, its atmosphere, and the boundless space of the universe. These world-straddling sciences have been responsible for a surprising degree of worldwide cooperation, even among countries harboring great political differences. In the field of meteorology, our current program involves the cooperation of more than 100 other countries. In our space program we have the cooperation of more than 50 countries and are beginning to co-operate directly with the Soviet Union in this field. In addition, we have had much success with the Soviets in exchanging information and ideas in the nuclear energy field.

I think that all this has brought us face to face with the fact that we can no longer live in a world where only a small percentage of the people enjoy the benefits of 20th-century life. Each year brings us closer to the realization that it is a technical, social, political, and moral necessity that we learn to live together in peace and understanding, sharing more and more of the knowledge we gain and the abundance that knowledge brings, until such time when all have the ability to share the workload evenly and all can enjoy the benefits which only some of us enjoy today. We no longer are a world of local or regional civilizations which can flourish or wither away by themselves. Our civilization is now global and absolute, and the actions of each nation, and to some degree of each individual, strongly affect our collective destiny.

There are many people who fear the current explosion of science and technology, who see in it a dehumanizing effort, who believe that it is running away with us and that we are becoming its slaves instead of remaining its masters. I cannot agree with these thoughts. . . .

I believe we *can be* masters of our fate. We *need not* be trapped by the onrush of our technology—simply because we recognize it. We realize (and not too late, as some would have us believe) its speed, its effects, and their cumulative impact. And in the light of this we can predict, plan, and work to shape our future.

Most of you are aware of the massive challenges facing mankind today. You read about them in your newspapers and magazines, see and hear about them on television and radio—environmental pollution, hunger, water shortages, the population explosion, the problems associated with urban growth, and, above all, that plague which mankind has not yet eliminated, the threat of war, compounded today by the overwhelming destructiveness of nuclear weapons.

Yet I believe that none of these problems are insoluble if we face them without delay and work hard toward their solution. There is an enormous amount of national and international effort already going into the meeting of every one of these problems. . . .

Essential to the meeting of all the challenges ahead of us is education—

education on all levels. A technologically developing world and an uneducated one are incompatible. Stating its support for the goal of universal education, UNESCO's Advisory Committee on Science and Technology has said:

> Governments of many developing countries must find the quickest formulae to teach children of largely illiterate people how to read and write and, at the same time, to train engineers and scholars drawn from among the same people. This is a phenomenon of the present century in which supersonic aircraft will be used as a means of transportation, while inside these same countries, traffic is still carried on donkeys.

The problem of hunger, still with us in so many areas of the world, is being attacked on an international scale by the work of many U.N. organizations. Under the leadership of the U.N.'s Food and Agriculture Organization, a Freedom From Hunger Campaign has been launched which involves over 80 countries working with UNESCO, the United Nations Children's Fund, the World Health Organization, the International Atomic Energy Agency, the International Labor Organization, and the World Meteorological Organization. This formidable combination of international scientific and educational groups is exploring every natural, technological, economic, and social means of providing basic food staples for all human beings everywhere. . . .

Under the sponsorship of UNESCO, FAO, and the World Meteorological Organization, an International Hydrological *Decade* has been proclaimed, during which a massive program will be undertaken to find ways of averting the water crisis that so many nations face. During the IHD, a sustained and coordinated program of scientific research will be carried on to find out, among many other things, where the sources of fresh water lie, how we can recover them, what the best methods are for desalting water, what can be done to salvage the water that evaporates or runs into the sea—and what all of these operations will cost. . . .

Finally, I call your attention to the work of the International Atomic Energy Agency, mentioned briefly before because of its cooperation in the Freedom From Hunger Campaign. The IAEA is not only making an important contribution to the world's efforts in developing the many peaceful benefits of nuclear energy, but it is also playing a leading role in seeing that the atom remains peaceful, in controlling the proliferation of nuclear weapons.

This organization, with its 95 member nations, oversees and administers an international "safeguards" system, a system of inspection and control designed to assure that the nuclear materials, facilities, and technology furnished for peaceful uses are not diverted to military applications. Right now—today—the IAEA safeguards inspection system is at work. It is the first program of international inspection in the arms limitation field to be put into operation, and it is operating with the blessing and encouragement of both the United States and the Soviet Union. Such an organization truly deserves our strongest praise and support.

We look to the IAEA, to UNESCO, and to all the organizations of the U.N. to help us achieve world peace—true peace, not just stalemates of political and military power but lasting peace based on reason and understanding, on world stability, and on the well-being of all men sharing a newly created abundance on this earth.

I believe that it is possible, through science and technology, to achieve these long-unfulfilled dreams of mankind. Our progress of the past few decades has, indeed, widened our horizons. It has given us much new knowledge and many remarkable new tools. It has also given us a glimmer of a better new world which can be reached with these accomplishments as a beginning. Let us not sit back then and revel in what we have done. Let us continue our progress. Let us continue to grow in knowledge, to apply that knowledge, and to work hard with our new tools so that we can continue to move toward those wide horizons and the greater promise they hold for all mankind.

Section 4

Changing national interests

The commonwealth turned upside down

Dennis Austin

Much is said of the evils of imperialism, but former colonies still come regularly, even after as much as 20 years, to the Commonwealth Prime Ministers' Meeting in London. The basis of Afro-Asian ties to the Commonwealth are not explained here. But Mr. Austin does say that British interests are being increasingly drawn away from Commonwealth nations toward such organizations as the Common Market. There has been a reversal of the original reason for the ties—the exclusive imperial interests of Great Britain—and the Commonwealth is "turned upside down."

This article originally appeared in The World Today *(October 1966), the monthly journal published by the Royal Institute of International Affairs, London. Mr. Austin is reader in Commonwealth studies, Institute of Commonwealth Studies, University of London.*

The Commonwealth Prime Ministers' meeting in September was the fifteenth since 1944. And in recent years virtually every one of these gatherings has been heralded as the beginning of the end, if not the end itself, of the association. Which is the more significant—the fact that the Prime Ministers and Presidents come so frequently to London, or the constant prophecies of doom which hang above their heads when they arrive? It is not yet possible to say, but there must surely be something of value in this extraordinary outgrowth of empire which continues to attract to its meetings the leaders of over twenty States. It can hardly be a matter of habit, since many of the member countries are of too recent an origin to have fallen into an unquestioned acceptance of Commonwealth virtues. The explanation usually advanced in these difficult years of economic stringency is that of 'mutual advantage' or, in less elegant phraseology, the recognition by each of the twenty-three member Governments that the Commonwealth is a 'concert of convenience.' This is not a very satisfactory explanation for so oddly assorted a group of countries, and a more plausible argument might be that the Commonwealth survives not because of a rational weighing of the advantages and disadvantages of membership in the cold scales of national interest but because of a deep-seated emotional view of Britain on the part of her former colonies. Just as empire was built on something stronger than force or profit, so the ties which link even the smallest and newest member country with Britain have their origin in an emotion which cannot be explained simply in terms of material advantage. There remains, it would seem, a fascinated attachment to Britain and a genuine liking for British ways of behaviour (however exasperating British *policies* may be in practice), whether at the highest level of Prime Ministers and Presidents or at the lowest level of Ph.D. students and undergraduates. This is an unusual conclusion to arrive at, especially following a meeting in which fierce debates are said to have been conducted between the United Kingdom and the African representatives. But affection and angry debate are not incompatible: indeed it would probably be impossible to hold such meetings if there were not also a common fund of affection and goodwill.

Are such feelings reciprocated in Britain? In earlier years, yes, certainly: the ties of loyalty and understanding between Britain and the overseas Dominions were mutual, though stronger no doubt on the side of Australia, Canada, and New Zealand, since the horizon of their interests was filled by a view of Britain and British society which they could not hope to achieve in comparable terms within the broad range of interests which engaged the attention of the United Kingdom. But today? Other attitudes can be detected in this country. The affection for—and interest in—Britain which draws the Commonwealth leaders so regularly to London has to be set against a double threat to the Commonwealth from Britain herself. The first arises from an uneasy doubt on the part of the U.K. Government and among many individuals about the price which these ties may exact in terms of non-Commonwealth interests; the second, and more harmful, development is a growing indifference as to whether these ties are maintained or not.

These are unfamiliar truths, and therefore all the more harsh since they lead to the conclusion that in the long run the worth of the Commonwealth has to be measured in terms of the price put upon it by the United Kingdom. And it is in this sense that one can talk of the Commonwealth being 'turned upside down.' For what was generally assumed to be the basis of the association—namely, its ground of existence in British policy and aims—can no longer be taken for granted. At the same time, those countries whose membership was once thought to be very conditional—held as it were only on approval—can now be seen as uncertain and anxious about the effect not of their remaining in the Commonwealth but of their withdrawal from it. . . .

The most obvious way in which the Commonwealth is now being stood on its head can be seen in the long debate over Rhodesia. The U.K. Government has clearly reached the position where its main desire is simply to be rid of the problem. It is Afro-Asian pressure which prevents it from reaching an agreement with Mr Smith. And, beset with domestic problems, Mr Wilson can hardly look forward with enthusiasm to the time when he may have to go to the United Nations for help in a programme of selected mandatory sanctions. One may reasonably conclude that he would like nothing better than to do nothing, and that it is a majority among the Afro-Asian-Caribbean members of the Commonwealth who are urging him forward. This, too, is a novel situation. For in the past, certainly before 1939 and up to 1956, it was Britain which tried to gain Commonwealth approval for action which she proposed to take overseas, and it was the attendant Commonwealth Governments which applied the brake. The measure of the change may be seen in the reluctance on the part of the United Kingdom to re-shoulder the burden of imperial rule in Africa, and in the arguments used by the African leaders to remind her of her need to act. . . .

It is true that emotions may ebb, though less quickly perhaps than an awareness of common interests can fade; one has no means of knowing what the next generation of Afro-Asian leaders will feel towards Britain and their (then remote) colonial past. But, considered on this time scale, the Commonwealth may go on for a surprisingly long time, despite the emergence of issues as difficult as that of Rhodesia. Nor should one overlook the practical advantages that the Commonwealth has as an international group. They can be summarized quite simply by noting the extraordinary diversity of the association. There are rich, moderately rich, poor, and very poor societies among its member countries; there are powerful, less powerful, and very weak States—and one may note the fact that Britain is no longer so powerful a State as to be a source of disquiet, as the United States has been in Latin and Central America, nor so feeble as to be unimportant. The Commonwealth also has the advantages—contrary to current forebodings—of variety and number, whereby a very representative, but manageable, proportion of the world's nations are able to meet regularly together. One has only to attend a U.N.-

sized conference to become aware of the immense advantages in the existence of a group of countries whose representatives are able to communicate directly with each other, not only through a common language but on the basis of a certain degree of familiarity with each other's history. Nor is the Commonwealth divided quite so simply in terms of 'race'—whatever meaning can be given to this very imprecise term—as is sometime suggested. If Australia and New Zealand were less concerned about Rhodesia at the recent conference than some of the African leaders would like them to be, Canada was able to mediate effectively between British and African opinion.

If one notes these advantages, it is possible to go on to argue that the Commonwealth is a useful meeting-ground for the examination of common interests among a group of twenty or more States which have grown accustomed to discuss such matters without commitment to a written Charter of rules. And there is no clear evidence from the Marlborough House conference that those who attended have reached the end of their willingness to go on meeting and arguing.

With one exception? Britain? Here one returns to the point made earlier, that the interesting feature of the September conference was to see how many of the former assumptions of Commonwealth behaviour were turned upside down, including the once commonly accepted belief that Britain had everything, and the newer members very little, to lose from the Commonwealth's disappearance. Admittedly, it would be wrong to argue that a large section of British opinion, or even of the Labour Government, had reached the conclusion that the dissolution of the Commonwealth would be a blessing in very thin disguise; but it would also be wrong to assume that there is a strong and persistent will to keep it alive. Such a policy and attitude may, however, be very blind. The Commonwealth having come to an end, we may find that Britain has become a little more insular in outlook, a little more racial-minded, a little less generous, and we shall not be able to recreate what was lost.

Panama and American national interests

J. William Fulbright

This excerpt from Senator Fulbright's famous "Old Myths and New Realities" asks the searching question whether a nation as powerful as the United States would not find it beneficial to yield a little more than half way to the interests of a weak and perennially unstable Panama. He feels that the realities of the present interests of both countries and not the "old myths" should form the basis for settlement.

Congressional Record, Senate, Vol. 110, No. 56 (March 25, 1964). Mr. Fulbright is a senator from Arkansas and chairman of the Foreign Relations Committee.

Latin America is one of the areas of the world in which American policy is weakened by a growing divergency between old myths and new realities.

The crisis over the Panama Canal has been unnecessarily protracted for reasons and sensitivity on both sides—for reasons, that is, of only marginal relevance to the merits of the dispute. I think the Panamanians have unquestionably been more emotional about the dispute than has the United States. I also think that there is less reason for emotionalism on the part of the United States than on the part of Panama. It is important for us to remember that the issue over the canal is only one of a great many in which the United States is involved, and by no means the most important. For Panama, on the other hand, a small nation with a weak economy and an unstable government, the canal is the preeminent factor in the nation's economy and in its foreign relations. Surely in a confrontation so unequal, it is not unreasonable to expect the United States to go a little farther than halfway in the search for a fair settlement.

We Americans would do well, for a start, to divest ourselves of the silly notion that the issue with Panama is a test of our courage and resolve. I believe that the Cuban missile crisis of 1962, involving a confrontation with nuclear weapons and intercontinental missiles, was indeed a test of our courage, and we acquitted ourselves extremely well in that instance. I am unable to understand how a controversy with a small and poor country, with virtually no military capacity, can possibly be regarded as a test of our bravery and will to defend our interests. It takes stubbornness but not courage to reject the entreaties of the weak. The real test in Panama is not of our valor but of our wisdom and judgment and common sense.

We would also do well to disabuse ourselves of the myth that there is something morally sacred about the treaty of 1903. The fact of the matter is that the treaty was concluded under circumstances that reflect little credit on the United States. It was made possible by Panama's separation from Colombia which probably could not have occurred at that time without the dispatch of U.S. warships to prevent the landing of Colombian troops on the isthmus to put down the Panamanian rebellion. The United States not only intervened in Colombia's internal affairs but did so in violation of a treaty concluded in 1846 under which the United States had guaranteed Colombian sovereignty over the isthmus. President Theodore Roosevelt, as he boasted, "took Panama," and proceeded to negotiate the canal treaty with a compliant Panamanian regime. Panamanians contend that they were "shotgunned" into the treaty of 1903 as the price of U.S. protection against a possible effort by Colombia to recover the isthmus. The contention is not without substance.

It is not my purpose here to relate the events of 60 years ago but only to suggest that there is little basis for a posture of injured innocence and self-righteousness by either side and that we would do much better to resolve the issue on the basis of present realities rather than old myths.

The central reality is that the treaty of 1903 is in certain respects obsolete. The treaty has been revised only twice, in 1936 when the annual rental was raised from $250,000 to $430,000 and other modifications were made, and in 1955 when further changes were made, including an increase in the annual rental to $1.9 million, where it now stands. The canal, of course, contributes far more to the Panamanian economy in the form of wages paid to Panamanian workers and purchases made in Panama. The fact remains, nonetheless, that the annual rental of $1.9 million is a modest sum and should probably be increased. There are other issues, relating to hiring policies for Panamanian workers in the zone, the flying of flags, and other symbols of national pride and sovereignty. The basic problem about the treaty, however, is the exercise of American control over a part of the territory of Panama in this age of intense nationalist and anticolonialist feeling. Justly or not, the Panamanians feel that they are being treated as a colony, or a quasi-colony, of the United States, and this feeling is accentuated by the contrast between the standard of living of the Panamanians, with a per capita income of about $429 a year, and that of the Americans living in the Canal Zone—immediately adjacent to Panama, of course, and within it—with a per capita income of $4,228 a year. That is approximately 10 times greater. It is the profound social and economic alienation between Panama and the Canal Zone, and its impact on the national feeling of the Panamanians, that underlies the current crisis.

Under these circumstances, it seems to me entirely proper and necessary for the United States to take the initiative in proposing new arrangements that would redress some of Panama's grievances against the treaty as it now stands. I see no reason—certainly no reason of "weakness" or "dishonor"—why the United States cannot put an end to the semantic debate over whether treaty revisions are to be "negotiated" or "discussed" by stating positively and clearly that it is prepared to negotiate revisions in the canal treaty and to submit such changes as are made to the Senate for its advice and consent.

I think it is necessary for the United States to do this even though a commitment to revise the treaty may be widely criticized at home. It is the responsibility of the President and his advisers, in situations of this sort, to exercise their own best judgment as to where the national interest lies even though this may necessitate unpopular decisions.

An agreement to "negotiate" revisions is not an agreement to negotiate any particular revision. It would leave us completely free to determine what revisions, and how many revisions, we would be willing to accept. If there is any doubt about this, one can find ample reassurance in the proceedings at Geneva, where several years of "negotiations" for "general and complete disarmament" still leave us with the greatest arsenal of weapons in the history of the world.

The Panama Canal: A reply

Strom Thurmond

Are the proposed treaties which grew out of requests similar to that of Senator Fulbright's for a new look in reality a "give-away" of "United States jurisdiction and sovereignty"? Senator Thurmond sees it as "the greatest *giveaway since God gave man the world for his dominion." He sees a conflict between American* sovereignty *and the* independence *of Panama which has been won by the United States. He sees extreme nationalism and communism combining together against the best interests of the United States. This view of national interests is in contrast to that of the preceding article.*

Delivered before the Young Americans for Freedom National Convention, Pittsburgh, Pennsylvania, on September 2, 1967. Mr. Thurmond is a senator from South Carolina.

The most recent dispatches from Panama have been telling a perplexing story. Last June [1967] President Johnson and President Marco Robles announced that the two countries of the United States and the Republic of Panama had completed negotiations on three *new* treaties regarding the Panama Canal. Although the official texts of these treaties have never been released, the details are fully known.

From the American point of view, there is only one word to describe their contents. These treaties are the *greatest* giveaway since God gave man the world for his dominion. They give away United States jurisdiction and sovereignty. They give away United States land and property. They give away United States operating facilities and engineering works. In short, they give away the entire U.S. Canal—and indeed any new canal that the United States might build in Panama—to a dubious operating authority whose sole strength is the slender reed of promises by the Republic of Panama. Let me take just a moment to describe the batch of three treaties. The first and most important treaty is the basic re-negotiated Panama Canal Treaty. This treaty sets up an *organization* described as "International Juridical Entity" which would be the administrative agency for operating the Canal. All of the property that *now* belongs to the United States Government would be turned over *free* of charge to the operating agency. The present Canal Zone would be diminished from the 10-mile wide strip to an area approximately 1 mile wide. The Canal Administration would operate its own *court system* and its own *police* forces in the Canal area.

So you can see that it will be very crucial for the *safety* of the Canal to make sure that the United States has *control.* Ultimate control of the Canal is in a governing board of 9 men. The United States has a 1-man majority on this board. But I want to point out that Congress will relinquish *all* control over the appointment of these men and has *no* recourse if even *one* of them should turn out to be incompetent or acts against the best interests of the country. . . .

The second treaty is the proposed status of forces treaty which defines the rights and privileges of our territory forces stationed to defend the Canal. One of the most serious drawbacks of this treaty is that it provides for a committee to confer when any special action is necessary to defend outbreaks of insurrection or enemy attack. The treaty stipulates that in the event that the committee fails to come to agreement on *what* measure can be taken that the controversy will be directed toward the respective governments through proper channels. This is an extremely cumbersome arrangement, and is another example of civilians dictating a no-win military policy without any consideration for the experience and professional judgment of the military experts.

Another feature of this treaty is a provision that the Panamanian Flag shall fly over *all* United States bases on Panamanian soil. The United States Flag *cannot* fly unless Panama gives *special* permission. No other base agreement that we have anywhere in the world stoops so low as to strike the American Flag.

The third treaty gives us an option to build a so-called sea level canal somewhere in Panama. At this point we do *not* know whether a sea level canal is technically or economically feasible. Congress currently has authorized a study which will take at least three years to complete. It is insane to propose a treaty for building a sea level canal when we don't even know that *such* a canal *can* be built. At the very least, these treaties should be held up until the sea level canal study is complete. Furthermore, if a sea level canal is built, the control structure will be virtually identical to the proposal in the new treaties with one exception: The door is held open to internationalization in the construction and financing of a sea level canal. *This* would dilute our control *even* more.

But in spite of this give-away, the most recent dispatches from Panama are indeed perplexing. These dispatches report that there is tremendous opposition growing within the ranks of Panamanian politics to approval of the treaties. . . .

These reports have caused great concern and puzzlement throughout many quarters in the United States. Many men thought that the generous give-away attitude reflected in these treaties would appease Panamanian nationalism. When the treaty negotiators sat down two years ago, the United States held almost all the cards.

We had, first of all, *sovereignty*—operating sovereignty in the Canal Zone. Secondly, we had won *independence* for Panama and furnished Panama with the main source of development and support. Thirdly, we have had a history of generous concessions and easy relations with Panama since the first treaty was signed in 1903.

The only card that Panama held was the somewhat dubious power of *blackmail*, a power growing out of *extreme* Nationalist activities. There was absolutely no reason why a strong powerful nation like the United States should give in to the petty blackmail on the fluctuating Panamanian political scene. . . .

From statements in the Spanish language press, it was clear that the Nationalists were prepared to urge extreme measures. Among their objectives were: First, that Panama aspires to have the *same* relation to the Panama Canal that Egypt has to the Suez Canal and proposes to nationalize it. Second, that Panama repudiates the idea of *internationalization*. Third, that Panama is determined to have *complete* sovereignty over the Canal Zone. Fourth, that Panama is considering closing territorial waters around the Canal Zone—a jurisdiction not recognized by the United States—as a *trap* to get its demands. . . .

The latest word is that even the most responsible of the forces opposing the treaty for principal objections are demanding that President Robles re-negotiate *four* principal items in the treaty which give minimum safeguards for the extensive U.S. interests in the Canal. These four objections are: First, that the provisions in the treaties for special *courts* in the area of the Canal would result in courts that would be outside Panamanian juridical control. Second, the special *police* force in the Canal area would have exclusive authority and not be under the direct control of Panama. Third, the *governing body* of the Canal administration would be weighted with 5 to 4 in favor of the United States; the Nationalists would prefer the other way around. Fourth, the provision for the use of Panamanian territory by U.S. armed forces defending the Canal is regarded as an imposition upon Panamanian sovereignty.

Now, as a matter of fact, the *actual* U.S. control exerted through these four points is so weak as to be extremely dangerous to our interests. The special Canal courts would be employing a new body of law which would not necessarily have the same protection as U.S. law. The police force would be under the control of a weak authority which would have difficulty coping with unexpected or large disturbances. The 5 to 4 margin on the governing body of the administration depends entirely upon the character and ability and inclination of the men who are appointed to the United States seats by the United States President.

Finally, the provisions for the United States defense bases in Panama are weakened by the giving of priority to Panamanian uses. Although the Panamanians want more than this, these protections are ridiculously weak when compared to the *firm* position which we *now* enjoy and seem intent upon abandoning. The question *then* is, *why* is Panamanian Nationalism intent upon rejecting the United States give-away?

The *answer* is that in terms of political action, Panamanian *Nationalism* is nearly impossible to distinguish from *Communism.* Now I grant that the *motives* of many Nationalists may be quite different from those of the Communists. I grant that many Panamanian politicians are not looking beyond their shores. On the other hand, the Communists have had their eye on the Panama Canal from the very first days when Communism seized power in the Soviet Union. In the famous memoirs of John Reed, *Ten Days That Shook the World,* this American observer of the Bolshevik Revolution reported that the Soviet representative to the Paris Peace Conference in 1919, Comrade Skobelev, was instructed by the Soviet executive Committee to demand that "all straits opening into inland seas as well as the Suez and Panama Canals be neutralized." This grand strategy of the Communists has endured down to the most recent days when, during the Suez crises in June, the Soviets once more demanded that *all* great waterways be internationalized.

It is easy to see *why* the Soviets have their eye on the Panama Canal. This is, of course, an important waterway in world trade. But it is even more important as a *vital* artery to *American* trade. Two-thirds of *all* cargo going through the Panama Canal is either bound to an American port or is coming from an American port. Those who wish to *bury* the United States must begin by blocking the Panama Canal.

But in time of war the Canal takes on an entirely *new* significance.

During the Second World War, 5,300 combat vessels used the Canal and 8,500 other ships carried troops or military cargo through it. For reasons of safety, no Axis ships could be permitted to go through. Of course, none would have dared come within hailing distance of the entrance to the Canal. Similarly, during the Korean war, over 1,000 U.S. Government vessels transited the Panama Canal to carry troops, supplies, and war material to U.S. troops in Korea.

Despite . . . those who say that the Canal is outmoded in an age of nuclear warfare, it continues to be an important supply line to Vietnam. U.S. Government and U.S. Government chartered vessels transiting the Canal increased in number from 394 to 725 in the period of fiscal year 1965-66. The cargo carried jumped from 1.9 million to 3.2 million long tons. Although these figures are the most recent available, they are for the year ending June

30, 1966, in the period before escalation really began in the buildup of military supplies in Southeast Asia. . . .

Even if the Canal were closed in peace time, the cost to the United States would be great. Millions of dollars would be added to U.S. shipping costs, and as much as two weeks time in ocean shipments. Japan, one of the largest buyers of U.S. coal, would probably have to seek other sources of supply. California and other West Coast states would begin to feel an almost instantaneous blight. Steel shortages would quickly begin to affect almost all West Coast manufacturing. On the East Coast, many of the canned foods which we take for granted, such as pears and pineapples, would become very expensive. . . .

I think that no one would disagree that the closing of the Panama Canal, or its take-over by a hostile nation, would be disastrous for the U.S. economy. It is no wonder, then, that the Communists have given it the No. 1 long-range priority. . . .

The *World Marxist Review* has already laid forth the Communist strategy for the take-over of Panama. . . . This article was published in March, 1965, almost contemporaneous with the beginning of the negotiation of the present Panama treaties that have been proposed by the Johnson and Robles administrations. Let me quote:

> In the opinion of our party, the national liberation revolution in Panama will pass through *two* stages. In the first stage, the task will be to set up a national, democratic, peoples government which will consistently carry out an agrarian reform, pursue an independent foreign policy, do away with corruption, take vigorous steps to develop the national industry, and embark on deep-going economic and social reforms.
>
> It is extremely important in the first stage to pursue a policy of unity, an alliance with all the forces interested in these changes (irrespective of their ideology). The party resolutions state that only a revolutionary peoples government, uniting all segments of the nation opposed to the oligarchy will be able in the second stage of the revolution to combat the U.S. and its monopolies, to remove the imperialist ulcer and pave the way to nationalization of the Canal.

The impossibility of distinguishing true Nationalist aims from issues which the Communists can use to agitate their two-part plan should make us wary of any arrangement in the Canal Zone which would weaken our control. Despite so-called safeguards written into the Treaty, we will no longer have the direct physical control of the territory in security of the Canal area which we now have.

If we *accept* these treaties in the hope of solidifying a fairly moderate government in Panama, the only thing we will accomplish is to make that government the target of increasingly strong Communist pressures. By throwing upon a small nation a responsibility which it doesn't have the capability to exercise, we are endangering the freedom and independence of that government.

I do not believe that any arrangement under which the United States gives up its effective sovereignty can be made to work for the benefit of the United States. There cannot possibly be any *better* way of protecting the Canal than to protect it *ourselves*.

We have the *sovereignty* and *jurisdiction* over the Canal by treaty. We *own* the land by separate purchase. We are twice owners of the Canal by *treaty* and *purchase*. There is no compelling reason to turn over its administration to a complicated *international* administration, under the direct sovereignty of a weak country.

If we accept the blackmail of Panamanian politics, then we will be following a policy which accurately complements the two-stage Communist plan outlined in the *World Marxist Review*. We see that plan already operating in the daily headlines of our newspapers today. If we are to avoid a stunning defeat, we must immediately change course. . . .

We must *not* jeopardize the security of our nation by allowing the confirmation of these proposed treaties with Panama.

Section 5

The new ideologies

Asian revolution and American ideology

Raul S. Manglapus

What is the relevance of American ideology to Asian traditions of conformity? Mr. Manglapus suggests that America light torches to become beacons of hope and direction, but that the actual direction and speed of the revolution to overcome poverty, traditionalism, and injustice be allowed to arise from within. Just as America "first had to slay the European father" to achieve its greatness, so must the American father image be slain, "or at least cut down to brotherly size," so that new ideologies may develop the "Asian revolution."

Foreign Affairs (January 1967). Reprinted by special permission. Copyright by the Council on Foreign Relations, Inc., New York. Mr. Manglapus is a member of the Committee on Foreign Relations of the Philippine Senate and former Undersecretary of the Department of Foreign Affairs in the Philippine government.

Asia wants revolution; Asia needs revolution. . . . Once all of Asia was in a state of equilibrium, with its agrarian societies relying for survival on a delicate balance between land and population. Land suitable for rice-growing was limited and rice-eating populations struggled for subsistence; they had neither the time, ability nor energy to think of governing themselves or even of participating in government. The task of governing was left to the few, a small, specialized class of scholar-officials. To labor and obey was left to the many. Thus the centralized state came into being, strong enough to protect these precarious balances from ever-threatening natural or artificial forces, skilled enough to undertake the control of the flow of water, the life-blood of the staple production.

In the centers of Asian culture, in India, Java, Cambodia, Japan and most especially in China, there was strong central government and a statically arranged society. In China, it was a pyramid, the peasants at the bottom, the land-owning gentry above them, still higher the scholar-administrators and at the summit the emperor, the divine maintainer of the equilibrium between land and population, man and nature, heaven and earth.

Confucius gave this stability a philosophic base which sanctified harmony and reverence for authority. But if the balance were disturbed, if the emperor could not control the avarice of landlords, the corruption of officials, the looting by invading barbarians, and if therefore the masses starved, the sacred work-cycle stopped and there was chaos, there yet was a remedy: the ruler ceased to be divine. Rebellion was permitted, nay called for, and the successful rebel was by his victory ipso facto vested with divine power. A new dynasty was born and the balance was restored. The Chinese formula was adopted, with modifications, throughout East Asia.

This kind of equilibrium was to last four thousand years, until one day Western man arrived with ideas more explosive than the powder the Chinese had invented for firecrackers at the harvest festival (and which the Westerner would later push into the mouths of cannon). Among these new ideas were Christianity, proclaiming human rights superior to those of the state; science, substituting immutable laws for the capricious will of the gods; parliamentary government, making the governor responsible to the governed; and new techniques for mass production and the control of disease.

Asian society was shaken to its roots. European governors replaced indigenous rulers, and the land once tilled only for the subsistence of the population was now made to produce raw materials for the colonial power.

When the Manchus fell in China, there was no other dynasty to take their place. The cluster of Western ideas, which the Europeans had never bothered to knit together into one harmonious whole to replace the old Asian equilibrium, fell on Asian ground as separate elements, breeding hope and despair in expectations that could not soon be fulfilled. Mass populations grew, unchecked by the old natural levellers, plague and epidemic; plantation economies stagnated because they were geared to export crops whose markets had faded away with the departure of the colonials.

Asia is left today with more ambition and less fullfillment, more people and less food. The equilibrium is gone. And no new rebel can assume the divine mantle and restore the harmony. The Asian, converted to the ideas of the West, now wants to control his government and his destiny. . . .

This now is the question: Is America ready to face the necessity of revolution? Many Americans would probably find the question impertinent. Are they not the first revolutionaries of the modern age? Is not their Declaration of Independence a ringing revolutionary document for men of all time to invoke in the cause of justice and equality?

They are, indeed, entitled to be proud. But recalling one's own revolution is perhaps not enough, or at least is a different thing from understanding another's hunger for revolutionary change. It becomes even less adequate when America's original revolution and its ideological underpinnings no longer seem relevant to the deep current of human events where men now need revolution most—among the masses of the developing world.

In another era, one of limited population and pure libertarian motives, the American Revolution was surely relevant. When America snatched independence from the first Philippine Republic at the turn of the century, William Jennings Bryan replied to the imperialists' justification of "educating the Filipinos":

> The educated Filipinos are now in revolt against us, and the most ignorant ones have made the least resistance to our domination. If we are to govern them without their consent and give them no voice in determining the taxes which they must pay, we dare not educate them, lest they learn to read the Declaration of Independence and Constitution of the United States and mock us for our inconsistency.

But the reasoning of John Locke and the precepts of Isaac Newton, which were the wellsprings of the principles of the American Constitution and Declaration of Independence, seem to have little bearing on questions like the pressures of population, the closing of the breach between rich and poor, the rapid demolition of the barriers of race and creed.

Equality is good, but in the newly emerging nations there is now too much equality in destitution. Dignity would be better. . . . In a world searching for an ideology that will bestow this dignity, where even the youth of America seeks a "national purpose," America's only answer seems to be pragmatic improvisation, meeting crises on a "case-to-case" basis.

And all the while, Americans are unpragmatically espousing or rejecting ideas because of associations that are either imprecise or no longer applicable. The idea of capitalism is a primary example. America is a monument to the genius of free enterprise, and American propagandists abroad would like to credit her unabated economic growth to completely free initiative, almost to classic laissez-faire. . . . No mention is made of American government controls and subsidies that enable the "free-enterprise" economy to accommodate the concern for the national welfare.

Americans are proud to be known as alert opponents of socialism . . . and are proud of their crusading anti-Communism. . . .

Even America's allies and non-Communist friends are beginning to tire of negative anti-Communism. As early as 1963, Don Van Sung, the Vietnamese patriot, warned: "By emphasizing anti-Communism rather than positive revolutionary goals and from lack of a better adaptation to the local situation, the United States has reduced its anti-Communist efforts in Viet Nam to the maintenance of an administrative machine and of an army." To Eduardo Frei, the Christian Democratic President of Chile, "the anti-Communisms of fear, of preservation of 'order,' and of forces manifested in military coups are doomed to failure and are constantly in rout. They have nothing to say to youth or the people."

But, it will be asked, what need is there of ideology? Did not pragmatism cure the ills of America? We may largely agree. The histories of other nations are always divided into periods, of rise and decay, of benevolent kings and lecherous kings, of the ascendancy of reason and the rise of faith, of progress and reaction. American history is singularly lacking in these periods and in this respect it is monotonous. But it is the unique, consistent and gloriously monotonous American condition which accounts for the fact that every minute an American is born free, free in every sense, to develop himself and his country according to his own will and initiative.

There will never be one single man known as the builder of America. And this just might be America's guarantee for greatness without end. . . . What shall we call this guarantee? Capitalism? Free enterprise? . . . Spontaneity may be the key. And as America built itself spontaneously, so also could we build Asia.

But Asia is not ready for spontaneity. There is at present little enthusiasm in Asia for the American example; for it is apparent that patchwork democracy requires conditions which do not exist in the developing world. One such condition is the challenge of the open frontier—the response to which was the beginning of the American miracle. There are no such frontiers to challenge Asians. The Asian peasant must respond not to the heartening call of the rich wild but to the demoralizing prospect of having to make productive two hectares of unowned land, his tenancy having emanated from some unwritten ancestral contract or royal decree which his ancestor could not read. . . .

A second condition nowhere prevalent in Asia is the American tradition of dissent. The very act of crossing the Atlantic by the original American settlers was one of dissent—dissent from oppression, from tyranny, simple dissent from opposing opinion. No such tradition motivates the Asian. The waves of Malays and Proto-Malays that landed on the shores of Luzon, Visayas and Mindanao, the early Filipinos . . . these men were no fugitives from tyranny. They came in groups of families . . . and their tradition was conformism—conformism to the will of the chief. . . . Soon it would be conformism to the will of the white colonial governor. But whether the supreme will was native or foreign, nonconformism would never be a right, and the penalty for it would invariably be heavy.

There is yet a third condition—the richness of the land. The pioneers found in the American continent a prodigious wealth of resources. Indeed there are pockets of great natural wealth in parts of Asia. . . . But most Asians work barren land and must overcome superstition before putting to use the fertilizer that will fatten the soil.

No wonder, then, that Asia is not yet ready to understand spontaneity. No wonder that Asians, having almost always been servants, have developed the habits of the servant, a resistance to change, a willingness to obey only the gods of superstition. . . . No wonder that when the Asian is told, "Go and be free, develop yourself, face and overcome each problem as it comes with your own genius," he does not understand.

It is quite possible that something akin to American spontaneity can come from other antecedents. The Filipino writer, Nick Joaquin, reported after a recent visit to Red China that "responsiveness to challenges is the spirit that is Americanizing the Chinese." He says that the party line this year in New China sounds like Babbitt at a salesmen's pep talk: "Go all out, aim high, get results! Think big! Act big!" "What could be more Damn Yankee?" he asks. "If you bumped into it in the dark, could you guess this was Chinese, not Rotarian; that this was Slave State, not Rugged Individualism?"

Responsiveness without freedom. Is this paradox really possible? If it is, it is the result of an upheaval the premises of which have been easier for Asians to understand: the simple dichotomy of the rich and the poor, the oppressor and the oppressed, the few and the many. The rich are the few, the poor are the many. Let the many rise in revolution and redistribute the fruits of the earth—this is something Asians may understand, a revolution an Asian may indeed find easy to join, because he knows the poverty, the inequality, the oppression and all the rest. It is certainly easier to join than that complicated revolt against stultifying tradition, that rebellion against self through which he would have to go before he could enjoy the privilege of "pragmatic" spontaneity.

This is not to say that Americans are incapable of magnificent responses to challenges that excite other men and other nations. . . . But for Asians, what chance has such a performance, however brilliant, against the sustained, persistent, unequivocal panorama of revolution projected from other capitals? America is perfectly capable of lighting torches, and men will at times follow, but as Jacques Maritain has put it, "for lack of adequate ideology, her lights cannot be seen. I think," he adds, "it is too much modesty."

Call it modesty, call it indifference, call it overconfidence; whatever it may be, I do not suggest that America stop lighting torches, for even though they may not last, they will always be useful in the dark. But America could also light a beacon, project a permanent beam steadily proclaiming what she stands for and informing the peoples of the world what it is they might gain from her leadership in the elevation of each human life.

Americans are almost organically averse to traditional ideology. This aversion may have been fitting to the early American, but how proper is it to the modern American—the American with a global commitment to leadership? Unless it is his desire to withdraw into isolation, he must collect his bundle of brilliant improvisations and distill from them an ideology relevant to the problems of this age and the lives of those millions who are touched by his commitment.

It is up to the Americans to draw the ideological possibilities out of their pragmatic experience, but an Asian is perhaps entitled to a few expressions of hope. He hopes that the beacon will show the way to a sustained social revolution that will lift men to a level where they may begin to enjoy the freedom and the privilege to be spontaneous. He also hopes this ideology will enable Americans to give better reasons than they have so far given for needed changes. Land must be redistributed because "it is the absolute right of the proletariat," says *Das Kapital;* "because of the social character of property," says *Quadragesimo Anno.* "Because without land reform American aid is wasted," says the American. Will Americans always limit themselves so? . . .

An Englishman has said: "The trouble with Americans is that they want to be on top of the world and still expect to be loved. It simply can't be done, you know."

Is this true, or not? When America has shown the world how she can leap over her barriers of race, of creed, of poverty—not "case-to-case" but by the propulsion of ideas so universal, so understandable that they reach the hearts of all men—who knows? Americans may yet manage to be on top of the world and be loved. But that is not the important thing. Even without reward for the work of world leadership, there is enough return in the urgency and value of flinging in the teeth of those who would create an anonymous and faceless society the idea of a world of men endowed with individual dignity.

The first false god to be toppled in the Asian revolution is paternalism. The family of young nations wants no more of the father image. Max Lerner has pointed out that in the days when American nationalism was taking shape, the Americans first had to slay the European father so that they could then without inhibition use the European heritage in their own drive to greatness. The Indians had to slay the British father to work out their own destiny through British constitutional traditions. The young Filipino entrepreneur must either slay the American father image or at least cut it down to brotherly size so that he can collaborate or compete on equal terms—using the techniques of the Harvard Business School. The Filipino leader must also slay the image so that he can lead his country without self-consciousness to its own version of American constitutional democracy, and negotiate treaties with America on the basis of mutual respect.

We are told we need not worry that the Americans will resist the slaying of an image which so ill befits them. A leader among equals, yes, but not a paternalist—not the American with his passion for brotherhood, his sporting blood that will preclude his taking advantage.

So let there be social revolution. Let it fight injustice, give hope. Let it produce wealth, but also close the gap between those who enjoy the wealth and those who do not. Let it not surrender to the simplistic idea that the only problem in Asia is productivity, "the enlarging of the pie," and that the exploitation of man by man will resolve itself with this enlargement. Let it persevere until the millions of Asia are released from the bonds of tradition, feudal tenancy and centralized power. Let America help to fire it, but do not make it an American revolution. Let it be so universal in meaning, so pregnant with hope for all races, that each nation will take it for its own.

Section 6

The new forms of imperialism

Pax-humanica?

Lee W. Farnsworth

Will national security always be threatened by the existence of imperialism in one of its many forms? The result of a Russian proposal for a U.N. declaration against "intervention in the domestic affairs of States" was a full-scale debate on modern forms of imperialism. What began as a Communist attempt to criticize the United States resulted in a consensus of small nations that there be "a plague on both your houses." The small nations want peace without interference of any kind.

The material for this article is edited from United Nations General Assembly, Twentieth Session, Official Records, *pp. 243–294, A/C.1/SR. 1395–1400 (General Debate of the First Committee) and United Nations* Yearbook, *Twentieth Session (1965), Chapter 6, pp. 87–95. This is the first publication of this article.*

It seems to many that imperialism is a thing of the past. The doubling of the number of members of the United Nations and a count of the few remaining colonial subjects indicates how far the world has traveled since Woodrow Wilson first proclaimed the concept of the right of national self-determination.

It used to be fairly easy to recognize imperialism. Through the use of power, one nation imposed its will on another to achieve its own economic, political, social, or military goals, regardless of the weaker nation's will. The colonies of Great Britain, France, and the Netherlands, among others, in Asia and Africa clearly fit within this definition. Less clear-cut but nevertheless recognizable as imperialism were the relationships of several Western nations with China and the United States with several Latin American states. It is also proper to include as imperialism the relationships between the Soviet Union and the Eastern European satellites, at least until the end of the Khrushchev era.

Imperialism is now taking on a new look, even though the central idea that it is the imposition of the will of the powerful on the weak remains. The two giants of the world, the United States and the Soviet Union, possessing predominant power, almost inevitably seek to expand their influence, albeit with different motivations. Other nations are also engaged in the process of influence, generally using modern communications techniques as the primary means. For instance, it is clear that South Vietnam is no longer a French colony, yet France works very hard through its cultural affairs office in Saigon to expand French cultural and economic influence over the nation—and it is quite successful in its efforts. Switzerland's main contact with other nations is also through a cultural office.

This article is principally concerned with the imperialism of the two giant powers. In recent years each has cited the behavior of the other as imperialism while calling its own behavior the "liberation" or "defense" of oppressed or subverted peoples.

The Soviet delegate to the United Nations requested on September 24, 1965, that an item be placed on the agenda of the General Assembly entitled "The inadmissibility of intervention in the domestic affairs of States and the protection of their independence and sovereignty." In the accompanying memorandum the Soviet Union noted that "certain powers" were impeding the political, economic, and social development of certain states by aggression and intervention in the domestic affairs of states whose peoples were fighting against "colonial domination" and for "national liberation." The USSR therefore submitted a draft declaration which has been summarized officially as follows:

> The General Assembly would regard it as its duty to: (1) reaffirm that every sovereign State and every people had an inalienable right to freedom and independence and to defend its sovereignty, and that this right must be fully protected; (2) urge all Member States to fulfill their Charter obligations; (3) demand that acts constituting armed or any other type of intervention in the domestic affairs of States, as well as those against the just struggle of peoples

> for national independence and freedom, should be halted forthwith and not be permitted in the future; (4) call on all States to abide by the principle of mutual respect and non-intervention in domestic affairs for any reason whatsoever. Finally, the Assembly would warn those States which, in defiance of the Charter of the United Nations, were engaged in intervention in the domestic affairs of other States that in so doing, they were assuming a heavy burden of international responsibility before all peoples.

This resolution was referred on September 28 to the First Committee of the General Assembly, where it was debated by 68 nations. The United States and others offered amendments to the USSR draft, and three other drafts were ultimately prepared. The fourth draft was sponsored by 57 member states and finally adopted by both the First Committee and the General Assembly.

The debate clearly illuminates the various charges, countercharges, and statements of defense on the issue of imperialism in the last third of this century. A summary of the debate follows.

The Soviet Union and its satellites took first crack at the United States; they cited Vietnam, the Congo, and the Dominican Republic. The brunt of the attack was concentrated on Vietnam. The United States, they charged, by escalating the war was committing aggression against the sovereign state of the Democratic Republic of Vietnam (North Vietnam) in complete disregard of international law, the United Nations Charter, and international agreements. In support of this effort and linked to it, the Soviet delegate Fedorenko further charged that the United States had troops in Vietnam, Thailand, Taiwan, South Korea, Guam, Okinawa, and elsewhere for "purposes of blackmail, and even for intervention in the domestic affairs of States." Moreover, the real representative of the South Vietnamese people was the National Liberation Front, which stood for "independence, democracy, peace, and end to imperialist intervention, and the establishment of a democratic coalition Government pursuing a policy of independence and neutrality in accordance with the Geneva Agreements of 1954." He concluded by saying that it is a "socialist principle" that peoples are entitled to their own social and political order without outside interference. Revolutions cannot be ordered from outside. Therefore, it was the duty of the United Nations to condemn "all foreign intervention in the domestic affairs of States."

The Cuban delegate, Alarcon Quesada, joined in the attack by saying that the United States and its puppet government in South Vietnam had prevented the peaceful unification of the country through general elections free from external interference. By providing military assistance, military advisers, and funds, the United States had engaged in a "cynical and shameless war of neo-colonialist aggression" in the guise of cooperation with and assistance to a friendly government. He concluded that "a small people which was trying to exercise its legitimate right to independence, sovereignty and peace" was being "subjected to criminal acts by the most aggressive imperialist Power in history." He then volunteered troops and supplies to fight against the United States in Vietnam.

The American delegate, Mr. Yost, charged in response that the Soviet Union had not presented the proposal as a sincere attack on intervention as such but rather as a pretext to attack the Western states. As for Vietnam, he noted that had North Vietnam fulfilled its commitment to leave South Vietnam alone, "there would be no war and no United States troops in that part of the world; aggression had come from the North, not the South." The United States had successfully stood up against previous Communist interventions in Greece and Korea. Vietnam was only different in that it was planned as part of the current Chinese Communist doctrine of intervention, falsely labeled as the doctrine of "wars of national liberation." A war of this kind had also been "unleashed against non-Communist Governments in Africa."

As for imperialism, Yost charged that "the most serious source of intervention in the domestic affairs of other States in the twentieth century had been the Soviet Union," at least until the advent of Communist China. He cited examples of the armed takeover of Estonia, Latvia, and Lithuania in 1940. The Soviet Union now includes parts of Finland, Poland, Czechoslovakia (which the Czech delegate later said had been offered up voluntarily), Romania, and Japan. In all these areas and in East Germany as well, "the people had never been allowed to exercise their right to self-determination."

The United States congratulated the Soviet Union for replacing the doctrine of the inevitability of war with the doctrine of peaceful coexistence. To make the declaration "more impartial, just and generally acceptable," however, the United States suggested amendments which would emphasize the idea that intervention "could not be justified for any reason, whether economic, political or ideological." After all, the greatest need for newly independent nations is not "wars of liberation" but protection against intervention for ideological reasons. He cited as examples the training of young African people in Communist China "for the purpose of mounting subversive movements against their own Governments" and young Latin Americans being trained in Cuba for similar purposes.

The United States also wanted a change designed to emphasize the unlawfulness of covert as well as overt interventions. Under the new Chinese doctrine of intervention, guerrilla bands were being encouraged, trained, and armed to attack insidiously their own governments from within. Such attacks were just as dangerous as armed attacks across international frontiers. The goals of these agents of a foreign power and ideology were to terrorize and murder innocent people and to impose "the will of another Government and another ideology."

Yost stated in conclusion that the United States willingly supported an amended declaration of this sort which would allow "all peoples, whether or not they were independent, to determine their own destinies through the exercise of the right of self-determination, in whatever manner they chose."

The British delegate, Sir Roger Jackling, generally supported the U.S. position. He particularly wondered why the USSR, as co-chairman with the United Kingdom of the Geneva Conference, had consistently refused to call a meeting of all parties concerned to resolve the question of who was guilty of intervention. He further questioned the merit of specifically mentioning direct and armed attack while making no mention of subversive activities, "particularly the training of dissident nationals of independent States who were receiving military or militant training inside communist countries." He even agreed to the plausibility, although it was still objectionable, of these activities for aiding "peoples' revolution" or "national liberation" in the case of colonial territories; it was, however, "indefensible in the case of independent States where subversion was fostered against the will of the people."

The delegate of Colombia denounced indirect aggression and fomenting revolution from outside, as had occurred in Latin America. The party that carried out these acts was acting under the orders of a "foreign Power." However, he added, intervention from another source to combat the subversive infiltration was also inadmissable. Colombia was opposed "to intervention of any kind, regardless of its motives, origin, or methods."

A number of less involved nations participated in the debate. Among the significant contributions was the Afghanistan delegate's suggestion that the declaration should affirm not only non-intervention but also the "closely related principles of non-aggression, co-existence, and international cooperation." He seemed concerned about a variety of the forms of intrusion and asked that there be reference beyond political sovereignty to include economic, social, and cultural independence as well.

The delegate from Uganda welcomed the opportunity for the small countries to unite in rejecting "the attempts of some of the great Powers to undermine their sovereignty and independence and reduce them to the status of political appendages." It was "painful" after struggling for independence and sovereignty to have some powers interfere in their internal affairs. He seemed to include both powers when he charged that interference had taken place by both military intervention and intrigue directed from inside or outside the country concerned. Such intervention was always in defense of some vital interest or ideology, usually called "democracy" by all concerned. He did not consider it very democratic, however, to promote coup d'etats, take military action, promote sabotage or "try to dislodge a Government because it had different ideological views or was regarded as a puppet regime." Democracy implies freedom of expression and acceptance of the voice of the majority; therefore, "the decision to change a Government should be left to the people of the country concerned." He felt that if the small and nonaligned nations could be left alone and without danger of outside interference, they could devote their scarce resources to economic and social development rather than to the establishment of security forces.

The delegate of Rwanda called for a condemnation of any direct or indirect act of aggression. "The small countries which had been the victims of colonialism for many years would not tolerate a neocolonialism aimed at the forcible imposition of a particular political or economic ideology." The intervention of the great powers on the pretext of protecting freedom or independence "in fact only sowed disorder in these States and set back their development." The delegate also condemned "the practice of training groups of young people or political refugees to sow death and destruction in their own countries." He hoped that the United Nations would have an assured future and that mankind would be saved from "the cataclysm of a nuclear war by the General Assembly defining and proclaiming against both direct and indirect aggression and intervention in the domestic affairs of States."

Finally, the delegate from Kenya noted that his country accepted the theory of liberation movements against "colonial and racist regimes." He even suggested that under certain circumstances it might be justifiable for the people of a given country to seek a change of government. He did not feel that the "overthrow of a popularly elected government" is a legitimate objective; according to him, that kind of revolution must be condemned as "inspired or engineered from outside to serve the interests of a foreign Power or foreign Powers."

The Kenya delegate was vociferous in attacking both U.S. intervention on the pretext of containing communism and Soviet and Chinese encouragement of infiltration, subversion, and propaganda for wars of liberation. Both were neocolonialism. No state had any right by virtue of its wealth or military or economic power "to dictate to less powerful States." "No foreign Power should assume," he said, "that it has a better understanding of the needs and aspirations of the Kenyan people than the Government which had been voted into power by that people."

It is obvious from the debate that great concern continues about imperialism among both the great and the small of the world. Each seems to stress his own problems and interests, but out of the argument emerges the reality that there is indeed intervention in "the domestic affairs of States" and that it is resented as a threat to domestic order and feared as a possible prelude to a general war.

The final Resolution 2131 (*xx*) was adopted by the General Assembly on December 21, 1965, by a vote of 109 to 0, with 1 abstention (the United Kingdom). The text was as follows:

> The General Assembly,
> Deeply concerned at the gravity of the international situation and the increasing threat to universal peace due to armed intervention and other direct or

indirect forms of interference threatening the sovereign personality and the political independence of States,

Considering that the United Nations, in accordance with their aim to eliminate war, threats to the peace and acts of aggression, created an Organization, based on the sovereign equality of States, whose friendly relations would be based on respect for the principle of equal rights and self-determination of peoples and on the obligation of its Members to refrain from the threat or use of force against the territorial integrity or political independence of any state,

Recognizing that, in fulfilment of the principle of self-determination, the General Assembly, in the Declaration on the Granting of Independence to Colonial Countries and Peoples contained in resolution 1514 (XV) of 14 December 1960, stated its conviction that all peoples have an inalienable right to complete freedom, the exercise of their sovereignty and the integrity of their national territory, and that, by virtue of that right, they freely determine their political status and freely pursue their economic, social, and cultural development,

Recalling that in the Universal Declaration of Human Rights the General Assembly proclaimed that recognition of the inherent dignity and of the equal and inalienable rights of all members of the human family is the foundation of freedom, justice and peace in the world, without distinction of any kind . . .

Recognizing that full observance of the principle of the non-intervention of States in the internal and external affairs of other States is essential to the fulfilment of the purposes and principles of the United Nations,

Considering that armed intervention is synonymous with aggression and, as such, is contrary to the basic principles on which peaceful international co-operation between States should be built,

Considering further that direct intervention, subversion and all forms of indirect intervention are contrary to these principles and, consequently, constitute a violation of the Charter of the United Nations,

Mindful that violation of the principle of non-intervention poses a threat to the independence, freedom and normal political, economic, social and cultural development of countries, particularly those which have freed themselves from colonialism, and can pose a serious threat to the maintenance of peace,

Fully aware of the imperative need to create appropriate conditions which would enable all States, and in particular the developing countries, to choose without duress or coercion their own political, economic and social institutions,

In the light of the foregoing considerations, solemnly declares:

1. No State has the right to intervene, directly or indirectly, for any reason whatever, in the internal or external affairs of any other State. Consequently, armed intervention and all other forms of interference or attempted threats against the personality of the State or against its political, economic and cultural elements are condemned.

2. No State may use or encourage the use of economic, political or any other type of measures to coerce another State in order to obtain from it the subordination of the exercise of its sovereign rights or to secure from it advantages of any kind. Also, no State shall organize, assist, foment, finance, incite or tolerate subversive, terrorist or armed activities directed towards the violent overthrow of the regime of another State, or interfere in civil strife in another State.

3. The use of force to deprive peoples of their national identity constitutes a violation of their inalienable rights and of the principle of non-intervention.

4. The strict observance of these obligations is an essential condition to ensure that nations live together in peace with one another, since the practice of any form of intervention not only violates the spirit and letter of the Charter of the United Nations but also leads to the creation of situations which threaten international peace and security.

5. Every State has an inalienable right to choose its political, economic, social and cultural systems, without interference in any form by another State.

6. All States shall respect the right of self-determination and independence of peoples and nations, to be freely exercised without any foreign pressure, and with absolute respect for human rights and fundamental freedoms. Consequently, all States shall contribute to the complete elimination of racial discrimination and colonialism in all its forms and manifestations.

7. For the purpose of the present Declaration, the term "State" covers both individual States and groups of States.

8. Nothing in this Declaration shall be construed as affecting in any manner the relevant provisions of the Charter of the United Nations relating to the maintenance of international peace and security, in particular those contained in Chapters VI, VII and VIII.

Unfortunately, events since 1965 do not indicate that any of the great powers nor several of the smaller ones have taken this declaration seriously in developing and practicing their foreign policy. Neoimperialism is a condition of our time, one with which all concerned are familiar. There has been talk of a "pax-Americana" and some even of a "pax-Russo-Americana," but both of these, by their very essence, are neoimperialism. However, judging from some of the remarks of the smaller nations, they may instead be hopeful of an eventual "pax-humanica."

Section 7

The law of change

Change and international relations

Zbigniew Brzezinski

Professor Brzezinski analyzes five major changes that he feels will vastly alter the system of international relations. These changes relate closely to the other concepts in this chapter.

"The Implications of Change for United States Foreign Policy," Department of State Bulletin, *July 3, 1967. Mr. Brzezinski is a member of the Department of State Policy Planning Council.*

International politics is dominated by crises. The result is that we often mistake these crises for the reality of international politics. Going from crisis to crisis, we simply lose sight of the more basic and often more important changes that imperceptibly reshape the world in which we live.

It is useful, therefore, sometimes to pause and ask in a detached way: What is the nature of our era? What is really changing in international politics? . . .

As I look at international politics, I see five major changes taking place, together fundamentally altering the nature of international relations in our day. The changes are not obvious, because they are slow; but their cumulative impact is most important.

1. *The first involves the waning of ideological conflicts among the more developed nations of the world.* Since the time of the French Revolution, conflicts between states have been profoundly emotionalized by mass struggles induced by a mixture of ideology and nationalism. Where that mixture was particularly intense, as in the case of nazism, the conflicts which resulted were particularly bloody and destructive. By and large, during the last 150 years or so relations among the more advanced states, particularly in Europe, have been poisoned by the emotionalizing impact of absolute doctrinal answers concerning most of the basic issues of humanity.

This condition is waning due to a variety of factors.

First of all, nuclear weapons have necessitated greater and greater restraint in relations among states. . . . Hitherto one could calculate the cost and the potential advantages of war; today, this simply is no longer possible, and thus even the most bitter ideological hatreds have to be restrained by common sense.

Secondly, just as important, we are realizing more fully that social change is such an enormously complex and interrelated process, with so many variables, that it cannot be reduced to a few simple ideological formulas, as was the case in the early stages of industrialization. . . .

Thirdly, communism, the principal, and until recently the most militant, revolutionary ideology of our day, is dead—communism is dead as an ideology in the sense that it is no longer capable of mobilizing unified global support. On the contrary, it is increasingly fragmented by conflicts among constituent units and parties. This has contributed to ideological disillusionment among its members. Communist states, Communist movements, and Communist subversion are still very important on the international scene, but Communist ideology as a vital force is no longer with us.

Revolutionary movements in different parts of the world instead relate themselves more specifically to local radical traditions and try to exploit local opportunities. Thus, the common doctrine and its alleged universal validity are being diluted by specific adaptations. . . .

The role of ideology is still quite important in relations among the less developed states, where problems are simpler, where issues can be translated into black-and-white propositions, and where absolute doctrinal categories still appear superficially relevant.

2. *Closely connected with the waning ideological conflicts among the more developed nations of the world is the decline of violence among these states.* During approximately the last 150 years, the international scene has been dominated by conflicts fought principally among the more advanced and largely

European nations of the world. The focus of violence today is shifting to the third world. Increasingly, conflicts are either between some of the developed nations and the less developed nations; or increasingly, instability in the underdeveloped world is itself the source of global tensions. It is thus a basic reversal of the dominant pattern of the recent past.

The new restraint on violence displayed by the more advanced states in relations among one another is also largely due to the nuclear age. . . . Given the range of conflicts, the frequent tensions, and the occasional clashes between the United States and the Soviet Union, in almost any other era in history a war between them probably would have ensued. . . .

This restraint is still largely absent insofar as relations among the less developed states are concerned. Moreover, the ideological passions and the nationalist tensions have not yet run their full course; and consequently the propensity toward total reactions, total commitment, and total violence is still quite high.

Without discussing the pros and cons of the Vietnamese war, it offers a good example of the generalization made above. It reflects the shift of focus in global affairs from conflicts between the developed states to a conflict that involves a wealthy and highly advanced country in an effort to create regional stability. The unwillingness of the Soviet Union to become totally involved in the conflict stems from the greater realization of its own interest in preserving peace in the nuclear age and also from the gradual waning of its ideology, which weakens its sense of total identification with every revolutionary movement in the world.

3. *The third generalization is the proposition that we are witnessing the end of the supremacy of the nation-state on the international scene.* This process is far from consummated, but nonetheless the trend seems to me to be irreversible. It is not only a matter of security interdependence among allied states. It is also a matter of psychological change. People through history have expanded their sense of identification. At first, men identified themselves with their families, then with their villages, then with their towns, then with their regions and provinces, then with their nations. Now increasingly people are beginning to identify with their continents and regions. This change has been induced by the necessities of economic development and of the technological revolution, by changes in the means of communication—all of which cause people to identify themselves more and more with wider, more global human interests.

4. *The fourth major change which has taken place in our times is the emergence of the United States as the preponderant world power.* The conventional view is that since 1945 we have seen three basic stages of international development: First of all, U.S. nuclear monopoly; secondly, bipolarity, based on two homogeneous alliances rigidly confronting each other; and now increasingly polycentrism, with many states playing the international game.

I submit that this is a wrong perspective; in fact, the sequence has been the opposite. The first postwar era—1945–50—was essentially a polycentric era. The United States was largely disarmed. It had a nuclear monopoly, to be sure, but its nuclear power was essentially apocalyptic; it was not applicable—it was only usable in circumstances which everyone wished to avoid—hence it was not politically relevant. The United States was disarmed, it was only beginning to be involved in Europe, hardly involved in Asia—and there were still two major empires on the scene, the French and the British. The Russians were asserting their regional control over Central Europe, but they were not yet involved in Asia. Asia itself was in turmoil. This truly was the polycentric era.

It gave way to the era of bipolarity, of dichotomic confrontation, if you will, between two alliances—one led by the Soviet Union, one led by the United States. The Soviet Union during this time acquired nuclear capacity, and under Khrushchev it misjudged its nuclear power and attempted to pursue between 1958 and 1962 a policy designed to assert Soviet global supremacy. These years were dominated by the Soviet effort to throw the West out of Berlin, to put missiles in Cuba and to force a showdown. However, Khrushchev discovered in 1962 that the Soviet Union still had only apocalyptic power. Its nuclear power was not relevant when faced with U.S. power, which by then had become much more complex and much more usable in a far greater diversity of situations.

Thus in the last few years the United States successfully stared Khrushchev down in Cuba, it protected its interests in the Dominican Republic and in the Congo—and today it is doing it in Viet-Nam. Yet the Soviet Union did not dare to react even in the area of its regional domination: Berlin. Today, the Soviet Union is in effect a regional power, concentrating primarily on Europe and on the growing danger from China. Our power during this ensuing period has become applicable power, with a long-range delivery system, with the means of asserting itself on the basis of a global reach.

Moreover, recent years—and this is much more important—have witnessed continued economic growth in this country; they have seen the expansion and appearance on the world scene of U.S. technological know-how. Increasingly, the U.S. way of life, our styles, our patterns of living, are setting the example. Today, if there is a creative society in the world, it is the United States—in the sense that everyone, very frequently without knowing it, is imitating it. However, paradoxically because the United States is the only global power, it finds it increasingly difficult to concentrate its resources or its policy on any specific region of the world. This often creates sharp dilemmas and difficulties, difficulties with which we will have to live because our involvement is also a major factor of stability in the world.

5. *The fifth major change involves the growing fragmentation of the world, not only between the developed states and the underdeveloped—which*

is, of course, much talked about—but the increasing fragmentation of the developed world. I have particularly in mind the growing difference between the United States and the rest of the advanced world. The United States is becoming a new society, a society no longer shaped by the impact of the industrial process on social, economic, and political life. That impact still shapes European life; if you look at the changes in the nature of the European political elite, if you look at problems of employment or unemployment or welfare, if you look at efforts to create greater access to education in Europe—all of these are manifestations of the impact of the industrial process on a formerly rural and traditional society.

The United States is no longer in this kind of historical era. Increasingly, our social dilemmas are of leisure, well-being, automation, psychic well-being, alienation of the youth (usually from well-to-do middle-class families). All of that is connected with a standard of living which has become relatively stable and high, connected with a society which is well-to-do but in many respects has new dilemmas of purpose and meaning. We are becoming, in effect, a post-industrial society, in which computers and communications are shaping more and more our way of life. . . .

All of this induces new perspectives and new attitudes and sharpens the difference between us and the rest of the developed world. . . .

Ever hear of a two-pants suit?

Russell Baker

A striking and humorous example of change is this column by Russell Baker. But even this young man from the time machine may already be outdated in style and dress in today's fast-moving world.

After the last gun was silenced in World War II, a man in a six-button suit and Beatle haircut appeared from a time machine one night and wandered among a barracks full of servicemen who were awaiting discharges.

"Do you understand what this war was all about?" he asked a GI. "Sure," the GI said. "We fought to save the Brooklyn Dodgers, the two-pants suit and Mom's apple pie."

"Then you have lost," said the man from the time machine. "Within 20 years, the Dodgers will be sold out to Los Angeles. The two-pants suit is even now gone from the haberdashery rack. And by the time all of you are Dads, Mom's apple pie, like almost everything else Mom used to whip up in the kitchen before Pearl Harbor, will be delivered by teamsters, frozen or ready-mixed."

The men in the barracks hooted and said that if they were not so tired of fighting they would bloody the visitor's nose on account of his feminine haircut.

A cynic interrupted, however.

"That Mom's-apple-pie is just a crude way of saying we fought for democracy," he said. "Pure applesauce. Actually, we fought to save the British Empire."

"Then you have lost," said the visitor. "The British Empire will be dissolved, at American insistence, within the decade."

"You talk like a Nazi propagandist," said a sailor. "You're trying to drive a wedge between us and the British. Next you'll be trying to divide us and our great Soviet allies."

"Within five years," the visitor said, "any of you who calls them 'our great Soviet allies' will be accused of treason."

"Throw the bum out," shouted a corporal of infantry.

"What did you fight for, corporal?" the visitor asked.

"Easy," the corporal said. "Germany had to be destroyed."

"Then you have lost," the visitor said, "for within five years, you will be paying to rebuild Germany out of your salary. For 15 years after that, America will risk new wars to help put Germany back together again."

The men laughed and laughed. "Tell us about Asia!!" shouted a marine. "Yea," said an air corps private, "tell us how we're all going to wind up loving the Japs and fighting the Chinese," and the barracks rocked with laughter.

"Don't tell me you fought to destroy Japan, too," the visitor said. "What else?" a sergeant asked.

"Then you have lost," said the visitor. "Within 20 years you will rebuild Japan. It will be your warmest friend in the Pacific. When your children are born, you will teach them not to say 'Japs.' You will train them to say 'our Japanese friends.'"

"That'll be the day," said a waist gunner. "The Jap bombing of Pearl Harbor will live in infamy. We've fought to guarantee that."

"Then you have lost," said the visitor. "Within 20 years you will have large unhappy children who will not remember Pearl Harbor. They will say, however, that our own bombing of Hiroshima and Nagasaki were acts of infamy."

"If any of my kids ever say that," a staff sergeant said, "they get a punch in the nose. What I fought for was none of that fancy stuff—just the good old American right to beat some sense into your own kids."

"Then you have lost," said the visitor, "for within 20 years, children who don't remember a thing about your war will outnumber you in the population, and though you may punch a few it will make no difference because your legs will be shot and your wind will be gone and your stomachs will be flabby with steaks and beer."

A supply clerk who had listened solemnly spoke up, "I fought to keep America the way it is," he said.

"That's right," said a Navy gunner. "I hear Jimmy Stewart say that in the movies. I fought because I didn't want anybody changing things around in America."

"Then you have lost," said the visitor, "for within 20 years everything will change. Farmers will live in the cities. City people will live in the suburbs. The country will be covered with asphalt. The cities you have known will be torn down. Money will be replaced by the credit card. Major Bowes, Charlie McCarthy, and The Singing Lady will disappear.

"Your children—" here he paused to display his six-button jacket, his stovepipe, leprechaun boots, and his seaweed hair—"will look like me."

"All right, men," roared the top sergeant, "grab the Fascist rat!" The visitor disappeared under a mass of uniformed bodies. "We'd better take him up to Intelligence for interrogation," the sergeant said. "He's probably part of a die-hard Axis scheme to destroy American morale."

When the men had untangled, of course, the visitor had spun off through time-space continuum into 1965 and was dancing the Jerk at the Go Go. "Tell me, Bird," he asked his partner between twitches, "did you ever hear of a two-pants suit?"

Chapter Two

Contemporary patterns of foreign policy

The drive for national security takes place in an international context. Continental security in isolation—such as the United States experienced in the nineteenth century—is no longer feasible in an age of ICBM's, supersonic transports, and communications and observation satellites. Today there is continuous and intimate contact between peoples throughout the world, and this contact creates a variety of problems. Foreign policy is the means by which nation-states approach these problems.

"National interest" is the foundation for foreign policy. Chapter One illustrated that national interest is a concept involving interests of varying intensities and that, particularly in free societies, the nature of this interest is the subject of much debate. Certain decision-makers, usually in the executive branch of government, having weighed the state's interests and various competing demands, are responsible for establishing foreign policy. Senator Fulbright feels that too often these interpretations of the national interest are based more on myth than on reality. Once made, though, this policy becomes a reality in the international arena.

Foreign policy is more often an abstract statement of goals than a specific statement of means. Although Red China's foreign policy statement is the only one of the five included that does not speak of a vision of peace, the Chinese goal of "victory in people's wars" is still a visionary and abstract goal rather than a specific program of action.

A foreign policy is only as successful as its ability to achieve its goals. If the goals are security or peace and insecurity or war are the result, then that foreign policy has failed. Faulty premises are often the basis for failures in programs of action.

More than a determination of means and ends, a successful foreign policy depends on a long-range program of strategic goals and a strategy of means. In his article, Lerche illustrates how U.S.–USSR differences in strategic styles have been essentially differences between short-range and long-range planning and behavior.

Diplomacy is the tool for nation-to-nation communication. Prior to World War II diplomats were more independent and isolated in their posts. The term *plenipotentiary*—most powerful—aptly describes their standing. More recently, diplomacy has become a personal tool manipulated directly by decision-makers as a result of the increasingly direct relationship between world affairs and national security and of the communications revolution, including the "hot line" communication now available to negotiators.

Diplomacy takes many forms. The establishment of permanent missions in foreign countries as official representatives of one state to another is the most obvious of these. Normal communication takes place through messages transmitted through and by diplomats. Normal foreign policy formulation uses information and analyses gathered by these embassies and based on local sources and experience. This process constitutes a vital part of foreign policy formulation.

Offering the "good offices" of a third party for negotiation between belligerents constitutes another form of diplomacy. This party acts as arbiter between two or more parties whose security is at stake while his security is not. He can offer suggestions or solutions which provide a retreat without loss of face and which appear to be compromise rather than defeat. One of the most recent of these instances was the USSR's invitation to Pakistan and India to meet at Tashkent for mediation of the Kashmir hostilities.

The Tashkent conference exhibited a third form of diplomacy—a summit conference attended by chiefs of state. Premier Kosygin took the role of mediator there. He later met with President Johnson at Glassboro, New Jersey, in a brief summit conference to discuss problems of mutual concern.

Chiefs of state also find the exchange of personal letters an expedient if more indirect form of diplomacy. An illustration of this form is the letters exchanged by President Johnson and President Ho Chi Minh in search of common ground for the opening of talks on the Vietnam War.

Section 1

Myth and reality

Foreign policy: Old myths and new realities

J. William Fulbright

"It has become one of the self-evident truths of the postwar era that just as the President resides in Washington and the Pope in Rome, the Devil resides immutably in Moscow." In these words Senator Fulbright focuses on what he considers to be the master myth challenging our confrontation of ever changing reality in the creation of a successful and realistic foreign policy.

Congressional Record, *Senate, Vol. 110, No. 56 (March 25, 1964). Mr. Fulbright is a senator from Arkansas and chairman of the Foreign Relations Committee.*

[T]here is an inevitable divergence, attributable to the imperfections of the human mind, between the world as it is and the world as men perceive it. As long as our perceptions are reasonably close to objective reality, it is possible for us to act upon our problems in a rational and appropriate manner. But when our perceptions fail to keep pace with events, when we refuse to believe something because it displeases or frightens us, or because it is simply startlingly unfamiliar, then the gap between fact and perception becomes a chasm, and action becomes irrelevant and irrational.

There has always—and inevitably—been some divergence between the realities of foreign policy and our ideas about it. This divergence has in certain respects been growing, rather than narrowing; and we are handicapped, accordingly, by policies based on old myths, rather than current realities. This divergence is, in my opinion, dangerous and unnecessary—dangerous, because it can reduce foreign policy to a fraudulent game of imagery and appearances; unnecessary, because it can be overcome by the determination of men in high office to dispel prevailing misconceptions by the candid dissemination of unpleasant, but inescapable, facts. . . .

I should like to suggest two possible reasons for the growing divergence between the realities and our perceptions of current world politics. The first is the radical change in relations between and within the Communist and the free world; and the second is the tendency of too many of us to confuse means with ends and, accordingly, to adhere to prevailing practices with a fervor befitting immutable principles.

Although it is too soon to render a definitive judgment, there is mounting evidence that events of recent years have wrought profound changes in the character of East-West relations. In the Cuban missile crisis of October 1962, the United States proved to the Soviet Union that a policy of aggression and adventure involved unacceptable risks. In the signing of the test ban treaty, each side in effect assured the other that it was prepared to forego, at least for the present, any bid for a decisive military or political breakthrough. These occurrences, it should be added, took place against the background of the clearly understood strategic superiority—but not supremacy—of the United States.

It seems reasonable, therefore, to suggest that the character of the cold war has, for the present, at least, been profoundly altered: by the drawing back of the Soviet Union from extremely aggressive policies; by the implicit repudiation by both sides of a policy of "total victory"; and by the establishment of an American strategic superiority which the Soviet Union appears to have tacitly accepted because it has been accompanied by assurances that it will be exercised by the United States with responsibility and restraint. . . .

Another of the results of the lowering of tensions between East and West is that each is now free to enjoy the luxury of accelerated strife and squabbling within its own domain. The ideological thunderbolts between Washington and Moscow which until a few years ago seemed a permanent part of our daily lives have become a pale shadow of their former selves. Now instead the United States waits in fascinated apprehension for the Olympian pronouncements that issue from Paris at 6-month intervals while the Russians respond to the crude epithets of Peiping with almost plaintive rejoinders about "those who want to start a war against everybody."

These astonishing changes in the configuration of the postwar world have had an unsettling effect on both public and official opinion in the United States. One reason for this, I believe, lies in the fact that we are a people used to looking at the world, and indeed at ourselves, in moralistic rather than empirical terms. We are predisposed to regard any conflict as a clash between good and evil rather than as simply a clash between conflicting interests. We are inclined to confuse freedom and democracy, which we regard as moral principles, with the way in which they are practiced in America—with capitalism, federalism, and the two-party system, which are not moral principles but simply the preferred and accepted practices of the American people. There is much cant in American moralism and not a little inconsistency. It resembles in some ways the religious faith of the many respectable people who, in Samuel Butler's words, "would be equally horrified to hear the Christian religion doubted or to see it practiced."

Our national vocabulary is full of "self-evident truths" not only about "life, liberty, and happiness," but about a vast number of personal and public issues, including the cold war. It has become one of the "self-evident truths" of the postwar era that just as the President resides in Washington and the Pope in Rome, the Devil resides immutably in Moscow. We have come to regard the Kremlin as the permanent seat of his power and we have grown almost comfortable with a menace which, though unspeakably evil, has had the redeeming virtues of constancy, predictability, and familiarity. Now the Devil has betrayed us by traveling abroad and, worse still, by dispersing himself, turning up now here, now there, and in many places at once, with a devilish disregard for the laboriously constructed frontiers of ideology.

We are confronted with a complex and fluid world situation and we are not adapting ourselves to it. We are clinging to old myths in the face of new realities and we are seeking to escape the contradictions by narrowing the permissible bounds of public discussion, by relegating an increasing number of ideas and viewpoints to a growing category of "unthinkable thoughts." I believe that this tendency can and should be reversed, that it is within our ability, and unquestionably in our interests, to cut loose from established myths and to start thinking some "unthinkable thoughts"—about the cold war and East-West relations, about the underdeveloped countries and particularly those in Latin America, about the changing nature of the Chinese Communist threat in Asia and about the festering war in Vietnam.

The master myth of the cold war is that the Communist bloc is a monolith composed of governments which are not really governments at all but organized conspiracies, divided among themselves perhaps in certain matters of tactics, but all equally resolute and implacable in their determination to destroy the free world.

I believe that the Communist world is indeed hostile to the free world in its general and long-term intentions but that the existence of this animosity in principle is far less important for our foreign policy than the great variations in its intensity and character both in time and among the individual members of the Communist bloc. Only if we recognize these variations, ranging from China, which poses immediate threats to the free world, to Poland and Yugoslavia, which pose none, can we hope to act effectively upon the bloc and to turn its internal differences to our own advantage and to the advantage of those bloc countries which wish to maximize their independence. It is the responsibility of our national leaders both in the executive branch and in Congress, to acknowledge and act upon these realities, even at the cost of saying things which will not win immediate widespread enthusiasm.

For a start, we can acknowledge the fact that the Soviet Union, though still a most formidable adversary, has ceased to be totally and implacably hostile to the West. It has shown a new willingness to enter mutually advantageous arrangements with the West and, thus far at least, to honor them. It has therefore become possible to divert some of our energies from the prosecution of the cold war to the relaxation of the cold war and to deal with the Soviet Union, for certain purposes, as a normal state with normal and traditional interests.

If we are to do these things effectively, we must distinguish between communism as an ideology and the power and policy of the Soviet state. It is not communism as a doctrine, or communism as it is practiced within the Soviet Union or within any other country, that threatens us. How the Soviet Union organizes its internal life, the gods and doctrines that it worships, are matters for the Soviet Union to determine. It is not Communist dogma as espoused within Russia but Communist imperialism that threatens us and other peoples of the non-Communist world. Insofar as a great nation mobilizes its power and resources for aggressive purposes, that nation, regardless of ideology, makes itself our enemy. Insofar as a nation is content to practice its doctrines within its own frontiers, that nation, however repugnant its ideology, is one with which we have no proper quarrel. We must deal with the Soviet Union as a great power, quite apart from differences of ideology. To the extent that the Soviet leaders abandon the global ambitions of Marxist ideology, in fact if not in words, it becomes possible for us to engage in normal relations with them, relations which probably cannot be close or trusting for many years to come but which can be gradually freed of the terror and the tensions of the cold war. . . .

Important opportunities have been created for Western policy by the development of "polycentrism" in the Communist bloc. The Communist nations, as George Kennan has pointed out, are, like the Western nations, currently caught up in a crisis of indecision about their relations with countries outside their own ideological bloc. The choices open to the satellite states are limited but by no means insignificant. They can adhere slavishly to Soviet preferences or they can strike out on their own, within limits, to enter into mutually advantageous relations with the West.

Whether they do so, and to what extent, is to some extent at least within the power of the West to determine. If we persist in the view that all Communist regimes are equally hostile and equally threatening to the West, and that we can have no policy toward the captive nations except the eventual overthrow of their Communist regimes, then the West may enforce upon the Communist bloc a degree of unity which the Soviet Union has shown itself to be quite incapable of imposing. . . . If, on the other hand, we are willing to re-examine the view that all Communist regimes are alike in the threat which they pose for the West—a view which had a certain validity in Stalin's time—then we may be able to exert an important influence on the course of events within a divided Communist world. . . .

We consider it a form of subversion of the free world . . . when the Russians enter trade relations or conclude a consular convention or establish airline connections with a free country in Asia, Africa or Latin America—and to a certain extent we are right. On the other hand, when it is proposed that we adopt the same strategy in reverse—by extending commercial credits to Poland or Yugoslavia . . . —then the same patriots who are so alarmed by Soviet activities in the free world charge our policymakers with "giving aid and comfort to the enemy" and with innumerable other categories of idiocy and immorality.

It is time that we resolved this contradiction and separated myth from reality. The myth is that every Communist state is an unmitigated evil and a relentless enemy of the free world; the reality is that some Communist regimes pose a threat to the free world while others pose little or none, and that if we will recognize these distinctions, we ourselves will be able to influence events in the Communist bloc in a way favorable to the security of the free world. . . .

There are numerous areas in which we can seek to reduce the tensions of the cold war and to bring a degree of normalcy into our relations with the Soviet Union and other Communist countries. . . . We have already taken important steps in this direction: the Antarctic and Austrian treaties and the nuclear test ban treaty, the broadening of East-West cultural and educational relations, and the expansion of trade. . . .

A modest increase in East-West trade may . . . serve as a modest instrument of East-West detente—provided that we are able to overcome the myth that trade with Communist countries is a compact with the Devil and to recognize that, on the contrary, trade can serve as an effective and honorable means of advancing both peace and human welfare. . . .

The world's major exporting nations are slowly but steadily increasing their trade with the Communist bloc and the bloc countries are showing themselves to be reliable customers. Since 1958 Western Europe has been increasing its exports to the East at the rate of about 7 percent a year, which is nearly the same rate at which its overall world sales have been increasing.

West Germany—one of our close friends—is by far the leading Western nation in trade with the Sino-Soviet bloc. West German exports to bloc countries in 1962 were valued at $749.9 million. Britain was in second place—although not a close second—with exports to Communist countries amounting to $393 million in 1962. France followed with exports worth $313.4 million, and the figure for the United States—consisting largely of surplus food sales to Poland under Public Law 480—stood far below at $125.1 million. . . .

In light of these facts, it is difficult to see what effect the tight American trade restrictions have other than to deny the United States a substantial share of a profitable market.

The inability of the United States to prevent its partners from trading extensively with the Communist bloc is one good reason for relaxing our own restrictions, but there is a better reason: the potential value of trade—a moderate volume of trade in nonstrategic items—as an instrument for reducing world tensions and strengthening the foundations of peace. I do not think that trade or the nuclear test ban, or any other prospective East-West accommodation, will lead to a grand reconciliation that will end the cold war and usher in the brotherhood of man. At the most, the cumulative effect of all the agreements that are likely to be attainable in the foreseeable future will be the alleviation of the extreme tensions and animosities that threaten the world with nuclear devastation and the gradual conversion of the struggle between communism and the free world into a safer and more tolerable international rivalry, one which may be with us for years and decades to come but which need not be so terrifying and so costly as to distract the nations of the world from the creative pursuits of civilized societies.

There is little in history to justify the expectation that we can either win the cold war or end it immediately and completely. These are favored myths, respectively, of the American right and of the American left. They are, I believe, equal in their unreality and in their disregard for the feasibilities of history. We must disabuse ourselves of them and come to terms, at last, with the realities of a world in which neither good nor evil is absolute and in which those who move events and make history are those who have understood not how much but how little it is within our power to change. . . .

Section 2

The unchanging purposes of foreign policy

The purpose of United States foreign policy: Peace and progress

Dean Rusk

The former U.S. Secretary of State tries to show that reality and not myth shapes the foreign policy of the United States. He discusses both the problems of conflict (Vietnam) and of cooperation (foreign aid) and the reasons for a commitment to them in the search for national and international security.

"*The Central Purpose of United States Foreign Policy,*" Department of State Bulletin, *August 28, 1967. Address by Secretary of State Rusk before the Catholic War Veterans convention at Washington, D.C., August 5, 1967.*

Now the central purpose of our foreign policy is the security of the United States—in a familiar phrase in the preamble of our Constitution, to "secure the Blessings of Liberty to ourselves and our Posterity." Our foreign policy also reflects our basic convictions, the enduring values to which we a people are dedicated: a belief in human dignity—not just a phrase; in government with the consent of the governed, the most powerful and revolutionary political idea in the world today; in freedom of worship and other freedoms for all in the brotherhood of man. Both our national security and our basic convictions compel us to work for a peaceful and orderly world and impel us to help our fellow man to achieve a more decent life. . . .

World peace the first imperative

The goal of the foreign policy of the United States is, and must be, a lasting peace in which free societies can thrive, the kind of world order sketched out in the preamble and article 1 of the United Nations Charter: a world of independent nations, each free to choose its own institutions but cooperating with each other to prevent aggression, to preserve peace, and to promote their mutual interests; a world in which all nations and people can make economic and social and human progress; a world which increasingly respects the rule of law; a world which also encourages, in the words of the charter, "respect for human rights and for fundamental freedoms for all without distinction as to race, sex, language, or religion."

Now, this kind of world we strive for is not a static world; change is the order of the day. We expect and desire a changing world, one which changes for the better and in which change comes through peaceful means and not through the violent use of force. Tragically, not all governments have abided by the purposes and principles of that charter. Some have not respected the right of self-determination of people, have not joined in collective measures for the suppression of acts of aggression, but have themselves promoted and indulged in acts of aggression.

And so we and other peoples who value independence and liberty have found it necessary to make clear our determination to exercise the right of individual and collective self-defense, and all of us here are aware of the nature of the threats to freedom and peace with which we have had to deal since the end of the Second World War. And all of us are aware of the crises caused by the Communist threats or use of force in such places as Iran, Greece and Turkey, the Berlin blockade, Korea, Laos, and in the Cuban missile crisis, and in Viet-Nam.

Now, the Communist world itself has been evolving; the two largest Communist nations are presently hostile to each other, and most of the smaller Communist states have displayed increasing independence.

Now, in the most recent years the Soviet Union and we have manifested a certain prudence in our mutual relations—a prudence which we welcome and we try to reciprocate—and we have earnestly sought and shall continue to seek areas of common interest with our adversaries, especially agreements or arrangements which would reduce the danger of a great war.

I wish I could tell you that it would be safe to relax our safeguards and our watchfulness, but I can't. The leaders of the Soviet Union remain committed to the Communist world revolution and in principle to what the Communists call "wars of national liberation" but which in reality are wars to impose Communist rule. They are actively engaged in trying to extend and increase their influence in the less developed areas of the world. They continue to spend vast amounts on armaments and to improve and enlarge their nuclear arsenals.

The conflict in Viet-Nam

The Asian Communists are openly committed to the use of force to impose Communist rule on other nations, and so are Castro and many of his adherents in Latin America. And so it would be imprudent for us and our allies and friends to relax or to falter in our efforts to defend liberty and to move the world toward a reliable peace. And a first essential in organizing a lasting peace is of course to eliminate aggression—hopefully, by deterring it. To that end, we have defensive alliances with more than 40 other nations, and to that end we are fighting now in Viet-Nam.

Some people still claim or cling to the mistaken notion that the conflict in Viet-Nam is just a civil war or an assertion of nationalism. There is, of course, a local southern element in the war against the Republic of Viet-Nam, but that is not why the United States has combat forces there. Our men are there because of the aggression from the North, and in accordance with a treaty commitment approved by the United States Senate with only one negative vote. That this is an aggression is recognized generally among the non-Communist governments of East Asia and the Western Pacific. Every one of them would be dismayed if we and our allies were to withdraw before securing the right of the people of Viet-Nam to live in peace under a government of their own choice. As one of the leading newspapers of Malaysia put it just the other day, there is not a non-Communist country in the area which is not confronted by the barrel of a Communist gun.

It is important for us to try to be clear about what is involved. It's not just a civil war; there is an aggression. We're not asking for unconditional surrender; we're not asking North Viet-Nam to surrender anything—an acre of ground or a dozen men—or to change their regime; we're asking them simply to stop shooting at their neighbors. If that is unconditional surrender, I don't understand the English language.

The word "escalation" is usually reserved only for what the United States and its allies do. The other side can mine the rivers of the Saigon harbor, they can put substantial forces into Cambodia, they can disrupt the demilitarized zone, without having it called escalation. We need to look at this with a certain reciprocity.

There are those now who are using the slogan "Negotiate now." Let us be quite clear about that. The United States is prepared to talk seriously about peace, literally tomorrow, without any conditions whatsoever. If the other side raises some conditions, as they have with respect to the bombing, we're prepared to sit down with them tomorrow and talk about the conditions.

What we have felt that we could not do is to stop one-half of the war while the other half goes on full steam ahead. Surely the resources of diplomacy are such that contacts, direct or indirect, public or private, can ascertain when the time comes for a serious talk with the other side about peace. There have been many, many opportunities for Hanoi to engage in such discussion, and thus far they have been unwilling to do so. It is curious to me that after all that has been done by our own government, by other governments and groups of governments, and by leading personalities all over the world that no one at any time has been able to produce a North Vietnamese anywhere in the world for serious discussions about the possibilities of peace. . . .

Economic and social assistance

I'd like to just say a few words, if I may, about foreign aid. Because when budgets are tight and we have problems here at home and there are demands upon us for the war in Viet-Nam, there is a tendency to think that we can neglect some of these great undertakings which all of mankind now faces in economic and social development.

But I have no doubt that economic and social assistance as an instrument of our foreign policy is very important to the longer range safety of this country. We now have more than a million men in uniform outside the continental United States in many different parts of the world. Surely we would not begrudge six-tenths of 1 percent of our gross national product, and the relatively small fraction of our own national budget, to try to get that job done without committing those men to combat, if possible.

Now, it has served our long-range security interests to provide this assistance, because the prospects for enduring peace and stability would die in a world in which a few nations are rich and the rest live in poverty. It is true that poor nations and peoples and the relatively rich nations and peoples have lived side by side throughout history. But today men everywhere are realizing that they are not doomed by the Almighty or by nature to live at a bare level of subsistence, and they realize that science and technology make it possible for them to improve their living standards, and men everywhere are resolved to make better lives for themselves and their children. . . .

We have learned that development is a slow process; and we have learned that our own role is secondary, that the job must be done primarily by the governments and peoples of the less developed nations; and we have learned—

indeed, we already knew from our own experience—that modernization will be very slow unless private enterprise is allowed to flourish. We have learned that agricultural development must be given first priority.

The food-population problem

The fact is that underdeveloped countries overall import today more food than they export, reversing the situation which existed before World War II. We have become aware that the food-population problem is already acute and that unless it is dealt with promptly and effectively mass starvation lies only a decade or two away from us.

As President Johnson said in his State of the Union message in January this year:

> Next to the pursuit of peace, the really greatest challenge to the human family is the race between food supply and population increase. That race tonight is being lost.
>
> The time for rhetoric is clearly past. The time for concerted action is here and we must get on with the job.

And it was that grim reality that caused President Johnson to propose that the United States lead the world in a war against hunger. . . .

In the Western Hemisphere the great cooperative economic and social enterprise, the Alliance for Progress, has produced substantial gains. The needs for development assistance are too great throughout the world to be met by the United States alone, and in fact other economically developed nations have been shouldering increasing shares of the load. But as by far the richest and technically and economically most advanced nation, the United States is properly the largest single contributor.

We understand the great calls being made upon us, for defense, for domestic burdens, for space, for other purposes. We sometimes forget how productive our economy is. We forget that our gross national product is as large as all of the NATO countries and Japan combined, that it is 10 times the gross national product of all of Latin America. We forget that our defense budget this year is just about equal to the gross national product of all of Latin America combined. Our productivity is more than twice that of the Soviet Union, and the gap is widening. It is 10 times that of Communist China, with a population of some 700 million people. So we have to be a little careful that we not find ourselves in the position of a voracious economy, calling upon the peoples of the rest of the world to send us their materials—their raw materials—their minerals and their services and to absorb our own goods in their markets, while we ourselves are neglectful or negligent about their own most pressing needs. . . .

I'd like to close with one or two personal observations. I would hope that we could understand what is really involved when the United States pledges itself to work together with someone else in mutual security; the integrity of the American commitment is the principal support of peace in the world. If those who are, or would be, our adversaries should ever suppose that our pledges are not worth very much, then we shall be well on the way down the slippery slopes of general war, and that we must not have.

This question of keeping our word is very important—that is what is involved in Viet-Nam, reaching beyond Viet-Nam itself and beyond Southeast Asia—for we have been tested time and again; and it was gambling on the part of aggressors that they would not encounter the United States that led to some of our frightful catastrophes in the past 25 or 30 years.

Secondly, please don't sell your country short in terms of our basic purposes. There are cynics abroad. There are those who would undermine confidence in what we're all about. But if you want to know what our foreign policy is all about, look in your own homes and your own communities, your own hearts. We're trying to build a little peace in the world, where men can live alongside of each other without being constantly at each other's throats. We believe in "Live and let live." We should like to see tomorrow better than today for our families; we should like to see the ancient burdens of illiteracy and misery, poor health, relieved from the back of mankind. We should like to see free institutions in which there is no knock of the terrorist's hand on the door at midnight. In other words, we should like to have a chance to build upon the most elementary commitments of our nation and to lend a hand to those abroad who are trying to build a decent world of that type.

This should not be strange, because these simple and decent ideas are shared by simple and decent people throughout the world, including many of them behind the so-called curtains. That, too, is not strange because these simple notions are perhaps a part of the very character of man himself, the very nature of man, and his most ancient commitments to his God and to his spirit. And so these are the bases for our common past with ordinary men, when we set out to build some peace, to enlarge our range of cooperation, to join hands in building a world in which our young people will be glad to have a chance to live, not overridden by terror, not living under the threat of destruction at noonday. That's what it's all about, and on that, thank you for your help.

The purpose of French foreign policy: Progress, independence, and peace

Charles de Gaulle

This foreign policy statement by General de Gaulle is a classic example of the close relationship between nationalism and foreign policy. Peace, for the French, will be obtained by withdrawal from NATO, exclusion of Great Britain from the Common Market, interference in French Canada, and recognition of Communist China.

Broadcast over French radio and television from the Elysée Palace, August 10, 1967. Reprinted in Vital Speeches of the Day, *September 1, 1967.*

Ordinarily every one—and it is quite normal—is absorbed in his daily life and circumstances and only once in awhile takes an overall look at what can become of our country. And, yet, everything depends on that. For who could doubt that the fate of each French person is bound up with the fate of France? Inversely, where would France head if the French took no interest in her? Because, in the rather tense situation in which the world finds itself, what our people do weighs heavily on France's future, and there is reason to point out today . . . what goals are being sighted in the conduct of the nation and what path is being followed to attain them.

The first of these goals, which governs the others, is peace. This is not said, as it has often been, to flatter, rather commonly, everyone's instinctive desire. For peace is in no way ensured by making statements. And proof is the fact that, since the beginning of the century and up to recently, although we were governed by eminently peaceful schools of thought and political groups, we never fought so much. While, during that period, everything in our country, official or unofficial, relentlessly proclaimed, "war against war," we had to wage two world wars, unprecedented in extent, before which, during which and after which we did not cease, in addition, to fight in Africa, in the Middle East or in Asia. Certainly, the principal cause of these dramas was an empire's ambition to dominate. But, faced with the threats that it was lengthily preparing, our generous entreaties did not drive away the storms, while our political inconsistency and our military weaknesses drew the lightning down upon us.

For, what peace requires is, on the outside, energetic and constant action, action all the more difficult that, in the midst of the conflicting of ideologies and the clashing of interests that fill the world, it must be free of foreign allegiances and episodic swayings of opinion. At the same time, peace demands, on the inside, the preparation of defense means suited to their times, which, for the same reasons, is also very difficult. This means that today, for France, peace should be not only desired but rigorously sought. After the enormous losses that we experienced in fighting for some fifty years, considering the state of a dangerous and upset world, taking into account the unheard of capacity for destruction of nuclear arms, nothing, absolutely nothing, is so important to us as to rebuild, through peace, our substance, our influence and our power.

That is why, despite burning passions and painful consequences, we deliberately put an end to the vain fighting in Algeria and established with our former territories of Africa, now independent, fruitful and fraternal relations. That is why, and to our credit, we class our conflicts with Germany as past history and practice friendly cooperation with it. That is why, however powerful may be America's attraction for the Europeans, we are working to convince the Community of the Six to become, for its part and on its account, a political reality and, thereby, an essential element of a peaceful world equilibrium. That is why, despite preconceived ideas and preformed inclinations, we are replacing the dangerous tension of yesterday with Eastern Europe with cordial and fruitful relations. That is why, even if the immediate advantage may not be very apparent, we have objectively made contact with Peking. That is why, however clamorous may be the stands taken, we condemn, on the part of whatever State, all armed intervention on the territory of others, precisely as it is taking place in Southeast Asia and the Middle East, because, in our times, the fire is from the start detestable and, once lit, it risks spreading afar. But also, this is why we are equipping ourselves with a deterrent weapon so that no country in the world can want to strike ours without knowing that, in the event, it would suffer terrible damage.

However, for France to have a hold on peace, as regards herself and, as much as possible, as regards others, she must have independence. Therefore, she has ensured it for herself. As America and the Soviet Union—colossal in their size, their population, their resources, their nuclear forces—are permanent rivals everywhere and in all areas, each has naturally formed around itself a block of States which are directly tied to it, over which it exercises its hegemony and to which it promises its protection. As a result, these States conform their policy willy-nilly to that of their great ally, submit their defense to it, confide their destiny to it.

By withdrawing from NATO, France, for her part, extricated herself from such subjection. Thus she would not find herself drawn, eventually, into any quarrel that would not be hers and into any war action that she would not herself have wished. . . .

But in order to keep and make the most of her personality, it is not sufficient for France to have her own policy and armed forces. The spirit and the movement of our era also force her to achieve modern development which, without failing to cooperate actively with others, she is to make a national task. For independence, today, must go hand in hand with progress. Now, as it is difficult, in diplomatic and military matters, to break with the insidious theories and the convenient practices of subordination, thus it is not without difficulties that, despite the accumulated routines and contrary pressures, we are seeing to it that in economic, social, financial, monetary, scientific and technical domains our country follows its own road by walking at its own pace. . . .

When we transform all French activity in accordance with our Plan, it is because we want our country, in its progress, to be itself within and without. Progress, independence, peace, these therefore are the combined goals toward which our policy aims. . . . Thus the fact that France, without in any way denying the friendship she has for the Anglo-Saxon nations, but breaking with the absurd and outdated conformity of self-effacement, should take a really French stand on the war in Vietnam, on the Middle East conflict, on the building of a European Europe, on the upheaval that would result in the Community of the Six from Britain's admission and that of four or five other States, on relations with the East, on the international monetary question or, not later than yesterday, on the unanimous and indescribable desire for affranchisement that the French of Canada have shown around the President of the French Republic, stuns the apostles of decline and fills them with indignation. Thus, because France has taken back possession of her forces and has undertaken to provide herself with a means of deterrence; because, in the event of a war between the two giants—a war which, perhaps, without striking one another directly, they might wage in Europe which lies between them—France would not be automatically the humble assistant of one of them and would provide herself with the opportunity of becoming something other than a battlefield for their expeditionary forces and a target for their alternating bombs; lastly, because France, by leaving the bloc system, has perhaps given the signal for a general evolution toward international détente, she appears to the votaries of Atlantic obedience, condemned to what they call isolation whereas a huge mass of humanity in the world approves her action and gives her credit for it. . . .

Rejecting doubt, that demon of all declines, let us continue on our way. It is the way of a France who believes in herself and who, in so doing, opens the future for herself.

Long live the Republic!

Long live France!

The purpose of Soviet foreign policy: Peaceful co-existence

L. I. Brezhnev

As in most Communist speeches, propaganda and policy are blended together in this Brezhnev report to the Congress of the Communist Party of the Soviet Union. Three themes are interwoven: (1) the need for unity among the Socialist nations; (2) the need to support "the peoples' struggle against colonial oppression"; and (3) the need to establish peaceful economic, scientific, and cultural ties with "the capitalist countries." The most important task for diplomacy for Brezhnev is to settle the issue of the Federal Republic of Germany (West Germany) and to end the arms race, so that security in Europe and the world might ensue. This speech relates to the Arthur Larson article in Chapter 5 in assessing the theme of "wars of national liberation."

Excerpt from "23rd Congress of the Communist Party of the Soviet Union: Report of the C.P.S.U. Central Committee to the 23rd Congress of the Communist Party of the Soviet Union," The Current Digest of the Soviet Press, *Vol. 18, No. 12., pp. 5–13. The author is chairman of the Communist Party of the Soviet Union.*

---

1. *The U.S.S.R.'S International Position. The Foreign-Policy Activity of the C.P.S.U.—1. The World System of Socialism, the C.P.S.U.'s Struggle for the Strengthening of Its Unity and Might.*—Comrades! In all the diversified foreign-policy activity of our party and state, an especially important place belongs to efforts to strengthen the might and solidarity of the commonwealth of socialist countries. We see in the world system of socialism a tremendous historical victory of the international working class, the principal revolutionary force of our epoch, the most reliable bulwark of all peoples who are fighting for peace, national freedom, democracy and socialism. In the past years the world system of the countries of socialism has grown considerably stronger; its international prestige and its influence on the destinies of mankind have increased.

In the sphere of the political cooperation of the socialist countries, the period under review has been characterized by the development of relations among fraternal parties on the basis of Marxism-Leninism, socialist internationalism and mutual support, on principles of equality, noninterference and respect for one another, the independence of parties and states. In the period under review our relations with the Communist and workers' parties of the countries of the socialist commonwealth and with the socialist states have undoubtedly become richer, closer and more cordial. . . .

In the sphere of the economic cooperation of the countries of socialism, our relations have developed successfully and risen to a new stage in the past years. There has been a considerable expansion of both bilateral and multilateral economic ties. The trade turnover between socialist countries has increased substantially. . . .

In the sphere of military cooperation, in the face of the intensified aggressive actions of the imperialist forces headed by the U.S.A., there has been a process of further strengthening of our ties with the socialist countries, a process of strengthening and perfecting the mechanism of the Warsaw pact. . . .

Speaking of the strengthening of the world socialist system, it is necessary at the same time, comrades, to point out that our relations with the parties of two socialist countries—with the Communist Party of China and the Albanian Party of Labor—unfortunately remain unsatisfactory.

Our party and the Soviet people would sincerely like friendship with people's China and its Communist Party. We are prepared to do everything possible to improve our relations with people's Albania, with the Albanian Party of Labor. . . .

The C.P.S.U. Central Committee sets forth for the future, too, as *one of the principal directions of the foreign-policy activity of the Party and the Soviet state the development and consolidation of ideological and political ties with the Communist Parties of all the countries of socialism on the principles of Marxism-Leninism, the development and consolidation of the U.S.S.R.'s political, economic and other ties with socialist states, the promotion in every possible way of the solidarity of the socialist commonwealth and the strengthening of its might and influence. For its part, the C.P.S.U. will do everything that depends on it so that the world socialist system may become ever more powerful and proceed from victory to victory.*

2. *The Deepening of the Contradictions of the Capitalist System. Development of the Class Struggle of the Proletariat.*—Comrades! The C.P.S.U. Central Committee has conducted its foreign policy activities taking into account the processes under way in the capitalist world. The capitalist system as a whole is experiencing a general crisis; its internal contradictions are becoming deeper. . . .

The basic contradiction of capitalist society—the contradiction between labor and capital—continues to operate with full force in the world of capitalism.

The monopolies are trying to place increasingly heavy burdens on the shoulders of the working class and other sections of the working people. . . .

The Communists and all the people of the Soviet land express their ardent solidarity with the working people of the bourgeois countries. The Soviet people are inspired by the knowledge that the achievements of the working class of the Land of Soviets and other socialist countries are a support to our class brothers in their courageous struggle for their rights, for the future of their children, for the victory of the new social system.

3. *The C.P.S.U. in the Struggle for the Solidarity of the World Communist Movement.*— . . . Half a century ago, when our party, under the leadership of Vladimir Ilyich Lenin, first roused the people to storm capitalism, there were 400,000 Communists in the world. Today 88 Communist Parties on all continents have a membership of almost 50,000,000 fighters. . . .

Since 1960 the number of Communists in the world has increased by 14,000,000. Their ties with the masses have grown even stronger. The international Communist movement has consolidated its position as the most influential political force of modern times.

The Communist Parties of the socialist countries are doing tremendous constructive work. They are resolving complex tasks of economic development, new social relations and the communist education of the masses; they are ensuring the defense of socialist gains. This work is of historical importance. It strengthens the international positions of socialism and increases the attractive force of its ideas throughout the world. . . .

The Communist Parties of the capitalist countries head the struggle of the masses against the monopolies and are forging in class battles the political army of the revolution. In many of those countries the Communist Parties today exert a profound influence on the whole of national life. . . .

What concrete ways, then, does our party see in the present-day situation for strengthening the unity of the Communist movement? . . .

Our party, like the other Marxist-Leninist parties, believes that even when there are differences, it is possible and necessary to work for unity of action of the Communists of all countries in the interests of the struggle against imperialism and intensification of the rebuff to its aggressive actions, in the name of the freedom and independence of peoples. The struggle to halt the American aggression in Vietnam, the support of the progressive forces of Africa, Asia and Latin America against the encroachments of imperialism, and the defense of our brother Communists in a number of countries from the terror of reaction —all these and other important tasks of the anti-imperialist struggle of our time will be accomplished the more successfully the greater the solidarity of the worldwide army of Communists. . . .

The Communist Party of the Soviet Union is unswervingly loyal to its internationalist revolutionary duty. From the rostrum of our Congress we assure the representatives of the world Communist movement, and through them the Communists of the whole world:

> The C.P.S.U. is fighting unswervingly for the strengthening of the international unity of all the fraternal parties on the basis of the great teaching of Marx, Engels and Lenin, on the basis of the line evolved collectively by the world Communist movement.
>
> And we shall continue to wage an irreconcilable struggle against revisionism, dogmatism, against nationalist manifestations, we shall work for the creative development of the Marxist-Leninist teaching.
>
> Our party will continue to carry out the line of joint action of the Communist Parties of the whole world in the struggle against imperialism and for the great goals of peace, democracy and national independence, for socialism and communism.

4. *Development of the National-Liberation Movement. Our Party's Support for the National-Liberation Struggle of the Peoples.*—Comrades! All these years the C.P.S.U. Central Committee has consistently carried out a policy of giving all possible support to the peoples' struggle against colonial oppression, of all-round cooperation with the liberated states on the basis of equality, strict respect for sovereignty and noninterference in their internal affairs. . . .

The Communist Party of the Soviet Union sees its internationalist duty in continuing to do everything in its power to support the struggle of the peoples for final liberation from colonial and neocolonial oppression.

Our party and the Soviet state will continue to:

> extend all possible support to the peoples who are fighting for their liberation, to work for the immediate granting of independence to all colonial countries and peoples;
>
> develop all-round cooperation with the countries that have achieved national independence and help them in developing their economies, in training national cadres and in their struggle against neocolonialism;
>
> strengthen the fraternal ties of the C.P.S.U. with the Communist Parties and revolutionary-democratic organizations in the countries of Asia, Africa and Latin America. . . .

5. *The Soviet Union's Struggle Against the Aggressive Policies of Imperialism and for Peace and International Security.*—Comrade delegates! In the sphere of foreign relations, the Soviet Union consistently pursues a policy of peace that stems from the very nature of our state, all of whose actions are determined by the interests of the working people. The founder of this policy was V. I. Lenin, and we unswervingly adhere to the Leninist approach in international affairs. . . .

In speaking of the mounting international tension and the danger of the outbreak of a world war, special mention must be made of the aggression against Vietnam by American imperialism. . . .

We state vigorously: In "escalating" the shameful war against the Vietnamese people, the aggressors will encounter mounting support for Vietnam from the Soviet Union and other of its socialist friends and brothers. The Vietnamese people will become the masters of their own land. And no one will ever succeed in extinguishing the torch of socialism that the Democratic Republic of Vietnam has raised aloft.

In connection with American aggression in Vietnam and other aggressive actions by American imperialism, our relations with the United States of America have deteriorated. And the U.S. ruling circles are to blame for this.

As for the U.S.S.R., it is prepared to live in peace with all countries, but it will not tolerate imperialist lawlessness with regard to other peoples. We have repeatedly declared our willingness to develop our relations with the U.S.A., and we adhere to the same position now. But for this it is necessary that the U.S.A. cease its policies of aggression. . . .

In exposing the aggressive policy of imperialism, we at the same time consistently and unswervingly pursue a course of the peaceful coexistence of states with different social systems. This means that the Soviet Union, while it regards the coexistence of states with different social systems as a form of the class struggle between socialism and capitalism, at the same time consistently advocates the maintenance of normal, peaceful relations with the capitalist countries, the solution of controversial interstate issues through negotiations and not through war. The Soviet Union firmly stands for noninterference in the internal affairs of all states, for respect for their sovereign rights and the inviolability of their territories.

Naturally, there can be no peaceful coexistence when it comes to internal processes of the class and national-liberation struggle in the capitalist countries or in the colonies. The principle of peaceful coexistence is not applicable to the relations between the oppressors and the oppressed, between the colonialists and the victims of colonial oppression.

As for interstate relations with the capitalist countries, we hold that such relations not only should be peaceful but should also include the broadest possible mutually advantageous economic, scientific, and cultural ties. . . .

The U.S.S.R. has always attached great importance to relations with neighboring countries, and we are pleased that our good-neighbor policy is yielding excellent results. . . .

The question of the removal of foreign military bases from the territories of foreign countries and the withdrawal of foreign troops from those territories was and remains a major international problem. The imperialist powers, first of all the United States of America, have scattered numerous military bases throughout the world and have deployed contingents of their armed forces on the territories of other countries. These bases and armed forces are employed in interests alien to peace, as a means of exerting pressure on peace-loving states and frequently for direct armed intervention in their internal affairs. The Soviet Union believes that the time has long since come to put an end to this situation that threatens peace and the security of states, to remove military bases located on the territories of foreign countries and to withdraw foreign armed forces from such territories. We shall continue to pursue a policy aimed at achieving this purpose in the interests of strengthening universal peace and the security of peoples.

Expressing the fundamental interests not only of the Soviet people but also of the broad popular masses in all countries, the Soviet Union is consistently struggling for the slowing down and complete cessation of the arms race unleashed by the imperialists, for the achieving of agreement concerning practical steps to be taken in this field in order to attain general and complete disarmament. . . .

During the period under review, the U.S.S.R. continued to participate actively in the work of the United Nations. . . . We shall continue to regard the U.N. as an arena of active political struggle against aggression and for the cause of peace and the security of all peoples.

The Communist Party of the Soviet Union considers that at the present stage in the struggle to improve the international situation, strengthen peace and develop peaceful cooperation among the peoples, the most important measures to be taken are, specifically:

> To put an end to U.S. aggression in Vietnam, withdraw all American and other foreign troops from South Vietnam and give the Vietnamese people the opportunity to decide their internal affairs themselves. To take as a basis for the settlement of the Vietnamese problem the position set forth by the D.R.V. government and the National Liberation Front of South Vietnam.
>
> To ensure strict fulfillment of the principle of noninterference in the internal affairs of states.
>
> To conclude an international treaty on the nonproliferation of nuclear weapons; to eliminate the question of nuclear arms for the F.R.G. [West Germany] or the F.R.G.'s access to nuclear arms in any form; to implement the aspiration of the peoples for the establishment of non-nuclear zones in various parts of the world; to obtain a solemn undertaking from the states that possess nuclear weapons not to use them first; to conclude an agreement on the banning of underground nuclear explosions. The implementation of these measures directed against the threat of nuclear war would open up the road for a further advance to the complete banning and destruction of nuclear weapons.
>
> To enter into negotiations on matters of European security. To discuss the existing proposals of the socialist and other states of Europe concerning a military detente and the reduction of armaments in Europe and the development of peaceful, mutually advantageous ties among all European states. To convene an appropriate international conference for this purpose. To continue

to seek ways for solving one of the cardinal tasks of European security—the peaceful settlement of the German question with a view to eliminating completely the vestiges of World War II in Europe on the basis of recognition of the now existing European frontiers, including those of the two German states.

Such are our proposals. Many of them have already been set forth earlier. We do not, naturally, regard them as all-inclusive, and we are prepared to give attention to all other proposals directed toward improving the international situation and strengthening peace. . . .

The purpose of Chinese foreign policy: The victory of people's wars

Lin Piao

Even the Chinese Communists look for ultimate peace, but the immediate foreign policy goal is the support of "people's wars." Such a war is one based on the ideology and experience of the Chinese revolution, especially of the encirclement of the "imperialist" cities by the rural village peasants. In terms of world strategy, the "rural villages" are the developing nations, and the "cities," which will be surrounded in the final world revolution, are the industrial nations.

Excerpts from a speech by Red China's Defense Minister on September 3, 1965. Translated from Jenmin Jihpao (People's Daily) *by William R. Heaton, Jr., a Fellow at the Center for Chinese Studies, the University of California, Berkeley.*

It must be emphatically pointed out that the dictum of Comrade Mao Tsetung concerning construction of rural revolutionary bases and encompassing the cities by the rural areas has obvious concrete, universal, and timely significance for all of the revolutionary struggles of all the oppressed peoples and nations of the world today, particularly the revolutionary struggles of those oppressed peoples of Asia, Africa, and Latin America who are trying to deal with imperialism and its lackeys.

Presently, many peoples and nations of Asia, Africa, and Latin America, are suffering from serious aggression and enslavement by the imperialists headed by the United States and their lackeys. The basic political and economic circumstances of many countries have many similarities with those of old China. In those places, the problems of the peasants are critically important—just as in China. The peasants are the main force in the national-democratic revolution against imperialism and its lackeys. When the imperialists are committing aggression against these countries they will always first occupy the main cities and communications channels; however, there is no method in which they can impose their jurisdiction over the vast number of rural villages. In the villages, and only in the villages, can the revolutionaries have freedom of movement—all over from east to west. The villages and only the villages can be the revolutionary bases in which the revolutionaries send out troops to win the final victory. It is precisely because of this that the dictum of Comrade Mao Tse-tung relating first to the establishment of rural revolutionary bases and then surrounding the cities from the countryside has a powerful attraction . . . for the people in these various areas.

Looking at the problem from the scope of the entire world, if we say that North America and Western Europe are the "world cities," then Asia, Africa, and Latin America are the "world rural villages." Since the Second World War, the proletarian revolutionary movements in the capitalist nations of North America and Western Europe have been temporarily halted for many reasons, but the peoples' revolutionary movements in Asia, Africa, and Latin America are developing at a rapid pace. Whatever "ism" one may choose to call it, today's world revolution is taking the form of "rural villages" encompassing the "cities." The entire success of the world revolution must finally hinge on the revolutionary struggle of the peoples of Asia, Africa, and Latin America who compose the majority of the world's population. The socialist nations must accept their own international responsibility of supporting the people's revolutionary struggles in Asia, Africa, and Latin America. . . .

Great changes have taken place in China and the world in the twenty years since victory in the war of resistance against Japan—and the changes are more to the advantage of the world's revolutionary peoples and to the disadvantage of imperialism and its lackeys.

During the time Japanese imperialism carried on its war of aggression against China, the Chinese people only had a small people's army and a few small revolutionary bases standing opposite the great oriental military despot. During this same time Comrade Mao Tse-tung said that victory could be won in the Chinese people's war and that Japanese imperialism could be overthrown. Today, the revolutionary bases of the peoples of the world are unprecedentedly strong, the revolutionary movements of the peoples of the world are rising at an extremely rapid rate, imperialism is weaker than ever, and the head of imperialism—United States imperialism—is on the verge of defeat. We can say with even greater faith that the people's wars of each nation can be victorious, and that United States imperialism can be overthrown.

The peoples of the world have the experience of the October Revolution, the experience of the anti-fascist war, the experience of the Chinese people's war of resistance against Japan and the war of liberation, experience in the Korean people's war against the United States, the experience of the Vietnamese people's war of liberation and war against the United States, and also have the experience of the people's armed revolutionary struggles in many other nations. They need only be good at taking advantage of these experiences and in creatively combining them with the concrete practice of the revolution in their own countries; then, on the stage of the people's war in each of the various countries, the revolutionary peoples will perform an even more powerful, grand historical play, finally burying the common enemy of the peoples of each nation—United States imperialism and its lackeys. . . .

United States imperialism is in the process of preparing a world war. However, can this save the life of United States imperialism? After World War I a whole series of socialist nations emerged, as well as many independent nations. If United States imperialism persists in fomenting World War III, then we can predict that the results will be that many hundreds of millions of peoples will turn to socialism, and there won't be much territory left for imperialism; the entire imperialist system will likely collapse.

We are optimistic about the future of the world. We resolutely believe that the era of war in the life of mankind will be concluded in the hands of the people. Comrade Mao Tse-tung formerly pointed out that the monster of war "will be finally eliminated by the progress of human society, and in the not too distant future, too. But there is only one way to eliminate it, and that is to oppose war with war, to oppose counter-revolutionary war with revolutionary war."

All peoples who have suffered the aggression, oppression, and exploitation of United States imperialism, unite! Raise high the righteous standard of people's war! Struggle for the work of world peace, people's liberation, people's democracy, and socialism! Victory belongs to the entire peoples of the world!

Long live the victory of people's war!

The purpose of nonaligned foreign policy: International harmony

C. S. Jha

Nonalignment is not a static and passive policy, according to Ambassador Jha, but rather a living policy embodying an individual search for security, peace, and harmony through noninvolvement in great power arguments. But nonalignment does not require noninvolvement in the world's problems or in the defense of national interests.

The text of an address delivered in August 1967 at the International Diplomatic Seminar held at Klesheim Salzburg. Mr. Jha, until recently India's Foreign Secretary, is at present her Ambassador to France.

For two decades, nonalignment as a creed has influenced the policies and ethos of many nations and the course of international relations. Some call it a third force, others say it is a euphemism for inertia. Many have hailed the policy of nonalignment as making a positive contribution to international peace and to a realisation of the purposes and principles of the United Nations. Yet some have characterised it as "immoral." Be that as it may, there is no doubt that the policy of nonalignment today stands adopted by well over fifty countries of the world. It has had a profound influence on inter-state relations and it has helped to steer the world in many troubled situations to the haven of peace.

The psychological origin of nonalignment lies in the natural desire of man individually and in groups to live in peace and friendship with his neighbours. In a small community, the wise man minds his own business, does not try to interfere with others and endeavours to cultivate friendly and good-neighbourly relations with others of his community. He lives righteously and adopts the policy of live and let live. On quarrels between neighbours the wise individual frowns; he keeps himself away from these. He desires and often succeeds in bringing about a *rapprochement* between feuding factions, thus contributing to the establishment of harmony and goodwill in the environments in which he lives. In that way his own position and interests are best secured. Transferred to the larger sphere of international relations, the behaviour pattern of the individual in a small community becomes the national policy of nonalignment in international relations.

Conditions posterior to World War II were favourable to the development of nonalignment. At the Paris Peace Conference of 1946, a rift between the allied powers was already evident. The honeymoon of the war period had ended and was replaced, after the allied victory, by competitive jockeying for power and for sharing the spoils of victory. The spirit of Yalta and Potsdam was disappearing. The drums of the cold war, though muffled at that time, were first beaten in . . . the First Session of the General Assembly in 1946. . . .

India had made her debut as an independent delegation at the United Nations in October, 1946. This was even before her formal independence on August 15, 1947. Power politics at the United Nations in 1946 and 1947 created a natural revulsion in India against the idea of following one ideological bloc or another. India decided to keep aloof from either bloc and to take an independent view on merits on the various issues coming up before the United Nations. . . .

It is a historical fact that India was in the vanguard of new independent nations which had previously been under foreign domination. . . . The task before India with its teeming millions was to build a society based on social justice and equality in the framework of democracy. The neglect of centuries of colonial rule had to be made good and India's millions had to be transformed from a state of poverty, illiteracy and disease into a modern society enjoying the fruits of scientific and technological progress and decent standards of living. The task was by no means easy. It was obvious that the energies of the Indian people had to be devoted primarily to rebuilding India into a modern nation and democracy had to be given economic and sociological content.

In order to achieve rapid economic development, it was necessary that the maximum available resources be devoted to nation-building activities. For the realisation of the aspirations of the people of India, world peace was a paramount consideration, as without that peace, its freedom and that of other newly independent countries would be caught in the maelstrom of war and big power conflict and would again become a casualty. It was necessary that scarce resources should not have to be frittered away for military purposes. For this, as for other reasons, security had to be assured. It was essential to cultivate friendly relations with all countries. . . . Peace was to be further assured by taking a constructive part in the United Nations for the maintenance of world peace and for the development of international cooperation in the social and economic fields. It was necessary, therefore, to avoid entanglements in the conflicts and tensions among the Big Powers and not to assume military postures or enter into military alliances with either of the Power Blocs. With security assured, India would devote all her energies and resources to the reconstruction of her national life and play her rightful role in international affairs for the maintenance of peace and strengthening of the United Nations.

These were the profound motivations of what has come to be known as the policy of nonalignment. The chief exponent and principal architect of this whole new philosophy was Jawaharlal Nehru. . . . The totality of India's policy was, in Nehru's words in an address to the University of Columbia on October 17, 1949,

> . . . the pursuit of peace, not through alignment with any major power or groups of powers but through an independent approach to each controversial or disputed issue, the liberation of subject peoples, the maintenance of freedom, both national and individual, the elimination of racial discrimination, elimination of want, disease and ignorance which afflict the greater part of the world's population.

Jawaharlal Nehru envisioned a new world, with the newly independent and developing countries in Asia and Africa struggling to clear the debris of centuries of foreign domination and striving to give content to their freedom and independence. . . . More and more developing countries have adopted the policy of nonalignment. In the Belgrade conference of nonaligned countries in 1961, the participants numbered 25; and there were 3 observers from Latin America. At the Cairo conference of nonaligned countries in October 1964, the participants had increased to 47, and the observers from Europe and Latin America to 10. Today there are well over 50 nations which adhere to this policy.

The essential character of nonalignment is:

> First, that nonalignment is not an end in itself but only a means to an end . . .
>
> Second, though nonalignment, semantically speaking, has a negative connotation in the sense of not joining the power alignments, it is a positive concept and requires active pursuit of internal and foreign policy objectives.
>
> Third, nonalignment is to be distinguished from neutrality. In the words of Jawaharlal Nehru before the US Congress in 1955: "Where freedom is menaced or justice threatened or where aggression takes place, we cannot be and shall not be neutral." . . . Thus India, in contrast to countries which have been traditionally neutral, has been an active participant in the United Nations in the discussions on the burning questions of the day, including colonial questions and problems affecting the freedom of peoples, the question of racial discrimination, disarmament, the United Nations peacekeeping operations, etc., etc.
>
> Fourth, peaceful coexistence and other principles of Panchsheel, namely, noninterference, non-aggression, respect for each other's sovereignty and in-

> dependence and equality and mutual benefit are the essential pillars of nonalignment. . . .

Having indicated the philosophy of the policy of nonalignment, it is relevant to consider to what extent that policy has served the aims of the countries adopting it. How far has the policy of nonalignment succeeded and proved beneficial in the two decades of its existence?

Nonalignment was intended to serve the needs of a developing country by keeping it free from military entanglements and postures and enabling it to devote its energy and resources primarily to the development of the standards of living of its own people. There is no doubt that this purpose has been adequately served by a policy of nonalignment. . . .

In the external field, the policy of nonalignment has eminently contributed to the maintenance of peace. . . .

On the Korean question in particular, it was India's efforts as a nonaligned country in the United Nations and outside, that helped bring an end to the Korean war. When the war was over, India was appointed Chairman of the Neutral Nations Repatriation Commission and provided the Custodian Forces to supervise the prisoners of war. . . . It is the voice of the nonaligned, neutral and other peace-loving countries in the United Nations which eventually culminated in the Moscow Test Ban Treaty. . . . The UN Operation in the Congo owes not a little for its success to the efforts of the nonaligned, neutral and other peace-loving countries in the United Nations.

The policy of nonalignment, from the very beginning, encountered heavy weather. During the days of the cold war, it incurred the odium of one or the other Power Blocs. . . . The United States Government in the earlier years seemed definitely to regard nonalignment as hostile to US aims and policies and sometimes equated it with communism. Secretary of State John Foster Dulles even went so far as to characterise nonalignment as "immoral." . . . As the number of nonaligned countries grew, the nonalignment policy became an increasingly important moderating force—some regarded it as a "third force"—in the United Nations. The US view is now reconciled to the validity of the policy of nonalignment for the countries adopting it; and the Soviet Union has repeatedly acknowledged in official pronouncements, joint communiques, etc., the important contributions of nonalignment in maintaining and strengthening the forces of peace and peaceful coexistence.

Notwithstanding such acceptance by the Big Powers, there have been various kinds of pressures which have put the fabric of nonalignment to severe tests. . . .

Perhaps the worst example was the Chinese aggression against India in 1962. Chinese motivations are as inscrutable as the face of the Sphinx. Nevertheless, it may be said that whatever might appear to be the superficial reasons for such attack, it was principally aimed against the policy of nonalignment which had helped India attain stability, economic progress and respect and influence among other nations. China wished to demonstrate the *faiblesse* of nonalignment. This, China did in spite of its subscription to "Panchsheel" in the Treaty of 1954 between India and China in regard to trade with Tibet. The Chinese aggression shattered India's sense of security, built up by a steadfast pursuit of nonalignment, and led to a questioning for the first time by some within the country itself of the efficacy and validity of the policy of nonalignment. It also compelled India to take measures for safeguarding its security, which meant diversion of part of her scarce resources from economic development to increased defence expenditure and which, in turn, meant another blow to the foundations of nonalignment.

Nonalignment has also been subjected to political pressures by powerful countries wishing to establish their hegemony over one or the other part of the world. . . . It has often taken the form of direct or indirect interference in the affairs of other states by powerful countries under one guise or another.

Aside from military and political pressures, there have also developed economic pressures. Newly independent countries, most of whom are nonaligned, have, during the last two decades, experienced the agony of economic development with scarce internal resources. They have, not unoften, received step-motherly treatment from developed countries in the matter of securing external resources so badly needed for development. The phenomenon of alternately or simultaneously incurring the wrath of one or the other Power Bloc, has been adequately reflected in the attitude of such Power Blocs to the question of providing economic assistance. In general, nonaligned countries have received less external assistance than those countries which are members of military blocs.

Further questions that need to be answered are: what is the present status of nonalignment? Is it the same force it used to be? How has it stood up to the test of the last two decades, and to what extent it has validity in the changed world conditions? These questions demand an answer, as on these depends the future of nonalignment.

A frequent comment on nonalignment is that with the ending of the cold war and the growing detente between the East and the West, the *raison d'être* for nonalignment has disappeared and, therefore, whatever force or validity this policy had in the earlier years, it is somewhat of an anachronism today. Such a view is superficial. The abatement of the cold war and the growing understanding between the East and the West are not antagonistic to nonalignment; on the contrary, nonalignment has helped to bring about a detente. An essential purpose of the policy of nonalignment is the reduction of tensions and the creation of accord and international harmony among nations. Therefore, the improvement in relations between the East and the West amounts to a vindication of the policy of nonalignment, towards which the nonaligned countries have never ceased to strive in the United Nations and outside. The establishment of a detente between the Soviet Union and the United States and its necessary concomitant, namely, the loosening, and the likely eventual breaking up of the military blocs, could perhaps nullify to some extent the negative aspect of the policy of nonalignment, that is, not joining any military alliances, since the military blocs would themselves have disappeared; but it does not affect the positive aspects of nonalignment, the principles of which are universal in application and embody immutable and permanent values in international relations. These are the cultivation of friendship with all countries; dedication to the United Nations; noninterference in each other's internal affairs; struggle for the freedom of dependent peoples; developing international economic cooperation etc., etc.

Another criticism levelled at the policy of nonalignment is that it has not saved nonaligned countries from becoming victims of aggression. For example, India and UAR, which are among the principal adherents to the policy of nonalignment, have both been victims of external attacks. Speaking of India, such a criticism is frequently voiced by our own people. . . . Nonalignment is a two-way traffic and, therefore, so far as China is concerned, India cannot be a nonaligned country. Nevertheless, it must be conceded that the experiences of India and UAR have cast some doubts in the minds of some about the adequacy of the policy of nonalignment in so far as the security of a nonaligned country is concerned.

It is obvious that conditions today have changed from those in which nonalignment was born and took root. The cold war, as one knew it in the 1950s and the 1960s, has all but disappeared and there is a welcome and growing detente between the Eastern and the Western blocs. . . . The favourable trends for a detente in Europe are among the important factors contributing to a lessening of the importance and validity of the classic military alliances such as the NATO and the Warsaw Pact. Another factor has been the development of ICBMs with nuclear warheads, creating a nuclear stalemate among the Super Powers and eliminating the need for foreign military bases.

As a political consequence of these developments, Power Blocs are becoming less solicitous of the opinion and support of the nonaligned countries than before. A cynic might say that the political market value of nonalignment has been diminishing during the last few years.

Another factor affecting nonalignment is the curious triangular situation in the world—the confrontation between the People's Republic of China and the two classic Power Blocs on the one hand, and China and nonaligned countries in Asia on the other. Among the latter are principally India, Burma and other nonaligned countries on the periphery of China. This is a new situation which was not envisaged in the earlier years of the policy of nonalignment. In such a complicated situation, nonaligned countries, particularly those not directly affected, have found it difficult to steer a meaningful course and have tended to equate nonalignment with neutrality. They have played for safety, and it will be correct to say that in recent years for many nonaligned countries the distinction between nonalignment and passive neutrality has tended in practice to disappear.

A striking example of the confusion in which nonaligned countries were thrown, was provided during the Chinese attack on India in 1962. Many nonaligned countries of Asia and Africa on that occasion mistakenly abstained from what they described as "taking sides," even though they were quite clear as to the merits of the case, namely, that India had been subjected to a deep and massive invasion by the Chinese armed forces. . . .

This tendency to adopt a passive and neutral attitude in the face of glaring injustice and violations of the Charter of the United Nations, has been among the principal factors tending to besmirch and shake the foundations of nonalignment and to weaken that policy in playing the role of an effective force for peace. . . .

Today, it is recognised by all that in order to safeguard their independence, nonaligned countries have no escape from building up their military strength for defensive purposes. This is the reluctant and painful conclusion to which many countries like India have been forced in the light of their experience in recent years.

Despite the various difficulties and pressures, most nonaligned countries have been convinced that they must continue on their chosen path. The alternative sometimes put forward by national elements in nonaligned countries of giving up the policy of nonalignment and joining military blocs, is not realistic.

In the first place, in the changed world conditions, there is little desire on the part of military blocs to extend the scope and area of their respective military alliances. Secondly, nonaligned countries, most of whom have gone through the unhappy experience of colonial domination, are fiercely jealous of their freedom and independence and have a built-in resistance to joining military blocs and thereby mortgaging their freedom of action. Nonaligned nations do not wish to toe the line whatever and whosesoever the line may be. Thirdly, in many nonaligned countries abandonment of the policy of nonalignment will inevitably lead to polarisation of internal forces with disastrous consequences to internal peace and stability. . . .

The application and execution of the policy of nonalignment needs, however, adaptation and change in the existing world circumstances. It is obvious that the ending of the last vestiges of colonial and foreign domination and the consolidation of the freedom and independence of newly independent countries are the crying needs of the day. The disparity between the developed and developing countries, which is widening, is leading to an increase of social, economic and political tensions. Nonaligned and developing countries are faced with the prime task of economic growth and raising the standards of living of their people and, as a concomitant to these, of scientific and technological progress. The fulfilment of these tasks, which alone can give contentment to the peoples and true meaning to their independence, depends primarily on the developing countries themselves. International economic cooperation, both vertical with the affluent countries and horizontal among themselves to the extent possible is, therefore, of paramount importance and must now claim the special attention of nonaligned countries. . . .

Nonaligned countries should have no hesitation in having close economic and other relations with aligned countries on a basis of equality and mutual benefit and peaceful coexistence. In fact, such wider contacts and relations are desirable and are likely to contribute towards wider international understanding which is essential for world peace. A movement in this direction has already started. In the reverse direction, leading countries of one power bloc are now forging closer relations with countries which are traditionally and officially aligned with the other power bloc.

It is sometimes said that the policy of nonalignment has no important role to play in the changed conditions of the world. This view is not correct. In the turbulent world of today, there is need for redoubled efforts for the realisation of the basic objectives of nonalignment. Nonaligned countries continue to play a significant role in crisis situations. . . .

Finally, it would be well to deal with the popular view of nonalignment which has been sometimes expressed in my own country that when there is a military conflict elsewhere, nonaligned countries should not take sides. . . . Likewise, there is a fallacy that a nonaligned country by receiving military assistance or support from another country, particularly a Big Power, violates the policy of nonalignment. While nonalignment does not contemplate that a country should tie itself up with a formal military alliance with either of the Power Blocs and thereby compromise its freedom of reaction and predetermine its attitude on important questions, a sovereign nonaligned state does not lose the inherent right of individual and collective defence which means the right of defending its own territory, either alone or with the assistance of friends when its own security and territorial integrity are endangered.

Thus, in the changing world we live in, the picture of nonalignment is somewhat different from what it was a decade ago. In a dynamic world situation, no policy can remain in a static state, and nonalignment itself must respond to the winds of change. Adaptation in its application is obviously called for, but the policy of nonalignment itself retains its validity and character. Indeed, in many ways, its positive aspects, namely peace and peaceful coexistence, need to be pursued more vigorously in the turbulent world of today. Nonaligned countries will continue to play in the future, as they have played in the past, a vital role in the promotion of peace and international harmony.

Section 3

Contemporary diplomatic practice

Contrasting strategic styles of diplomacy

Charles O. Lerche

In this essay on "cold war diplomacy," Professor Lerche shows how differences in diplomatic styles are related to differences in national temperament and illustrates with the games of chess and poker. Both diplomatic strategies are searching for national security, but are both capable of the continual adjustment needed in a dynamic world?

"Contrasting Strategic Styles in the Cold War," U.S. Naval Institute Proceedings, *Vol. 88 (May 1962).* *The late Professor Lerche was on the faculty of the School of International Service of the American University and author of numerous articles and books on international relations.*

In spite of 15 years of experience gathered in the course of day-by-day struggle with the Kremlin, most Americans feel themselves no better qualified today to anticipate trends in the cold war than they were in 1946. The "Soviet enigma" seems no nearer solution than ever; the United States retains its belief in the existence of some mysterious but clearly sinister "blueprint," "master plan," or "time-table" that the Soviet bosses obstinately insist on hiding from honest God-fearing Americans by means of the infamous "closed society." Operationally, therefore, the dominant American strategic concept ever since 1946 has been one of "response" to whatever "challenges" the Soviet cares to initiate, whether "ambiguous" or "explicit."

The image of a great people resting its security and survival on nothing more substantial than its ability always to improvise an effective response to an external threat—over a time span usually measured at least in several decades—has proved galling to most Americans. As long as the nation admits itself to be unable to penetrate Soviet intentions, however (and avoids attempting to do so by relying on near-cosmic and operationally useless postulates of "world domination" and "the spread of Communism"), no more rewarding approach is possible. Actually, granted American assumptions, the only viable alternative to the contemporary posture of the United States is a suicidally risky pre-emptive (sometimes called "forward") strategy of dubious rationale and low potential productivity.

Part of the obvious inability of American political and opinion leadership to come to grips effectively with the Cold War is due to the great dissimilarity in what can be termed the "strategic styles" of the two nations: the distinctive fashion in which each formulates its operative problems and devises techniques for their solution. Completely apart from their opposing concepts of national mission and ideological orientation, the U.S.S.R. and the United States approach the narrower field of political and strategic analysis from radically different points of view and varying patterns of assumptions.

The bulk of official, journalistic, and public discussion of the issues of the Cold War in the United States centers about the conflict of purpose that is painfully obvious between the antagonists. Far too little attention has been paid to the matter of style. Very few Americans seem at all sensitive to the fact that the United States conducts its Cold-War policy in a very different way than does the Soviet. Yet victory or defeat for the nation will be finally registered only in the real world. It does not seem unreasonable to argue, therefore, that deeper insight into the actual conditions of the global struggle will bear fruit in a more realistic and effective American policy.

This is not merely to argue that the United States should forthwith make still another massive effort to "understand the menace of Communism," although obviously the more that Americans learn about the reality of Soviet motivation and action (as opposed to the myths industriously propagated by several schools of doctrinaires), the better for the nation. But Americans stand in even greater need of self-analysis; it is shockingly apparent to any serious student that the American people understand themselves and their government's policy only marginally better than they do the Soviet. Intensive study of the U.S.S.R. can be no more than a waste of time unless the United States couples this effort with an equally serious attempt to come to terms with itself. Only in this way can the struggle with the Soviet be placed in its true perspective.

Probably the most basic difference in strategic style between the Soviet Union and the United States is dramatically suggested by the Russian preference for chess as an intellectual pastime in contrast to the American predilection for either poker or contract bridge. This is in no sense an invidious comparison; poker and contract bridge are both serious games of strategy that require intellectual and analytical gifts of at least as high an order as does chess. But—and this is the key point—the conditions under which strategic choices are made are radically different in chess than in the games favored by Americans.

The essence of strategy in chess—especially as the game is played by the Russian masters, who are the best in the world—is its integral unity. The entire plan of attack is tied together from the very first move. The successful conclusion of a game is the result of an interlocked series of operating decisions, each of which is dependent upon those preceding it and in turn affects and eventually governs those that follow. There are no breaks in the strategic web, no opportunity to "fall back and regroup." The chess player, once he has committed himself to a strategic plan, must stand or fall on it to the end.

Poker and bridge, on the other hand, both consist of a series of analytically independent strategic confrontations (deals) tied together only loosely by a central strategic purpose. "Victory" in bridge or poker is achieved by amassing a large enough margin of profit out of an indefinitely prolonged series of separate strategic situations to emerge the winner. Each situation, furthermore, is operationally unique, with its controlling characteristics determined by the chance fall of the cards. An evening of bridge or poker demands as many strategies as there are deals.

In chess, victory (checkmate) is won by one move made *at the end of the game*. In games of cards, however, pay-offs are maximized by capitalizing on favorable opportunities that are at least partially fortuitous—an unusually large pot or a redoubled slam—*whenever they arise*. Chess problems are formulated as ways of ending a game ("white to play and win in three moves"); bridge problems, however, involve the solution of an entire hand examined with no reference to the over-all state of the competition. Chess begins with the players exactly equal in strength (except for "the move"), while poker or bridge allocates strength to each player by an arbitrary distribution of cards. Chess, in a word, demands a strategy of finality; poker or bridge, a strategy of opportunity.

American behavior in the Cold War is rooted—possibly unwittingly—in the bridge-poker school of strategy. Operationally, foreign policy seems to be conceived as a set of beads on a string, held together only by the single thread of time. Each bead is a single crisis, conflict, or "situation" (Berlin, Laos, Cuba, the Congo, Suez, Korea, and so on). Each situation (deal) is complete in itself, with its own unique context, its largely fortuitous conditions, and its own strategic imperatives and opportunities. Each is deemed susceptible of "solution" within its own terms. The United States thus moves through time dealing with one foreign policy crisis after another, with top priority being assigned in practice to the current or most recent one.

Thus the nation is confronted with an endless series of new strategic situations, each calling for a fresh approach that is forcibly reminiscent of the bridge player picking up a new hand. Within each such "problem" the United States seeks "victory"—or at least an escape from "defeat." Victory and defeat in these cold-war "hands" are reciprocal: the United States "wins" if the Soviet is balked and "loses" if Moscow has its way. After all, in a poker hand "there can be only one winner"; setting an opponent's contract frequently scores more points for the bridge player than he could possibly make on his own initiative. And although defeat is irksome, it can often be borne by reflecting that "we just didn't have the cards" or by giving voice to the perennial hopeful cry of the loser: "Deal!"

In strict bridge-poker terms, this piece-by-piece approach to strategy is beyond criticism; this is the way one wins such games. But do Americans really believe that enough American "victories" in individual crisis situations can be accumulated ever to persuade Khrushchev to throw in his cards? Nevertheless, political and journalistic figures thunder for "victory" in each confrontation with the Soviet, and American success in the cold war is usually computed on some "box-score" basis for mass consumption.

The essentials of Soviet strategy can all be found in the literature of chess. The U.S.S.R. has a policy that is unified, both in time and in space. The Kremlin is adept at the "orchestration of crisis," using a bewildering variety of tactics simultaneously in many parts of the world in a co-ordinated effort to achieve its ends. The Soviet, unlike the United States, does not have a "Latin American policy," a "southeast Asian policy," or even a "German policy"; there is only a single Soviet policy that governs action in any situation.

Another analogy that highlights the difference between the two approaches is drawn from sports. Soviet calculations are much like those used in managing a professional baseball team; U.S. policy-makers, on the other hand, react more like the coaching staff of a "big-time" intercollegiate football team.

Organized baseball is a game of percentages. Each team in a league will win some games and lose some; the championship goes to the one that compiles the highest winning percentage. There is no premium on winning any particular contest (except the final game of the World Series—the baseball counterpart of checkmate). Throughout a long season there is a single strategic goal to which the team's effort is constantly directed; a single victory (even a spectacular one) is only one small step toward the championship that can be balanced off the next day by a loss. Any one game is much less important in itself than in relation to the team's performance over the whole season and to the record of the other teams in the league.

This is a fair characterization of Soviet policy. To use a tired cliché, the Kremlin "keeps its eye on the ball"; any single issue gains policy significance only in terms of an over-all strategic design. Thus Soviet planners have no reason to fear a dangerous relaxation of effort in a moment of triumph nor does Moscow disintegrate in dismay and shock after a defeat. The U.S.S.R. plays the percentages; Soviet strategy is aimed at winning the final game of the international World Series.

There is nothing either novel or vicious, or uniquely Communist, about this approach; on the contrary, it is in the grand tradition of statecraft. It was long ago pointed out—frequently, at least by some Germans and Americans, with some scorn—that "Britain always loses every battle but the last one." It is a tribute to British reticence that only seldom did London point out the obvious fact that the last battle is the only one really worth winning. It is, however, a difficult concept for Americans to grasp, since so many of them think in categories appropriate to high-pressure college football.

The modern football coach in an institution taking the game seriously has his mission imposed upon him by the nature of the system in which he operates. He must strive for an undefeated season, or at least a sufficiently impressive won-lost record to attain the stratospheric regions of the "top ten." . . .

The coach must, therefore, win ten or 11 games, evenly spaced throughout a three-and-a-half month season. . . . For most coaches, their record and their job security are placed in absolute jeopardy each Saturday. A football team "plays one game at a time" in a special and excruciating sense. . . .

Thus for most football teams, there is no World Series. The season does not build to a climax, but instead is spent on a plateau of tension with no release until the very end. A final strategic influence is the distinctive rhythm of the football season: a week of preparation for a game, the game itself, another week of practice, another game, and so on. . . .

The national proclivity to conceive policy as a series of direct Soviet-American confrontations separated by more or less static pauses for practice strongly affects the planning of American action. The United States has found it difficult either to see beyond the end of the crisis it is engaged in at the moment or to deal with more than one at a time.

Any American Secretary of State, once a major Soviet-American crisis is touched off, must feel akin to the college football coach at the moment of kick-off. Now his preparations will be tested; now his true worth as a strategist (testable, according to this doctrine only in face-to-face struggle—"the battle is the pay-off") will be measured. He knows also that like the coach an undisguisable failure will touch off a popular demand for his official scalp. Humiliation and punishment of "those responsible" for "defeat" is part of the

American way of doing business. And even a real success cannot console him, for he knows that there is another game to be played next Saturday.

Most significantly, however, the "football touch" is revealed in the pursuit of the undefeated season. Once the whistle blows and the United States becomes locked in open conflict with the Soviet, the nation demands "the old college try" from its servants. Each crisis is as important as any other; all are absolutely critical and call into question far-reaching matters of national prestige, survival, and world role. Each victory, no matter how trivial, vindicates the entire American position and induces visions of total success at some future time; each defeat (especially as interpreted by the mass media) plunges the nation into gloom and an orgy of Spenglerian despondency about the failure of American "vitality" and "will."

Where the baseball-chess orientation of Soviet strategy pays off best is in its possession of a built-in device for the rationalization of operational priorities. Secure in their appreciation of an overriding and well-formulated set of objectives, Soviet planners avoid the trap of assigning each issue the same—necessarily absolute and transcendent—importance. Instead, Moscow can quickly determine how far it is appropriate to go in any situation, how much risk can be justifiably assumed, and how many human and material resources may be thrown into the struggle. Thus stabilized by a central strategic concept, Soviet policy has a consistency and a tenacity that make it very difficult to throw off the track.

The United States, relying on its football-poker calculus, finds it much more troublesome to govern its operations by any such tight strategic pattern. . . . As a result, the objectives of American policy usually find expression as abstractions with a vague operational ring rather than as formulations of concrete states-of-affairs the United States is seeking to bring about: "stop Communism," "advance the cause of freedom," "strengthen the Free World," "stand firm," and the like. None of these is of any use as a guide to action in an actual situation, and the United States usually contents itself with trying to "win" the pot on the table with the cards it has been dealt.

A student of chess soon learns the value of the "gambit": the deliberate sacrifice of a piece in order to gain an immediate advantage in time or position that will make possible the later recapture of the lost piece under more favorable circumstances. Soviet strategists are adept at this maneuver, but it would be a foolhardy American policy-maker who would dare seriously to propose any such move. After all, no football team ever deliberately lost a game, no bridge player ever accepted an avoidable set, and very few poker players permit a pot to go by the board just to bait their opponents into over-extending themselves. . . .

In still another way the baseball-football contrast is visible in the respective national styles. Football is a game governed by a clock; everything takes place within a predetermined and, at least for the losing team, frequently too short period of time. Success demands strategies that produce quick results, or at the very least pay off within the fixed playing time. Baseball, on the other hand, has no time limit; the game is governed by the number of times each team comes to bat. No matter how long a team may prolong an inning, its opponents will have exactly as many opportunities—under identical rules and conditions—to score in its turn. Thus there is no premium on playing a "possession" game or in seeking to monopolize the initiative. Defense and offense are two sides of the same coin.

The analogy is almost disturbingly apropos to the Soviet and the United States. American expectations are geared to quick results, "crash programs," "breakthroughs," and winning "races" with the Soviet. The recurrent demand that the United States "seize the initiative" is clearly linked to the equally pervasive plaint that "time is running out," so beloved of the nation's editorialists. "You can't score," football wiseacres intone, "unless you have the ball," and Americans see themselves committed to scoring the winning touchdown soon, before the final gun goes off. The Soviet, however, is not at all obsessed with time; the game is yet in its early innings and by the time the last man is put out, many years hence, Moscow is certain it will be the winner. Early leads do not count, except as a measure of how much catching up is to be done. It is the score at the end of the game that is all-important. . . .

Americans are fond of reminding themselves at every opportunity that they are involved in a struggle of long duration, but very few seem to have grasped the strategic implications of this platitude. The Soviet has been and obviously still is planning for the long term, building strategy upon the assumption that its goals are important and worthy enough to justify intensive and coordinated effort for many years. The United States, orienting itself primarily to crisis, has demonstrated astonishing ingenuity in extemporizing strategies and tactics in times of stress, but it has never developed a generalized strategic concept to rationalize its many policies and programs. The chess player, in a word, must think ahead to the consequences of any move he makes; the poker player cannot plan until he sees the cards he has drawn.

Bluff is a key element in poker, with the explicit strategic function of forcing an uncomfortable burden of choice upon one's opponent. A skillful poker player can, under appropriate circumstances, maximize winnings otherwise unobtainable by the forthright and vigorous employment of a bluff. But chess is also replete with analogous situations, and the chess strategist has a major advantage over the poker player in evaluating a bluff. He has a broader strategic outlook and many more analytical criteria. He has the entire sweep of the game to help him decide whether or not to call the bluff, while the poker player must operate largely within the limits of the single hand. The Soviet leaders have repeatedly shown much greater sophistication than the United

States in handling bluffs. For Americans, a called bluff means either defeat or a dangerous escalation of the crisis. For the Soviet, it is only a side-clip to another prepared position.

The crisis of decision facing the United States at this point in history is whether the nation can safely go on playing poker with a chess master. Against an enemy who is always thinking several moves ahead, how long can the United States afford the luxury of not adopting a strategy until it sees the cards it has been dealt, until the crisis actually breaks? Under the conditions of military and political technology in the latter half of the 20th century, what chance has a strategy of opportunity against a strategy of finality?

Fifteen years of cold war have undermined most of the fundamental postulates on which the United States has based its approach. The result is a serious erosion in the American position:

(1) International crises are not independent and self-contained events, capable of being attacked as isolated decisional systems; instead, each development in world affairs is part of a seamless web of international interaction.

(2) All crises are not of equal importance, nor is one victory as meaningful as another. The real measure of American success or failure is relative, not to the embarrassment the Soviet bloc may suffer, but rather only to the central strategic purpose the United States may be serving.

(3) No state, no matter how powerful, can realistically hope for an undefeated season every year. A certain proportion of American moves are bound to fail, even under optimum circumstances; the best any strategist can dream of is a winning percentage adequate to move him toward his own goals.

(4) The complex and swift-moving nature of contemporary world affairs places a high premium upon explicit and operative concepts of national purpose. No other device can prevent American policy from deteriorating into a welter of unrelated and often self-contradictory undertakings.

With the world so emphatically refuting the American assumptions about the nature of the game, a massive overhaul in American strategic thinking is long overdue. It is past time for the United States to learn to play international political chess itself. Only by a strategic technique that takes into full account both the peculiarities of the environment and the tactics of the enemy can the nation significantly improve its capabilities for rewarding effort.

The elements of such a new strategic style have been already suggested; here they may be briefly summarized: (1) a clear formulation of national purpose that can serve as a constant criterion of choice; (2) a unitary strategy that integrates American action across time and in any part of the world; (3) an articulated system of priorities, derived from postulated goals, that imparts a sense of proportion to American planning; (4) a capacity to accept either a victory or a defeat with confidence and poise; (5) a sense of time that permits long-term planning and operations in pursuit of vital objectives.

None of these is especially esoteric, nor is any inherently impossible of adoption by the United States. Their realization requires only a greater measure of maturity in the American people and a display of greater courage and determination by their leaders. To embark on such a course, however, will undoubtedly generate painful political tensions within the United States and upset many cherished ways of thinking and acting. To fail to develop a viable strategic style, however, is to condemn the United States to a static policy in a dynamic world and the American people to a steady diet of eroding prestige and bewildered frustration. There would seem to be little doubt about which road the United States should take.

The USSR as peacemaker: Tashkent and after

The Soviet Union's role as mediator in the Indo-Pakistani conflict over Kashmir is analyzed by The World Today. *In addition to being a good example of the role of a third party in resolving a conflict, it illustrates how Soviet foreign policy operates in practice in achieving national interests.*

This material appeared originally in The World Today *(February 1966), the monthly journal published by the Royal Institute of Foreign Affairs, London. Reprinted by permission.*

Of the parties to the Tashkent Conference, the host country alone appeared unquestionably a beneficiary. Following Mr Kosygin's offer . . . of Soviet 'good offices' as a step towards a settlement of the Indo-Pakistan dispute, the reservations expressed first by Pakistan and then by India aroused doubts as to whether this Soviet debut in the field of international peacemaking would materialize. Even when Mr Shastri and President Ayub

Khan finally agreed to the detailed arrangements, scepticism about the outcome of the meeting persisted and, in many quarters, was dispelled only by the signing, on 10 January [1966], of the Joint Declaration. Modest though the content of the Declaration may be, however, the very fact that such a document could be agreed [upon] appears to constitute a significant achievement of Soviet diplomacy.

The immediate Soviet gains from this initiative are considerable. First, they have gained the gratitude of both India and Pakistan and, by their appearance of scrupulous impartiality, have, without alienating the former, increased their influence with the latter. Second, they have won, in greater or less measure, the plaudits of all save the Chinese (who, apart from a brief factual report, studiously ignored the conference) and their associates. Third, they have been able to represent the meeting as a defeat for Western 'scepticism' and 'pessimism' (an *Izvestiya* editorial of 13 January [1966] commented: 'As for Western commentators, many of them find it hard to conceal their irritation at the fact that as a result of the meeting the international prestige of the land of the Soviets has grown still greater'). Fourth, they have strikingly reaffirmed their interest in Asia and will have further undermined the Chinese contention that the Soviet Union 'is not an Asian Power'. Finally, thanks to the venue of the meeting, they have elicited tributes from the Indian and Pakistani leaders to the achievements of a Soviet Asian Republic and to the goodwill of its inhabitants.

The conference was, not least, a personal triumph for Mr Kosygin. While the Russians, in preparing the ground for the meeting, stressed its bilateral character and offered Mr Kosygin's assistance only 'if both sides deem this useful', it became clear from the comments of participants and observers that his role, particularly on the penultimate day, must have gone beyond that of affording 'good offices'. Thus an Indian spokesman characterized the Soviet Premier's conduct of the opening day's session as 'correct, cautious, and constructive', but a report in the Pakistani *Dawn* two days later asserted: 'Premier Kosygin's role in the Tashkent talks, though behind the scenes, holds the key to their successful conclusion'; and Mr Shastri, in his last statement to correspondents, spoke of the 'great and noble role' which he had played.

It should perhaps be noted that Mr Kosygin, in the cause of bringing the parties together, did not hesitate to awaken memories of the former colonial status of the sub-continent or directly to describe the dispute as 'the heritage of the long period of domination by the colonisers, who set the enslaved peoples against one another'. The leading Soviet commentators Zhukov and Maevsky (in *Pravda* of 10 January), expanding this theme, set the outcome of the meeting in the context of the East-West struggle as a whole: 'Friendship between India and Pakistan strengthens both the two countries and peace in Asia; enmity between them weakens each of them and plays into the hands of those who do not desire peaceable, good-neighbourly relations between Pakistan and India and who are fanning the flames of the war of aggression in Vietnam in their endeavour to undermine the successes of the national liberation movement on the Asiatic continent.'

What of the implications of the Soviet initiative for the future? As far as Soviet relations with the sub-continent are concerned, it might seem to require scrupulous adherence to the line of impartiality which has marked the treatment of the dispute by Soviet publicity since last autumn. Certainly, the Russians have, during the last twelve months or more, been genuinely anxious, without prejudice to their good relations with India, to bring about a *rapprochement* with Pakistan. They may, moreover, consider that a by-product of the 'spirit of Tashkent' should be the elimination from the Pakistani press of the frequent anti-Soviet items which have gratefully been reproduced by the Chinese. However, a Pakistani correspondent who inferred that 'the Soviet Government's initiative in calling the Tashkent meeting is itself evidence of their neutralist stance in the Indo-Pakistan dispute' may have been in some measure mistaking appearance for reality. Unquestionably, the Russians will sincerely welcome a *détente* between India and Pakistan; but there are no grounds for supposing that they will cease assistance to India. It is not without interest that during the period of the Tashkent meeting a new long-term Soviet-Indian trade agreement, envisaging an increase by 1970 in the volume of trade between the two countries to almost double the 1964 level, was concluded in New Delhi.

At the same time, it will have been clear to the Russians that the Pakistanis, in accepting their offer of good offices, risked incurring the displeasure of the Chinese. The latter virtually ignored the conference, but chose on 6 January to deliver a sharp Note to India alleging that the Indian Government had of late made a 'frenzied effort to create tension by armed force along the Sino-Indian border and the China-Sikkim border'. The timing of this Note was, as an Indian spokesman at Tashkent remarked, 'odd' and appeared designed (as even a Soviet commentator conceded) to stiffen the Pakistani delegation's attitude.

Finally, could the limited success achieved at Tashkent be a harbinger of a Soviet conciliation initiative in Vietnam? This appears extremely unlikely. While the Soviet press hailed the 'good example' of the Tashkent Declaration, a Soviet delegation to Hanoi reaffirmed support for the 'four points' and signed an agreement for supplementary Soviet aid to North Vietnam. Moreover, the Indo-Pakistan dispute and the Vietnam conflict are scarcely analogous either in dimensions or as regards the political and ideological standing of the contestants *vis-à-vis* the Soviet Union.

In search of a peacemaker: The United States and North Vietnam

Letters of Lyndon B. Johnson and Ho Chi Minh

Many events have transpired since the exchange of these letters, but they are still powerful examples of the use of diplomatic exchange in propagandizing and in rationalizing behavior. Their failure to produce immediate results illustrates how slowly the wheels of diplomacy, like those of justice, turn.

The text of a letter from President Johnson to President Ho Chi Minh dated February 2, 1967, and the North Vietnamese leader's reply, dated February 15, 1967. Congressional Record, *Senate, Vol. 113, No. 72 (May 9, 1967).*

President Johnson's letter

Dear Mr. President: I am writing to you in the hope that the conflict in Vietnam can be brought to an end. That conflict has already taken a heavy toll—in lives lost, in wounds inflicted, in property destroyed and in simple human misery. If we fail to find a just and peaceful solution, history will judge us harshly.

Therefore, I believe that we both have a heavy obligation to seek earnestly the path to peace. It is in response to that obligation that I am writing directly to you.

We have tried over the past several years, in a variety of ways and through a number of channels, to convey to you and your colleagues our desire to achieve a peaceful settlement. For whatever reasons, these efforts have not achieved any results.

It may be that our thoughts and yours, our attitudes and yours, have been distorted or misinterpreted as they passed through these various channels. Certainly that is always a danger in indirect communication.

There is one good way to overcome this problem and to move forward in search for a peaceful settlement. That is for us to arrange for direct talks between trusted representatives in a secure setting and away from the glare of publicity. Such talks should not be used as a propaganda exercise, but should be a serious effort to find a workable and mutually acceptable solution.

In the past two weeks, I have noted public statements by representatives of your Government suggesting that you would be prepared to enter into direct bilateral talks with representatives of the U.S. Government, provided that we ceased 'unconditionally' and permanently our bombing operations against your country and all military actions against it. In the last day, serious and responsible parties have assured us indirectly that this is in fact your proposal.

Let me frankly state that I see two great difficulties with this proposal. In view of your public position, such action on our part would inevitably produce worldwide speculation that discussions were under way and would impair the privacy and secrecy of those discussions. Secondly, there would inevitably be grave concern on our part whether your Government would make use of such action by us to improve its military position.

With these problems in mind, I am prepared to move even further toward an ending of hostilities than your Government has proposed in either public statements or through private diplomatic channels. I am prepared to order a cessation of bombing against your country and the stopping of further augmentation of United States forces in South Vietnam as soon as I am assured that infiltration into South Vietnam by land and by sea has stopped. These acts of restraint on both sides would, I believe, make it possible for us to conduct serious and private discussions leading toward an early peace.

I make this proposal to you now with a specific sense of urgency arising from the imminent new year holidays in Vietnam. If you are able to accept this proposal I see no reason why it could not take effect at the end of the new year, or Tet, holidays. The proposal I have made would be greatly strengthened if your military authorities and those of the Government of South Vietnam could promptly negotiate an extension of the Tet truce.

As to the site of the bilateral discussions I propose, there are several possibilities. We could, for example, have our representatives meet in Moscow where contacts have already occurred. They could meet in some other country such as Burma. You may have other arrangements or sites in mind, and I would try to meet your suggestions.

The important thing is to end a conflict that has brought burdens to both our peoples, and above all to the people of South Vietnam. If you have any thoughts about the actions I propose, it would be most important that I receive them as soon as possible.

Ho Chi Minh's reply

Your Excellency: On 10 February 1967, I received your message. This is my reply.

Vietnam is thousands of miles away from the United States. The Vietnamese people have never done any harm to the United States. But contrary to the pledges made by its representative at the 1954 Geneva conference, the U.S. Government has ceaselessly intervened in Vietnam; it has unleashed and intensified the war of aggression in South Vietnam with a view to prolonging the partition of Vietnam and turning South Vietnam into a neocolony and a military base of the United States. For over two years now, the U.S. Government has with its air and naval forces carried the war to the Democratic Republic of Vietnam, an independent and sovereign country.

The U.S. Government has committed war crimes, crimes against peace and against mankind. In South Vietnam, half a million U.S. and satellite troops have resorted to the most inhuman weapons and the most barbarous methods of warfare, such as napalm, toxic chemicals and gases, to massacre our compatriots, destroy crops and raze villages to the ground.

In North Vietnam, thousands of U.S. aircraft have dropped hundreds of thousands of tons of bombs, destroying towns, villages, factories, roads, bridges, dikes, dams and even churches, pagodas, hospitals, schools. In your message, you apparently deplored the sufferings and destructions in Vietnam. May I ask you: Who has perpetrated these monstrous crimes? It is the U.S. and satellite troops. The U.S. Government is entirely responsible for the extremely serious situation in Vietnam.

The U.S. war of aggression against the Vietnamese people constitutes a challenge to the countries of the Socialist camp, a threat to the national independence movement and a serious danger to peace in Asia and the world.

The Vietnamese people deeply love independence, freedom and peace. But in the face of the U.S. aggression, they have risen up, united as one man. Fearless of sacrifices and hardships, they are determined to carry on their resistance until they have won genuine independence and freedom and true peace. Our just cause enjoys strong sympathy and support from the peoples of the whole world, including broad sections of the American people.

The U.S. Government has unleashed the war of aggression in Vietnam. It must cease this aggression. That is the only way to the restoration of peace. The U.S. Government must stop definitively and unconditionally its bombing raids and all other acts of war against the Democratic Republic of Vietnam, withdraw from South Vietnam all U.S. and satellite troops, and let the Vietnamese people settle [for] themselves their own affairs. Such [is the basic] content of the four-point stand of the Government of the D.R.V., which embodies the essential principles and provisions of the 1954 Geneva agreements on Vietnam. It is the basis of a correct political solution to the Vietnam problem.

In your message, you suggested direct talks between the D.R.V. and the United States. If the U.S. Government really wants these talks, it must first of all stop unconditionally its bombing raids and all other acts of war against the

D.R.V. It is only after the unconditional cessation of the U.S. bombing raids and all other acts of war against the D.R.V. that the D.R.V. would enter into talks and discuss questions concerning the two sides.

The Vietnamese people will never submit to force, they will never accept talks under the threat of bombs.

Our cause is absolutely just. It is to be hoped that the U.S. Government will act in accordance with reason.

Chapter Three

The struggle for power

There are two basic routes to national security—through national power or through international order. Power and order are not mutually exclusive, for even international order is forced to rely on military power. Political and economic power are evident in international organization and in peaceful bilateral arrangements. These categories are chosen instead to help organize a study of the real struggle—for security in a changing and still basically unorganized world.

Nationalism and sovereignty have limited international cooperation and organization and have limited the search for security to a basis of individual effort. After each of the last three major wars—the Napoleonic Wars and World Wars I and II—attempts were made to avoid future wars and gain mutual security through world organization. Each attempt has failed. Only in the case of a mutual threat too large for effective unilateral action have nation-states found it expedient to trust their national security to others. The threats of Napoleon, of the Central Powers, and of the Axis Powers faded after each of the wars, as did the viability of the new international security organization when faced with increasing individual national drives for security.

The fading of old threats has often seen their replacement by new ones. When a state becomes a sovereign actor responsible for its own security, every other state becomes a potential enemy. In fact, complete security could only be obtained by controlling most of the world's offensive power, because only then is a nation immune to successful attack by any combination of forces. This would result, paradoxically, in greater insecurity for all other nations.

The threat that causes war or preparation for war is one directed against vital national interests. These interests are not always clear since each state determines them unilaterally, but clarification of these interests, if only for internal use, often prevents war. The Korean War may have occurred principally because in 1950 the United States publicly announced that Korea and the Taiwan Straits were not within her "perimeter of defense." North Korean troops invaded South Korea within three months with the intention of accomplishing by force what international organization had failed to do by peaceful means—unify Korea. America several months later ignored the warning by the new People's Republic of China that she considered it against her vital interest of territorial integrity to have troops along the Sino-Korean Yalu River border. Only after proceeding to the border was it found that Red China was serious about being willing to fight for this interest. In another instance war was avoided when a firm declaration of vital interests was made. In the Cuban Crisis of 1962, the United States clearly made it known that the placement of Soviet missiles in Cuba constituted a threat to American security. The Soviet Union withdrew the missiles under the counterthreat of a naval blockade (a limited act of war). Especially in an age of accurate intercontinental ballistic missiles, the Soviet Union clearly had no vital interest in maintaining missiles in Cuba.

In both the Korean and the Cuban cases, each nation's decision was determined not only by its vital interests but also by the availability of power. U.S. power, together with a clear statement of vital interest, might have prevented the war in Korea. In Cuba this combination made the difference, regardless of Cuba's claims to her own vital interests.

The underlying theme of the post-World War II era has been the cold war. This hostility between the Western and Communist blocs began even before their allied forces completed the "crusade" against the Axis Powers of Germany, Italy, and Japan in World War II. The basic cause of this war was fear for security and doubts about the intentions of the other side—fears and doubts which the United Nations, with neither power nor authority, was unable to moderate. There is some feeling that the internal disruptions within each of the large camps and a stalemate in power are bringing the cold war to an end. Frankel's article elaborates on the theme of the Fulbright and Lerche articles in Chapter Two that a more realistic approach is needed.

The Korean War faded in an armistice rather than a peace treaty, and it continues to smolder some fifteen years later with armies still squared off across the 38th parallel. It remains a classic example of a war started by strategic error and unable to be ended while the cold war lingers on. The year 1968 saw the possibility of a reopening of active hostilities. The North Koreans seemed bent on reopening the war by such blatant violations of vital interests as an attempt on the life of President Park of South Korea and the capture of the American reconnaissance ship the U.S.S. Pueblo and its crew. Numerous border violations have also been recorded. Atkinson reports on this "pantomime" of war as an example of the continuing hostility short of all-out war that also occurs periodically in the Middle East and Cyprus.

The tension of the cold war has led to concrete preparation for hot wars.

The arms race, a classic attempt at "oneupmanship," has seen the great powers seeking security through superior weaponry. We have advanced from sophisticated conventional weaponry to the development and testing of nuclear, chemical, and biological weapons deliverable by rocket via outer space. Any superiority of one power is, of course, untenable to the other, and the upward-spiraling game goes on, together with the possibility of an Armageddon of unimaginable destruction.

Currently the two superpowers each possess not only second-strike capability but also an effective mutual deterrent—a situation which has led to a tenuous and highly volatile feeling of security within each state. There is constant temptation to build better guarantees of security. The offensive striking power of each state has reached the level where further development becomes redundancy, and the emphasis now is on defense through the development of an antiballistic missile (ABM) system. Erickson talks about the USSR's move toward the establishment of an ABM umbrella over Moscow and other concentrations of industry and power, while former Secretary of Defense McNamara presents the inevitable American countermove. Both these moves seem directed as much at China as they are at each other. The probable net result will be a higher explosive level of mutual deterrent capability.

The idea of deterrence is that an attack becomes unlikely as a result of the retaliatory capability of the target nation. The number of past wars is a measurement of both the failure of deterrence and the attempt to achieve security (among other goals) by conquering others. This failure is noted with a suitable warning in a special report prepared for the United Nations by the Secretariat and included here. Nuclear war has been avoided so far, but the growth of the "nuclear club" entails security problems for the hundred-odd nations which have neither the defensive nor the offensive capability to deter a nuclear attack.

The problem of credibility is equal to that of capability. A nation relying solely on nuclear weapons would be more vulnerable in a series of minor wars where the use of nuclear weapons would be impractical. General McConnell in a speech included here calls for more varieties of strategic military power. Another general, James M. Gavin, writing about the limits of military power, suggests that economic strength and technological changes may be more important tools of persuasion in the long run. Stabilization of the power balance at a certain level or complete disarmament are the alternatives to pursuing security through the arms race.

The problem of arms control occurs on nuclear and non-nuclear levels. A nuclear test-ban treaty has already been ratified by most nations. Of those who agreed not to test, most could not test anyway, but among those with nuclear capability, France and Red China, on the conviction it is necessary to their national security, continue to test. If no program beyond the mere cessation of testing is soon devised, even such nations as India, Israel, and Egypt are contemplating attaining nuclear capability. The frustrations of arriving at an agreement in an area where every nation has a vital interest at stake are described, with his views on the matter, by Arthur H. Dean, one of the negotiators. The official Soviet reaction to the recent treaty on the nonproliferation of nuclear weapons, as well as attitudes on disarmament in general, is presented by Premier Kosygin and by an official government memorandum.

The problems of nuclear power are not relative to the potential conflicts among the smaller nations of the world which have created an arms race at a lower and more conventional level. In recent years small-scale wars between the Israelis and the Arabs, the Pakistanis and the Indians, and the Turks and the Greeks have all necessitated appropriate weaponry. In some cases the arms sources are both Communist and non-Communist, but often both sides in the dispute are supplied by the United States, which has given or sold arms on the basis of its own prescription for world security—resistance to Communist aggression. The recipients of this aid, however, have utilized their arms from their own, regional viewpoint of security. It has not been the United States' intention that this arms supply for NATO allies would be used by them to destroy each other, as the Turks and the Greeks may well do over Cyprus. McCarthy discusses the possible repercussions of this problem. Kemp's article deals with the arms control problem in the Middle East, where the Soviet Union is busily engaged in supplying arms to the Arab side.

Assuming that both nuclear and non-nuclear disarmament are possible, what are the prospects for security? The "disarmers" of the 1920s found that disarmament without guarantees for security will be short-lived. A realistic discussion of this volatile issue must also account for national sovereignty. Two scientists, Rich and Platt, discuss the complexities of a disarmed world of sovereign nations.

The logical end to the arms race is the use of these arms in open conflict. The nuclear powers have avoided direct confrontation, but there has been indirect confrontation in Korea and in Vietnam. The United States is involved in Vietnam because of its announced commitment to protect "the Free World" from Communist aggression. The wisdom of the goal may be challenged, but none can doubt the reality of the war. The other protagonists see this war as one for the achievement of their own vital interests—independence and security from external interference. The Senate Republican Policy Committee has prepared a summation of the Vietnam War which asks some pertinent questions about the interests at stake.

In many ways Vietnam differs from previous wars. These differences are in terms of the commitments and the methods of warfare. Two humorous accounts, one by Buchwald and one by Baker, are presented, despite the seriousness of the issue, to illustrate the nature of this change.

Conflict has also taken place between the Arabs and the Israelis. Here again, each side feels that it is engaged in protecting its true vital interests. The Arabs feel that the very existence of Israel is a mockery of justice, territorial integrity, and the sovereignty of nations. In 1967 they began to make the necessary noises and to move in the direction of correcting this mockery of twenty years' standing. The young Israeli nation could not accept this threat of destruction. After all, what nation-state has come into existence except at the expense of others or at the cost of violence? And every state has the obligation to protect its peoples' security with all available and necessary power. Despite the presence of a U.N. peace-keeping force, war began when the two sides declared the existence of incompatible and overlapping vital interests in the area of national security. Yost presents a summary of the beginning of that war.

Each new outbreak of war, however small, raises the possibility that escalation will lead to the involvement of the nuclear powers and another world war. Martin's article deals with these questions.

We have talked much about change in this book. Although the causes of war remain constant, the styles of war change. Vietnam, in particular, is a different kind of war, a fact reflected by the difficulties America has in fighting it. There are no fronts, the enemy is not clearly recognizable, the goals are not the seizure and control of geographical locations, and there is no clear definition of the interests at stake. For the Americans and the North Vietnamese alike, the war is a political war, an attempt to win "the hearts and minds of the people." The frustrations of not only combatting but also participating in this new kind of war are discussed by Hillam. Slover discusses the solution of the problem in a wider scope—the new role of "civic action" by military units. Perhaps out of this we can learn the uses of political, economic, and technological power which stabilize people and the way in which destructive military power can be avoided in the search for security.

Section 1

The continuing cold war

Can we end the cold war?

Max Frankel

What is the cold war, and where, when, how, and why did it begin? Mr. Frankel explains the complexities of this phenomenon and its effect on the interacting behavior of men and nations.

The New York Times Magazine, *January 29, 1967. © 1967 by The New York Times Company. Reprinted by permission. Mr. Frankel is a diplomatic correspondent for* The New York Times.

The great hope surrounding Vietnam is that the end of the hot war there may begin to finish off the cold war everywhere.

Whatever the deal that finally becalms Southeast Asia, Communists around the world may reckon at last with the costs of their rash rhetoric about wars of liberation while Americans learn to reckon with the costs of incautious commitments and the cant of containment. Korea taught the folly of direct military invasions—in both directions—but it only exacerbated the hostilities that produced the battle. With any luck, an imperfect outcome in Vietnam will demonstrate not only the folly of indirect military intrusions—by both sides—but also the menace of ideological passions.

For passion as well as power must be curbed before the cold war can end. Though it began as a rather conventional struggle between two superpowers, the Soviet Union and the United States, for European territories and resources of obvious value, it soon expanded into a universal contest for what were called "the hearts and minds" of all humanity and for rival conceptions of a new world order. And eventually the main antagonists were joined by a third, Communist China, with each waging cold war against the other two.

The territorial joust in Europe expired in deadlock, but only after its hatreds and fears had confused and corrupted conflicts everywhere. It also corrupted the values of otherwise humble men. Russians learned to gloat when Americans lost their jobs or went on relief. Americans came to cheer when Soviet food stocks ran low.

In place of international politics, there developed only polemics, understandably, perhaps, about the future of Germany but also ludicrously about the fate of Zanzibar. What was denounced as terror by one side was celebrated as valor by the other. What was invasion here was liberation there. Whoever was not with, was against, until the habits of conflict prevailed even where its causes had long been forgotten.

That all this may at last be drawing to an end is already a subject of lively speculation among American scholars. The "end of ideology" has been one of their major themes for some time; "beyond the cold war" has been another. A search for "alternatives" dominates much of their literature.

The periodic efforts of the Soviet Union and the United States to probe for a peaceful settlement in Vietnam, and their halting steps to preserve cordial relations in other matters even while their missiles and planes are engaged in direct combat in North Vietnam, suggest the extent to which realism already has conquered ideological fervor. Despite the shooting, as President Johnson remarked in his State of the Union message, "we have avoided both the acts and the rhetoric of the cold war." The objective now, he said, was to end it. . . .

Even a sketchy review of the major stages of the cold war suggests that it was much more than the Soviet-American conflict we usually imagine, much more than the product of simple Western resistance to simple Communist threats. It sprouted from deep roots and developed with a terrifying logic.

In a sense, the cold war began 50 years ago, when Moscow and Washington first proclaimed rival ideologies to which they only gradually devoted their national energies. Lenin envisioned a world of revolutionary transition to Communism, sweeping away old economic institutions and, in time, even the frontiers of nations. At almost the same time, Woodrow Wilson proclaimed a revolution for a new order to make the world safe for those very institutions and nations. . . .

In their bones and in their rhetoric, if not always in their policies, Soviet Communists came to feel duty-bound to assist *any* Marxist rebellion, while Americans, applying what they took to be the lessons of two world wars, came to regard *any* Communist advance, domestic or international, as a threat to their security.

The collision of these conceptions made it impossible for Moscow and Washington to wage an ordinary, "sordid" power struggle after World War II, the kind that would end in a conventional balance of forces. Instead, they talked so much of great crusades that at important junctures they talked themselves into messianic adventure.

The first and probably main engagement of the cold war did not require these emotional commitments. It was actually quite short. It was largely confined to Europe. It could be explained in entirely rational terms.

Though devastated by war, Europe possessed enormous latent human, economic and military resources that neither the United States nor the Soviet Union dared to lose to the other. . . .

Moscow drew first, by moving to dominate most of the areas the Soviet armies had occupied. When it threatened to move even farther, in Iran in 1946 and in Greece and Turkey in 1947, and actually moved farther by seizing Czechoslovakia in a 1948 coup, it evoked a hasty American response.

It does not really matter whether the Soviet leaders actually planned to march the Red Army clear across Europe to the Atlantic. The United States had reason to fear that they did and Western Europe alone was plainly too weak to resist Soviet challenge from the outside or Communist subversion from the inside.

The United States responded with massive military and economic assistance, embodied in the Truman Doctrine of aid to Greece and Turkey, the Marshall Plan of $12.5 billion for Western Europe's economic recovery and the North Atlantic Treaty Organization, representing a threat of nuclear retaliation for any direct Soviet attack.

Within a few years, this territorial struggle ended essentially where it began. Moscow had tightened its hold on the lands east of the Elbe while the anti-Communist societies recovered in the western regions beyond. A number of times, particularly in the Berlin blockade of 1948–49, both sides showed themselves eager to avoid a direct military clash. Neither seemed to feel greatly menaced by the division of Europe that ensued.

Winston Churchill, who had been among the first to rally the West against Soviet advances in 1946, felt by 1950 that the time had come to press for a final settlement. The balance of power, he predicted, would not again be so favorable to the West. . . .

But his American cousins were by now too obsessed with a sense of mission and of fear to acquiesce in a sordid power balance. When President Truman had set out in 1947 to obtain Congressional support for $400-million in anti-Soviet aid to Greece and Turkey, Senator Arthur Vandenberg, his influential Republican ally, told him he would have to "scare hell out of the country" to put the measure through. And scare the country he did, in Wilsonian absolutes that the country has not shaken off yet.

Instead of saying what he meant, which was that Greece and Turkey and Western Europe should not be allowed for solid strategic reasons to fall under the control of Communist agents of the Soviet Union, Mr. Truman gave his doctrine a soaring definition and ambition: "Totalitarian regimes imposed on free peoples, by direct or indirect aggression, undermine the foundations of international peace and hence the security of the United States," he said.

Carefully specifying that he did not wish to intervene with American troops, the President nonetheless proclaimed an unlimited policy "to support free peoples who are resisting attempted subjugation by armed minorities or by outside pressures." He meant only Communist minorities that were then clear projections of Soviet power, but that is not what he said.

From that day forward, the challenge of Soviet power, which Churchill deemed manageable in 1950, came to be seen in the United States as the challenge also of Soviet and all Communist ideology. Thus when China fell into Communist hands in 1949, it seemed to Americans to be not just a major event, but a major "defeat." And within a few months, the struggle reached right into the midst of American society; Senator Joseph McCarthy ignited a domestic crusade that equated every Communist idea with a full Soviet division.

By 1950, the United States was emotionally unfit to accept the consequences of the brief postwar struggle even if the Soviet Union had accepted Churchill's modest estimate of its power. It had become impossible to think of a settlement or even of customary diplomatic dealings with the "evil" and "godless" men in the Kremlin.

And then came Korea.

In early 1950 President Truman's Secretary of State, Dean Acheson, could still envision a policy of shrewd opportunism in Asia. It would be foolish, he said to "deflect from the Russians to ourselves the righteous anger and the wrath and the hatred of the Chinese people, which must develop." Much of Asia would long be unstable, he added, but "we can help only where we are wanted and only where the conditions of help are really sensible and possible."

The war broke these barriers of restraint. It began with a Communist aggression that has never been properly explained. Mr. Acheson may have tempted North Korea by neglecting to place South Korea inside a well-defined Western defense perimeter. Moscow seized the opportunity, probably because it wished to prevent Japan's progressive adhesion to the Western camp.

Whatever the cause, the Korean war propelled the United States into a firm commitment to the Chinese Nationalists on Taiwan, into a counterinvasion of North Korea and, therefore, into direct, costly and inconclusive combat against the Chinese Communists.

Above all, the war became for many Americans the final proof that a single Communist conspiracy, centered in Moscow, was hell-bent on conquest of the entire world, with hundreds of millions of Chinese now prepared to march on its signal.

Success in defending South Korea was no longer enough. In a crucial psychological turn, a moralistic Eisenhower Administration now accepted Communism's portrait of itself as a monolithic, well-nigh invincible force. Diplomacy was turned wholly from its traditional function of compromise and placed in the service of a worldwide crusade for freedom, self-determination and order, American style.

John Foster Dulles, Mr. Eisenhower's Secretary of State, delivered pious promises to "liberate" the "captive peoples" of Eastern Europe, to "roll back" Communism everywhere, to undo his predecessors' "negative, futile and immoral" policy of "containment." Washington would not "tolerate," said Mr. Dulles, the "welding of the 450 million people of China into servile instruments of Soviet aggression."

Events would soon expose these slogans as hollow, but they were not therefore meaningless. For they spoiled what balance there might have been for earnest negotiation with Stalin's insecure successors in Moscow. By including also a hypocritical "unleashing" of the Chinese Nationalists to reconquer the mainland, the slogans also spoiled what little chance there might have remained to exploit, as Mr. Acheson had advised, Peking's developing hostility toward the Soviet Union.

The Eisenhower crusade became a worldwide imitation of the successful policies in postwar Europe. Every inch of non-Communist territory, including worthless rocks off the coast of China, were embraced in Dulles and Eisenhower Doctrines that defined their "loss" as matters affecting the vital interests of the United States.

Washington sought not only bases from which to defend itself against Soviet or Chinese attack. It tried to convert the poor and unstable societies of Asia into allies as reliable and congenial as the recovered nations of Western Europe. It built them armies with which to guarantee domestic stability and tested their allegiance by demanding strident expressions of anti-Communism. . . .

For a time the worldwide contest of good guys vs. bad guys led Americans to cast even neutrals in the role of "immoral" spectators. It perpetuated the threat that Eastern Europe and mainland China were some day to be "recaptured." It justified alignment with regimes of any totalitarian or corrupt color so long as it was not Red. It forced the United States to suspect and oppose many rebellious nationalist movements and led it to meddle in the affairs of many governments—in Indochina, Iran, Indonesia, Latin America.

The crusade turned the United Nations into a blatant instrument of American policy. Above all, it blinded Americans to the evidence of real unrest and change in the Communist nations of Europe and to the possibilities of a profound rift between Peking and Moscow. . . .

This new phase of the cold war was not, of course, a one-sided contest. In Europe, Nikita Khrushchev and his fellow heirs to Soviet power appeared eager for acceptance of the status quo, but elsewhere they mounted their own crusade, imitating Western techniques of economic bribery and military assistance in packages labeled "peaceful coexistence."

Probably more often than Americans the Russians managed to separate the interests of Soviet power from those of local Communists in places such as Egypt, India and Indonesia. They let many a Marxist rot in jail while they courted his jailer. They, too, were unwilling or unable to relinquish the ideological doctrines of Communist revolt, and measured their progress principally by American failure.

Fortunately, neither side really had the courage of its crusading convictions. Moscow made its peace with many post-colonial regimes whose revolutions stopped far short of Communism and whose policies were rarely dominated by anti-Americanism. And during the East German uprising of 1953, the collapse of the French in Indochina in 1954 and, most spectacularly, the Hungarian revolt of 1956, American inaction made a mockery of the Dulles doctrine of liberation. . . .

The year 1956 might thus have become a turning point in the cold war, for the simultaneous uprising in Hungary and the British-French invasion of Suez exposed deep fissures in both major alliances. By avoiding conflict in Hungary and even cooperating diplomatically over Suez, Moscow and Washington again demonstrated not only eagerness to avoid a direct clash but an inchoate yearning to structure the world jointly.

Both Stalinism and McCarthyism were in decline, leaving each society more prepared to deal realistically with the other. Out of the new humility there might have evolved a new diplomacy.

But in mid-1957 Mr. Khrushchev suddenly acquired the intercontinental missiles which he was to rattle for five years to force terms upon the West. He had spent enormous amounts of real and political capital, with little to show for the investment abroad or at home. The Chinese pressed him to use the missile threats in support of their Asian interests, but Khrushchev set out to demonstrate that a shrewd mixture of ultimatum and blandishment could bag really big game: a favorable settlement in the heart of Europe.

With simultaneous threats to Berlin, offers of total disarmament, colorful journeys through neighboring lands and a bellicose junket around the United States, he demanded the respect that he thought Soviet power and purposes deserved. But he suffered only humiliation, as in the U-2 spy-plane episode, and rebuff, as in Berlin; the sputniks had panicked Americans and again shattered their confidence in negotiation.

Belligerent in the eyes of Washington and cowardly in the eyes of Peking, Khrushchev spent the years of his greatest power at home in frantic and confused efforts abroad. Cuba's turn to Communism—an aberration that neither Moscow nor Washington had expected—only made matters worse, for it rekindled the Russians' revolutionary dreams and tempted them strategically while further frightening Washington, on both counts.

Thus did the cold war persist through the last two, least messianic, years of the Eisenhower Administration and through two of the three years of the Kennedy Administration.

In 1961, after humiliation at the Bay of Pigs, bitter confrontation with Khrushchev at Vienna, deterioration of non-Communist positions in Laos, construction of the wall in Berlin and resumption of nuclear testing by both sides, the cold war took on the added dimension of a resumed arms race.

Threatened directly for the first time by Soviet missiles, the United States strained to keep ahead. It also redesigned its conventional forces in the hope that conflict, if it came, might be fought without the ultimate weapons. And with this new capability President Kennedy began to inject men and resources into South Vietnam to prevent yet another "loss" of face or territory.

Nor until Mr. Kennedy had proved his nuclear-age virility and Khrushchev's strategic inferiority in the Cuban missile crisis of 1962 did the two sides return to the search for alternatives to the cold war. The time was right because the missile crisis and China's brief invasion of India had aggravated the conflict between Peking and Moscow almost beyond repair, certainly beyond denial.

The Russians secretly and hastily installed long-range missiles in Cuba, it is thought, because all else had failed in their desperate bid to close the strategic gap. Here was a chance to threaten American soil as much as American weapons were then threatening Soviet territory. And the humiliation of the United States from this sudden build-up was probably counted on to bring unexpected diplomatic gains throughout Latin America and perhaps as far away as Berlin. But by forcing a showdown and enforcing a humiliating Soviet retreat instead, Washington only dramatized Moscow's strategic inferiority at the time. Whether tactically, to gain a prolonged breathing spell, or for all time, as some insist, the Russians withdrew not only their missiles but also the whole panoply of challenge to the United States.

Tentatively, but simultaneously at last, Moscow and Washington sought accommodation, notably in the treaty to ban nuclear testing. There was an echo of the old frenzy among Americans when a few Cubans were suspected of "exporting" their revolution to, of all places, Zanzibar, on Africa's east coast, but confidence finally overcame such ridiculous fright.

A Communist Cuba, it was found, could be easily and effectively isolated and tolerated so long as the rhetoric of liberation was not taken too seriously. An opportunistic United Arab Republic, though often the paid agent of Soviet diplomacy, could not only be tolerated but, it was found, at times even manipulated. Iraq, Guinea, Ghana and Algeria, all of which had at one time turned away from the West and toward Communism, were not, in fact, "lost"; they proved quite adept at defending themselves against it without the American military embrace.

The independence of a nation, it was found, did not, after all, always depend upon American protection or intervention. In fact, the Communist nations of Eastern Europe, long closed even to American propaganda, had developed healthy appetites and capacities for independent maneuver. Not only Yugoslavia, whose independent career began in 1948 with American military aid, but also Albania and Rumania, became more defiant of the Soviet Union than even the "liberalized" regimes of Poland and Hungary. Though run by Communists, they probably gained greater freedom of action than some Central American republics.

Independence and Communism were no longer simple opposites; in some cases they became quite compatible. Certainly no nation was more doggedly "independent" than Communist China. Her defection from the "international Communist conspiracy," if ever there was one, certainly wrecked the "master plan" of conquest, if ever there was one. Some American officials actually came to hope that Moscow would retain a greater, presumably moderating influence over Peking. . . .

Yet in situations of turmoil, in the Congo, in Vietnam, in the Dominican Republic, Washington could not quite shake the old habits of thought and rhetoric. The defeat of every incipient Marxist or Communist movement everywhere had been for too long the principal aim of American foreign policy. Washington's reflexes obeyed this early training even where the mind resisted.

Although they comprehend the conflicts among Communist nations and the changes inside many Communist societies, Americans continue to equate the goal of "containing" Soviet or Chinese power with the obliteration of each Communist challenge in every place, no matter how remote.

And the new Soviet leaders, too, continue to confuse their ideological sense of duty with their more narrow national interests. Goaded now by the competition with Communist China for authority in the Communist world, the Russians have gone perhaps farther than they might otherwise wish in the support of Communist subversion and wars of liberation. And where local Communists have clear territorial ambitions, as in Korea and Vietnam, Moscow would probably support even more aggressive tactics if American power did not block the path.

Events keep conspiring, therefore, to keep the cold war alive.

As a conflict between what is loosely called Communism and anti-

Communism, it still magnifies, exaggerates and perhaps even generates conflicts of interest between the Soviet Union and the United States in places and situations that neither might otherwise care about or which might, at worse, be the occasion for quite routine economic and diplomatic competition.

The emergence of Communist China has temporarily inflamed the ideological conflict; so has the continuation of the arms race and the eruption of hot war in Vietnam.

But Vietnam should also help to demonstrate the threats posed by the ideologies of both sides. Neither the Communists nor the anti-Communists of that unhappy country have played the docile parts assigned to them by their big-power patrons.

Few Communists anywhere, in fact, have behaved as the Russians or Chinese wished or as the Americans feared. More and more anti-Communists are similarly breaking the cold-war restraints. Europe, where it all began, is relatively stable and therefore also restive; East and West, it is beginning to share the distaste of other regions for the forms of stability prescribed by Moscow and Washington.

The collapse of the postwar bipolar structure and the conversion of the cold war into a triangular contest may not bring peace, but it should corrode the rival theologies.

As Peking develops gradually into a significant power, there will be more and more occasions for two of the large powers to line up in uneasy coalition against the third: Moscow and Peking against Washington in a Korea or Vietnam; Moscow and Washington against Peking in a Kashmir; Peking and Washington against Moscow in the encouragement of East European independence. (An interesting example of the potential attraction between China and the West is the serious if somewhat premature talk in West Germany about how Peking might be strengthened so that Moscow will feel threatened in its rear and compelled to seek a more durable settlement in central Europe.)

If it teaches anything, the history of the cold war suggests that none of the major parties is blameless for its long life. It suggests also that in periods of swift international change there is little virtue in mere consistency, in the perpetuation of old, even successful tactics.

The dreams of worldwide revolution for democracy or for Communism can possess the heart without forcing the hand. A step back from interventionism need not be a retreat to isolationism. Big powers can be involved in almost everything without becoming doctrinally and militarily engaged almost everywhere. The end of the cold war would not automatically bring harmony and stability; it would mean only that in the quest for peace we prefer the political deal to religious zeal.

The pantomime at Panmunjom

Basil Atkinson

One of the longest running performances of diplomacy is that taking place at the 38th parallel in Korea. The actors have changed many times, but the roles change very little. Mr. Atkinson's description of this part of the cold war as a pantomime is apt.

Saturday Review, *October 9, 1966.* *Mr. Atkinson is manager of the Australian National Tourist Association, Melbourne.*

Panmunjom is really too long for a dateline but the word slips easily off the tongue or typewriter. It sounds friendly, euphonious, almost melodious. But a name can mislead. Panmunjom in Korea is the essence of cold hostility. Men in yellow or red armbands pass silently by. They may stop to glare at one another, but they do not speak. The men in yellow armbands are mostly big men; the men in red armbands are invariably little men. Their skins are white, black or brown, but their attitudes are uniform: grim, unsmiling, businesslike, determined, tough. Here man shows no sympathy or feeling for his fellowman if his armband is of a different color. . . .

There is no respite from the grimness at Panmunjom. Even on festive occasions the faces are set just as firm and silently. The Americans put up a Christmas tree last year hoping it might bring some cheer. Instead, it brought a charge that it had been put there for purposes of provocation.

Officially, Korea is still in a state of war. A peace treaty has never been signed, although the armistice has lasted since July 27, 1953—the longest ceasefire in history. Panmunjom is the place where the peace is being kept. It sits precariously on the 38th Parallel at the western side of the demilitarized zone which winds 151 miles across the Korean peninsula. This zone, which was the line of ground contact between the opposing forces at the moment of ceasefire, has now grown thick with underbrush and is about two-and-a-half miles wide stretching to the east to just below the 39th Parallel. The center of the strip is marked every few hundred yards with signs in Korean and English that it is the military demarcation line.

The border is too well known and too frightening a prospect for Koreans to stumble across it by accident. Those who go there go by design—stealing into the South or stealing into the North. They are driven to it by desire to escape, or to be reunited with family, or to spy. Many get no further. . . .

All military equipment and forces have been withdrawn from the buffer zone, but each side is allowed to have 1,000 military police in its half of the zone. In the southern part, some 300 Americans and 700 Republic of Korea military personnel are engaged in regular patrols, while a similar number of Communist forces patrol the northern part. These groups frequently meet and it is not unusual for shots to be exchanged. Charges and counter-charges then follow at a meeting of the Military Armistice Commission.

The Commission meets in the joint security area at Panmunjom, which is roughly circular and half-a-mile wide. Here nerves of steel are needed, for buildings of the United Nations Command and the Communists adjoin, and troops pass one another stiffly and silently as they go about their duties.

Rival guard posts are within a few yards of each other. One of the loneliest and most foreboding sentinel posts for any American is near here on the edge of Communist territory at "The Bridge of No Return." An American Negro as big as Joe Louis was on duty there during my recent visit. A few yards away from him at the Communist post was a diminutive, brown-skinned North Korean. They stood almost at spaghetti distance, but glumly silent. Even the birds had ceased to sing.

Each side is permitted only thirty-five military police on duty at one time in the joint security area. Only six are allowed to carry arms. To the south beyond the Freedom Gate Bridge at the Imjin River, American and South Korean troops move about with their normal military equipment. But in the joint security area at Panmunjom one walks on tiptoe. Little wonder that its unique elements—surprise, danger and tension—have combined to make it one of Korea's main tourist attractions. We were told that 25,000 United Nations guests visited the area last year compared with 1,100 brought in by the Communists. Since the cease-fire in 1953 the total number of visitors from the two sides has been 145,000 and 11,000 respectively. It can be reached in less than three hours by road from Seoul and the United Nations Command welcomes visitors provided they have prior notice. . . .

Visitors are given strict instructions before they are allowed into the area. Each person is issued a white distinguishing badge and is required to sign a form to the effect that he will:

1. Remain in a group and will not leave his escort.
2. Undertake not to fraternize, including speaking or making gestures,

with the Communists (military personnel, red armbands; press representatives, green armbands; Communist visitors, green piece of cloth at the upper pocket).

3. Agree not to enter any Communist building (painted a tired green) or enter a United Nations Command building (painted a tired blue) without permission of his escort.
4. Avoid standing in the way of military formations of either side.
5. Cease to take pictures if the Communists interfere with picture-taking.
6. Remain calm if any incidents should occur.

The focal point for visitors of both sides is the Military Armistice Commission building. Here visitors can eavesdrop at meetings at which the sullen silence is replaced by torrents of words. There are five members from each side whose purpose is to supervise implementation of the truce terms.

Since meetings can be called by either side at twenty-four hours' notice, they take place most weeks. Chiefly they concern alleged truce violations—charges of aircraft straying over the line, espionage and military infiltration, ships poaching in one another's territorial waters, and the like. No prior notice is given of any charge.

There is no chairman or agenda, yet the proceedings are highly formal. The accusing side enters first at 11 a.m. followed by the other side through a separate door. The five men from each side sit facing one another across a green, felt-covered conference table. The center of the table is set plumb on the military demarcation line. Those sitting to the south are in South Korea and represent the United Nations Command. Those to the north are in North Korea and they are the Communists. The frosty proceedings leave no doubt that the line is not imaginary. To show it is real, a microphone cord bisects the table on the line.

The accusing side first lodges its complaint usually in forthright terms in its own language. Translations follow. This is a time-consuming business because three languages (English, Korean, and Chinese) are used. A charge is usually followed by a countercharge and this may go on for hours. Members do not leave the table while the Commission is sitting. It is an arduous business.

The Communists use the proceedings largely as a propaganda forum. They lay most of the charges and see to it that they are well publicized. The Americans claim to be fastidious in their investigation of these charges, but say that only a small number—about 2 per cent—are valid. Where a genuine mistake or error of judgment has occurred, they say their policy is to admit it.

The participants from both sides are well schooled in psychological warfare, and search for any sign of weakness from the other. Strong words are used and tempers can become frayed. This is the greatest danger. To show irritation or annoyance on any point is to invite hours of continued pressure on that point.

Small matters can become big issues. There was the case of the size of the flags on the conference table. One day the Americans placed a small U.N. flag on their side of the table. The next day the Communists came in with their flag. It was an inch taller so it stood slightly over the U.N. flag. The U.N. flag was then lifted to the same height. At the next meeting there was a new Communist flagstand, which again made this flag an inch higher. And so the battle of the flags went on meeting by meeting until an agreement was reached. Now the tendency is to go in the other direction and make the flags smaller.

The Neutral Nations Supervisory Commission meets in the building next door. This comprises representatives of Sweden, Switzerland, Czechoslovakia, and Poland—four nations not involved in the Korean War—and apart from the inspection work they carry out, they are the intermediaries who help dampen situations when they become dangerously hot. . . .

Yet it is just as well that the Neutral Nations Supervisory Commission continues to be there. The members show that man can still have feeling for his fellowman regardless of his politics or color or creed. This is the one healthy sign at Panmunjom. Without it life would be intolerable. Instead there is just plain cold hostility—a safely-exciting tourist attraction if one abides by the rules.

Were it not so serious, it could make quite a pantomime.

Section 2

The arms race and the limits of power

"The fly in outer space": The Soviet Union and the anti-ballistic missile

John Erickson

New innovations are sought in the constant struggle to maintain superiority or at least equality in the arms race. Professor Erickson analyzes the latest Soviet innovation—the ABM—and weighs its effect on the Soviet offense-defense balance and on American offensive power.

This article originally appeared in The World Today *(March 1967), the monthly journal published by the Royal Institute of International Affairs, London. Reprinted by permission. Mr. Erickson is a reader in the Department of Government, University of Manchester, and the author of* The Soviet High Command: A Military-Political History, 1918–41.

In his recent testimony before the U.S. Senate Foreign Relations Committee, Professor Kennan was apparently inclined to rate the Soviet decision to proceed with the development and the partial deployment of an anti-ballistic missile (ABM) defence system as unwise, a comment which seemed to chide rather than to condemn. Certainly at first sight purchasing only a sliver of security at the price of a possible spurt in the strategic arms-race does appear to be a questionable move; yet from the Soviet side the situation is the product of a certain logic, no small amount of which derives from eliminating the illogicalities of the final period of Mr Khrushchev's rule. For some, the Soviet commitment to the ABM is merely the well-known syndrome of Soviet strategy, 'defence-mindedness', a factor indeed in the Soviet outlook, but so gratifyingly simple an explanation hardly corresponds to all the nuances and implications of the post-Khrushchev 'reconstructionist' military policies.

The terms of this 'reconstruction', for such since 1964 it has been, merit some inspection. Not that the fundamental frame of reference for Soviet strategy has been recast: it remains what it was, a concept of war-waging based on a combination of offensive and defensive capabilities (in contrast to the U.S. strategy of war-deterrence based on an overwhelming offensive capability, 'assured destruction capability', as Mr McNamara defines it). There have been, however, shifts in some directions, involving modifications in doctrine and differentiation in capabilities. By attacking what was called 'one-variant war', and by improving both the qualitative and quantitative aspects of the Soviet strategic missile arsenal, the Soviet command has moved away from 'total deterrence' (Soviet threats of 'massive retaliation' which were losing both their credibility and their utility, a point the Chinese were quick to emphasize to Moscow's cost) and the 'minimum deterrence' which might have satisfied Mr Khrushchev as he cut the corners of cost but which failed to convince the military that it would work. . . . Credibility, therefore, was and is a major issue, and in this connection Soviet review of the escalation factor is important; no longer is there rigid insistence that escalation would be automatic, but instead the recognition—publicly affirmed—that the use of nuclear weapons might be conditional, that 'limited war' might develop and for such a commitment the Soviet Union should prepare. Thus the Soviet command disengages itself deliberately from commitment to 'one-variant war', moves towards 'flexible response' of a kind, and therefore reinforces credibility by giving notice of commitment not merely at the topmost rung of war-waging but also at intermediate levels—'all-out', unlimited war and 'limited' war. In short, by moving towards a form of 'flexible response', the Soviet command is extricating itself from the ambiguities and the damaging inconsistencies of a deterrence position whose credibility was eroding. 'Total deterrence' was in a number of senses obsolete: 'minimum deterrence' was at best unsatisfactory, at worst downright dangerous. 'Nuclear fetishism' was what Peking, with its propaganda guns trained on Moscow, chose to call it; now the Russians have moved out of that line of fire, or so they might calculate. . . .

The effect of the reconstruction policies on the Soviet strategic arsenal has been both quantitative and qualitative (with the latter perhaps of greater significance): the two 'significant' changes underlined by Mr McNamara for the past year are the increased rate of 'hardening' ICBM launching installations and the deployment of an ABM system. This corresponds generally to an outlook which casts its war-waging strategy in terms of offensive capability and 'active defence', one additional measure of which is apparently the establishment of new, distinctive 'military-political organs' to run the Soviet Union in the event of nuclear war and so described by Major-General Zemskov.

The Soviet armed forces, organized along the lines of their 'missions' or specific functions, fall into four main groupings: the strategic deterrence force (ICBMs, fleet ballistic missiles), the strategic offensive force (the Long-Range Air Force, strategic airborne or amphibious forces), the strategic defence forces (ABM defence, the 'aid defence command'), and theatre forces (ground troops, air and naval support). Numerically they present this appearance:

	Russian	*U.S.*
ICBMs	+340	934
Submarine-launched missiles (SLBMs)	+130	624
IRBMs, MRMs (medium-range)	750	
Long-range bombers	up to 200	over 600
Medium-range bombers	1,200	

This represents some shaving down of the U.S. 4:1 numerical superiority (a superiority which is 2:1 in terms of megatonnage, Soviet warheads running higher up the scale, from 10–30 megaton). The second-generation Soviet ICBMs (forming the bulk of present strength) have storable liquid fuels and thus lend themselves more easily to protection through 'hardened' sites. In addition to these qualitative improvements, the reconstruction period can point to the virtual doubling of Soviet land-based ICBM strength (from + 150 in 1964 to well over 300 now). This signifies steady progress rather than any drastic 'crash programme', a policy which might be assumed to apply also to the ABM system. . . .

A planned ABM defence, based initially on what might be a considerable technological break-through and conceived as 'city defence' (the power centres of the Soviet Union), seems to be a cogent Soviet design. It is therefore possible to guess that the Soviet command has an estimate of how much 'defence' it is buying, or more particularly, what it wants to buy. The other Soviet defensive system, 'Blue strip' or 'Blue belt', which may involve missile-firing submarines, is separate from this ABM system. An indicator of obvious importance (both for Soviet intentions and capabilities) is not only 'active defence' but also 'passive defence', the Soviet civil defence programme, particularly a mass shelter effort; the role of shelters has been described as 'problematical' in no less a work than Marshal Sokolovskii's *Military Strategy*, while elsewhere emphasis has been laid not only on shelters but more upon dispersal and evacuation of the civilian population. What is perhaps more important as an indicator is the recent revelation about new 'organs' to run the country in the event of nuclear war, indicating possibly a newly revised approach to survivability and what to make of it. It might be less population protection and more 'administrative-political protection', safeguarding the nucleus of the State.

With the budgetary bulge which the ABM has already produced, the Russians, or at least an important section of the leadership, must be convinced that they are buying more than just a pig in a nuclear poke. Exactly what they are buying remains, of necessity, somewhat unclear. The best that might be attempted by way of summary is to look at why they have taken up this commitment. First, some general considerations:

1. An ABM deployment, partial as well as massive, would conform to the deterrent requirements of Soviet policy as a whole and to defence necessities should 'deterrence' fail.

2. An ABM deployment would fit some of the requirements of 'stretched' counter-deterrence, and indeed it becomes an integral part of the Soviet style of 'flexible response'.

3. In terms of war-fighting capabilities, an ABM system, even in limited deployment, could augment Soviet survivability, especially if this were conceived in terms of protecting the 'power nucleus'.

4. As indicated by Major-General Talensky, an 'effective' ABM system would reduce Soviet 'dependence' on the 'good-will' of a potential enemy and by narrowing the options would limit the freedom of such an opponent to select counter-force or counter-city strategies.

5. The pursuit of the ABM is a move in the strategic power balance in favour of the Soviet Union, supplying a possible means to strategic superiority (in the event of a unilateral technological break-through) or favourable momentum which does not bring any particular danger of a spurt in the arms race (though this depends upon acceptance of the Soviet view that the ABM is *absolutely* a defensive weapon, the implications of which can be categorically curtailed).

6. On the other hand, significant Soviet progress with an ABM might produce a 'defence lead' with important political consequences, what John R. Thomas calls 'a political pay-off' through a down-grading of American offensive capabilities (and equally an up-grading of Soviet survivability in the context of a protracted conflict).

7. A numerically smaller (compared to the American) ICBM force, though one possessing warheads of very high yield, and an ABM system speedily and widely deployed could be a desirable combination of weapon systems, impinging directly on the U.S. ICBM lead and eliminating the need for a very large jump in Soviet ICBM strength.

8. A strategic force which could only inflict damage but in no way inhibit (or prevent) it within or upon the Soviet Union has an obvious deficiency which can be overcome only by correction on the 'active defence' side; this moreover improves over-all Soviet war-fighting capability if 'deterrence' does not 'deter', while in a non-war situation it brings political benefit.

There are, additionally, other factors which could contribute to the attractiveness of the ABM: introduction of it without a 'crash programme' yet bringing a significant gain (military and political) which could span several years; by-products like insurance against 'independent deterrents', European or Chinese; an 'umbrella' for Soviet counter-deterrence. In general, Soviet expectation of the military-operational efficiency and the political utility of a more widely deployed ABM system seems to be high. It is, therefore, not a little remarkable that this attainment has gone largely unsung in the Soviet press at large: the only official confirmation of partial deployment the Soviet reader could derive from his own press was in January, in *Za Rubezhom*. This may indicate either Soviet caution, the difficulty of publicizing a technological achievement of this nature (other than through sweeping phrases, such as 'the fly in space') or the intention to unroll the propagandistic wraps only when the deployment is more advanced.

Apparently Soviet opinion does not hold the introduction of the ABM to be an act of destabilization. On the contrary, it is intended to 'even up' the balance *vis-à-vis* the 'vast stockpile' held on 'the other side'. It could be a very promising combination of weapon systems, from which the Russians would take some dissuading. It could be an extremely promising military technology, indeed this seems to be the present value put upon it; exploitation both successful and rapid could hoist the Soviet forces on the way to that superiority, strategic superiority, which military doctrine makes mandatory. On the other hand, there is much more ground to cover: this can scarcely be the closing stage of the divergence between military and political views, between minimum deterrence and war-fighting capabilities. Certainly the gap has closed a little, but it is early days to conclude that Soviet strategy as a whole is being 'militarized'. The present 'militarization' may be due predominantly to the present circumstances of the leadership, where military counsel carries greater weight than was the case under Mr Khrushchev. There has been movement from 'minimum deterrence', though no radical shift. There is no evidence that this is the prelude to some inordinately ambitious political strategy. It could reflect a more sombre view of 'good-will', but above all it appears as a very much introverted Russian decision, deeply embedded in caution, even pessimism, and constructed as an elaborate compromise.

Anti-China missile defense and U.S. nuclear strategy

Robert S. McNamara

The American response to Soviet urban protection by ABM's came from former Defense Secretary McNamara. His thesis is that the United States can penetrate any ABM net merely by increasing the number of attacking missiles. The United States will build a small-scale system, however, to ward off any Communist Chinese threat. He discusses nuclear strategy in both the broad and the narrow sense.

This is the text of former Defense Secretary McNamara's address delivered in San Francisco on September 18, 1967, as issued by the Pentagon.

I want to discuss with you . . . the gravest problem that an American Secretary of Defense must face: the planning, preparation, and policy governing the possibility of thermonuclear war. It is a prospect most of mankind would prefer not to contemplate. . . . For technology has now circumscribed us all with a conceivable horizon of horror that could dwarf any catastrophe that has befallen man in his more than a million years on earth. . . .

If . . . man is to have a future at all, it will have to be a future overshadowed with the permanent possibility of thermonuclear holocaust. . . . No sane citizen; no sane political leader; no sane nation wants thermonuclear war. But merely not wanting it is not enough.

We must understand the difference between actions which increase its risk, those which reduce it, and those which, while costly, have little influence one way or another. . . .

. . . Nuclear strategy is exceptionally complex in its technical aspects. Unless these complexities are well understood, rational discussion and decision making are simply not possible.

What I want to do . . . is deal with these complexities and clarify them with as much precision and detail as time and security permit. . . .

The cornerstone of our strategic policy continues to be to deter deliberate nuclear attack upon the United States, or its allies, by maintaining a highly reliable ability to inflict an unacceptable degree of damage upon any single aggressor, or combination of aggressors, at any time during the course of a strategic nuclear exchange—even after our absorbing a surprise first strike.

This can be defined as our "assured destruction capability." . . .

We must possess an actual assured destruction capability. And that actual assured destruction capability must also be credible. . . .

The point is that a potential aggressor must himself believe that our assured destruction capability is in fact actual, and that our will to use it in retaliation to an attack is in fact unwavering.

The conclusion, then, is clear: If the United States is to deter a nuclear attack on itself or on our allies, it must possess an actual and a credible assured destruction capability. . . .

[W]e must be able to absorb the total weight of nuclear attack on our country—on our strike-back forces; on our command and control apparatus; on our industrial capacity; on our cities; and on our population—and still be fully capable of destroying the aggressor to the point that his society is simply no longer viable in any meaningful, twentieth century sense.

That is what deterrence to nuclear aggression means. It means the certainty of suicide to the aggressor—not merely to his military forces, but to his society as a whole.

Now let us consider another term: "First-strike capability." . . . [A]s it is normally used, it connotes: . . . The substantial elimination of the attacked nation's retaliatory second-strike forces. . . .

The United States cannot—and will not—ever permit itself to get into the position in which another nation, or combination of nations, would possess such a first-strike capability, which could be effectively used against it.

To get into such a position vis-à-vis any other nation or nations would not only constitute an intolerable threat to our security, but it would obviously remove our ability to deter nuclear aggression—both against ourselves and against our allies.

Now, we are not in that position today—and there is no foreseeable danger of our ever getting into that position.

Our strategic offensive forces are immense . . . and . . . these flexible and highly reliable forces are equipped with devices that insure their penetration of Soviet defenses.

Now what about the Soviet Union? Does it today possess a powerful nuclear arsenal? The answer is that it does.

Does it possess a first-strike capability against the United States? The answer is that it does not.

Can the Soviet Union, in the foreseeable future, acquire such a first-strike capability against the United States? The answer is that it cannot. . . .

But there is another question that is more relevant. And that is, do we—the United States—possess a first-strike capability against the Soviet Union? The answer is that we do not. . . .

We do not possess first-strike capability against the Soviet Union for precisely the same reason that they do not possess it against us.

And that is that we have both built up our "second-strike capability" to the point that a first-strike capability on either side has become unattainable. (A "second-strike capability" is the capability to absorb a surprise nuclear attack and survive with sufficient power to inflict unacceptable damage on the aggressor.) . . .

The blunt fact is, then, that neither the Soviet Union nor the United States can attack the other without being destroyed in retaliation; nor can either of us attain a first-strike capability in the foreseeable future.

The further fact is that both the Soviet Union and the United States presently possess an actual and credible second-strike capability against one another—and it is precisely this mutual capability that provides us both with the strongest possible motive to avoid a nuclear war.

The more frequent question that arises in this connection is whether or not the United States possesses nuclear superiority over the Soviet Union.

The answer is that we do.

But the answer is . . . technically complex. The complexity arises in part out of what measurement of superiority is most meaningful and realistic. . . . [T]he United States does have a substantial superiority over the Soviet Union in the weapons targeted against each other. . . . [but] . . . the most meaningful and realistic measurement of nuclear capability is neither gross megatonnage, nor the number of available missile launchers; but rather the number of separate warheads that are capable of being *delivered* with accuracy on individual high-priority targets with sufficient power to destroy them.

Gross megatonnage in itself is an inadequate indicator of assured destruction capability, since it is unrelated to survivability, accuracy, or penetrability, and poorly related to effective elimination of multiple high-priority targets. There is manifestly no advantage in over-destroying one target, at the expense of leaving undamaged other targets of equal importance.

Further, the number of missile launchers available is also an inadequate indicator of assured destruction capability, since the fact is that many of our launchers will carry multiple warheads. But by using the realistic measurement of the number of warheads available, capable of being reliably delivered with accuracy and effectiveness on the appropriate targets in the United States or Soviet Union, I can tell you that the United States currently possesses a superiority over the Soviet Union of at least three or four to one. Furthermore, we will maintain a superiority—by these same realistic criteria—over the Soviet Union for as far ahead in the future as we can realistically plan. . . .

[However,] in the larger equation of security, our "superiority" is of limited significance—since even with our current superiority, or indeed with any numerical superiority realistically attainable, the blunt, inescapable fact remains that the Soviet Union could still—with its present forces—effectively destroy the United States, even after absorbing the full weight of an American first strike. . . . [Moreover, it] is essential to understand . . . that the Soviet Union and the United States mutually influence one another's strategic plans. . . . It is precisely this action-reaction phenomenon that fuels an arms race. . . .

In recent years the Soviets have substantially increased their offensive forces. . . .

Clearly, the Soviet buildup is in part a reaction to our own buildup since the beginning of this decade. . . . Our intention was to assure that they—with their theoretical capacity to reach such a first-strike capability—would not in fact outdistance us. But they could not read our intentions with any greater accuracy than we could read theirs. And thus the result has been that we have both built up our forces to a point that far exceeds a credible second-strike capability against the forces we each started with. . . . [E]ach of us can deny the other a first-strike capability in the foreseeable future. . . .

We do not want a nuclear arms race with the Soviet Union—primarily because the action-reaction phenomenon makes it foolish and futile. . . . [W]hat we would much prefer to do is to come to a realistic and reasonably riskless agreement with the Soviet Union, which would effectively prevent such an arms race. . . . But since we now each possess a deterrent in excess of our individual needs, both of our nations would benefit from a properly safeguarded agreement first to limit, and later to reduce, both our offensive and defensive strategic nuclear forces. . . . And we believe such an agreement is fully feasible, since it is clearly in both our nations' interests. . . .

It would not be sensible for either side to launch a maximum effort to achieve a first-strike capability. It would not be sensible because the intelligence-gathering capability of each side being what it is, and the realities of lead-time from technological breakthrough to operational readiness being what they are, neither of us would be able to acquire a first-strike capability in secret.

Now, let me take a specific case in point.

The Soviets are now deploying an antiballistic missile system. If we react to this deployment intelligently, we have no reason for alarm.

The system does not impose any threat to our ability to penetrate and inflict massive and unacceptable damage on the Soviet Union. In other words, it does not presently affect in any significant manner our assured destruction capability.

It does not impose such a threat because we have already taken the steps necessary to assure that our land-based Minuteman missiles, our nuclear submarine-launched new Poseidon missiles, and our strategic bomber forces have the requisite penetration aids—and in the sum, constitute a force of such magnitude, that they guarantee us a force strong enough to survive a Soviet attack and penetrate the Soviet A.B.M. deployment.

Now let me come to the issue that has received so much attention recently: The question of whether or not we should deploy an A.B.M. system against the Soviet nuclear threat.

To begin with, this is not in any sense a new issue. We have had both the technical possibility and the strategic desirability of an American A.B.M. deployment under constant review since the late 1950s.

While we have substantially improved our technology in the field, it is important to understand that none of the systems at the present or foreseeable state of the art would provide an impenetrable shield over the United States. Were such a shield possible, we would certainly want it—and we would certainly build it. . . .

It has been alleged that we are opposed to deploying a large-scale A.B.M. system because it would carry the heavy price tag of $40 billion. . . . If we could build and deploy a genuinely impenetrable shield over the United States, we would be willing to spend not $40 billion, but any reasonable multiple of that amount that was necessary.

The money in itself is not the problem: The penetrability of the proposed shield is the problem. . . .

Every A.B.M. system that is now feasible involves firing defensive missiles at incoming offensive warheads in an effort to destroy them.

But what many commentators on this issue overlook is that any such system can rather obviously be defeated by an enemy simply sending more offensive warheads, or dummy warheads, than there are defensive missiles capable of disposing of them. . . .

Were we to deploy a heavy A.B.M. system throughout the United States, the Soviets would clearly be strongly motivated to so increase their offensive capability as to cancel out our defensive advantage.

It is futile for each of us to spend $4 billion, $40 billion, or $400 billion—and at the end of all the spending, and at the end of all the deployment, and at the end of all the effort, to be relatively at the same point of balance on the security scale that we are now.

In point of fact, we have already initiated offensive weapons programs costing several billions in order to offset the small present Soviet A.B.M. deployment, and the possibility of more extensive future Soviet A.B.M. deployments. . . .

If we in turn hope for heavy A.B.M. deployment—at whatever price—we can be certain that the Soviets will react to offset the advantage we would hope to gain. . . .

We must continue to be cautious and conservative in our estimates—leaving no room in our calculations for unnecessary talk. And at the same time, we must measure our own response in such a manner that it does not trigger a senseless upward spiral of nuclear arms.

Now, as I have emphasized, we have already taken the necessary steps to guarantee that our offensive strategic weapons will be able to penetrate future, more advanced, Soviet defenses.

Keeping in mind the careful clockwork of lead-time, we will be forced to continue that effort over the next few years if the evidence is that the Soviets intend to turn what is now a light and modest A.B.M. deployment into a massive one.

Should they elect to do so, we have both the lead-time and the technology available to so increase both the quality and quantity of our offensive strategic forces—with particular attention to highly reliable penetration aids—that their expensive defensive efforts will give them no edge in the nuclear balance whatever.

But we would prefer not to have to do that. For it is a profitless waste of resources, provided we and the Soviets can come to a realistic strategic arms-limitation agreement. . . . [R]ealism dictates that if the Soviets elect to deploy a heavy A.B.M. system, we must further expand our sophisticated offensive forces, and thus preserve our overwhelming assured destruction capability.

Having said that, it is important to distinguish between an A.B.M. system designed to protect against a Soviet attack on our cities, and A.B.M. systems which have other objectives.

One of the other uses of an A.B.M. system which we should seriously consider is the greater protection of our strategic offensive forces.

Another is in relation to the emerging nuclear capability of Communist China.

There is evidence that the Chinese are devoting very substantial resources to the development of both nuclear warheads and missile delivery systems. . . . [I]ndications are that they will have medium-range ballistic missiles within a year or so, an initial intercontinental ballistic missile capability in the early 1970s, and a modest force in the mid-70s.

Up to now, the lead-time factor has allowed us to postpone a decision on whether or not a light A.B.M. deployment might be advantageous as a countermeasure to Communist China's nuclear development. . . .

China at the moment is caught up in internal strifes, but it seems likely that her basic motivation in developing a strategic nuclear capability is an attempt to provide a basis for threatening her neighbors, and to clothe herself with the dubious prestige that the world pays to nuclear weaponry. . . .

We possess now, and will continue to possess for as far ahead as we can foresee, an overwhelming first-strike capability with respect to China. And despite the shrill and raucous propaganda directed at her own people that "the atomic bomb is a paper tiger," there is ample evidence that China well appreciates the destructive power of nuclear weapons.

China has been cautious to avoid any action that might end in a nuclear clash with the United States—however wild her words—and understandably so. We have the power not only to destroy completely her entire nuclear offensive forces, but to devastate her society as well.

Is there any possibility, then, that by the mid-1970's China might become so incautious as to attempt a nuclear attack on the United States or our allies?

It would be insane and suicidal for her to do so, but one can conceive conditions under which China might miscalculate. We wish to reduce such possibilities to a minimum.

And since, as I have noted, our strategic planning must always be conservative, and take into consideration even the possible irrational behavior of potential adversaries, there are marginal grounds for concluding that a light deployment of U. S. A.B.M.s against this possibility is prudent.

The system would be relatively inexpensive—preliminary estimates place the cost at about $5 billion—and would have a much higher degree of reliability against a Chinese attack than the much more massive and complicated system that some have recommended against a possible Soviet attack.

Moreover, such an A.B.M. deployment designed against a possible Chinese attack would have a number of other advantages. It would provide an additional indication to Asians that we intend to deter China from nuclear blackmail, and thus would contribute toward our goal of discouraging nuclear weapon proliferation among the present non-nuclear countries.

Further, the Chinese-oriented A.B.M. deployment would enable us to add—as a concurrent benefit—a further defense of our Minute-man sites against Soviet attack, which means that at a modest cost we would in fact be adding even greater effectiveness to our offensive missile force and avoiding a much more costly expansion of that force.

Finally, such a reasonably reliable A.B.M. system would add protection of our population against the improbable but possible accidental launch of an intercontinental missile by any of the nuclear powers.

After a detailed review of all these considerations, we have decided to go forward with this Chinese-oriented A.B.M. deployment, and we will begin actual production of such a system at the end of this year.

I want to emphasize that it contains two possible dangers—and we should guard carefully against each.

The first danger is that we may psychologically lapse into the old oversimplification about the adequacy of nuclear power. . . .

The second danger is also psychological. There is a kind of mad momentum intrinsic to the development of all new nuclear weaponry. If a weapon system works—and works well—there is strong pressure from many directions to produce and deploy the weapon out of all proportion to the prudent level required. . . .

The road leading from the stone axe to the I.C.B.M.—though it may have been more than a million years in the building—seems to have run in a single direction.

If one is inclined to be cynical, one might conclude that man's history seems to be characterized not so much by consistent periods of peace, occasionally punctuated by warfare; but rather by persistent outbreaks of warfare, wearily put aside from time to time by periods of exhaustion and recovery—that parade under the name of peace. . . .

However foolish unlimited war may have been in the past, it is now no longer merely foolish, but suicidal as well. . . .

The question is what is our determination in an era when unlimited war will mean the death of hundreds of millions—and the possible genetic impairment of a million generations to follow?

Man is clearly a compound of folly and wisdom—and history is clearly a consequence of the admixture of those two contradictory traits.

History has placed our particular lives in an area when the consequences of human folly are waxing more and more catastrophic in the matters of war and peace.

In the end, the root of man's security does not lie in his weaponry.

In the end, the root of man's security lies in his mind.

What the world requires in its 22nd Year of the Atomic Age is not a new race towards armament.

What the world requires in its 22nd Year of the Atomic Age is a new race towards reasonableness. . . .

Deterrence: Short-term interests versus world survival

Report of the U.N. Secretary-General

In this brief report the dangers of deterrence by means of nuclear arsenals are presented both in terms of the risk of failure to deter and of the potential danger of a nuclear exchange to all the world, including the attackers.

United Nations General Assembly, A/6858/Corr. 1, November 1, 1967. This is an excerpt taken from the report of a group of consulting experts.

Nuclear weapons constitute one of the dominant facts of modern world politics. They are at present deployed in thousands by the nuclear weapon Powers, with warheads ranging from kilotons to megatons. We have already witnessed the experimental explosion of a fifty to sixty-megaton bomb, i.e., of a weapon with about 3,000 times the power of the bomb used in 1945 against Japan. Hundred-megaton devices, weapons about 5,000 times the size of those used in 1945, are no more difficult to devise. They could be exploded just outside the atmosphere of any country, in order utterly to destroy hundreds, even thousands, of square kilometres by means of blast and spreading fire. It has been suggested on good authority that in certain geographical circumstances multi-megaton weapons could also be exploded in ships near coastlines in order to create enormous tidal waves which would engulf the coastal belt.

The effects of all-out nuclear war, regardless of where it started, could not be confined to the Powers engaged in that war. They themselves would have to suffer the immediate kind of destruction and the immediate and more enduring lethal fall-out, whose effects have already been described. But neighbouring countries, and even countries in parts of the world remote from the actual conflict, could soon become exposed to the hazards of radio-active fall-out precipitated at great distances from the explosion, after moving through the atmosphere as a vast cloud. Thus, at least within the same hemisphere, an enduring radio-active hazard could exist for distant as well as close human populations, through the ingestion of foods derived from contaminated vegetation, and the external irradiation due to fall-out particles deposited on the ground. The extent and nature of the hazard would depend upon the numbers and type of bombs exploded. Given a sufficient number, no part of the world would escape exposure to biologically significant levels of radiation. To a greater or lesser degree, a legacy of genetic damage could be incurred by the world's population.

It is to be expected that no major nuclear Power could attack another without provoking a nuclear counter-attack. It is even possible that an aggressor could suffer more in retaliation than the nuclear Power it first attacked. In this lies the concept of deterrence by the threat of nuclear destruction. Far from an all-out nuclear exchange being a rational action which could ever be justified by any set of conceivable political gains, it may be that no country would, in the pursuit of its political objectives, deliberately risk the total destruction of its own capital city, leave alone the destruction of all its major centres of population; or risk the resultant chaos which would leave in doubt a government's ability to remain in control of its people. But the fact that a state of mutual nuclear deterrence prevails between the Super Powers does not, as we know all too well, prevent the outbreak of wars with conventional weapons involving both nuclear and non-nuclear weapon nations; the risk of nuclear war remains as long as there are nuclear weapons.

The basic facts about the nuclear bomb and its use are harsh and terrifying for civilization; they have become lost in a mass of theoretical verbiage. It has been claimed that the world has learnt to live with the bomb; it is also said there is no need for it to drift unnecessarily into the position that it is prepared to die for it. The ultimate question for the world to decide in our nuclear age—and this applies both to nuclear and non-nuclear Powers—is what short-term interests it is prepared to sacrifice in exchange for an assurance of survival and security.

The fallacy of the "nuclear stalemate"

General J. P. McConnell

What is the acceptable limit of loss in a nuclear exchange? Calling this the "nuclear threshold," General McConnell suggests that such a limit is dynamic, variable, and unpredictable—dependent upon the particular nation. Therefore, the United States' most demanding challenge is to keep a safe margin of strategic superiority to challenge even the highest nuclear threshold.

Vital Speeches of the Day, *May 15, 1966. Address at the Air Force Association Luncheon, Carswell Air Force Base, Texas, March 24, 1966. General McConnell is Chief of Staff, U.S. Air Force.*

. . . I want to . . . discuss with you briefly some of the lessons we have learned during the past twenty years and what these lessons mean in terms of our future security. In particular, I want to talk about the lessons entailed in the evolution of modern airpower from its post-World War II role as a tool of massive retaliation to its present far-ranging role in Southeast Asia.

Let us go back, for a moment, to . . . 1946. . . . The United States had emerged from World War II as the most powerful nation in the world, politically and economically as well as militarily. The newly established Strategic Air Command, Tactical Air Command and Air Defense Command gave us such overwhelming aerial superiority that no nation or even combination of nations would have dared to challenge it. Most of all, we were the only country that had atomic bombs, and we had strategic bombers that could carry them to any spot on earth.

We did not exploit this unique position to impose our rule and will on anyone. We used our strategic supremacy merely as a military safeguard for what we hoped would be lasting peace and security from armed aggression throughout the world. How different would have been conditions then, and how different would conditions be today if the atomic monopoly had been in the hands of a Hitler or a Stalin!

And here is the first lesson. Military superiority is no longer possible without superior airpower, and superiority in the air cannot be achieved or maintained without superiority in technology. If a nation's technological superiority is large and broad enough, it is in a far better position to pursue its objectives, be those objectives universal peace and prosperity—or global aggression and dictatorship.

As we have learned this lesson, so have the Soviets. You will remember that, twenty years ago, our atomic monopoly made us feel secure for a long time to come. While the aggressive ideology of the communists created much unrest and disturbances, Soviet Russia seemed unlikely to pose a military threat to us throughout the foreseeable future. It had not only suffered some 20 million dead and the loss of a crippling percentage of its economy, but it was also very much backward in its technological development.

But the Soviets had learned from our example. Bent on achieving their avowed goal of global domination, they embarked on an all-out scientific and industrial effort designed to catch up with and, eventually, surpass us in the field of military technology. Having greatly underestimated their single-minded determination and inherent capabilities, we were shocked out of our complacency when, as early as in 1949, the Soviets managed to explode their first atomic device. That explosion was far more than a technological accomplishment of the first order. It also signaled the end of our atomic monopoly and the beginning of a mounting threat such as our country had never faced before.

And this is lesson number two. No matter how great our technological lead may be at the moment and how decisive a military advantage it may entail, we must accept the fact that we will enjoy that particular advantage for a limited time only. Nor must we ever again underestimate the determination and capability of any other nation to develop into a technological and military threat to us, regardless of how poor or backward or troubled that nation may appear at the time. . . .

The next lesson we learned during the past twenty years is a direct consequence of the previous two and, from the standpoint of our future security, perhaps the most significant and least understood. That lesson is that there is no such thing as a permanent "nuclear stalemate."

There is no need for me to recount the events that led to this so-called stalemate—the rapid build-up of the Soviets' nuclear capability during the 1950's and the steps we had to take, for our protection, in strengthening our own strategic posture. The point is that, now, both nations possess enough nuclear weapons as well as long-range delivery vehicles to make a nuclear war between them extremely costly for either side.

This does not mean, however, that there is now a permanent nuclear stalemate because this term implies that we have reached a stable condition of power balance which will remain stable for as long as everybody is mutually deterred. And therein lies the fallacy of this concept. What will deter *us* from risking nuclear war will not necessarily deter the Soviets or the Red Chinese—once they have achieved an operational nuclear capability—or any other potential aggressor nation that may join the nuclear club at some future date.

The Soviets and, eventually, the Red Chinese would base any decision to engage in nuclear war on their estimate of potential gain versus expected loss. The gain would be the elimination of the United States as the principal obstacle to the achievement of their expansionist goals, and they might be willing to gain this objective even at the price of a nuclear war, provided three conditions are met. First, all other means must have failed; second, they would feel certain of winning; third, their expected losses would be within acceptable limits.

It follows that each country has its own "nuclear threshold," that is, the point or level of restraint above which it may no longer be deterred from nuclear war. This threshold is by no means static but dynamic as it is determined by a number of factors which are both variable and unpredictable. . . .

Putting it differently, as long as a potential aggressor is persuaded that he cannot achieve his objective and, in trying to achieve it, would be destroyed regardless of the quality of his active and passive defenses, then his nuclear threshold is high enough to discourage him from initiating or even risking nuclear war. Our most demanding challenge, therefore, is to keep the nuclear threshold of any and all potential aggressors above that level, and that is why it is so vital to our future security to maintain a safe margin of strategic superiority.

Our Air Force has provided all or most of such a margin throughout the past twenty years. While that margin has been shrinking, it is still large enough to represent a compelling deterrent to nuclear aggression. However, recent history has made clear that the communists remain prepared to instigate or support conflicts at the lower levels, ranging from local crises to limited wars, such as the one that is presently being fought in Vietnam. At the same time, our strategic superiority not only serves to deter the Soviets from precipitating nuclear war but also permits our national leaders to take whatever action they deem necessary in resolving local conflicts without undue risk of sparking such a war.

It is not always realized that, in addition to its direct participation in the Vietnamese war, the Air Force also performs an indirect but all-important role, and that is to provide the nuclear back-up without which we could not have afforded to engage in a conventional conflict of that scope. Still representing some 80 percent of the Free World's entire nuclear capability, the strategic strike forces of the Air Force, now complemented by the Navy's Polaris submarines, assure us of a strategic superiority which neither the Soviets nor the Red Chinese are likely to challenge.

Our strategic airpower has had to serve the dual purpose of deterring nuclear aggression and insuring freedom of action in local conflicts for most of the past twenty years. As the record shows, it has served these purposes well. This would not have been possible, however, had it not been for the continuous strengthening and modernization of our strategic strike forces so as to keep up with the growing nuclear threat posed by the Soviets. . . .

As President Johnson has emphasized time and again, our political objective is not the destruction and unconditional surrender of North Vietnam but a negotiated settlement of the conflict which will assure the freedom and security of our South Vietnamese allies. In supporting that objective, certain military objectives have been assigned to all the armed forces on our team. You can be assured that these objectives have been and are being met fully and to the very limits established by the civilian authorities. . . .

I have no doubt that, eventually, we *will* achieve our political objectives and thus fulfill our promise to the people of South Vietnam. Nor do I have any doubt that the lessons of that war will help us to further improve our capability to counter any future acts of local aggression, wherever and under whatever conditions they may occur.

Perhaps the most important lesson in that respect is the emergence and recognition of airpower as a primary factor in local conflicts. Moreover, I hope that we will not only heed these lessons ourselves but also teach any potential aggressors a lesson to remember. And therein lies one of the most significant aspects of the Vietnamese war.

We must never forget that what happened in Vietnam is not merely an isolated incident; it is part and parcel of the communist scheme of either wearing us down through an unending series of local aggression or of destroying us through a nuclear war should we ever forfeit our strategic superiority.

Thus the lessons of the past twenty years have taught us that we must not be misled by the fallacy of the nuclear stalemate into the complacent and fatal belief that we have won the battle for strategic superiority. We could lose that battle and, with it, the battle for national survival should the Soviets ever succeed in confronting us with a technological surprise—in missile defense, in space weapons or in some still unimaginable area of strategic warfare.

Nor must we be satisfied just with keeping the nuclear thresholds of any potential aggressors above safe levels. Our aim should be to raise and keep up their thresholds for any kind of aggression through a posture of all-inclusive deterrence. I am confident that we can do so by demonstrating convincingly both our capability and determination to make aggression at any level both too costly and too unprofitable to warrant its risk. . . .

Military power: The limits of persuasion

James M. Gavin

This former top-level military strategic planner takes issue with the thesis that the answer to military threat is more military power; instead, he argues that economic and technological power will ultimately be more persuasive and therefore more powerful in achieving policy goals. The battles for Korea and Taiwan are being won by economic assistance behind a military shield. The world, Gavin argues, abhors military escalation, but the Communists fear economic, social, and technical assistance escalation even more, for these stabilize rather than disrupt.

Saturday Review, *July 30, 1966. © 1966. Reprinted by permission. Lt. General Gavin was a World War II paratroop commander and a senior Army planner until his retirement from the military in 1958. He has served as U.S. Ambassador to France and is now chairman of the board of Arthur D. Little, Inc., in Cambridge, Massachusetts. He is author of several books and articles dealing with the problems of war.*

Since the beginning of time power has been used to persuade. Yet, paradoxically, at a time when we possess more power than any nation on earth, we are not very persuasive. . . . Perhaps it would be well to examine the nature of our power and, more important, its changing character since World War II.

Usually we think of power in terms of military power—military weapons systems—and most of us have long considered these to be the primary source of power in world affairs. Of course, to exist, military power must have a base of economic support. In all past experience only a society that had the natural resources and, in addition, the inventiveness and industries to produce modern weapons systems, could bring them to combat and thus gain a decision in international conflict. Hence, from history we are inclined to think of military power as the dominant force, and the economic power which supports it as a *secondary* source of military strength. . . .

I believe that there is a fundamental change taking place, and indeed it has taken place, in this relationship between military and economic power. Fundamentally, today technology can, if wisely directed, provide adequate resources for humans to live comfortably on this earth. At the same time, technology can, if so exploited, provide the weapons systems to destroy a major portion of the human race. Finally, technology is having, and will continue to have, such a tremendous impact on world affairs that it is changing the balance between economics and military power significantly. It is this change that I would like to examine.

First, let me call attention to the talk given by our Secretary of Defense in Montreal on May 18, [1966]. He referred to the sources of unrest and discontent around the world, and emphasized that security is not military hardware; security means economic development. In fact, he stated flatly that, in his opinion, the concept that military hardware is the exclusive or even the primary ingredient of permanent peace in the mid-twentieth century is absurd.

During the past twenty years I have been closely associated with the use of military power, the planning and execution of national military policy, and, to a lesser extent, the conduct of foreign policy. To say that it has been an extremely active environment is an understatement, for we never have had such amounts of power available nor have we had so many problems associated with its use. And never has there been such widespread interest in our many commitments and involvements abroad, nor so much social turbulence at home.

Having been in the vortex of much of the discussion, I find it deeply disturbing that we have *yet* to get to the heart of the matter. To do so we must understand, and articulate, in much clearer terms than we have so far, our total *diplomatic* and *political* power, for this is the power that persuades: the economic, technological, and military components of such power. Part of this examination will be a consideration of the role that each of these will play in our national strategy.

Actually, we have been doing very well in the realm of economics and technology, especially during the past decade. It is in the area of applied military power, tactical military power, that most of the misunderstandings and frustrations seem to exist. In order to understand their cause, therefore, I believe that we should begin with an examination of the meaning of the most significant military event of our time—the detonation of the first nuclear weapon. . . .

Few realized in 1945 that the bomb was the beginning of the end, if not indeed the very end, of man's search for energy to be used as military force. The more prevalent view was that a new era was born—the age of atomic force. Now, twenty years later, we understand better the place of the bomb in the spectrum of history. It was the end, not the beginning of an era. It was the end of man's search for force and it marked a beginning of a new quest—the search to find new ways and means of influencing the behavior of other humans. It was to be the age when the earth would shrink rapidly due to high speed air travel, space exploration, satellite communications, and rapid data processing systems, for example. More and more the nations of the earth were to consider themselves part of one large world community; the logical end of an evolutionary process that began many thousands of years ago with the family, tribal, and city-state, and later, national groupings.

Furthermore, in the armed forces the physical effects of the bomb alone made plain for all to see that all the boundaries between the traditional arenas of combat, land, sea, and air, were wiped out. The earth was soon to become one theater of operations, shrunken to such small size that no area was immune from attack from any other point on the globe. And when, in the traditional manner, our military recalled its own experience for answers to deal with the new problems of the day, it did not find them. For the answers were not to be found in a remembrance of things past, they could be found only in a thoughtful analysis of the future, in a profound search for the meaning of the period that we were about to enter. The classical military formula of escalating power until total victory would be achieved was to become absolutely meaningless. For wars, if there were to be wars, and the means that would resolve them, were going to be many orders of magnitude different from what they had been in the past.

In 1950, five years after the end of World War II and Hiroshima, Soviet-equipped North Koreans invaded South Korea. It was a costly experience for us. Possessing the most powerful military establishment in the world, well-equipped with nuclear weapons, we suffered more than 140,000 casualties and had to accept terms less than victory. Yet, despite the Korean experience our national strategic policy in the mid-Fifties was still based on massive retaliation. Admittedly there was much argument and discussion about the validity of this view. Indeed, our Promethean achievement seemed to have left us in intellectual disarray.

But from the mid-Fifties on, our total power seemed to paralyze our intellectual processes, and our response to challenges of lesser magnitude than total war were of a diminishing degree of credibility. This was because a number of myths prevailed in our thinking, and they stemmed from a tendency to look inward to our experience rather than to postulate technology and political trends into the rather clouded and hazardous unknown of the future.

The first myth is that war is a continuation of politics by other means. This Clausewitzian orthodoxy holds that wars will be fought and won, and sufficient power will be applied until they are won. Then war will be followed by peace, a period in which politics as usual will be the preoccupation of the world powers. This, in turn, very likely will be followed by a period of war, and the difference between the two will be quite discernible. I believe that by now most of us realize that this no longer is true.

In his recent Montreal speech, our Secretary of Defense discussed conflicts of recent years and pointed out that in the past eight years "there have been no less than 164 internationally significant outbreaks of violence, each of them specifically designed as a serious challenge to the authority, or the very existence, of the government in question. . . . And not a single one of the 164 conflicts has been a formally declared war." From this experience, realistically, we must conclude that wars will not always be declared and that nations will not always commit their total resources to win in every confrontation. There will be wars that are not wars, if defined in terms of our experience before Hiroshima. In fact, for some nations it may be wiser to keep a shooting war limited and undeclared while pursuing national goals by other means, never admitting the existence of a war nor indeed a desire to bring it to an end.

The second myth is that if you destroy enough people and enough property you will overcome an enemy's will to resist. A corollary to this is that a nation should use as much force as necessary to win, since in war there is no substitute for victory. Actually, the nature of conflict being what it is, and the danger of a nuclear holocaust being ever present, it is compelling that solutions less than total war be found. The indiscriminate use of power has been further complicated by modern communications media that now bring more and more detailed information about the conduct of war into every home. The inevitable, and needless, loss of civilian lives has become the subject of concern to more than just the contending military forces. Thus, sensitivity to public opinion has made it necessary to consider restricting attacks to military targets whenever this is possible. Unless, of course, the nation's goal is to seek total war.

A third aspect of existing military thinking deserves mention. The thought still persists in many minds that the ultimate in sophistication and usefulness in weapons systems is the high-yield megaton bomb delivered by missile or aircraft. By its very nature it is believed that it should be able to cope with almost any threat to our survival. The fact is that it is the very effectiveness of our strategic air force, and the overwhelming, devastating potential of H-weapons, that prevents their employment in a conflict other than total war. And again, it is the devastation that would be caused by the use of these weapons by the strategic air arm that has given tremendous emphasis to the role of the other Services; those that have it in their ability to apply power with discrimination, flexibility, and restraint. It is this possibility of devastation that gives great emphasis to the need to find and understand the uses of other forms of power stemming from our science and technological programs and our great economic strength.

The changing nature of conflict today makes it imperative that we develop better means of dealing with limited wars, guerrilla wars, and other types of conflicts that we cannot yet anticipate with accuracy, but which will not be total war. Studies in these areas will require great effort not only in anticipation and planning, but in research and development as well.

Until World War II, we were protected by a shield of time and space. And while we were enjoying that protection, Hitler's forces ravaged Europe and, more important, his scientists developed the first surface-to-surface rockets, surface-to-air rockets, air-to-air rockets, the snorkel submarine, the first jet plane and the first rocket plane, nerve gas, etc. And he came close to developing the atomic bomb. After we entered the war, and finally overran his concentration camps, we found the gas ovens being enlarged—and he had already destroyed more than 6,000,000 human beings. Today we no longer enjoy the advantage of time and space. Our armed forces must be ready for every challenge that confronts our nation regardless of how sophisticated the weapon or the technology from which it springs. This will require a continuing expenditure of our national resources if we are to achieve an adequate state of readiness for every reasonable challenge. And this, in turn, necessitates a dynamic, imaginative, productive economy.

How good is our economy?

Most people will remember that after World War II the Soviets anticipated an economic collapse of the West, believing that our economy was entirely a war-based one. What we have accomplished has been truly remarkable, and during the past twenty years our economy at home has expanded at a tremendous rate. It is vital that we sustain this growth. . . .

One of the most remarkable and far-sighted programs ever undertaken by any country was the inauguration of our foreign assistance program in 1949. Through it, we were able to provide economic assistance, wherever it could be properly used, to the newly emerging nations as well as to many of the older powers. In 1949, this program amounted to a little over $4.5 billion and was 1.75 per cent of our Gross National Product. It has been overwhelmingly successful, and today South Korea, Taiwan, and Indonesia, for example, all are monuments to the achievements of this program. In addition, a country geographically almost a part of the Eastern bloc, Yugoslavia, was able to achieve economic prosperity and retain its political independence from Moscow.

Our foreign aid program has been overwhelmingly successful in areas where the Communists can least afford to have us succeed. In areas where they would like to accuse us of colonialism and, indeed, do accuse us of economic colonialism today, we have been able in many countries to help achieve an unprecedented standard of living, far superior to anything that the Communists could offer. . . .

Another area in which Americans have achieved great success has been in the exportation of products and business know-how. . . .

Maintenance of our position in the world community is based not only on those programs that we export abroad, but also on the kind of a society we have at home. World opinion will be formed by not only the prosperity and higher standard of living that we can help other nations achieve, but also by what the world knows that we are able to do in our own society. Through our ability to manage our own internal affairs, we export an image of America and of our way of life. And in this area there is much to be done.

We have made progress in dealing with some of the problems of the aged and of the very young, but, in my opinion, we have not yet begun to deal adequately with the problems of the teen-agers and the near teen-agers. We must completely revitalize our educational system by bringing together the vast industrial, scientific, and technological resources of this country with our educators, to the end that we can significantly improve the education and technical training of our young. In addition, we must provide opportunities for those out of school for some time to return to educational centers to update their knowledge and to learn new skills.

Equally as important as directing the intellectual energies of our young people into useful channels is the problem of helping them to develop their physical talents. . . .

Now, what does this discussion on the relationship between military power and economic programs mean when applied to problems of today? What, for example, does it mean in terms of Vietnam?

I think that we would all agree that we should not be in the predicament that we are in in Vietnam, but the fact is that we are there. The problem now is to handle our resources—men, weapons, aircraft, etc.—in such a manner as to neither impair our strategic efforts in other areas nor our tactical prospects in future conflicts. . . .

Obviously, we have reached the point where further escalation could seriously impair our strategic commitments—our exportation of capital and management skills, our foreign aid programs, and our science and technology programs—and our social programs at home. Perhaps we have passed this point. Furthermore, we should anticipate and be ready for a very serious struggle for Thailand and the Kra Peninsula. And if our involvement plunges us deeper into war in Southeast Asia, we should be prepared for a reopening of the Korean front. It is important, therefore, that we accelerate the measures to bring the Vietnam situation under control. Certainly, we should not willingly allow it to escalate. . . .

In the past two decades, the world has changed from a community of many independent nations, frequently remote from one another, to one small world community. It will look with great apprehension on any indiscriminate use of military power. In the meantime, from an unprecedented abundance of scientific and technological knowledge, man has acquired the potential for tremendous good and tremendous harm. This new knowledge must be channeled into the areas where the greatest good for the most can be realized; to help our Great Society at home and to help the emerging nations abroad. The most influential force in world affairs today is the economy of the United States. It should be sustained and enriched as a matter of sound strategic policy.

Tactical engagements that do occur should not be permitted to grow as uncontrollably as a malignant cancer. Fighting will certainly occur, from time to time, at any point along the abrasive interface between the Communist nations and the Free World. Our power must be used to persuade those who seek to improve their position through aggressive attacks upon their neighbors that they will be deterred and cannot possibly succeed. Concurrently, we should make clear our intention and ability to maintain a dominant position in global affairs. Our global power must be exercised with restraint and wisdom. At a time of Great Britain's greatness, Disraeli said, "All power is a trust—and we are accountable for its exercise." Now, we too are accountable, not only to the American people but to people of the world community of nations.

Section 3

The dilemmas of arms control and disarmament

The war on weapons: An insider's view

Arthur H. Dean

What is the relationship between arms control and national security? It must be a close relationship because these disarmament talks, as explained by insider Arthur H. Dean, have been among the most tenacious ever. Here he clarifies the harsh realities of disarmament and the basic fact that the "first-priority goal of any government . . . [is] the protection of the national security." Despite the frustrations of an imprecise and dangerous Soviet draft treaty, he favors continuation of the talks.

Saturday Review, *March 19, 1966. Based on chapter "Points of Emphasis" in* Test Ban and Disarmament: The Path of Negotiation. *© 1966 by Council on Foreign Relations. Reprinted by permission of Harper & Row, Publishers. The author is former chairman of the U.S. delegations to the nuclear test ban negotiations and the Eighteen-Nation Disarmament Conference in Geneva.*

Since 1946 the U.S. Government has expended more man-hours and more effort on questions of disarmament and arms control than on any other one subject of international negotiation in a comparable period of time. How much progress have we made? To take the briefest tally of a complicated subject, there has been no approach to agreement with the Soviet Union on the issues of general and complete disarmament, or even on limited measures for arms control, such as safeguards against surprise attack. On the other hand, we were able in 1963 to reach agreement on three limited matters which, though not technically disarmament measures, could help to set the scene for further agreements that might ultimately lead to disarmament: the so-called hot line, the partial test ban, and the resolution against placing nuclear weapons in outer space. And 1964 was the year of the mutual example, involving such steps as cutting back the production of fissionable material. Of limited inherent and indeed even practical value, nevertheless they held some promise for the future, for the immediate possibilities lie with limited measures. No matter how necessary or how sincerely desired and worked for, general and complete disarmament is a far-off will-o'-the-wisp.

This candid statement of a frustrating truth might need no elaboration were it not for the difficulty many well-intentioned people seem to have in accepting it. For understandable and irreproachable reasons people and nations yearn to avoid war, especially war among the big powers. Being human, they all too often eagerly embrace a slogan or a single concept as a kind of magical prescription and are bitterly disillusioned when, for want of having been thought through, the prescription doesn't work.

How much simpler it would be if there were more general awareness and understanding of four basic realities about disarmament: (1) the essential foundation for negotiation on arms control and disarmament is respectable military strength on both sides; (2) disarmament is as much a function of national security as is armament; (3) limited measures may open the way to general disarmament, while being of value in themselves; (4) there is no reason to assume that disarmament in and of itself will bring with it the disappearance of conflict any more than did the defeat of the Axis powers.

Take the matter of military strength. Like the arms race itself, the impulsion to negotiate for the control or abolition of arms by consent is rooted in a mutual respect among adversaries for each other's military strength. There would be no talks at Geneva at all were it not for the fact that both the United States (with Canada and its European allies) and the Soviet Union (and its allies) consider it a worthwhile goal of foreign policy to seek to reduce the military threat posed by the other.

Two conclusions follow. First, unilateral measures of disarmament or multilateral measures that inequitably bear on only one side and thus undermine the condition of mutual respect to the detriment of that side will most likely lead not to acceptable disarmament but to the political defeat of the weakened side and probably also to greater dangers to peace. The breakup of disarmament talks, for which there would no longer be a *raison d'être*, would follow. Thus the most ardent and the most emotional supporters of disarmament, the impatient ones who argue for unreciprocated unilateral or unbalanced measures, on the grounds that they will help to create the necessary confidence and inspire the other side to reply in kind, are in reality the worst enemies of any realistic disarmament. Unreciprocated measures would ultimately destroy the basis on which the negotiation of stable agreements rests.

The second conclusion stems from the first. If the basis of disarmament talks has been correctly stated, then it follows that disarmament can only proceed on the principle of balance, whereby the stock of existing arms and those from future production are reciprocally reduced without altering in any drastic way the existing relationship between the states concerned. If, on the other hand, a disarmament proposal would, in its practical effect, result in a considerable weakening of one side as against the other, then such a proposal may be considered an element of political warfare rather than a serious disarmament effort.

No matter what the propagandists say, disarmament is not the first-priority goal of any government in the world today. This priority everywhere goes to the protection of the national security. In the case of the United States, a major aspect of that security is the maintenance of an international environment in which we and our friends can live in peace and freedom. This is the simple reality of our times. There is no point in wasting time fulminating against it. The real, the significant question in disarmament is not which should come first, defense or disarmament, but how to utilize both in their manifold interrelationships to attain security and peace.

It is a lesson of our experience thus far that a great deal of time has been wasted on the sterile issue of which should come first, a treaty on general disarmament or limited measures of disarmament and arms control. It should be apparent that whichever is practically feasible should come first. Which this is can only be discovered by face-to-face exploration of specific proposals. It stands to reason that simpler measures that involve less adjustment, fewer concessions, and a minimum of domestic problems in the states concerned will usually be more readily acceptable and comparatively easier to work out. Therefore limited measures of disarmament and arms control should receive the greater immediate emphasis. In spite of appearances, this is what has happened at Geneva, especially after the agreements of 1963. Thus, although Soviet representatives still inveigh against "arms control without disarmament" and proclaim a strong preference for "general and complete disarmament first," in actual fact they have been discussing and proposing limited measures for quite some time. It is on such measures that we should in the immediate future be putting our strongest effort, always bearing in mind that the limited steps may be building blocks for an eventually far more comprehensive structure.

Finally, as was said earlier, it is not logical to expect a major reduction of arms or even total disarmament alone to bring with it an absence of conflict. Although there is much misunderstanding and wishful thinking on this point, it is clear that one cannot expect the unavailability of certain weapons to change the nature of man. Just as Cain slew Abel, as long as there is greed and ambition, so long will men and nations be tempted to take what is not theirs. As long as there is injustice, whether fancied or real, so long will men be tempted to take by force what they feel rightly belongs to them. In such a situation the absence of arms will merely amount to the removal of *one* means of influencing the conduct of other states. Some states will still remain bigger than others, wealthier, with better natural resources, industrially more developed, and with a larger or better-trained population, a larger internal police force, more sophisticated nuclear know-how, and a more advantageous geographic location. Though the list could be continued, it should be sufficient to show that vast opportunities for political blackmail and coercion will continue to exist. In other words, in the absence of arms, equations of political force will be drawn in different terms but they will still be drawn. It follows that it will be essential to provide both a disarming and a disarmed world with international peace-keeping forces that are appropriately financed and staffed and, above all, effective. Just how this can be done has not yet been answered; the problem of enforcement, as we saw in the Congo and elsewhere, raises issues on which we can now see no way to agreement. But it must be done if significant disarmament is to be anything more than a dream.

The quest for disarmament should be relentlessly pursued. Nevertheless, it is impossible to escape the conclusion that it is vain to expect rapid progress toward general and complete disarmament. The conclusion flows from the nature of the subject itself and from the basic differences in the goals which the United States, the Soviet Union, and Communist China (not to mention France and other states with strikingly independent policies) seek to achieve.

Disarmament is a supremely complicated subject. Among the difficulties in arriving at an equitable formula for reducing armed strength is the problem of balancing the various elements of a particular nation's power against those of another. The United States, for example, is primarily a sea and air power; the Soviet Union is a land-oriented continental power with growing naval and fishing fleets. What is the balance between one nation's tanks against another's aircraft carriers and nuclear-powered submarines, or between intermediate range missiles on one side and intercontinental ballistic missiles on the other? Even if there were no cold wars in Europe but a condition of "peaceful engagement" and the negotiating nations were on friendly terms, there would still be the problem of balancing out the differences among them. These would involve, in addition to arms themselves, the impact of the domestic political system on the successful implementation of disarmament agreements, geographic location, strategic doctrine and problems, industrial production and potential educational levels and the availability of highly trained personnel, reliance on foreign trade and raw materials, and a host of other factors. It is almost impossible to compare these elements in a meaningful way, but the relative positions on any such levels would affect the impact of a particular disarmament agreement on each of the nations involved.

In addition, we have only begun to take the measure of problems which are new to our times, at least in their urgent form. There are, for example, the particularly perplexing problems involved in deciding on the powers to be given the peace-keeping institutions that will be necessary in a disarming and disarmed world. In the exchanges at Geneva on the nature of the international force required to keep the peace, the Soviet representatives have argued for internal police forces equipped with small non-nuclear arms of various types, which would be called into international service by the Security Council if necessary. The American position has been that a standing international force should be created and that it might have to be equipped with nuclear weapons against the contingency that some still illegally retain such weapons and break the peace after the supposed completion of total disarmament. The matter is far from settled and indeed raises the most far-reaching questions.

If, as the U.S. draft outline of 1962 put it, the international force is to be strong enough "effectively to deter or suppress any threat or use of arms" then it must itself be more powerful than any combination that might be raised against it. If it is to be that powerful, how is it to be kept from becoming the most powerful organization in the world? Who is to control it? The Security Council, with the veto power intact? The General Assembly, with its 117 or more disparate members? The Secretary-General, without reference to the country from which he comes, the United Nations body to which he responds, or whoever pays the costs?

Or is the proposal for an effective international peace-keeping force, logically speaking, another way of urging world government? If this is so, and if the conditions for such world government do not exist, is it possible to have general and complete disarmament? Or must we be content for the time being with some halfway measures of limited disarmament and with limited peace-keeping forces, whose primary functions would be to keep the great powers out of conflicts in which their vital interests are not involved? It cannot be said that the United States or any other nation sees its way clearly in this problem. Nor have we even begun to probe deeply into a number of others, both general and technical, such as the difficulties of verifying the limitation or elimination of bacteriological and chemical warfare.

These differences and difficulties are very important. But they might conceivably be amenable to resolution if there were sufficient political consensus between the United States and the Soviet Union. The record of disagreement is, however, a reflection of basic differences on world goals. As President Kennedy expressed it after his chilling meeting with Premier Khrushchev in Vienna in 1961, "We have wholly different concepts of where the world is and where it is going."

The disarmament discussions became primarily explorations of these differences and of what common ground might exist in spite of them. Let us consider briefly some of the points that came to the fore in those talks, concentrating on the ways in which the two sides looked at the "how" of disarmament.

On the matter of sovereignty the Soviet draft treaty, not surprisingly, places its emphasis on a strictly defined, highly traditional, inviolable concept of state sovereignty. Accordingly, it does not provide for any central peace-keeping authority but calls instead for the use of internal police forces under Article 43 of the U.N. Charter and under the control of the Security Council. It further seeks to insure national control by providing that command of the national units to be provided under Article 43 should be made up on the "troika" formula, of "representatives of three principal groups of states existing in the world [capitalist, Communist, and nonaligned] on the basis of equal representation."

Unhampered by the great weight of suspicion and secrecy which the Soviet Union carries, the United States and Great Britain have tried to go beyond such a confining and unsatisfactory approach to deal with the real problem of how to organize the peace. They have tried to work out concrete measures toward the development of new institutions that would be adequate to the tasks that would confront them in a disarming and eventually disarmed world. Their efforts are still exploratory, but at least they do represent honest attempts to push aside obstacles that stand in the way of effective solutions.

The Soviet draft shows an impatient drive for measures that would immediately put the West at a military disadvantage, while the U.S. draft outline concentrates on a slower process of proportionate reduction of arms, coupled with the careful development of adequate institutions for the settlement of disputes and for peaceful change. The Soviet draft treaty, with slight modifications by Foreign Minister Gromyko in 1962 and 1963 and by Ambassador Tsarapkin in Geneva in February of 1964, provides for the immediate destruction of practically all nuclear weapon delivery vehicles (though not of the nuclear warheads themselves) in Stage 1 of disarmament and the immediate abandonment of all military bases, troop deployment, and missile sites maintained by one country on the territory of another country. It provides also for the prohibition of all joint maneuvers and for the establishment of denuclearized zones (including the territory of West Germany but not part of the Soviet Union). All these measures would have the effect of breaking down the military effectiveness of NATO while leaving Soviet defenses intact on its own vast geographical territory.

Furthermore, the Soviet government insisted, and continues to insist, that its proposals be accepted "in principle" before its representatives will consent to the discussion of what they call "details," such things as timing, inspection, verification, and how many and what kinds of weapons would be involved. In contemplating these aims, it is indeed hard to escape the conclusion that the

Soviet Union has, as my predecessor in Geneva, Ambassador James J. Wadsworth, put it, used arms control negotiations as "part of a grand strategy aimed at the eventual total defeat of the other side."

The Western nations, while mindful of the need to approach the problems in terms of their own security and world outlook, have nevertheless tried to devise proposals which are also responsive to legitimate Soviet concern for security. In spite of differences in detail, the United States and Great Britain have been in general agreement about how the goal of disarmament might be accomplished: through a balanced reduction of arms, to be carried out in fixed proportions during three stages, with verification at each stage. As I put it before the Eighteen-Nation Disarmament Conference on April 18, 1962, since the tolerable balance of forces existed in the world at that moment, "the nations of the world should seize a moment in time to stop the arms race, to freeze the military situation as it then appears and to shrink it progressively to zero, always keeping the relative military position of the parties to the treaty as near as possible to what it was at the beginning."

This balanced disarmament was to be accompanied by (1) a system of international inspection adequate to report any violations, including those that related to excessive levels of armaments retained illegally in contravention of the quantities authorized for that phase of the disarmament process; and (2) the simultaneous and pioneering development of stronger international institutions for keeping the peace and for insuring that all change would be peaceful, to the point, as Secretary of State Herter had said in 1960, "where aggression will be deterred by international rather than national force."

The keynotes of the Western draft are gradual and peaceful change, maintenance of the existing balance, open reassurance, and international peace-keeping. The keynotes of the Soviet draft are disruption of the existing balance, secrecy, reliance on verification largely under national management, and the big-power veto in the Security Council.

The Soviet draft treaty was and remains unacceptable to the United States and to Great Britain. As we put it at the time, it was not a true plan for disarmament but rather a plan to disarm the free world. It would virtually have forced the United States to give up at the start those arms on which it had placed a heavy reliance for the defense of itself and its allies, and in which, as a sea and air power, it had marked superiority. The plan would have forced the withdrawal of the United States from a number of overseas bases and gravely weakened its alliances. The result would have been to give a major advantage to the Soviet Union.

These Soviet proposals have not been significantly amended. For a while there seemed to be a glimmer of hope that some compromise suggestion on the immediate destruction of delivery vehicles might be in the making, when Foreign Minister Andrei Gromyko proposed at the General Assembly in September 1962 that in the process of destroying vehicles for the delivery of nuclear weapons during the first stage "exception be made for a strictly limited and agreed number of global intercontinental missiles, anti-missile missiles and anti-aircraft missiles of the ground-to-air type," which each nuclear power could keep, exclusively on its own territory, until the end of the second stage.

A year later Mr. Gromyko told the same body that "limited contingents of intercontinental, anti-missile and anti-aircraft missiles should remain at the disposal of the Soviet Union and the United States in their own territories until the end of the third stage," that is, until the end of the disarmament process. In February 1964 Mr. Tsarapkin indicated that as part of the proposed "nuclear umbrella" the two powers should retain the following: (1) intercontinental ballistic missiles, (2) antimissile missiles, and (3) antiaircraft missiles in the "ground-to-air" category. All of these would be located on Soviet and United States territory only, and under "strict control" at the launching pads. No further explanation has been offered.

It is clear from this brief summary that the hopeful estimates of the significance of Gromyko's 1962 statement were misplaced. There has been no forward movement. We have made numerous efforts to find out just what the Soviet government had in mind, to bring the discussion down to concrete details, to find out how many delivery vehicles would be included in the proposed "nuclear umbrella," and to ascertain how the desired end might then be verified effectively. We have met with a blanket refusal to go beyond the either-or demand that we either accept the idea "in principle" or not discuss it at all. Since we obviously cannot accept such a onesided proposal "in principle," there has been no progress on this crucial topic.

It may be worthwhile at this point to take cognizance of the argument so often advanced by the Soviet Union that the U.S. draft outline does not, *in Stage 1,* provide guarantees against nuclear war, whereas the Soviet proposal for the elimination (or virtual elimination) of nuclear delivery vehicles does. The fact of the matter is that there is a broad "twilight zone" in which it is factually impossible to draw the distinction between vehicles that are "capable" of delivering nuclear weapons and those that are not. The Soviet draft allows for the production of rockets subjectively characterized as being for "peaceful purposes."

Thus, in order to achieve the Soviet claim of a guarantee against nuclear war in Stage 1, the Soviet draft would have to provide for the elimination of every vehicle that *could* carry a nuclear weapon. This definition would include a large number of conventional aircraft, submarines, and surface warships. But the Soviet draft, as amended, proposes only to reduce conventional military aircraft by 30 percent during the first stage and does not deal with other conventional aircraft at all. This brief statement, given by way of example only, serves as the merest indication of the imprecision of the dangers concealed in the Soviet draft treaty.

Perhaps it will be clear by this time why the discussions have been so tedious and unproductive. Nevertheless, we continue to talk, because it cannot be predicted when some measure of agreement might suddenly become possible, and also because something may be learned in the process of analysis and talking.

The treaty on nonproliferation of nuclear weapons

A. N. Kosygin

In this official statement, Premier Kosygin and the Soviet government present the party line on disarmament. Some of the points are aimed specifically at the United States (such as points 4, 6, and 7), but one wonders how the Soviet Union would react in the future to a crisis like the 1968 Czechoslovakian reforms if points 7 and 8 and the ultimate "complete and general disarmament" were already in effect. What would then serve as the power base for control of the satellites?

A speech by Premier Kosygin introducing the official USSR government memorandum issued on the occasion of signing the Treaty on Nonproliferation of Nuclear Weapons. The official text appeared in Pravda *and* Izvestia *on July 2, 1968. Reprinted from* The Current Digest of the Soviet Press, *Vol. 20, No. 27 (July 1968), pp. 3–4.*

Esteemed comrades and gentlemen! Permit me, on the instructions of the Soviet government, to express profound satisfaction over the fact that today marks the start of the signing of the Treaty on Nonproliferation of Nuclear Weapons, an important international document that has been approved by the overwhelming majority of U.N. members. Conclusion of the Treaty on Nonproliferation of Nuclear Weapons is a major success for the cause of peace. From the time nuclear weapons first appeared, the Soviet Union has firmly and consistently favored delivering mankind from the nuclear threat. This treaty is an important step toward this goal in that it bars further proliferation of nuclear weapons and thereby reduces the danger of an outbreak of nuclear war.

The participation of a great number of states in today's signing of the treaty is convincing evidence that states are capable of finding mutually acceptable solutions to complex international problems of vital importance for all mankind. The elaboration of the treaty required great efforts and prolonged negotiations, in which states with different social systems, nuclear and non-nuclear countries, big and small, developed and developing, all took part. The treaty reflects the numerous wishes and suggestions expressed by the states and takes into account various points of view on solving the nonproliferation problem; at the same time, all the states approving it were agreed on the main point—the necessity of barring further proliferation of nuclear weapons.

The decision the Security Council adopted several days ago on security assurances for the non-nuclear countries party to the treaty is an important supplement to the treaty. As was stated in the Security Council, the Soviet government intends to comply strictly with this decision.

Five years ago here in Moscow we signed the Treaty Banning Nuclear Weapons Tests in Three Environments. After that a treaty was concluded prohibiting the use of outer space for military purposes. Along with the Treaty on Nonproliferation of Nuclear Weapons, these all constitute practical steps toward limiting the arms race and have created more favorable conditions for progress in disarmament.

The Soviet government, in ascribing great significance to the provisions of the Treaty on Nonproliferation of Nuclear Weapons obligating the parties thereto to conduct, in a spirit of good will, negotiations on effective measures for cessation of the nuclear arms race and for disarmament, decided on and sent to all governments a memorandum on several urgent measures for cessation of the arms race and for disarmament, including such measures as banning the use of nuclear weapons, halting the manufacture of nuclear weapons, reducing and liquidating their stockpiles, limiting and subsequently reducing strategic weapon delivery systems, and other measures. The Soviet government ascribes exceptionally great importance to this memorandum, since it is aimed at strengthening peace. Simultaneous or stage-by-stage implementation of the disarmament measures proposed by the Soviet government would be a serious contribution to the struggle for cessation of the arms race and for a radical solution of the disarmament problem.

Permit me to express the hope that the memorandum will be examined with due consideration by the governments of the world's states, that it will be the subject of comprehensive and constructive discussion in the 18-Nation Disarmament Committee, which is to resume its work in the near future, and that this will make it possible to achieve the concrete results in the field of disarmament that all the world's peoples are waiting for.

U.S.S.R. government memorandum on several urgent measures for cessation of the arms race

The Soviet state, from its very first days, has advanced the struggle against the imperialist policy of aggression and wars and for safeguarding peace among peoples as the foundation of its foreign-policy line. Following the course indicated by V. I. Lenin, the Soviet government has firmly and consistently favored carrying out a broad program of measures for cessation of the arms race and for disarmament and implementing a general and complete disarmament plan.

Active struggle by the socialist countries, all peace-loving states, has made it possible to take several practical steps to restrict the sphere of the nuclear arms race and achieve disarmament. The Treaty Banning Nuclear Weapons Tests in the Atmosphere, in Outer Space and Under Water was followed by the Treaty on Principles Governing the Activity of States in Outer Space, which closed outer space to nuclear weapons. The Treaty on Nonproliferation of Nuclear Weapons, which has now been drafted and is ready to be signed, is of great significance for the cause of strengthening peace and creates favorable conditions for further struggle to halt the arms race and implement effective measures for banning and destroying nuclear weapons.

The interests of safeguarding peace call for further steps to restrict the arms race and achieve disarmament. This is especially important in that the activation of aggressive forces has increased tensions in international relations, the U.S.A.'s aggressive war in Vietnam is being expanded, and Israel continues to occupy several Arab states' territories that had been seized by force.

After the conclusion of the Treaty on Nonproliferation of Nuclear Weapons, the Soviet government proposes that agreement be reached on implementation as soon as possible of the following urgent measures for cessation of the arms race and for disarmament.

1. *A ban on the use of nuclear weapons.* From the time nuclear weapons first appeared, the Soviet Union has consistently favored banning and completely liquidating these weapons of mass destruction. The conclusion of an international agreement banning the use of nuclear weapons would be an important advance toward solving this problem and eliminating the threat of nuclear war. Such an agreement would be a serious deterrent to all those who would want to use nuclear weapons. By dispelling the suspicions of some powers with respect to other powers' intentions to use nuclear weapons, this agreement would help to improve the international atmosphere.

In order to promote the earliest possible solution of this problem, the U.S.S.R. government submitted to the 22nd session of the U.N. General Assembly a draft convention on banning the use of nuclear weapons. A substantial majority of the delegations at the Assembly supported the idea that it was necessary to conclude such an international convention. The Assembly urged all states to study the draft convention on banning the use of nuclear weapons submitted by the Soviet Union, as well as other proposals that could be made on this question, and to hold talks concerning the conclusion of this convention by calling an international conference, in the 18-Nation Disarmament Committee or directly between states.

In order to achieve a practical solution to the problem of banning the use of nuclear weapons, the Soviet government proposes that the 18-Nation Committee discuss as a priority item the draft convention on banning the use of such weapons and exchange opinions on calling an international conference to sign this convention.

2. *Measures for ending the manufacture of nuclear weapons and reducing and liquidating their stockpiles.* Seeking to rid mankind of the threat of nuclear war, the Soviet government proposes that all nuclear powers immediately open talks on cessation of the manufacture of nuclear weapons, reduction of stockpiles of them and a subsequent total ban on and liquidation of nuclear weapons under the proper international control. The Soviet government expresses its readiness to start such talks with all other nuclear powers at any time. In so doing the Soviet government proceeds on the assumption that in the course of such talks an understanding can be reached both on the entire complex of measures leading to the destruction of nuclear weapons and on certain measures directed at this aim.

3. *Limitation and subsequent reduction of strategic systems for delivery of weapons.* The Soviet government proposes that an understanding be reached on concrete steps in the sphere of limiting and subsequently reducing strategic systems for delivery of nuclear weapons. In so doing the Soviet government proceeds on the assumption that destruction of the entire arsenal of strategic delivery systems or at any rate reduction of this arsenal to the absolute minimum, with retention of only a strictly limited quantity of such delivery systems—and this retention only temporarily—would be a measure leading to the elimination of the threat of nuclear war.

The Soviet government expresses its readiness to hold an exchange of opinions with concerned states on mutual limitation and subsequent reduction of strategic systems for delivery of nuclear weapons.

4. *Ban on flights of bombers carrying nuclear weapons beyond national frontiers; limitation of zones of voyages by submarines carrying missiles.* The Soviet government has repeatedly drawn the attention of the governments of other states and world public opinion to the danger presented by flights of bombers carrying nuclear weapons beyond national frontiers. The increasing instances of crashes of American bombers carrying nuclear weapons beyond the

territory of the United States arouse legitimate alarm among various countries. There is no guarantee that the next crash of a bomber carrying nuclear weapons will not lead to a nuclear explosion with all the consequences this might bring. In the present tense situation, such a nuclear explosion could set off a whole chain of grave events and lead to a conflict dangerous to all mankind. From a military point of view these bomber flights make no sense, in view of the existence of nuclear rocket weapons. They can have only one purpose: to aggravate international tension, without regard for the consequences of such a dangerous practice.

The Soviet government proposes that flights of bombers carrying nuclear weapons beyond national frontiers be banned without delay.

In order to reduce the risk of the outbreak of a nuclear war, the Soviet government also proposes that an agreement be reached on ending patrols by submarines carrying nuclear missiles within missile striking range of the contracting sides' borders.

5. *Ban on underground tests of nuclear weapons.* The Soviet Union has been and remains a firm supporter of a ban on all tests of nuclear weapons and believes that a ban on all tests would promote the strengthening of peace and the easing of the arms race. The Soviet government is prepared to reach an immediate understanding on banning underground tests of nuclear weapons on the basis of using national means of detection to exercise control over this ban.

6. *A ban on the use of chemical and bacteriological weapons.* The Soviet government has repeatedly drawn the attention of states to the threat posed to mankind by the use of chemical and bacteriological weapons. Reflecting the common anxiety of the peoples over this threat, the 21st session of the U.N. General Assembly passed a resolution calling for strict observance by all states of the principles of the 1925 Geneva Convention on a ban on the use of chemical and bacteriological weapons, denouncing all actions contradicting this aim, and proposing that all states adhere to the Geneva Convention.

However, some countries, first and foremost the United States of America, have failed to carry out this important General Assembly decision. Moreover, the U.S.A. uses chemical weapons in its aggressive war in Vietnam. In view of this, the Soviet government proposes that the 18-Nation Committee examine ways and means of ensuring that all states observe the Geneva Convention on banning the use of chemical and bacteriological weapons.

7. *Liquidation of foreign military bases.* Foreign military bases on alien territory create a serious threat to peace. Such bases serve as sources for the outbreak of military conflicts and threaten the freedom and independence of the peoples. This is convincingly borne out by the U.S.A.'s continuing aggressive war in Vietnam and by the tension and conflicts in other places where foreign bases are located.

The Soviet government proposes that, in conformity with the instructions of the 21st session of the U.N. General Assembly, the 18-Nation Disarmament Committee urgently examine the question of liquidating foreign military bases.

8. *Measures for regional disarmament.* The Soviet government supports the creation of denuclearized zones in various parts of the world. In so doing it proceeds on the assumption that the formation of such zones will effectively limit the sphere of deployment of nuclear weapons and fully accord with the task of preventing their direct or indirect proliferation.

The Soviet government believes that not only groups of states embracing whole continents or major geographic regions, but also more limited groups of states or even individual countries may assume commitments to establish denuclearized zones.

The Soviet government also supports proposals concerning the implementation of measures for regional disarmament and for arms reductions in various parts of the world, including the Near East. Needless to say, the question of such measures for limiting the arms race in the Near East could be considered only if the consequences of the Israeli aggression against the Arab countries are eliminated and, above all, if Israeli forces are fully evacuated from the Arab countries' territories they have occupied.

9. *Peaceful uses of the seabed and ocean floor.* Limitation on the military uses of the environments in which man lives and works and the prevention of such uses of new spheres of human activity are in accord with the interests of easing the arms race. The Soviet government has consistently made and continues to make efforts to attain these objectives and notes with satisfaction that the appropriate limitations, set forth in the Antarctic Treaty and the Treaty on the Principles Governing the Activity of States in the Exploration and Use of Outer Space, Including the Moon and Other Celestial Bodies, are important practical steps in this direction.

The progress of research and the prospects for development of the seabed and the ocean floor make it possible to raise the question of establishing soon and in proper form the conditions to ensure that the seabed, beyond the limits of territorial waters, be used exclusively for peaceful purposes. This would ban, specifically, the establishment of fixed military installations on the seabed, as well as any other military activity. The Soviet government proposes that the 18-Nation Committee open talks on the question of using the seabed, beyond the limits of territorial waters, exclusively for peaceful purposes.

In proposing these measures, the Soviet government calls attention to the need of making all possible efforts to achieve concrete results in solving the problem of *general and complete disarmament.* The Soviet government deems it necessary to activate talks on this question in the 18-Nation Disarmament Committee. At the same time it favors implementation of the U.N. General Assembly's decision to hold a world disarmament conference and is confident that convening such a conference will facilitate a solution to this highly important task that confronts mankind.

The Soviet Union, guided by its principled line on questions of the struggle for peace and in cooperation with the socialist countries and all peace-loving states, will seek to eliminate the threat of nuclear war, to curb the forces of aggression and to implement a broad program of disarmament. The Soviet government calls upon all states to do everything necessary to reach an understanding on urgent measures for cessation of the arms race and for disarmament.

The U.S.: Supplier of weapons to the world

Eugene J. McCarthy

Is the proliferation of non-nuclear weapons "an even more serious threat to peace" than nuclear proliferation? Senator McCarthy argues that with the Soviet Union and the western nations—especially the United States—actively engaged in arms competition, this possibility ought to be examined. In the name of world security, he calls for a moratorium on arms sales, which hopefully would avoid such disputes as Kashmir, the Arab-Israeli War, and Cyprus.

Saturday Review, *July 9, 1966.* © *1966. Reprinted by permission.* *Mr. McCarthy is a senator from Minnesota.*

In the Thirties, companies that sold weapons to foreign nations were called "Merchants of Death." Politicians reviled them. They were the subject of a sensational Senate investigation headed by former Republican Senator Gerald P. Nye of North Dakota.

Times have changed. The U.S. Government is now encouraging defense manufacturers to sell arms overseas.

—*Forbes* Magazine

Over the past fifteen years, the United States has given or sold to other countries some $35 billion worth of military assistance as part of our foreign aid. The major share of Defense Department arms supplied under our military assistance program has gone to industrialized countries in Europe and the Far East.

We have provided arms, equipment, and training to countries who are allied or associated with us through treaties—NATO, SEATO, CENTO, ANZUS—which are the legacy of the early years of the containment policy and of the John Foster Dulles era. In addition, we have provided military aid to a wide range of countries in such categories as: "forward defense" areas, including the Republic of China (Taiwan), Iran, Philippines, South Korea, Greece, and Turkey (the last two countries are also allied to us through NATO); countries that have given us military base rights such as Ethiopia, Libya, Spain and our NATO ally Portugal; "Alliance for Progress Security" countries—virtually every country in Latin America; and some twenty-three countries in Asia, Africa, and the Middle East that are regarded as having "free world orientation."

Our interest and concern over the threat of nuclear proliferation should not distract us from giving careful attention to what may be an even more serious threat to peace—the proliferation and distribution of non-nuclear weapons. Supplying non-nuclear arms has become a major activity—not only for the modern merchants of death or for illegal gunrunners, but for the governments of the major industrial countries.

France, long a major supplier of arms to the Middle East, is reported to be exporting nearly 40 per cent of its total aerospace production. The Soviet Union is also a major supplier of arms. Great Britain is actively engaged in the arms competition. But today the United States is the world's leading producer and supplier of arms.

In recent years, sales of arms have been taking the place of grants and gifts in U.S. military assistance programs. In 1950, the fourteen countries that obtained U.S. arms and military training all received these on a grant basis. In 1966, of the seventy countries that received any combination of grant aid, direct sales or credit assistance for arms, sixty-two were receiving grant aid, thirty-four were buying arms directly, and eighteen were the beneficiaries of credit assistance.

The principal purpose of most military aid, whether it be in the form of grants or sales, is, of course, to strengthen recipient countries against Communist aggression and subversion.

Secretary of Defense Robert McNamara, in testimony before the Senate Foreign Relations Committee on April 20, 1966, stated:

> The governing principle of our military assistance program has been and is that the vital interests of the United States and the defense of the Free World

are dependent upon the strength of the entire Free World and not merely upon the strength of the United States.

Over the past decade, however, inter-governmental trade in arms with the developing countries has involved more complex motivations and considerations. Several pressures have combined to increase the arms supply.

First, newly independent countries are frequently anxious to acquire arms for prestige purposes. Lions on golden chains no longer satisfy. To many nations, these arms are status symbols—the tangible manifestation of their nationhood and newly acquired sovereignty.

Second, supplying arms opens the way to influence on the military and also on the political policies of the recipient countries. Experience has demonstrated that when an arms deal is concluded, the military hardware is only the first step. Almost invariably, a training mission is needed and the recipient country becomes dependent on the supplier for spare parts and other ordnance.

Since the Cuban missile crisis, there has been an increasing inclination on the part of both the United States and the U.S.S.R. to compete in supplying military assistance in areas adjacent to the sphere of influence of the other power. Thus, we tend to concentrate our military assistance to developing areas in those countries, such as Iran and Pakistan, which are on the "forward-defense arc" that borders the Communist heartland. Almost three-fourths of the program proposed for 1967 is for countries adjacent to the borders of the U.S.S.R. and Communist China. . . .

The Soviet Union, on the other hand, tries to increase its influence by assistance to, for example, Cuba, close to our shores.

The third reason for increasing arms sales, and a relatively new one for the United States, is financial and budgetary. Our balance of payments deficit is, in large measure, the result of military expenditures overseas—money that leaves the United States to support our military forces abroad, in Europe, and, particularly now, in Vietnam. The Vietnam war effort is costing the United States some $16 billion this year. By encouraging other countries to buy arms from us, we can offset to some extent the outflow resulting from these programs. Now, for instance, the Pentagon reportedly is "encouraging" additional purchases of U.S. arms by Germany by threatening transfer of U.S. troops from Europe to Vietnam. . . .

Secretary McNamara appears to believe that there is no reasonable alternative to intensified sales of U.S. weapons and, with the traditional rationalization of arms salesmen through history, states that if nations cannot buy them from us they will buy them elsewhere—from Britain, France or the Soviet Union, at higher prices.

But what is the effect of this policy?

The outbreak of war between India and Pakistan is a prime example which was of great concern to this country. Pakistan, which has recently been receiving military assistance from Communist China, is formally allied to us through the Southeast Asia Treaty Organization and is reported to have received from $1.5 to $2 billion in military assistance in the last decade. India, the largest democratic nation in the world, refused United States military aid until its borders were attacked, but it had been receiving arms from England. When it became clear that United States–supplied weapons were being used in the Indo-Pakistani war, many Americans must have wondered how our government could have allowed itself to become caught in such a contradiction. Nor was it any comfort when John Kenneth Galbraith, former Ambassador to India, stated before the Foreign Relations Committee on April 25, 1966:

> The arms we supplied . . . caused the war between India and Pakistan . . . If we had not supplied arms, Pakistan would not have sought a military solution [to the Kashmir dispute]. . . .

Among President Johnson's recent proposals to the Disarmament Conference meeting in Geneva is a suggestion that "countries, on a regional basis, explore ways to limit competition among themselves for costly weapons often sought for reasons of illusory prestige." On April 19, 1966, the U.S. delegate to the Disarmament Conference elaborated further the principles by which nations might undertake, on a regional basis, to limit conventional arms. If such regional arrangements could be concluded, potential suppliers should pledge to respect them and not deliver arms to the area.

But the Defense Department's guidelines for its arms salesmen give little encouragement to those who would favor restraint. Its pamphlet, *Information and Guidance on Military Assistance,* states:

> The Department of Defense has embarked on an intensified military assistance sales program. . . .
>
> Achievement of . . . objectives calls for a very substantial increase over past sales levels. Success in this endeavor will be dependent in large measure upon effective sales promotion. The DOD has taken several steps to assist in the successful conclusion of military sales. . . . Foreign customer preference for U.S. material is being generated by developing an appreciation of its technical superiority, price, availability, and the offer of follow-on support through U.S. logistics systems.
>
> In many cases, credit arrangements may be made to facilitate military sales, on short or long term basis as needed.

It seems to be a case of the left hand of the government trying to control what the right hand is busily promoting.

Former Ambassador Galbraith has stated:

> The policy of arming the indigent . . . has long since acquired a momentum of its own. It owes its existence partly to habit, partly to vested bureau-

cratic interest, partly to the natural desire to avoid thought and partly because to stop doing what is wrong is to confess past error.

At a minimum, one would hope for some rationalization of the United States policy on arms sales. There is evidence that the Soviet Union might welcome an opportunity to disengage from arms competitions, at least in the Middle East. The United States should pursue any such possibility and, at the same time, use its influence to persuade other major suppliers to agree to some form of conventional arms moratorium. Such a moratorium would be a further step in the direction of the general disarmament and nuclear weapons control which most of mankind so earnestly desires.

Controlling arms in the Middle East

Geoffrey Kemp

In this article Mr. Kemp asks Senator McCarthy's questions about the Middle East. Can an arms regulation or embargo be successfully established in the light of such complexities as internal security, East-West competition for influence in the area, the intensely hostile feelings in the region, and even the technical capacity of Israel to build nuclear weapons? His answer is not a very optimistic one.

This article originally appeared in The World Today *(July 1967), the monthly journal published by the Royal Institute of International Affairs. Reprinted by permission. Mr. Kemp is a research associate at the Institute for Strategic Studies and the author with John L. Sutton of* Arms to the Developing Countries.

The speed and effectiveness of Israel's blitzkrieg war against the Arab world has temporarily solved the problem of controlling arms in the Middle East. The remnants of the Arab air forces and armoured units cannot be replenished overnight, however keen the Soviet Union may be to win back favour with her defeated beneficiaries. The rearmament of Egypt, Syria, and, possibly, Jordan may have begun already, but it will be a long time—years, not months—before these countries will be able to pose a serious military threat to Israel, assuming their benefactors are unwilling to provide them with 'volunteers' or nuclear weapons. Is it reasonable to hope that this period of time will be used to search for sensible arms control proposals that could prevent yet another Middle East arms race?

In 1950 Britain, France, and the United States attempted to balance the input of arms into the Middle East and outlined their intentions in the Tripartite Declaration. With reference to arms sales, the Declaration stated:

> The three Governments recognize that the Arab States and Israel all need to maintain a certain level of armed forces for the purposes of assuring their internal security and their legitimate self-defence, and to permit them to play their part in the defence of the area as a whole. All applications for arms or war materials for these countries will be considered in the light of these principles.

In so far as they were able, the three Powers did try to prevent a major arms race between the Arab countries and Israel, but their calculations were rudely upset by the Soviet-Egyptian arms deal in September 1955, and by Israel's relative superiority in conducting military operations. The entry of a fourth major weapons-supplier into the field—Russia—destroyed the last vestiges of Western arms policy and paved the way for the anarchical situation which existed up to 4 June 1967; Israel's successive victories over the Arab countries have rendered meaningless control policies based on a quantitative balance of arms transfers. . . .

The question of renewed arms supplies to the Middle East has been the subject of a certain amount of speculation. Some people have condemned the fact that American, British, French, and Russian weapons were used in the war, and have called for a joint *embargo* on future supplies. These critics might do well to reflect on the outcome of a religious war in the Middle East fought with small arms; the casualty figures would be colossal and the war would drag on interminably. Others have suggested a Quadripartite Agreement to *regulate* future weapons sales to the area; some people feel it unlikely that the Soviet Union would go along with this proposal, and have argued that the three Western Powers should unilaterally agree to regulate arms sales in the hope that world opinion and common sense would persuade the Russians to do likewise.

Before any of these ideas can be examined certain pertinent facts must be realized. First, Israel is at present in a very strong military position; she controls the important strategic areas in Jordan, Syria, and Egypt, and has effectively destroyed the bulk of the Arab armed forces. Second, the humiliation of the Arab military leaders must cause them to re-assess their future military capabilities and be prepared to settle for more limited strategic objectives. This *de facto* situation is unlikely to change for some time, though it is reasonable to suppose that Israel will eventually give up most of the territory in Sinai. How, if at all, could the external Powers use this interim period to influence the future pattern of re-armament in the area? The Arab countries will obviously re-equip up to a level commensurate with their capabilities and the generosity of their donors. It would be naïve to suppose that the Soviet Union will be unduly worried by possible 'bad debts'; her arms policies in the Middle East are dictated by political, not commercial, considerations and the extent of her possible monetary losses must be seen against the far more staggering costs of American activity in Vietnam. One can also discount any hope that Israel will be prepared to refrain from a measure of re-equipment, unless such a move was linked to a general political settlement.

It is unlikely that the Western Powers will agree to curtail further supplies to Israel, particularly if the Soviet Union continues to re-equip Egypt and Syria and the existing Anglo-American deals with the 'traditionalist' Arab States go ahead. An alternative proposal would be for the external Powers to refrain from selling certain types of weapons, preferably those that can best be described as 'offensive,' 'provocative,' or 'escalatory'; for example, bombers, submarines, and surface-to-surface missiles. Such suggestions make sense and might even be accepted by the Soviet Union, were it not for the fact that these weapons are precisely the ones the Arab countries will be clamouring to receive. The 80-Hour War demonstrated the effectiveness of pre-emptive air and sea strikes, the importance of low-level strike aircraft, and the necessity for a strategy based on offence. Assuming that, without a settlement, Israel will retain some of her territorial gains and will not be prepared to revert to the *status quo ante*, the Arab countries will feel compelled to plan for an aggressive campaign against her. It is therefore going to be difficult, perhaps impossible, to persuade them to accept weapons designed for defence rather than attack. . . .

The feasibility of Middle East arms control arrangements must be seen as part of a much broader settlement that tackles the thorny problems of Israel's territorial border, the refugee question, and the long-term possibility of an indigenous Israeli nuclear weapons programme. The outcome of the geographical settlement will probably influence Israel's future defence policy more than any other factor. If she retains some authority over West Bank Jordan as far east as the vital north–south high road on the Nablus–Jenin–Jerusalem–Bethlehem–Hebron axis, and the hills in Syria overlooking her previous north-east border, her security against external attack and infiltration will be enhanced. She will therefore have less justification for relying so overwhelmingly on an offensive, punitive, and pre-emptive strategy. If the Arab countries were prepared to accept terms that acknowledged the existence of Israel and solved the tragic refugee problem, then the chances of long-term stability would be eased. However, if the Arab countries, the Soviet Union, and the majority of the United Nations Assembly refuse to accept these terms and use diplomatic and economic pressures to force Israel to return to her pre-war boundaries, Israeli strategy will inevitably remain offensive. Further, Israel cannot guarantee that the Arab forces will remain indefinitely inferior; this will eventually force her to take up her option on nuclear weapons production and to supplement her offensive strategy with one based on nuclear deterrence.

The effect of an Israeli nuclear weapons programme on stability in the Middle East and the desire of the super-Powers to curb nuclear proliferation can only be guessed. Israel will presumably be subjected to great pressure from the U.S. to sign the non-proliferation treaty; she may only agree to sign if the U.S. is prepared to give her a cast-iron guarantee—in effect a bilateral defence treaty. Whether the U.S. would be prepared to pay the cost of such an alignment would, in turn, depend on Soviet attitudes. The Soviet Union has consistently preached the need for a non-proliferation treaty; whether she could afford to allow the U.S. to guarantee Israel as a price for an Israeli signature on the treaty, and, at the same time, avoid being drawn into a formal alliance with Egypt and Syria is problematic. It is conceivable that a non-proliferation treaty, for what it would be worth, could be obtained *without* an Israeli signature, in which case there would be no immediate need for the U.S. or the Soviet Union to underwrite Middle East security. However, the attitude of the Arabs, if Israel refused to sign, can be imagined; before the war, President Nasser said Egypt was prepared to sign a non-proliferation treaty but would launch a pre-emptive attack against Israel if it were known she were building a bomb. Clearly this last option is now out of the question, though it will not take Egypt long to have the capacity to mount a limited airstrike against the vulnerable Israeli nuclear research equipment in Dimona. The alternative would be for Egypt to develop her own nuclear capability with outside assistance, possibly from China; but this would take a long time, would be vulnerable to Israeli attack, and would prevent her, too, from signing the non-proliferation treaty. Or Egypt could ask for a Soviet guarantee against Israel.

It seems inevitable that the participation of the super-Powers in the security of the Middle East would be at best a holding operation. The dangers of a Great Power confrontation are enhanced the stronger the Arab countries become and the more involved the U.S. and the Soviet Union are in the security of their respective clients. The U.S. has no need to intervene on Israel's side so long as Israel retains such an overwhelming conventional superiority over her enemies; once this superiority begins to erode—this may take some time since the Arabs cannot be expected to maintain their solidarity indefinitely—the possibility of renewed military pressures against Israel becomes realistic. The most hopeful outcome would be for certain Arab States, preferably Jordan, to come to a bilateral agreement with Israel. The various options open to the Great Powers to provide for a more stable Middle East seem slender unless it is possible to envisage a joint Soviet-American declaration that guarantees Israel's territorial integrity and, at the same time, is acceptable to the Arab countries. Such an arrangement seems unrealistic; it is more sensible to assume that the national interests of the super-Powers militate against further involvement in the kaleidoscope of Middle East politics.

So long as the commercial interests of the Western Powers require them to reach a *modus vivendi* with the Arab world, it is unduly optimistic to imagine they will discontinue selling arms to the area although it is possible that a new pattern of arms supplies will emerge. It is equally short-sighted to expect the basic antagonisms between the Arabs and Israel to evaporate overnight, even if Israel were to show leniency in her territorial demands. In view of these gloomy prophecies, it is realistic to argue that the short-term stability of the Middle East will be best served if Israel remains the predominant conventional military Power in the area. Unfortunately the behaviour of the Great Powers and the United Nations during the recent crisis will inevitably reinforce pressures within Israel for an eventual nuclear weapons programme. However, though she has the technical capacity to produce a small nuclear bomb and does not face great difficulties with respect to a delivery system, the costs of a nuclear programme would add an unwelcome burden to her already inflated defence budget. It must be expected that Israeli expenditure on conventional forces will rise for the next few years—an occupation of Sharm-el Sheikh, West Jordan, and areas of Sinai and Syria could not be achieved for nothing.

This leads one to suppose Israel will definitely keep open her nuclear option but refrain from a large-scale programme until such time as she feels militarily vulnerable. If she can maintain her position of conventional military superiority, which in turn can only be achieved if her previous territorial boundaries are adjusted, her need to rely on a pre-emptive strategy will diminish. This is not to say she will no longer need to conduct *offensive* operations against Arab countries, but that a strategy based on pre-emption can be supplemented by one based on deterrence, as in the years immediately following the 1956 Suez war. Once the Arab countries have re-equipped and, more important, retrained their forces, a fourth Middle East war seems inevitable. All one can hope for is that this time-scale will be sufficiently long to find some way of reaching a negotiated settlement, however obscure the possibility may seem at present. The time-scale is likely to be shortened if capricious interference by the external Powers seriously upsets this strategic equation.

How to keep the peace in a disarmed world

Alexander Rich
John R. Platt

Rich and Platt feel that nuclear weapons offer less security than their abandonment and here illustrate the type of system of world organization that could be developed to "generate the security that weapons once provided" while allowing for the continuation of sovereign nation-states.

These excerpts from "How to Keep the Peace in a Disarmed World," by Alexander Rich and John R. Platt, are reprinted with permission from Bulletin of the Atomic Scientists *(April 1966). Copyright 1966 by the Educational Foundation for Nuclear Science. Alexander Rich is professor of biophysics at the Massachusetts Institute of Technology, and John R. Platt is associate director of the Mental Health Research Institute at the University of Michigan.*

It is a curious thing that relatively little attention has been directed toward working out methods for keeping the peace in a disarmed world. The technological developments of the last twenty years have made disarmament a major concern of most nations, for it has become apparent that war is no longer an effective means for settling disputes between the great powers. Both the United States and the USSR have committed themselves to the goal of "general and complete disarmament," and a great deal of effort is being directed toward working out techniques for carrying us through a critical transitional period of disarmament. But there has been relatively little discussion of the ultimate organization among states in a disarmed world and of the mechanisms which must be developed for settling disputes and providing security. We wish to emphasize some aspects of this problem, and to point out an historical analogy which may provide a background for discussion. It is probably no exaggeration to say that our survival depends upon how we approach and solve this central problem of keeping the peace.

Disarmament discussions have been enormously difficult. Armaments have traditionally been used by states to resist demands, obtain satisfaction, or provide symbolic backing in a dispute even if not overtly used. Thus armaments have fulfilled some very practical needs in the intercourse between states, and it is not surprising that considerable resistance develops to an attempt to discard them. In addition, disarmament discussions are difficult because they are concerned with dismantling large, intricate military and production establishments.

On the other hand, the question of the type of system under which states would live in a disarmed world is, to a large degree, independent of the substance of disarmament discussions. It does not involve the mechanics of disarmament but the far more important problem of the structural design of arrangements for keeping the peace. On the scale of history, the trying period during which disarmament will actually be carried out will be relatively short, while the length of time during which states will live in a disarmed world hopefully will be extremely long.

Our continued failure to discuss fully the organization of a disarmed world may itself be a considerable impediment to the progress of disarmament negotiations. During the last twenty years, the significance of armaments has changed. Weapons of mass destruction have become so threatening that their possession begins to offer less security than their abandonment. This realization is gradually spreading, yet there has been little consideration of the system which needs to be created to generate the security that weapons once provided. Countries may be displaying understandable reluctance to disarm in part because they cannot fully picture the society into which they will be moving. It is clear that some other methods need to be developed for satisfying states when disputes arise or when internal or external pressures begin to build up.

It should be emphasized further that there is a particular advantage in undertaking long-range discussions now, because attitudes have not yet polarized between the nations of the East and West on the nature of life in a disarmed world and the mechanisms for maintaining the peace. No government has yet suggested a complete blueprint, perhaps because its realization has seemed so remote. The only relevant statements have been those by the U.S. on the importance of inspection, and those by the Soviet Union that there can be complete inspection once there is complete disarmament. Since this is still an uncharted area, it offers the opportunity of carrying out a joint or collaborative discussion among individuals of the East and West concerning peacekeeping mechanisms. If it develops that a consensus can be reached, it is conceivable that this in itself would have a beneficial effect on the entire disarmament problem.

We feel that certain general features will be necessary in an organization of states designed to preserve the peace in a disarmed world.

First, it should be the minimum organization that is consistent with actually keeping the peace. We are not faced with the necessity for organizing a "world government." This might be a desirable goal, but at the present time, it is hardly a practicable one. What is needed is a system limited enough so that the major states could persuade themselves to accept it; one in which states will have to submit to as little interference with their present functions as possible and surrender as little of their present powers as possible. By the same token, the organization must be broad enough to encompass member states with completely different economic systems or cultural backgrounds.

Yet it is of fundamental importance that the system "work." The question of stability is one we are especially interested in, since instability would result in a breakdown of the system, with a consequent reversion to the increasing dangers of an armed world. One of the most important features affecting stability in any system of social engineering is the built-in "feedback controls": that is, the system has to be able to change without falling apart. It must be able to respond to many different types of pressure for change—economic alteration, technological evolution, rebellion, or government change. The pressures are so numerous that they cannot all be anticipated over the years, and yet the peace-keeping organization must remain stable even when the unexpected occurs. This may seem a paradoxical requirement, but such a problem is frequently faced by the mechanical or electronic design engineer, and his solution is to deliberately install compensating mechanisms throughout the system which allow it to operate effectively over a very wide range of stresses. Some such feedback mechanisms are equally relevant in considering the organization of many nations in a disarmed world.

Any system that is to be stable under changing conditions must have its feedback mechanisms designed with various time-constants so that some of them can act quickly while others act gradually. In a social system, mechanisms are needed to insure stability in the face of rapidly developing dangers, such as attempts by small groups or nations to subvert the system, or to prevent slow but steady increases in instability, such as those that might be due to corruption of the system or unforeseen evolution of technology. The system must have within itself mechanisms for making structural changes which are deliberate enough to insure adequate consideration of major alterations before they are adopted, but which are not so slow as to make for enormous stress before things can be altered.

Finally, it is important that "fail-safe" features be present so that if the entire system should collapse, nations will not feel that they must act precipitously to avoid being taken over by other nations. One way to provide such a feature might be to disperse geographically among the major nations those remnants of military authority which are necessary for keeping the peace. The major nations would then feel that if the system were to break up or be unilaterally abandoned they could revert to some form of stabilized deterrence, because they would still have physical possession of powerful weapons.

In formulating any peacekeeping system, it is important to assume that individuals or states may sometimes try to work against the system to evade or subvert it. It is safest to assume that men may sometimes have the worst of intentions and to design the system with stabilizing mechanisms which will tend to prevent any state or group of people from frustrating it. In short, the system must be hardheaded; it cannot rely on "men of good will," since that is too fragile a basis for developing a system secure against all the possible fluctuations of interests. . . .

Organization in a disarmed world

Let us consider some of these principles in more detail. Here we are assuming that disarmament has been achieved, and that the United Nations may be regarded as a precursor of another type of organization which would operate in the disarmed world. What could the nature of this new organization be, and what problems will it face?

One major problem is the mode of representation of states and peoples in this central organization. Today all states are represented in the U.N. General Assembly by one vote, while some more highly developed or populous nations are represented more strongly in the Security Council. Both types of representation are important, and it is valuable for stabilization to have two different bases of representation which turn over at different rates, and which, at the same time, permit double consideration of legislation.

Yet it would seem that a legislative body in a disarmed world could be more representative and even more effective. For example, one house might be organized like the present General Assembly with each state having an equal vote, while another house could be created in which the voting power of each state would be a function of both population and economic activity (perhaps as represented by something like the gross national product). The more highly developed states, which presumably would be shouldering more of the burden of financing the central organization, would then have a greater voice in this body, which would in some degree be appropriate to their greater power and their greater peacekeeping responsibility. The inclusion of both population and economic activity as bases of representation in this house would also provide a mechanism for change. As less developed regions became more fully developed, they would have correspondingly larger representation. In addition, this kind of representation would require a periodic census of both population and economic activity by the central organization, which would be valuable on several counts. It might even be integrated with the inspection function of the central organization which would be needed to insure that the states refrain from building any weapons of mass destruction.

In a legislature composed of two houses, an additional element of flexibility might be the use of different mechanisms for selecting the representatives in the bodies. Thus representation might be determined by the states in one house as an "Assembly of the Nations"; but by popular election as an "Assembly of the People." . . .

The executive authority

Perhaps the greatest problem in devising a design for a stable system revolves around the composition and powers of the executive authority. . . .

Two problems in particular must be faced in designing a safe but adequate executive authority. One is, of course, the composition, organization, and disposition of the armed forces available to the central authority. This is almost the central problem in devising a stable system in a disarmed world. The military authority must be organized to ensure energetic action when necessary and yet not enable any group of men or nations to corrupt or manipulate the system toward its own ends. One possible solution is that a series of organized regional military units might be formed, under the command of officers whose terms are staggered and whose geographical origin is so diverse as to prevent the take-over of this force by national groups. This is only one of a number of possible stabilizing feedback mechanisms which should be debated and decided on with great care in this critical area.

The other problem is whether the military authority should have nuclear weapons. Their possession may be a necessary consequence of the fact that it may become comparatively easy to manufacture these weapons covertly, and the central authority could then be blackmailed. If it is necessary to retain nuclear weapons (and perhaps even missiles with nuclear warheads), then it probably will be desirable to take a step which at first may seem to be even more dangerous: to disperse them widely. In particular it might be of considerable value to the stability of the system to locate them within the major powers, even though they would be under the jurisdiction of the central authority, as a kind of fail-safe mechanism. These few widely distributed nuclear missiles might come to represent a reassuring, symbolic focus of force distributed among the major powers. It would be a low level stabilizing deterrent even though the nations of the world had fully disarmed.

One of the central questions in the organization of a disarmed world is what to do when there is a revolution or internal change in a national government brought about by the force of small arms. If weapons of mass destruction have been eliminated, the availability of small arms represents a continuing last-ditch mechanism for a people's defense against government tyranny. It seems unlikely that the central authority in a disarmed world will be able to prevent this kind of change and it is not clear that it should attempt to do so if it is going to be a minimum peacekeeping structure pledged to avoid embroilment in internal affairs. Some nations with inflexible or poorly stabilized internal structures may tend to undergo government changes repeatedly in this way rather than by popular elections or legislative evolution.

What should be the general policy of the central military authority toward such events? One possibility is that the executive authority should partially seal off the country to prevent the inflow of small arms that would increase the bloodshed. However, it might not necessarily prevent the flow of economic assistance. In addition, regulations might be developed to provide for the intervention of the central authority if the revolution has not terminated after a certain period.

We think it is important to realize that competition, even intense and occasionally bloody competition between groups, nations, and economic systems, will continue in a disarmed world. This competition must be taken into account in generating any stabilized design for the organization of life in this world.

Economic support for the central organization

An important point . . . is the . . . necessity of obtaining financial support not from the sovereign states but rather from individuals or units within the states. The sad consequences of neglecting this principle can be seen today in the financial difficulties of the United Nations. In any league of independent states, the attempt to collect revenue directly from the states is fatal, because they can withdraw their support from the central organization whenever they begin to disagree with its policies.

But it might easily be possible for a peacekeeping organization to obtain financial support through more stable mechanisms. For example, revenue could be obtained from a small tariff placed on international trade. This would be both appropriate and easy. Trade is extensive and benefits greatly from the maintenance of peace; the percentage of taxation needed would be small and would not require repeated appeals to legislatures and governments; and trade flows through a small enough number of channels so that the revenue could be monitored and collected with comparative ease. Through this method, the central organization would be supported largely by those states which are sufficiently advanced economically to have a large foreign trade and which are therefore best able to bear the additional tax burden.

Alternative possibilities for revenue include the taxation of activities that involve all nations, like the orbiting satellite system that will eventually become an integral part of world communications, or the leasing of mineral and other rights in international areas like the oceans.

Another important financial consideration in a world structure is the method of paying delegates to the legislative body. If they are paid by the central organization rather than by the member states, a uniform salary level would be assured and a sense of loyalty to the central authority would also gradually develop, which would in time foster a greater degree of support for it . . . This is a typical example of a type of feedback control which may seem insignificant at first but which over many years may do a great deal to increase the overall stability of the organization. . . .

A course of action

Just before his death Leo Szilard suggested a crash program in which a small group of American and Soviet citizens would collaborate over a six-month period to try to outline peacekeeping problems and suggest possible solutions. Up to the present, there have been no statements by governments of either East or West about the nature of a disarmed world and this would facilitate independent thinking by such a group. In particular, the United States and the Soviet Union will have very similar interests in the composition and functioning of a central organization in a disarmed world. Both countries have large land areas and populations, are heavily industrialized, and are interested in being as powerful in a disarmed world as they are today. Thus, perhaps there are favorable prospects for developing a joint outlook on the organization required to keep the peace. Getting an East-West group together to discuss the design of such an organization is a plan we strongly endorse, especially if there can be incorporated into the designs at every step the essential ingredients of feedback stabilization. A major study of this type could point the way to the solution of many of our problems almost directly. . . .

It is our feeling that efforts to reach such a consensus would considerably clarify the direction in which all societies must inevitably move, and might also have a beneficial influence on the progress of disarmament discussions today.

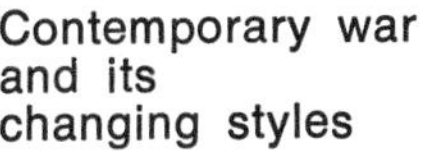

Section 4

Contemporary war and its changing styles

Dimensions of the war in Vietnam

Senate Republican Policy Committee

This is a brief but strong statement concerning the dimensions of the Vietnam War and asking some pointed questions about national interests.

This statement was prepared by the Senate Republican Policy Committee, Bourke B. Hickenlooper, Chairman. Congressional Record, *Senate, Vol. 113, No. 72 (May 9, 1967).*

As of April 1967, the war to contain Communist aggression in Vietnam has assumed for the United States these unusual dimensions:

It means a conflict that has escalated from a small force of 600 American technicians to over a half-million fighting men.

It means over 8,000 men killed.*

It means over 50,000 wounded.

* [Since May 1967, the number has risen to over 30,000.—Ed.]

It means greatly increased American conscription at a time when the rest of the Western world has done away with its draft.

It means our longest war since the American Revolution—six years—a weary nightmare and yet the men who fight are fighting with extraordinary bravery and skill.

It means not knowing at any given moment precisely who the enemy is.

It means a war which is not simply fought over this tiny land of Vietnam; for this war, unlike all others in American history, is more and more justified as much on geopolitical grounds as on the defense of one small government.

It means our relative isolation as the world's policeman, for here we have no Grand Alliance as in World War II, no United Nations Combined Forces as in Korea. In addition to South Vietnamese troops, four Pacific nations have provided some fighting help—with our financial assistance.

It means fighting a people who claim this is a civil war, and who in turn are spurred on by two giant powers quarrelling openly with each other.

It means that while we have committed 500,000 men to battle communism, neither the Soviet Union nor Red China—the great Communist powers—has found it necessary to commit troops.

It means the most frustrating sort of war, with no front lines, which breaks out here and there, even across national borders in Laos and Cambodia, neither of which is involved.

It means spending over $300,000 to kill each enemy soldier.

It means spending $24 billion a year, with another increase in taxes threatened, a further drain on an already inadequate gold supply, and an escalation of inflation.

It means enormous discretionary powers assumed by the President, with Congress asked to approve his actions after the fact.

It means the Nation which started the war—France—and lost it, now has become our most outspoken critic while profiting heavily from the war.

It means a war where, in the eyes of many Asiatics, we are fighting against indigenous Asiatic nationalism, much as France did in the past.

It means the first war in our history fought not only on the battlefield but brought into the American living room, every day, through the raw emotionalism of today's mass communications.

It means a war in which religious controversy between Catholic minority and Buddhist majority has come dangerously close to causing collapse of the successive governments of South Vietnam.

Here at home this confusion, this frustration, has raised challenges within Congress, within colleges and universities, within the press, within the military itself—and all to a degree not experienced in the United States since the Civil War. Conscientious objectors today outnumber their Korean counterparts 4 to 1. . . .

The national interest

. . . Before making any further decisions to support or differ with the President, Republicans might agree to seek hard, realistic answers to two basic questions:

1. What precisely is our national interest in Thailand, Cambodia, Vietnam, and Laos?
2. To what further lengths are we prepared to go in support of this interest? . . .

Exterminators create chaos (a moral's here—somewhere)

Russell Baker

Baker here offers a humorous critique on the merits of a great power's coming to the rescue of a small state. Any resemblance to a real war is purely intentional.

When the O'Flahertys discovered they had rats in their cellar, they immediately telephoned the United States Exterminating Co., which sent out Hogan and Wertham to clean up the situation.

Hogan and Wertham set out poison in small paper trays which the rats, being nobody's fools, declined to eat. After a few weeks Mr. O'Flaherty complained, and Hogan and Wertham returned. "If there's one thing I hate," said Wertham, examining the untouched trays of poison, "it's a smart rat."

"They are probably part of international rattism's scheme for world domination," said Hogan. "We're going to have to take severe measures."

That night Hogan and Wertham sat in the O'Flaherty's cellar with shotguns. There were half a dozen loud reports during the night. At dawn Wertham woke Mr. O'Flaherty with bad news. "Afraid we shot the side out of your hot-water heater," he said.

"Did you get any rats?"

"Can't say yet. You know that dog you got down there?"

"Old Rover? Of course, he's been in the family for years."

"Well, Hogan accidentally winged him in the hind quarter with a load of shot and he's running around so mad down there, we don't dare try to get a body count."

Mrs. O'Flaherty said that Hogan and Wertham would have to go, but Wertham was adamant. "If these rats are permitted to get away with taking over your cellar," he explained, "next they'll take over the cellar next door, and then the cellar next door to that, and before you know it they'll be all the way across town where we live. We've got to stop them right here."

Later that day Hogan and Wertham returned with reinforcements—a squad of 24 strapping young men apprenticed in the exterminating trade—to man a round-the-clock vigil. Under Wertham's leadership that night they conducted Operation Pied Piper.

Operation Pied Piper was based on the theory that, since the rats would not come out and fight in the open, they had to be concealing themselves someplace, possibly in the pipes. Bertham's strategy called for a direct frontal attack on the cellar pipes with sledge hammers. This was done.

In the wreckage next morning they found one dead rat and three mice. "We've got 'em on the run," said Wertham. That night he conducted Operation Pied Furnace, which resulted in demolition of the O'Flahertys' heating plant.

"How much longer is this going on?" demanded Mrs. O'Flaherty, whose kitchen was constantly overrun with off-duty exterminators given to pinching her daughter, flirting with her son's fiancee and complaining that her house was "the kind of dump that rats deserve."

"To tell you the truth, ma'am," said Hogan, "it could take three years, five years, maybe seven or eight years, but we're not going to falter. We're going to prove right here that rats can't get away with moving in on defenseless people like you. When we finally get the rats out of here we're going to build you the fanciest cellar in town."

That night while patrolling the crawl space under the sun porch, Wertham was bitten by a rat, or perhaps a spider—in the dark he could not be sure—and in an emotional retaliatory outburst he set fire to some old newspapers and burned down the entire north end of the house before the fire department arrived.

"At last," he told Mr. O'Flaherty, "we've severely limited their possible area of operations."

Two days later Hogan saw three rats dashing from the house next door, which belonged to the Smeeds, into the charred open end of the O'Flahertys' house. "That does it," Hogan told the Smeeds. "We're going to have to hit their infiltration routes, which lead right through your house."

Mr. Smeed went to Mr. O'Flaherty. "I don't know about you," he said, "but if those bunglers come looking for rats in my house, I'm going to court. I'd almost rather have Dean Rusk on my side."

Hogan and Wertham quickly gathered their forces and thrust a massive assault into the attic. The carnage was considerable, and at the peak of the battle the attic flooring, which had never been strong, buckled. Hogan, Wertham, 16 of their apprentices and sundry trunks crashed through to the second floor.

There the stunned forces of extermination, fearing an ambush, began smashing doors and windows in their search for escape routes. City inspectors arrived just at dinnertime to notify the O'Flahertys that the house was in hazardous condition and would have to be abandoned.

"Don't take it so hard," said Wertham to the sobbing Mrs. O'Flaherty. "At least you won't be leaving much to make life worthwhile for those rats."

The war of the Edsels

Art Buchwald

In this column Buchwald wonders out loud about the value of supporting commitments, no matter how tenuous and unsuccessful.

Los Angeles Times News Syndicate. © 1967. Reprinted by permission of the author. Mr. Buchwald is a syndicated columnist.

We were sitting around discussing the war in Vietnam the other night when somebody remembered that Secretary of Defense Robert McNamara used to work for the Ford company.

Then somebody else said, "I wonder what would have happened if Ford continued making the Edsel motor car?"

This is what we decided could have happened.

The year the Edsel came out a high-level conference was called.

The vice president in charge of sales made his report. "Sir, we might as well face it. The Edsel is a bomb. We can't sell enough of them to pay for one advertising spot on the Ed Sullivan show. I think we ought to take our losses and get out."

"Wait a minute," a board member said. "If the Edsel falls, the Ford might fall, then the Mercury and then finally the Continental. Psychologically this would be the greatest victory General Motors could possibly achieve, and our prestige in the motor industry would be impaired forever. We've got too much at stake for us to stop the Edsel now."

"I disagree with you, sir. I think we made a mistake and should admit it."

"Balderdash. The solution is to pour in more men and money. Surely with all our resources we can make the Edsel a big success, and we will show General Motors once and for all that if Ford makes a commitment to a car it will keep it."

"What's your plan, sir?"

"Let's send in our top engineers and develop the best car money can buy."

A year later, the high-level group stared glumly at the sales figures. "Sir, as you can see, we only sold 43 cars this year. The people just won't buy the Edsel. It's not their kind of car. Let's get out before it's too late."

"We can't just get out. We've got 50,000 workers committed to making a successful car and we'd be the laughing stock of the world if we quit now. The problem seems to be with the Edsel management team. Let's change the management, send in another 75,000 workers, add an additional $30 million, and we're bound to have a winner on our hands."

A year later the same group met to hear the news that only 23 Edsels had been sold. But one of the top-flight executives, who had just returned from a visit to the Edsel factory, was optimistic.

"It may take more time than we thought," he said, "but progress is being made. We have to concentrate harder on the customers to win them over before we'll see any results on the sales charts. Our industrial intelligence division says that General Motors is hurting badly and that with each new Edsel coming off the production line their morale is sinking to a new low. This is no time to let up. I propose we pour in another 125,000 workers and $50 million additional funds. GM must be made to realize that their hard-sell tactics won't pay off."

Three years later, with 550,000 workers on the production line and a billion dollars invested in the car, only one Edsel was sold—to the Smithsonian Institution.

"What do we do now?" someone asked.

"I think we should stop making Fords, Mercurys, Thunderbirds and Continentals and put all our resources into the Edsel. Our engineers say that all they need is 250,000 more workers and another billion dollars, and they'll have General Motors on their knees."

The Arab-Israeli war: How it began

Charles W. Yost

Yost's article has two theses: (1) "no government plotted or intended to start a war" and (2) no peace or security is possible without Arab recognition of Israel, Israeli reconciliation with her neighbors, and settlement of the Palestine refugee problem. A summary of the causes of the war is used to support the argument.

This article is reprinted by special permission from Foreign Affairs, *January 1968. Copyright by the Council on Foreign Relations, Inc., New York. Mr. Yost is a senior fellow on the permanent staff of the Council on Foreign Relations, former Deputy United States Representative to the United Nations, and former Ambassador to Laos, to Syria, and to Morocco. He now serves as U.S. Ambassador to the United Nations.*

The recent Six Day War in the Middle East grew out of the sterile confrontation to which the peoples of the region had committed themselves over the past twenty years. Both parties had frequently proclaimed their intention to go to war under certain circumstances. It seems unlikely, however, that any of them plotted and planned war for 1967. It seems more likely that they blundered into it.

Both sides might on many occasions have moved to end their confrontation by compromise, but this neither side showed the slightest willingness to do. The Israelis, feeling themselves beleaguered by fifty million hostile neighbors, acutely conscious of the recent fate of six million Jews in Europe, believed any significant concession would merely whet insatiable Arab appetites and start Israel down the slippery slope to extinction. The Arabs, looking upon the establishment of Israel as the latest in a series of imperialist occupations of their homeland, of which the presence of a million Palestine refugees was a constant reminder, found it emotionally and politically impossible to accept Israel as a permanent fact of life or to forego harassing it and conspiring against it.

This common intolerance and mutual harassment had brought on war in 1956. It is pertinent to note that, in his "Diary of the Sinai Campaign" published in 1966, General Dayan wrote that the three major objects of that campaign from the Israeli point of view were "freedom of shipping for Israeli vessels in the Gulf of Aqaba; an end to the Feydayen terrorism; and a neutralization of the threat of attack on Israel by the joint Egypt-Syria-Jordan military command." With slight variations, these were the issues that brought on war again eleven years later.

Through the latter part of 1966, so-called "El Fatah" incursions into Israel, sometimes carried out by Palestinian refugees, sometimes moving through Jordan or Lebanon, but for the most part mounted in Syria, grew in numbers and intensity. In October two particularly serious incidents . . . caused Israel to appeal, as it often had before, to the U.N. Security Council. However, a relatively mild resolution proposed by six of its members, calling on Syria to take stronger measures to prevent such incidents, was, as on previous occasions, vetoed by the Soviet Union in the supposed interests of its Arab friends.

A new and more radical Syrian government had come to power by coup d'etat earlier that year. It enthusiastically supported the claims and machinations of the so-called Palestine Liberation Army which mobilized and inflamed the refugees and carried out some of the raids. . . . Early in November, moreover, a "defense agreement" was concluded between Syria and the United Arab Republic, involving a joint military command and other measures of "coordination and integration" between the two countries.

It had long been Israel's practice, whenever it judged that Arab raids had reached an intolerable level, to retaliate massively. It did so on November 13 against Es Samu in Jordan where, according to U.N. observers, eighteen Jordanian soldiers and civilians were killed and fifty-four wounded. . . .

The U.N. Security Council, by a vote of fourteen to one abstention (New Zealand), censured Israel "for this large-scale military action in violation of the U.N. Charter and of the General Armistice Agreement between Israel and Jordan" and emphasized to Israel "that actions of military reprisal cannot be tolerated and that if they are repeated, the Security Council will have to consider further and more effective steps as envisaged in the Charter to ensure against the repetition of such acts."

Perhaps more important in its effect on subsequent events, the Jordanian Prime Minister in a press conference charged the U.A.R. and Syria, which had been denouncing King Hussein's government, with failing to bear their share of the confrontation against Israel. . . . The U.A.R. Commander-in-Chief of the Arab Command replied publicly with similar recriminations but the charges must have struck home to a regime so peculiarly sensitive to face and prestige. . . .

On April 7, 1967, one of these clashes escalated into what in retrospect appears to have been the curtain-raiser to the six-day war. An exchange of fire between tanks gave rise to intervention first by Israeli and then by Syrian aircraft. . . . Those knowing President Nasser's temperament could hardly have felt any assurance that he would hold aloof a third time.

On . . . May 11, Israeli Prime Minister Eshkol was saying in a public speech in Tel Aviv that his government regarded this wave of sabotage and infiltration gravely. "In view of the fourteen incidents of the past month alone," he said, "we may have to adopt measures no less drastic than those of April 7." . . . Two days later he declared: "It is quite clear to the Israeli Government that the focal point of the terrorists is in Syria, but we have laid down the principle that we shall choose the time, the place and the means to counter the aggressor." Eshkol went on to say that he intended to make Israeli defense forces powerful enough to deter aggression, to repel it and to strike a decisive blow within enemy territory. . . .

These Israeli exercises in verbal escalation provoked far more serious repercussions than they were no doubt intended to do and, far from sobering the exuberant Syrians and their allies, raised probably genuine fears in Damascus, Cairo and Moscow to a level which brought about the fatal decisions and events of the following week. . . .

The situation in mid-May was therefore the following: The aggravation of the El Fatah raids originating in Syria would seem to have brought the Israeli Government to the decision announced publicly in general terms by responsible officials . . . to retaliate sharply and substantially if the raids continued. There is no solid evidence, however, that they intended anything so massive as a drive on Damascus. Nevertheless, this prospect had in both Moscow and Cairo an impact which the Israelis probably did not fully anticipate or correctly assess. . . .

Nasser, for his part, saddled with responsibility for the unified Arab Command which was supposed to protect all the Arab states from Israel, jealous of his already damaged position as would-be leader of the Arab world, having been ridiculed by his allies and rivals for his failure to stir at the time of the Es Samu and April 7 affairs, categorically assured by Syrians and Soviets that Israel was about to attack Syria, for which public statements by Israeli leaders seemed to give warrant, may well have felt that he could no longer stand aside without fatal loss to his prestige and authority.

Israeli public statements between May 11 and 13, therefore, regardless of how they may have been intended, may well have been the spark that ignited the long accumulating tinder. . . .

May 16, General Rikhye, Commander of the U.N. Emergency Force in Sinai, was handed the following letter from General Fawzi, Chief of Staff of the Egyptian Armed Forces.

> To your information, I gave my instructions to all U.A.R. Armed Forces to be ready for action against Israel the moment it might carry out an aggressive action against any Arab country. Due to these instructions our troops are already concentrated in Sinai on our eastern borders. For the sake of complete security of all U.N. troops which install O.P.s along our border, I request that you issue your orders to withdraw all these troops immediately. . . . Inform back the fulfillment of this request.

Secretary-General Thant received General Rikhye's report . . . that same evening and . . . at his urgent request received the U.A.R. representative to the U.N., Ambassador El Kony, to whom he presented the following views: (1) General Rikhye could not take orders from anyone but the Secretary-General; (2) if General Fawzi was asking for a temporary withdrawal of UNEF from the Line this was unacceptable because UNEF "cannot be asked to stand aside in order to enable the two sides to resume fighting"; (3) if General Fawzi was asking for a general withdrawal of UNEF from Gaza and Sinai the request should have been addressed by the U.A.R. Government to the Secretary-General; (4) the U.A.R. Government had the right "to withdraw the consent which it gave in 1956 for the stationing of UNEF on the territory of the U.A.R."; (5) if the U.A.R. Government addressed such a request to the Secretary-General, he "would order the withdrawal of all UNEF troops from Gaza and Sinai, simultaneously informing the General Assembly of what he was doing and why"; (6) a U.A.R. request for a temporary withdrawal of UNEF from the Line would be considered by the Secretary-General "as tantamount to a request for the complete withdrawal of UNEF from Gaza and Sinai, since this would reduce UNEF to ineffectiveness."

Early the next morning, May 17, Egyptian troops began to move into and beyond some UNEF positions along the Armistice Line. . . .

Space permits only the briefest summary of the events which followed in rapid succession. On the afternoon of May 17 in New York the Secretary-General consulted with representatives of countries providing contingents to UNEF (Brazil, Canada, Denmark, India, Jugoslavia, Norway and Sweden). . . .

The next morning, May 18, Foreign Minister Riad informed representatives in Cairo of nations with troops in UNEF that "UNEF had terminated its tasks in the U.A.R. and in the Gaza Strip and must depart from the above territory forthwith." At noon New York time the Secretary-General received a formal request from the Egyptian Foreign Minister to the same effect. That afternoon he met with the UNEF Advisory Committee where he encountered the same divergence of views as at the meeting the previous day but where the members finally acquiesced in his belief that, in the absence of any proposal to convene the Assembly, he "had no alternative other than to comply with the U.A.R.'s demand." He did so that same evening by a message to Foreign Minister Riad and by instructions to the UNEF Commander.

The immediate reaction of Israel also deserves mention. On the morning of May 18 the Secretary-General received the Israeli representative who presented his Government's view "that the UNEF withdrawal should not be achieved by a unilateral U.A.R. request alone and asserting Israel's right to a voice in the matter." When, however, the Secretary-General raised the possibility of stationing UNEF on the Israeli side of the line, the Representative replied that this would be "entirely unacceptable to his Government," thus reaffirming the position in regard to UNEF which Israel had taken ever since the establishment of the Force in 1956.

The intent and rationale of the decisions taken in Cairo during those critical days in mid-May are still shrouded in obscurity, while those taken in response in New York are still bedeviled by controversy. What seems reasonably clear is that, as so often in the prelude to war, the control of events slipped from everyone's hands and limited decisions hastily taken had sweeping consequences no one desired.

No doubt the Egyptian Government decided sometime between May 13 and 16 that, in view of its assessment of the threat to Syria, it must move some of its armed forces up to the Sinai Armistice Line in order either to deter Israel or to come to Syria's assistance if deterrence failed. Reliable Arab sources maintain that: (1) the U.A.R. Government had as late as May 16 no intention to request the withdrawal of UNEF; (2) it desired merely the removal of several UNEF posts along the Sinai Line which would inhibit the contemplated redeployment of Egyptian forces; (3) it saw no incompatibility between this redeployment and the continuance of UNEF in its other positions, including Sharm el Sheikh; (4) the implementation of the redeployment was left to the military leaders who failed to consult the civilian authorities, including the President, about either the scope of the redeployment they intended to carry out or the demand addressed to General Rikhye on May 16; (5) when the Secretary-General confronted the U.A.R. Government with the naked choice between reversing the redeployment, to which its military leaders had publicly committed it, and requesting the withdrawal of UNEF, it felt obliged to choose the latter; (6) furthermore, when it unexpectedly found its forces once more in possession of Sharm el Sheikh, it felt it could not fail to exercise, as it had from 1954 to 1956, its "belligerent right" to forbid the passage of Israeli vessels and "war material" through the Strait.

As to the decisions taken in New York, the U.N. authorities have maintained that: (1) the indicated redeployment of U.A.R. forces was incompatible with the continuance of UNEF since it deprived UNEF of its essential function as a buffer between Egyptian and Israeli forces; (2) UNEF had hitherto been able to function effectively only because of an informal U.A.R. agreement that its forces would be held 2000 meters back from the Armistice Line in Sinai (Israeli forces patrolled right up to the Line); (3) once confrontation between the two forces was re-established, conflict between them was, in the existing state of tension, very probable and UNEF units scattered among them would be wholly unable to prevent it; (4) two of the troop-contributing states, India and Jugoslavia, had made clear their intention to withdraw their contingents whatever the Secretary-General decided and others were likely to follow suit, with the probable result that UNEF would disintegrate in a disordered and ignominious fashion; (5) the U.A.R. Government had the legal right both to move its troops where it wished in its own territory and to insist on the withdrawal of UNEF at any time, just as Israel had the right to refuse it admittance; (6) if the U.N. contested that right, peacekeeping would become "occupation" and other governments would not in the future admit U.N. peacekeeping forces to their territories; (7) a reference of the Egyptian request to the Security Council or the Assembly would merely have produced, as subsequent events proved, a prolonged debate during which UNEF would have either disintegrated or been helplessly involved in war.

No conclusive judgment can be pronounced on these two lines of argument. What does seem apparent is that both the U.A.R. and the U.N., like Israel a few days before, acted precipitately and with little resort to diplomacy. If the Egyptian account is accurate, temporization on the part of the U.N. might conceivably have led to some modification in U.A.R. military dispositions which had not been authorized by its own government. It seems very doubtful, however, that in the prevailing state of emotion, dispositions once taken, even without full authorization, could have been reversed. By May 17 the crisis had already acquired a momentum which seemed inexorably to sweep all parties toward and over the brink.

Nevertheless, we can hardly fail to note parenthetically the serious shortcomings of a peacekeeping procedure whereby, as in this case, a U.N. force can be ordered out of a critical area at the very moment when the danger of war, which it is stationed there to prevent, becomes most acute. The fault, however, lies not with the U.N. but with the great powers whose rivalries ever since 1945 have blocked the application of the enforcement procedures provided by Chapter VII of the Charter, under which a U.N. military force could be, for example, interposed between two prospective combatants regardless of the objections of either or both. In the absence of great-power willingness to permit the Security Council to apply compulsion of that type, the U.N. has been obliged for many years to rely on a much more fragile form of peacekeeping whereunder a U.N. force, whatever may have been the arrangements under which it entered the territory of a state, can in practice remain there only so long as its government consents. Such was the situation in Sinai before May 16.

To return to the concluding events of that month: President Nasser on May 22 announced his intention to reinstitute the blockade against Israel in the Strait of Tiran. This was the final fatal step. . . .

In any case, the reaction in Israel and elsewhere was immediate. On May 23 Prime Minister Eshkol declared in parliament: "The Knesset knows that any interference with freedom of shipping in the Gulf and in the Straits constitutes a flagrant violation of international law. . . . It constitutes an act of aggression against Israel." On the same day President Johnson declared in Washington: "The United States considers the Gulf to be an international waterway and feels that a blockade of Israeli shipping is illegal and potentially disastrous to the cause of peace. The right of free, innocent passage of the international waterway is a vital interest of the international community." . . .

In the meantime, however, the crisis had assumed proportions far beyond an argument over maritime rights. The advance of the Egyptian forces to the Armistice Line, the ouster of UNEF and the reimposition of the blockade were received with enormous enthusiasm throughout the Arab world. . . .

Nasser's prestige, which had been falling for some time, rebounded overnight. Expressions of solidarity poured in. Iraq, Algeria, Kuwait and Sudan promised troops. In a startling reversal of long-standing hostility, King Hussein of Jordan appeared in Cairo on May 30 and concluded a mutual defense pact with the U.A.R. which a few days later was extended to Iraq. The armed forces of Egypt, Jordan and Syria were more and more concentrated around Israel's frontiers and there seemed every likelihood they would soon be reinforced by other Arab states. . . .

In any case the Israeli Government obviously decided that it could not wait. All the factors which had induced it to go to war in 1956—a multiplication of raids into its territory, a substantial build-up of Egyptian and other hostile forces on its borders, the blockade of the Strait—had reappeared in even more aggravated form. Efforts of the U.N. and the U.S. to relieve them by international action seemed unavailing. On May 30 Foreign Minister Eban said in a press conference in Jerusalem:

> Less than two weeks ago a change took place in the security balance in this region. The two most spectacular signs of this change were the illegal attempt to blockade the international passageway at the Strait of Tiran and the Gulf of Aqaba and the abnormal buildup of Egyptian troops on the Israeli frontier. The Government and people of Israel intend to insure that these two changes are rescinded, and in the shortest possible time.

Six days later Israel struck with this end in view; twelve days later it had achieved its objective, and much more beside.

It is not difficult in retrospect to identify the ventures and responses on both sides which over preceding months and weeks, compounding the hatreds which had been allowed to fester for twenty years, led almost inevitably to war.

First were the El Fatah raids, organized from Syria, involving the "Palestine Liberation Army," subjecting peaceful Israeli villages to recurrent jeopardy and terror, building up through the months from October to May, unpunished and, because of the Soviet veto, even uncensured by the U.N. Security Council. Remembering the history of the previous twelve years, it is difficult to see how any Arab or Soviet leader could have failed to realize that this murderous campaign would eventually bring forth a murderous response.

Second were the Israeli "massive retaliations" at Es Samu in November and in the air over Syria and Jordan in April, designed to punish and deter, but disproportionate in size, visibility and political impact, causing also the death of innocent people, condemned by the Security Council in the strongest terms in November, as similar disproportionate retaliations had been repeatedly condemned in the past. It is difficult to see how any Israeli leader could have failed to foresee that such repeated massive reprisals must eventually place the leader of the Arab coalition in a position where he would have to respond.

Third were the public and private statements by high Israeli authorities in mid-May which indicated the probability of even more drastic retaliation against Syria in the near future if the El Fatah raids continued. These statements, even though no doubt designed to deter the raids, almost certainly convinced the Syrian and U.A.R. Governments that such retaliation was definitely projected and may well have persuaded them and the Soviets that the Syrian regime itself was in jeopardy.

Fourth was the decision by the U.A.R. Government, presumably encouraged by Soviets and Syrians, to move its armed forces up to the Sinai Armistice Line, thus reestablishing at a moment of acute tension the direct Egyptian-Israeli military confrontation which had been the major immediate cause of the 1956 war. This redeployment of Egyptian forces was under the circumstances critical whether or not it was originally intended to be accompanied by a demand that UNEF be withdrawn.

Fifth and finally was the decision of the U.A.R. Government, finding itself whether by intent or accident once more in command of the Strait of Tiran, to exercise its "belligerent rights" by reimposing the blockade, thus reproducing the third of the elements which had brought on the 1956 war. The likely consequences of this step were indeed foreseen but, in the climate of fear, passion and "national honor" which by then prevailed, were faced with fatalism and desperation.

It remains, however, the thesis of this article that no government plotted or intended to start a war in the Middle East in the spring of 1967. Syria mounted raids against Israel as it had been doing for years, but more intensively and effectively; Israel retaliated disproportionately as it often had before, but in more rapid succession and in a way that seemed to threaten the existence of the Arab government; Nasser felt his responsibilities and ambitions in the Arab world did not permit him again to stand aside in such a contingency and took hasty and ill-calculated measures which made major conflict, already probable, practically certain. All concerned overreacted outrageously. Yet there is no evidence—quite the contrary—that either Nasser or the Israeli Government or even the Syrian Government wanted and sought a major war at this juncture.

Of course the fault of all of them, and indeed of the great powers and the United Nations, lay not so much in their actions or omissions in May and June 1967 as in their failure, indeed their common blunt refusal, to face the facts of life in the Middle East during the twenty years before that date.

There will be no peace there, no security for its inhabitants or for the great powers involved there, until the Arabs recognize that Israel, however unjust its creation appears to them, is a fact of life, that it has as much right to exist as they have, that to threaten and harass it, to arouse among their people false hopes about its dissolution, is actually as much a threat to Arab as to Israeli security, that the two equally have more to gain than lose by peaceful co-existence. On the other hand, there will also be no peace in the Middle East until the Israelis recognize that the condition of their long-term survival as a nation is reconciliation with their much more numerous Arab neighbors, that survival cannot indefinitely be preserved by military force or territorial expansion, that displays of inflexibility and arrogance are not effective modes of international intercourse, and that in particular there will be no security for Israel until, whatever the political and financial cost, the million or more Palestine refugees have been compensated, resettled and restored to dignity.

Is world war inevitable?

Kingsley Martin

Are U Thant and Einstein correct in predicting the near inevitability of another world war? Taking into account contemporary regional wars, the arms race, and the irrational nature of man, Mr. Martin concludes that perhaps they are (or are not).

New Statesman, *July 14, 1967. Reprinted by permission. Mr. Martin is a professional writer on world affairs.*

On 11 May [1967], U Thant remarked that he feared that "the initial phase of World War Three had begun." Einstein stated that when it came it would be fought with H-bombs which would "annihilate all life on earth." Such a war was, he thought, "inexorable." So, if we are to believe these remarkably well-informed men, we have none of us long to live. The question is whether they were right. My own view is that U Thant was right in believing that the Third World War had begun, but that Einstein may have been exaggerating about the "inexorable" result.

You must not dismiss U Thant's analysis; he is a cool, very able, far-seeing man, with less patriotic bias than other men and, as Secretary General of the UN, probably better informed about world politics than anyone else alive. Note that he did not say, as Bertrand Russell has sometimes rashly done, that the human race will shortly be wiped out; he spoke of various phases through which we are likely to pass, drew a parallel with events in Europe just before the Second World War, and pointed out that the "psychological climate" for war took time to develop. "When conditions were ripe, then a global war was triggered." He spoke before the Israeli-Arab war and found the danger of "direct confrontation between Washington and Peking" in Vietnam quite a sufficient basis for prophecy. Since then, apart from the war in the Middle East, China has exploded an H-bomb, and Mr. William Bundy, U.S. Assistant

Secretary of State, has said that if China enters the Vietnam war, the U.S. would use "everything we have."

The analogy between the political situation today and that of the years preceding the Second World War is only too easy to draw. We are apparently back at the stage of anarchy in which we lived after the failure of the League of Nations. It is another period of absolute cynicism, gross cruelty and total disregard for human life. The parallel between the Spanish war and the Vietnam war is horribly close. Both were civil wars in which great military powers intervened, nominally for ideological reasons. In Spain we know now that Germany was trying out her weapons for a European war. We were not then habituated to the bombing of open cities and were shocked by the destruction at Guernica, but it was no doubt useful to the German general staff to train pilots by the massacre of real people, instead of dummies. The United States is following this pattern in Vietnam; if it does not fear reprisals from Russia it may, according to Mr. Bundy, experiment with nuclear weapons. It has not been able to do this since killing Asians in 1945.

The cynicism of current international politics has never before been equalled. There was still a notion of world order when Baldwin betrayed the League of Nations in 1935. That was the last occasion in which a sovereign nation pretended to stand by any principle, or paid regard to any policy beyond its immediate national interests. Telling lies to the House of Commons about non-intervention in Spain was almost as flagrant as telling lies about the Suez affair in 1956. But hypocrisy has probably never reached to the point that we are now witnessing about the Middle East.

Israel is arraigned as the aggressor (which, of course, she was, with the collusion of Britain and France, in 1956) although Egypt and other Arab powers had simultaneously mobilised on her frontiers, demanded a withdrawal of the UN Peace Force, increased their boycott into a stranglehold by closing the Gulf of Aqaba and stated categorically and often that they were about to destroy Israel and drive its inhabitants into the sea. They never recognized the right of Israel to exist and were always technically at war with her. The Israeli reply was swift and predictable; her only alternative was tamely to wait for destruction from the air. A recent observer who flew over the Sinai desert described to me how it was littered, as he put it, like the floor of a children's nursery, with hundreds of Soviet weapons, some destroyed, many not even damaged. Today, as if to prove it is determined to promote another Arab war with Israel, the U.S.S.R. is transporting a large, though unknown, quantity of weapons to Egypt and other Arab states, which, if they were not rearmed, might now have been tempted to recognise Israel and establish a *modus vivendi.*

The unfortunate Arab peoples have been told nothing but lies. First, they were cozened into believing they had won the war, then that the Jews, in Kosygin's words, had committed "Hitlerite atrocities" upon their prisoners, and that they had been defeated by Western military forces. They are now told the Israelis will be compelled to retire, not only from the territory where they are responsible for tens of thousands of luckless refugees, but also from security points which would give them some guarantee against renewed Arab attack. No attempt has yet been made to find any general solution for the Middle Eastern situation and all we know at present is that the Russians are helping to maintain Arab fanaticism and ignorance. Here, clearly, is the prospect of a second dangerous confrontation. . . .

No one any longer believes that statesmanlike policies will lead to a general settlement either in Vietnam or the Middle East. The hawks of the Pentagon will not admit that Hanoi and the Viet Cong cannot be treated separately, nor indeed is it likely that they wish to call a halt to a war which may give them an excuse for bombing China's industrial and nuclear bases.

Even in the Thirties, which people now ridicule as idealistic, thoughtful men, who did not in those days seem powerless, advocated such far-reaching propositions as bringing the great sea highways—the Suez, Panama, Straits of Gibraltar, Gulf of Aqaba—under international control, that industrial nations would be well advised to cooperate in the development of backward areas and to use for universal benefit the extraordinary advances of modern science. It is to me grotesque that today, when the Soviet Union proposes to develop an anti-missile device for its defense, it should be at once assumed that the Americans must reply, not only by developing such a device themselves, but by spending billions of dollars on increasing their offensive power.

This is a gloomy picture. I do not, however, believe that Einstein was right in saying that the H-bomb would "inexorably" lead to the annihilation of all life on this earth. In suggesting other alternatives, it may just be that my mind boggles at the thought of general annihilation, and though my reason tells me that it is possible, and even probable, I can conceive of alternatives. There could be a war, for instance, between nuclear powers which stopped before humanity committed suicide. I recall the hideous picture which Aldous Huxley painted in *Ape and Essence* of a world in which a debased humanity survived after a nuclear war. Perhaps it would be better that the species should not survive rather than that any such mutations should remain after it. Again, it is by no means impossible that some great power might resort, with incalculable results, to the chemical and biological horrors which we know governments are now preparing.

If there is a better hope on the horizon, it may lie in the balance of fear, producing amongst the powers a new kind of diplomacy. We no longer make the mistake of imagining, as we did in the Thirties, that economics would prove more powerful than nationalism or than the complex of factors which lead nations to prefer death rather than yield an inch of territory. Biologists are now explaining the part that aggressive impulses play in the human composition. We understand that the human species is almost alone in preferring to die rather than to yield when defeated in combat. According to the great biologist,

Konrad Lorenz, only the dove (ironically enough) is unlike other animals and birds in insisting upon fighting to the death. It looks as if, confronted with suicide as an alternative to surrender, nations may be learning the same convention. Great nations are now playing a monstrous game of "Chicken."

That this can happen we learnt when the U.S. and the U.S.S.R. confronted each other over Cuba. The United Nations have recently made loud, bellicose noises, poured abuse upon each other, but stopped short of recommending suicide. In short, aggression may be ritualized and mutual abuse substituted for final war. There is perhaps not much comfort in this. The game is terribly dangerous and, at best, allows comparatively small wars to continue all over the world. Worst of all, owing to U.S. folly in isolating China, Peking has not yet learnt this ritual game. Conceivably, now that it has the H-bomb, China will play it, too. All this is somewhat theoretical in a world in which the only certainty is the continuation of war. The one prospect which seems ruled out is that sanity will take possession of humanity's rulers. All prophecy is impossible. The only thing one can say is that the expected never happens. It is always something else.

Vietnam: The frustrations of a political war

Ray Cole Hillam

Why the frustrations of the war in Vietnam? Professor Hillam suggests that the unique nature of guerrilla war is one answer and that the existence of a comprehensive Viet Cong infrastructure throughout South Vietnamese society is another. The tactics for combating such an enemy are necessarily complex and long-term, so that the inevitable result is continued frustration.

Professor Hillam is chairman of the Department of Political Science at Brigham Young University. In 1966–1967 he was a Fulbright-Hayes professor in Vietnam and adviser to the Political Warfare College at Dalat. He is the author of several articles on Vietnam. This is the first publication of this article.

The war in Vietnam is presenting a new challenge to traditional American concepts of warfare. In the past we liked to keep our wars simple, and we liked to wage them for one purpose—victory. The present war has not met these criteria. We have been frustrated by the "political approach" of guerrilla communism.

The objectives and strategy of the enemy

The objectives of the enemy in Vietnam help to explicate the nature of this different kind of multifaceted war and reveal that it has a depth that traditional wars, whatever their scale, lack. The enemy intends not only to seize power or to exchange one government system for another but also to restructure the entire South Vietnamese society, including the destruction of the prevailing myths that bind this society together. In this sense, the objective is total. To achieve this objective, the enemy has resorted to a war of persuasion, manipulation, and compulsion as well as of violence. Thus, the war takes on political, economic, social, and psychological as well as military significance.

The strategy of the enemy in South Vietnam is based partly on a mixture of aphorisms accumulated over the years from the writings of Chinese and Vietnamese revolutionaries and partly on pragmatic assumptions of how best to come to power in South Vietnam. Recently captured enemy diaries and notebooks clearly indicate the emphasis the enemy places on the writings of Mao Tse-tung and Vo Nguyen Giap, the North Vietnamese theoretician. They both describe the political character of war. Indeed, they are advocates of a war which is more political than military. The continual reference to the military maxims and political aphorisms of these two prominent revolutionaries suggests the importance the enemy places on the ideology of guerrilla communism as a motivating and directing factor.

In discussing the strategy of the enemy, it is important to refer to the earlier strategies of Mao and Giap. Mao, in his 1938 lectures, *On Protracted War*, speaks of a three-phased protracted strategy: the defensive, stalemate, and offensive strategy. In his book entitled *Peoples War, Peoples Army*, Giap adds two preliminary phases which provide first for the psychological milieu for the insurgency and second for the organizational base for launching the protracted war. The next three phases, which tend to be operational rather than preparatory, are similar to Mao's description of the three-phased protracted war.

In an effort to simplify the description of the enemy's strategy, both as it is based on the Mao-Giap formula and the present environment, perhaps it is best to speak in terms of four phases: the organizational, the nonviolent, the violent, and the legitimization phases.

In the organizational phase, the professional revolutionary and the functional cadre develop a network of clandestine organizations and lay the foundation for a comprehensive infrastructure. It is also during this incipient phase that a strategy is developed for launching organized resistance against the constituted authorities.

In the next phase, which is the initial operational phase and which is best characterized by the emphasis placed on nonviolent activities, the cadre is actively engaged in political agitation and indoctrination. He organizes and directs study groups, fronts, and other overt organizations designed to enlist popular support for his clandestine movement. This organizational base, both overt and covert, continues to broaden during this phase and subsequent phases of the protracted strategy.

The third phase is characterized by violence. There are assassinations, kidnappings, and guerrilla attacks on outposts, police patrols, and convoys. Initially, the enemy employs defensive tactics of hit, run, and hide. The government is in hot pursuit but eventually becomes overextended. Yet it still tries to hold on. Throughout this phase, the enemy is building and consolidating his position. Continued emphasis is placed on clandestine activity and organizational work. Political agitation and indoctrination as well as acts of terror continue.

The final phase is one primarily of force rather than issues. The guerrilla units become mobile, conventional military units which initiate frontal assaults and attack fortified positions. The war becomes conventional, and much of the ideological emphasis is replaced by the long-hoped-for military victory. It is during this phase that the movement hopes to achieve legitimacy and general acceptance, both locally and abroad.

In the enemy's protracted strategy, the transition from one phase to the next is not precise and can be reversed, and one phase is not necessarily a prerequisite for another. Figure 1 illustrates the fluid nature of the enemy's phased strategy of protracted war. Note that each stage, while evolving into an advanced stage, continues its existence until the end of the conflict.

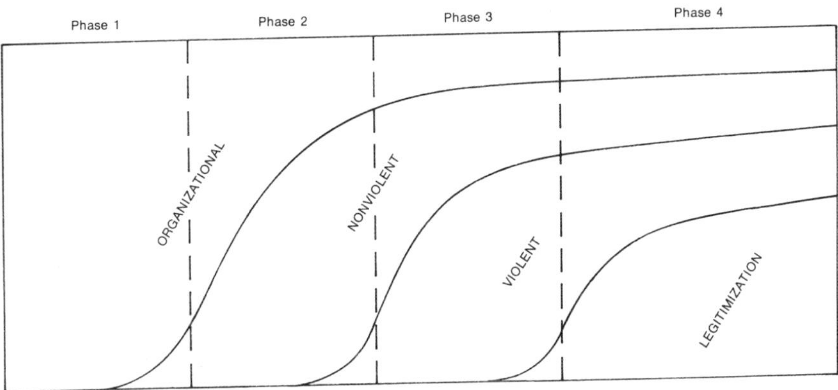

Figure 1. Strategy for protracted war

There are expressions of all four phases in different areas of South Vietnam. In the Mekong Delta, except for An Giang Province, the enemy is in phase three. In the northern provinces of South Vietnam, he is in phase four. In the An Giang and Tuyen Duc provinces, he has never extended much beyond the second phase. In late 1964, the enemy was passing into the fourth phase, but because of the direct and escalated commitment of U.S. troops, the enemy has had to revert back to earlier phases in some areas.

The present situation

There are indications that some military, political, and economic gains have been made by the allies in the war. There have been military successes against Viet Cong battalion-size forces, and North Vietnamese units and enemy strength appears to be waning in some areas. The runaway inflation of 1965 has been curbed, and the programs for education, public works, and agriculture continue. There is evidence that more people are being brought under the control of the Saigon government and that this government is extending its admittedly meager aura of legitimacy.

However, there are factors which counterbalance these gains. Though conventional-size enemy units have been defeated, the guerrillas are still a formidable enemy. The enemy has progressed from fighting with captured rifles and limited supplies to using automatic weapons, heavy mortars, artillery, and rockets that have been brought into South Vietnam. The cost of the war has been extremely high in terms of dollars, destruction, and lives, both to Vietnam and her allies. More than a million troops have been able to secure only a fraction of a country slightly larger than Utah. Both economic and political progress could be abruptly reversed; if the U.S. were to withdraw, the newly elected government would rapidly collapse. Why is it that the militarily inferior enemy is able to wage war successfully against the allied giant? Why is it that we have been frustrated in our efforts to achieve substantial military progress?

The infrastructure

The strength of the enemy in South Vietnam lies in his organization—the infrastructure. The term *infrastructure* is appropriate since it implies an arrangement of constituent parts beneath the surface. Indeed, the infrastructure is a sophisticated network of parallel, horizontal, and vertical intermediate structures designed to enmesh populations and retain commitments. It is this complex organization which has been used to mobilize and manipulate the rural population and to prevent the Saigon government from governing.

The question may be properly raised as to how the infrastructure was able to

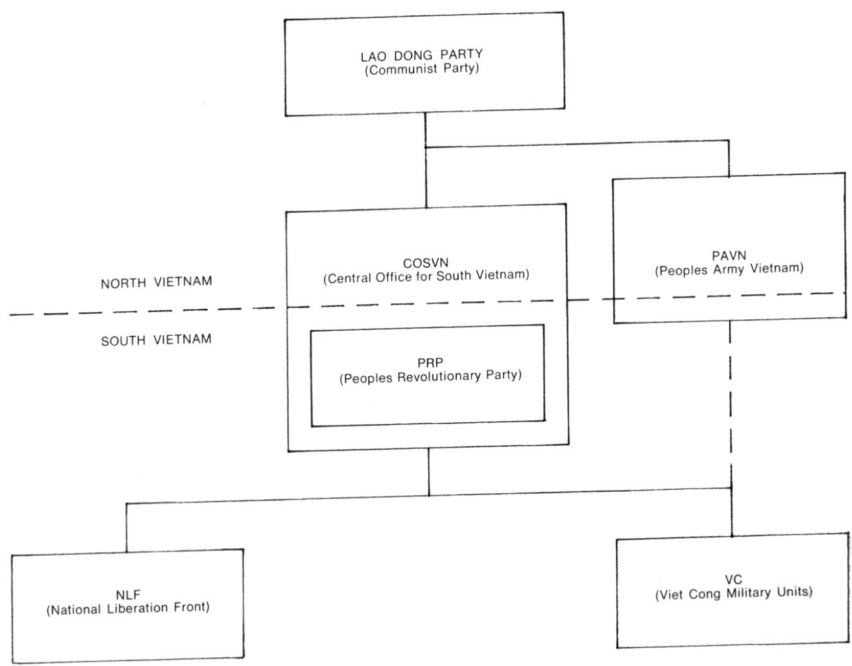

Figure 2. Chain of command of infrastructure (simplified)

gain this stronghold. The roots are in its predecessor, the Viet Minh movement, through which Ho Chi Minh obtained power in the North. The Viet Minh was a nationalistic movement of Vietnamese against the French colonialists. Ho, through political and organizational genius, was able to seize control of the movement, so that it became a Communist front organization. Not long after the Geneva agreements of 1954, the enemy began to strengthen and extend the clandestine war against the Ngo Dinh Diem regime. An administrative vacuum existed throughout much of South Vietnam, partly because Diem was never able to extend effective control over the entire nation and partly because officials in those areas under nominal control of the Diem government preferred to govern in the traditional mandarin manner—"Let the peasants come to you, do not go to them."

The vacuum was filled by the remnants of the Viet Minh infrastructure, who restructured the existing apparatus, recruited and trained additional cadre, and broadened their popular base. Thus, the infrastructure began to evolve not wholly as an indigenous clandestine revolutionary movement but as one which had been partially transplanted. Figure 2 indicates the line organization of the infrastructure. Direction of the infrastructure is provided by the Central Office for South Vietnam (COSVN) with headquarters in North Vietnam. This is a hard-core Communist organization with lines running into South Vietnam, particularly to the People's Revolutionary party (PRP), which is composed of Communist cadre, most of whom are South Vietnamese. This party is the intermediary between the leadership for the National Liberation Front (NLF) which, like its predecessor, the Viet Minh, is a Communist front organization. The purpose of the NLF is to serve as a gathering point for all opposition to the Saigon government, and it includes both Communists and non-Communists. The Viet Cong armed units are the military forces subordinate to the PRP.

The infrastructure has three levels. At the top are the dedicated North and South Vietnamese Communists who provide direction for the movement. In the middle are the cadre who are perhaps more motivated by career and professional incentives than revolutionary fervor. Whatever their motivation, they are the backbone of the movement and provide the necessary link between the leadership and the masses. The lower level consists of the peasants who belong to mass organizations, who provide men, provisions, and cover for the military effort, and who are loyal to whichever government is currently in control. The rank and file are often motivated to support the movement through grievances against the government, promises of a better future, or intimidation and terror.

The infrastructure has a great advantage over the government since its organization, as designed, thoroughly penetrates every level of society and has been in operation for a number of years.

Defeating the infrastructure

How can the infrastructure be rendered ineffective? The most meaningful strategy is to dry up its resources. This requires more effectively restricting the infiltration of supplies and manpower from North Vietnam and, more important, reducing the local sources of supplies, manpower, and popular support.

Past strategies of interdiction are clearly insufficient. Infiltration has been so great that the enemy has been able to escalate its military effort, particularly in I Corp (the northern provinces of South Vietnam) from the third to the fourth phase. Bombing the access routes from North Vietnam has been of limited value. Enemy infiltration has been made more difficult by military operations in the demilitarized zone and along the Laotian and Cambodian borders, but it has not been reduced. In fact, it has increased because of the requirements of the enemy in the South.

The futility of the present strategy of interdiction is reflected in the recent statement of the South Vietnamese Defense Minister, General Cao Van Vien, who said that bombing in North Vietnam would not in itself stop infiltration. The problems, he said, are the infiltration routes and base areas the enemy has in Laos and Cambodia; so long as these problems cannot be resolved, infiltration will not cease. He believes the war will last another twenty to thirty years unless infiltration of men and supplies through Laos is halted.

Since present military measures have not curbed effectively the enemy's infiltration into the South, some argue that negotiations with Hanoi are the only other alternative. Negotiations, while they might be desirable, are no guarantee against infiltration. The attitude of Hanoi is to continue the effort in the South, and the Central Office for South Vietnam has been instructed not to deviate from the original goals, even though there are negotiations with the Americans.

The strategy of interdiction has been of limited value. Although negotiations are taking place in Paris, it is questionable whether infiltration will stop. The cessation of bombing and a deescalation of the conventional war may reduce enemy infiltration voluntarily. However, some alternative methods should be considered. Perhaps the construction of a fortified belt or barrier south of the demilitarized zone, later followed by building a system of strategically situated barriers down the Laotian and Cambodian borders or erecting a fortified barrier across Laos to the Mekong River, should be more seriously considered. These barriers, if properly maintained and enforced, could more successfully restrict the huge flow of supplies and manpower and possibly dry up the infrastructure's external source of support. These measures, however, seem costly and could contribute to a renewal and undesirable escalation of the war.

More significant than infiltration from the North is the availability of support to the enemy in the South. The locally recruited hamlet and village cadre who provide the necessary link between the hard-core leadership and masses are the backbone of the enemy infrastructure. It is through these middle-range cadre, who in many cases have their own political base, that the enemy is able to secure recruits and supplies to carry on the war.

How can the recruitment of young men in the hamlets and the collection of food and other supplies be curbed if not eliminated? How can the enemy's resources within South Vietnam be dried up? The answer lies partly in the full implementation of a comprehensive pacification program.

Pacification is an integrated military and civil process to restore, consolidate, and expand government control so that "nation-building" can succeed. It consists of coordinated military and civil actions to free the people from enemy control, restore public security, initiate political, social, and economic development, extend effective government authority, and win the support of the people, even many within the enemy's infrastructure. It is a comprehensive, balanced, and integrated approach to provide security and to transform South Vietnam into a free, viable, and enduring society. It recognizes that neither the military war nor the "other war" by itself is adequate. In concept, it ties together all sides of the struggle—military, political, economic, and social. As a result, the marginal man (middle cadre) of the infrastructure becomes the most significant target.

In most of South Vietnam, the heart of the problem is providing security. Many hamlets have been under enemy control for as long as twenty years. Clearing the area of main-force enemy units, rooting out the infrastructure, and transforming the political loyalties of the people cannot be achieved overnight. Past crash programs have not been realistic. For instance, in the first part of 1967 it was announced that the Khan Van hamlet, just miles from Saigon, had been "pacified" again—for the *fifth* time.

Unfortunately, the pacification programs have always been under constant pressure from Saigon and Washington to show results. This pressure often corrupted the reporting process and thus resulted in overplayed success stories and false optimism. The current pacification program has been plagued from the beginning by the lack of expertise in leadership and the recruitment of incompetent workers. Many of the teams which are sent into the hamlets to live with the people for six months or longer for purposes of pacification have been more of a drain on the economy and manpower pool than an asset to pacification. Some have deserted en masse. Others, however, have been effective where adequate security has been maintained.

The slow and disappointing beginning of the present program and its recent setback during the Tet offensive does not mean there is a need for a new program. Rather, it needs to be perfected, specifically, by being more adaptable to the requirements of each hamlet and to the nation as a whole. Moreover, since pacification is basic to national policy, both the Vietnamese effort and that of their American advisors must be more thoroughly integrated, and the themes of pacification should be a rallying point for military and civil effort.

Conclusions

The war in Vietnam is frustrating to most Americans who have served there because of its complexity, protraction, and current stalemate. Frustration also stems from the failure of not knowing what to do next. Withdrawal is virtually impossible, even if desirable, and continued military escalation will have little impact on the infrastructure unless it leads to the kind of massive destruction most Americans consider unthinkable.

The newly elected government and its allies must focus more on the challenge of drying up the enemy infrastructure. The current military situation is perhaps meaningful if the positive trends toward constitutional government and economic progress can continue; however, these trends are not assured unless the power of the infrastructure is substantially reduced.

Guns or plowshares? Military civic action

Robert H. Slover

In this essay Colonel Slover shows how the military, as the best organized group in many societies, can perform nonmilitary economic and social roles in building and stabilizing a country. Assuming an initial build-up of security necessary for the change from military to civic action, successful experiences in South Korea and the Philippines offer a blueprint for similar operations in Vietnam.

Professor Slover is associate professor of political science at Brigham Young University and was a pioneer in the field of civic action as a colonel in civil affairs and military government in the U.S. Army. This is the first publication of this article.

Poverty, hunger, and disease are the way of life for millions of people in countries around the world. The causes for this are many and varied but can roughly be categorized as stemming from economic underdevelopment, social inequities, exploitation, and political instability. Under such conditions, subversion and insurgency are inevitably at or near the surface, so that the country often becomes engaged in a struggle between the two major ideologies of the world—communism and democracy.

In any phase of such a struggle, the desires of the people must be a major consideration. Thus, the issue becomes one of winning the support of the people. This is a role which can be played by the military elements of a country. This new role was expressed by President John F. Kennedy in a statement he made to the diplomatic corps of the Latin American nations. He told these dignitaries, "The new generation of military leaders has shown an increasing awareness that armies cannot only defend their countries—they can help build them."

Military capabilities required to perform the normal military missions include such specialist talents as health and medicine, sanitation, public works and engineering, transportation, safety, communications, administration, and education. Military agencies or selected personnel from the armed forces are in a position to offer material and constructive assistance toward a country's development in each of these fields. In many instances, the training of the armed forces has objectives closely paralleling their civilian counterparts, and the equipment used is the same type. With organization, training, and modernization, the soldier and his military unit become stabilizing forces in developing societies.

One of the U.S. Air Force officers who has been instrumental in encouraging developing countries to use their military forces for nation building has summarized their role as follows:

> In some of the 40 countries the U.S. gives military assistance to, the armed forces are the only government organization within the nation which is organized on a national scale, which is readily identifiable with the government, which is disciplined and thus responsive to central authority, and which is able to communicate quickly with all of its elements throughout the country. It is within the armed forces that leadership is generated and from which demands in time of crisis are made for national duties far beyond the conventional military interests.

The objective, then, is to make full and effective use of the military forces of a nation. Their training must include the best methods of employing the principles of military-civil relations to ensure the voluntary support and cooperation of the people. The action of the military can become a program to assist the people to improve their living standards and realize their economic and social aspirations. Such a military program, which utilizes the capabilities and resources of the military force to help alleviate want, poverty, and suffering and to improve the economic base of a nation, has been termed *military civic action.* Civic action has become a technique for welding together an effective military-civilian team that counters insurgency in its many forms.

Military civic action is a many sided program ranging from the proper actions and attitudes of the individual soldier toward the people to the performance of projects by military units. From past and current experience, certain basic principles underlying successful military civic action have been formulated. These are as follows:

1. Military civic action is essentially a host country program. The United States gives assistance, but the major effort must come from and be desired by the government and the armed forces of the country itself.
2. In putting its many professional skills to use in helping the people to better their living conditions, the military forces should work with the people, not just for them.

3. By working side by side with the military on civic action projects, the people not only develop better relations with their armed forces but also learn that the military can contribute to economic and social development.

4. Because the maximum benefits are obtained when the people participate, the projects must be ones they desire. Small, immediate-impact, short-term-completion projects have a high priority. Projects must be aimed directly at the people, for it is essential not only that the various projects address themselves to the people's needs, but also that the people are willing to participate in these projects. For example, concrete and adobe blocks are used for construction in many developing countries. A hand-operated machine into which is shoveled a mixture of sand, gravel, cement, and water will turn out pressed blocks which, when dried in the sun, provide the building blocks for many useful buildings. The machine needs no operating fuel, no spare parts, is not subject to costly upkeep, and can be operated on the project by the people or the military unit. A regiment in Guatemala using such a hand-operated machine saw the cement blocks they made rise into a school for the children of a depressed area. This contribution incorporated the work of the local community, the central government, and the military forces.

In Korea we have been able to realize the potential of the military structure as a force for economic and social development and for bringing stability to a country in need of help. That story is the story of AFAK, the Armed Forces Assistance to Korea Program.

In 1953, shortly after the cease-fire agreement in Korea, General Maxwell D. Taylor—then commander of all the forces defending the Republic of Korea—proposed that approximately $15 million worth of U.S. construction materials in Korea, not then required for the original combat projects, should be utilized by U.S. forces personnel in helping to rebuild, at least on a small scale, the war-ravaged nation.

This was the formal beginning of the AFAK Program—a U.S.-sponsored effort aimed at helping the proud citizens of a courageous nation help themselves. As one of the Eighth U.S. Army publications stated, "It is the rebuilding of a country, the rehabilitation of its people; it is American personnel extending the hand of friendship to their Korean allies." Never before has there been, on so large a scale and in so short a time, such a beating of swords into plowshares. Military units sponsored and helped with such projects as school buildings, hospitals, roads, churches, orphanages, and other programs needed throughout the country.

Although the AFAK Program was sponsored by U.S. forces, they set an example and encouraged the Korean military forces to adopt this kind of program to help their own people. Moreover, the techniques learned in Korea have been used to spread the civic action program around the world.

The great success of AFAK has been due to several factors. The need for cooperative assistance was very real and very great in Korea. U.S. forces had a large concentration of highly skilled personnel in the theatre and a relatively large stock of supplies and equipment. And above all, the program had the encouragement and support of the commanders in the field as well as government agencies in Washington and Seoul. It has been well coordinated and well directed, has served a distinctly worthwhile purpose, and has exemplified the possibilities of using military resources to assist in the social-economic field without detriment to the military mission.

This same approach has been adopted by the government in the Philippines, where the military forces have been effective in the establishment of law and order, civic leadership, local improvements, and development of virgin areas by resettlement.

The story of the anti-Huk campaign in the Philippines becomes increasingly important as tactics are developed for countering insurgency. The reason for the rise of the Huks (Communist insurrectionists) was instability in the country, which was just getting back on its feet after World War II.

Arms were available, and the Communists felt they had enough popular support to overthrow the government by defeating its constabulary and army. They almost did. The Philippine Army was most puzzled as to why they could not find or destroy the 15,000 armed insurgents.

Thousands of poor Filipinos supported, hid, and informed the Communist Huks. Why had these Filipinos turned against their own government? Their government, represented by unscrupulous politicians and a military indifferent to their needs, had turned against them. Absentee landlords preyed on them, elections were dishonest, prices were exorbitant, and living standards were low. The Huks urged the people in the barrios (villages) to pick up weapons and change the government by force. Thus, the rural communities came more and more under Huk control because of the general popular discontent.

The late Ramon Magsaysay then stepped into the picture, first as Secretary of Defense and then as President. He took a look at the conventional, frequently terrifying operations of his military and other governmental agencies and found the common people were as afraid of his own forces as they were of the Huks.

President Magsaysay, a barrio man himself, knew that the Tao (Filipino common man) wanted help in agricultural pursuits, medical assistance, education, and some improvement in basic public works. He convinced the Tao that he would help them. He told them he would retrain his military forces to help and protect the common man. In turn, he asked that the Tao stop supporting the Huks and getting information for them.

Under President Magsaysay's concept the military soon became a favorable symbol of the Philippine government and undertook a wide range of social operations. First they helped the people by protecting them so they could work. Then the military went into community development, care for the sick, school construction, resettlement of Huk sympathizers on land in government holdings. They helped with roads; troop behavior at checkpoints and on patrol was improved. Poor farmers were given legal assistance in the land courts in tenancy cases. By word and deed, President Magsaysay demonstrated to the Tao that it was in their best interests to support the government—not the Communist insurrectionists. As he put it, the armed forces offered the Huks and their sympathizers the hand of all-out force or all-out friendship. The army called this effort civic action.

One major civic endeavor of the armed forces of the Philippines was the Economic Development Corps (EDCOR). It was initiated in 1950 to rehabilitate Huk prisoners held by the army but grew in scope in subsequent years. Four farm communities were constructed, a vocational rehabilitation center established, and one complete village moved and re-established in a more favorable area. Farm communities were formed from selected Huk prisoners, volunteer retired military personnel, and civilian applicants. In establishing farm communities, the army moved small units to the area (12 officers and 91 enlisted men) to build dirt roads, establish security, and construct temporary housing to receive the settlers upon arrival. Troops and settlers then worked together to clear the jungle for farming and to construct housing, community centers, schools, chapels, dispensaries, sawmills, wells, markets, and sanitary facilities. The army arranged for settlers to earn title to the land. The EDCOR administration soon reported healthy progress in making these farm communities independent and in collecting debts from the settlers.

An analysis of the Philippine civic action program was given at a SEATO meeting in November 1957 by Jesus Vargas, then Secretary of Defense. Secretary Vargas said:

> In this psychological action, the men in uniform themselves were not spared. The Armed Forces were fully reformed, with their members disciplined, in high morale and reoriented to a virtually new and ideal type of soldier. We re-indoctrinated every individual soldier in his constitutional role as a public servant and protector of the people and not his master or superior. We taught him how to be gallant and helpful to the civilians, especially to the needy who are more susceptible to the forces of communism. Before we sent him to the field where he would surely come in contact with civilians, we made sure he had been properly oriented in his new role. The results were amazing. It became no exception to see soldiers actually doubling as sanitary inspectors, arbitrators of family disputes and other trouble, and doing other odd jobs which, coupled with sheer efficiency in performance, brought them closest to the hearts of their people. When peasants, convinced of the adequate and continuing protection of the military, returned to their farms, soldiers actually helped in reclaiming their lands from thick forest vegetation which by that time had already covered the area. Thus, the spectacle hitherto unseen in all Asia. Against the wiles and false promises of communism, the results became evident.

Perhaps the most vital area where the military civic action program is now being tested is in South Vietnam—both by the Vietnamese and the U.S. forces. It is a basic element of the pacification and counterinsurgency program, termed the Revolutionary Development Program. There are many examples and incidents of the program to draw on, some successful, others less successful, but all designed to win the people to the side of the government and to defeat the Viet Cong.

One example of a basic military civic action project is Operation LANIKAI, put into effect by a unit of the 25th U.S. Infantry Division. This was a three-pronged operation designed to free the village of Rach Kien in the province of Long An from the Viet Cong, re-establish government control, and help improve the villagers' living conditions.

Rach Kien had once been a prosperous market town of over 4,000 people, but the Viet Cong had taken it over, destroyed many of the facilities, taken the harvested crops, and, through force and terrorist tactics, reduced the village to less than 400 people. The U.S. 25th Infantry Division soldiers moved into the village area in force and set up a base perimeter around the town and a rigid line of defense farther out. Numerous times the Vietnamese and U.S. forces had to fight the Viet Cong, who were attempting to re-enter the village, but the village defenses held.

The first task for the civil affairs section of the division was that of relocating displaced persons, controlling population movement, and caring for refugees. As a part of the operation, the province chief sent in a 110-man team of Vietnamese composed of refugee specialists, information officials, health and welfare specialists, and national police. By working together, these groups secured the village area, re-established government control, and started rehabilitation. The civic action program expanded from one designed to give emergency care to an operation capable of improving the health, education, and economy of the entire community.

The aid station operated by the 25th Division doctors and medics treated nearly 200 people a week and arranged for medical evacuation for patients requiring better equipped hospitals. Sanitary conditions were improved, a water tank was provided for potable water, the schoolhouse was repaired, and the troops built and painted desks, built new blackboards, and procured school supplies and playground equipment. The Engineer Battalion moved in and reopened the roads leading northward to profitable trade centers and rebuilt the marketplace facilities.

Property, security, and government control once again slowly returned to the village of Rach Kien. This process must be repeated hundreds of times in many villages and hamlets in Vietnam if the second war is to be won. Military civic action will have its place in each operation.

President Lyndon Johnson, recognizing the civic action role of the military forces, told Congress in his message on the Foreign Aid Program for the five year period beginning in 1966, "We shall give new stress to civic action programs through which local troops build schools and roads, and provide literary training and health services. Through these programs, military personnel are able to play a more constructive role in their security, and to establish better relations with the civilian population."

Chapter Four

The struggle for international order

In the struggle for security, men have traditionally organized themselves under a government based on laws and possessing the means to enforce those laws. Men have seen fit to expand this system only to the nation-state level. Beyond that, on the international level, there is no effective law, only power and inconsistent influence battling confusion and anarchy.

As the article by Rich and Platt in Chapter Three has shown, resistance to international government is due principally to two factors: the sovereignty of states and the fear that world organization will fail to bring security—security of ideology as well as cultural, military, and economic security. Such security is felt to exist under nationalism.

Nationalism's roots include common language and literature, common ethnic and cultural background, folk heroes and historical myth, geographic unity, and a common ideology. The difficulties of a South Vietnam, an India, or an Indonesia in building a unified nation involve overcoming tremendous diversities. The building of a world-state would mean a huge multiplying of these problems. The language riots in India and the religious disputes in South Vietnam would be multiplied a hundredfold. Many of the new states are only now realizing national independence, and it is unlikely that they would be willing or able to step beyond this long sought after goal—despite its many failings. The world is not ready to understand the notion of Barbara Ward, the British economist, that the Earth is a spaceship hurtling precariously through space and in need of cooperation and development for survival.

There are advocates for attaining security through cooperation and rudimentary law. The World Peace through World Law movement sees peace as coming only through commonly accepted law, but such law requires both legislating and enforcing agencies to make it effective. As Chief Justice Warren's speech to that organization makes clear, current international law is self-proclaimed and nearly self-enforcing and exists primarily in the form of treaties.

Treaties, unlike domestic laws, are not easily amendable by either judicial or executive interpretation or by legislative act; there is only the tedious process of nation by nation ratification. Arnold Toynbee, never a friend of nationalism, pins part of the blame for the inability to achieve world government on this Western-developed ideology. Law and government, he argues, cannot exist apart from each other.

Despite their many shortcomings, the United Nations and its various affiliated organizations are the only form of world government we have. Will it be able to fulfill its original, rather idealistic goals of world peace and security? U Thant, in his summary of the U.N.'s first twenty years, urges some better system than the "unsteady balance of nationalistic power and aspiration" as at present under the nation-state system. The United Nations has been much more successful in promoting cooperation in areas of mutual benefit (health, communications, and so on) than it has been in keeping peace where the mutuality was not of benefit but of hostility. Most programs seeking peace and security through order have too often been disrupted and stifled by war—both in terms of the destruction itself and in terms of the priority of war in the allocation of national resources.

The nature of the U.N. peace-keeping effort is discussed by Cox and its failure to keep the peace by Hudson, who includes a brief suggestion on reform. Niebuhr rejects this reform because of its failure to compensate for national sovereignty and power.

The United Nations' peace-keeping problems stem primarily from what Morgenthau refers to as its "constitutional" weakness. It has the appearance of a parliament and debates as a parliament, but it cannot act as a parliament. It has over 120 members and each casts one vote in the General Assembly. The two superpowers, as Toynbee notes, have only one-sixtieth of the total vote, which is obviously a constitutional weakness; states with 90 percent of the world's power will yield only reluctantly or not at all to the rest of the world if it is against their national interests, particularly if they are vital interests. The Soviet Union cannot be forced to pay peace-keeping dues, and even Rhodesia and Israel are capable of resisting the "will" of the United Nations. A solution to the problem of better balance based on power is suggested in the Whitaker article, with suitable comment on the problem in a column by Hoppe.

The problems that these differences in national power present to international order exist on the regional level, too. Similar problems also exist on this level in terms of the need for law and organization contrasted with the built-in opposition of nationalism and sovereignty. The need for security beyond the nation-state also exists on the regional level. And, again, this security is not only military security but also economic and political security. The article by Rostow traces the rationale for the development of regionalism as a new kind of economic world order.

The cold war in the fifties created a climate in which military security took precedence over this economic type of security. Under the direction and with the financial support of the United States, a string of defense pacts spread from Latin America and the Western Hemisphere to Europe and from there to East Asia via the Middle East and Southeast Asia. All of these pacts were anti-Communist, and an "aggressive" Soviet Union, Red China, or both were the principal targets. None of these pacts has been utilized in open hostilities, and SEATO, despite the Vietnam situation, has been conspicuously absent from the scene in Southeast Asia.

NATO has been the most viable collective defense organization. A debate between the United States and the USSR over NATO shows that the United States views it as an organization for peace, while Russia calls it the prime threat to European security. So great is Soviet fear of NATO and particularly of a rearmed West Germany that Soviets have established the economic and military counterforce of the Warsaw Pact, which is analyzed by Wolfe.

The "model" for cooperative regional organization has been the European Economic Community (Common Market). Many anticipated the gradual development of a supranational organization in which European interests would gradually take precedence over national interests. Despite its economic and technical successes, as Aron argues, the Common Market has failed as a political unit. Its two strongest members disagree strongly on security matters and are unwilling to yield in questions of political decision-making to any organization superior to their respective national governments.

Other regions of the world seem to desire mutual economic cooperation similar to the Common Market. If the desire to exercise power and sovereignty solely on the national level can be overcome, the political failure of the European Economic Community may provide valuable lessons and aid the success of these attempts. Bradbury discusses the prospects for such a "market" in Latin America. The Arab attempt to establish an even broader regional unity is analyzed by Kelidar. Another significant regional organization working toward unity of the economic type is the Organization of African Unity. An article is found in the recommended readings at the conclusion of this book.

Most of the order that exists in the world, as we have indicated, exists because of unilateral acts on the part of nation-states, especially treaties. Such treaties again focus on the conflicting forces of power and order. We want to concentrate on those agreements that seek order, particularly those that are nonmilitary in nature.

It has been argued that the development of greater interdependence in trade constitutes a major step toward peace. Pearson is a strong supporter of trade liberalization. To many people, this means ignoring the cold war barriers to trade. Boycotts and expansion of trade are both advocated in the name of security and other national interests. The boycotters generally argue that trade expansion will release resources that will then be utilized to attack the "free nations." The contrary argument is that increased trade is mutually beneficial and encourages the development of peaceful appetites (such as the desire for consumer goods) and peaceful industry. It is further argued that trade with satellite nations helps remove their over-reliance on the Soviet Union and might also lead gradually to greater political independence—perhaps even to a moderation of ideology. Ball discusses the merits of these arguments, generally supporting the expansion of nonstrategic trade.

International investment is closely related to trade. The economic security of many states depends largely on the influx of capital from abroad. Control of this investment is a crucial problem for both the investor and the receiving state. In a debate over this problem, Ball and French disagree over the motivation and the effect of international investment; the latter suggests a kind of exploitation by the United States.

Related to international investment is international cooperation in the development of "non-national" resources. There has been international cooperation in scientific exploration of the Antarctic regions, of the seas, and, increasingly, of space. This cooperation has had some implications for national interests but has progressed despite this because of the nonvital nature of the subject matter. The seas have come increasingly under scrutiny as a possible resource in the battle to feed and support the expanding human population. Humphrey and Clift cite examples of the value of international cooperation in the development of the seas.

Much of the orderly development and stability evident in the newer states is due to various assistance programs. American aid following World War II enabled Europe to feel secure again—even in relation to the supplier of this aid. Since then aid has become institutionalized as part of the program of international order. Money grants, project development, technical assistance, credit grants, and long-term and short-term loans are only a few of its many and varied forms. This aid has been practiced bilaterally, multilaterally, and also through international organization.

However, the entire international aid program is being reviewed by both the donors and the recipients. The article by Nehru expresses his concern over the entire philosophy of assistance. The Tun article illustrates the new thinking of many people in the developing areas that this development involves more than the rich giving to the poor. It requires the cooperation and encouragement of those nations. The developing nations resent being encouraged through aid to develop and then discouraged through trade barriers and restrictions from continuing that development. Since 1964 the smaller nations have expressed this concern in the United Nations Conference on Trade and Development (UNCTAD). From March to June 1964, over 2,000 delegates from 119 nations met in the largest intergovernmental conference ever held. According to Richard Gardner, it presented a North-South, or developed-underdeveloped, split rather than one drawn on customary East-West cold war lines. This conference led to the establishment of a permanent organization with headquarters in Geneva, where numerous committees and subcommittees work on the problems of trade and development. UNCTAD has become a major focal point for the discussion of economic problems of particular interest to the less developed countries.

The major donor, the United States, is undergoing a sharp and critical review of its foreign aid policy. The 1968 Congress authorized the lowest figures for aid in the program's twenty year history. The debate over this cutback is presented here by Hare and Passman, who represent the administration and congressional views, respectively. Sigel evaluates his experience with the Peace Corps, a new and significant variety of technical assistance.

Most Americans have assumed that their country is single-handedly supporting world aid programs. This is not the case; even many former recipients of U.S. aid, including Japan, West Germany, France, and Great Britain, now have their own aid programs in the form of grants, credits, and loans. Not too surprisingly, the Soviet Union also sees her national interests served in her aid program, which is described by Goldman. More surprising is the possibility presented by Mondale of the poor nations providing aid—aid which they can ill afford to give—to the rich nations.

The struggle for security is always the basis of national activity. The problems of the orderly achievement of that security through law, organization, trade, investment, cooperation, and various forms of aid appear so complex and overwhelming at times that resorting to the much simpler use of power is a common occurrence. The question of which of these conflicting means will be able to bring more enduring peace and security to the "spaceship Earth" still remains unanswered.

Section 1

World peace through law and government

Peace with justice

Earl Warren

Two basic questions are raised by Chief Justice Warren: (1) What is the role of law in bringing world peace, and (2) does world law require the yielding of national sovereignty? His answer is that world law is a prerequisite to peace and actually enhances national sovereignty.

Vital Speeches of the Day, *August 15, 1967. Address before the Geneva Conference on World Peace through Law, First World Assembly of World Association of Judges, Geneva, Switzerland, July 10, 1967. Mr. Warren is Chief Justice of the United States Supreme Court.*

It is indeed wonderful to be here with so many old friends and to meet so many for the first time who we henceforth shall claim as friends. We greet all of you as co-workers in the cause of peace with justice, peace under the rule of law. Peace which after all is in the ultimate a system of order and security under just law.

I especially greet most warmly my fellow judges from all over the world. I look forward with much pleasure to participating with you in our first meeting as a World Association of Judges.

In this shrunken world where all men are now neighbors, we judges must decide more and more cases involving transnational facts and law, many of you lawyers have clients who trade or travel in many countries, those of you who are professors of law have expanded your teaching to encompass the growing volume of international law, and you law students will live and practice with the world community as your area of effort and interest. All segments of our great profession are thus involved, deeply involved, in the vast changes in the world which are rapidly affecting the field of law. We of the law have expanded our horizons world-wide. We have embraced new ideas, new concepts and new techniques such as the computer. Our times present for the law profession the greatest challenge and the greatest opportunity in the history of mankind.

We do indeed meet at a time of enormous change and at a time of some unfortunate turmoil. Change and turmoil growing in part out of landmark scientific and technological achievements. Achievements which have split the atom, enabled man to traverse outer space and which will soon allow us to place a man on the moon. Change and turmoil caused in part by the shrinking of time and distance and the ever growing closer relationships and interdependence of all mankind. Change and turmoil exemplified by the restlessness on college campuses and among peoples world-wide who are deprived of social and economic benefits which should redound to all men from the scientific and technological advances of our day. Change and turmoil which require that man develop ways and means whereby all can share equally in a better life. Ways and means whereby men can live together in peace and avoid almost certain extinction if the holocaust of nuclear war explodes.

Against humankind's great accomplishments and the changes thereby wrought we must recognize that some of our current turmoil is caused by mankind's failure to develop adequate ways and means to avoid international conflict or to channel that conflict into institutions for peaceful resolution. This failure is the greatest gap in the peace structure of the world community. Law is the substance out of which man has most successfully fashioned ways and means to avoid or peacefully resolve conflict. We of the law must accept a large measure of the responsibility for this failure, this gap in the world's peace structure.

As we meet here to face our tremendously important responsibility, let me remind that each of us are here as individuals to express personal views only. We are not here as representatives of the governments of the countries from which we come. We are not here to espouse or defend the policies of our governments. We are not here to argue for or against the conflicts or troubles of our own or other governments. In fact, our Conference rules prohibit this.

In this connection let me remind also that we come from nearly all nations.

We live under many different systems of government. We speak many different languages. We adhere to many different customs, religions and beliefs. But we of the legal profession hold in common a belief in and respect for the concepts of the rule of law which provides us a common foundation upon which to carry out our joint endeavors to forward our great objective of a peaceful world community which provides justice for all men and all nations.

To stand here in this great Hall brings to mind the great men who have spoken for peace from this rostrum. By inaugurating our joint endeavors in this Hall we both honor these renowned workers for peace and recall that it is their efforts which should enable our generation to achieve that peaceful world which mankind has sought in vain since the beginnings of civilization.

Just to recall the memories of these leaders of the past should inspire us to extraordinary efforts in our week's work for peace that is here begun.

We are beyond the beginning of the beginning of our work together for peace. Our organized cooperative labors are now four years old. In the four years since the Center was born in ancient Athens we have assembled manpower and world-wide knowledge of existing law to an extent never before accomplished. We have contacted, met with, and organized the leaders in the field of law in 121 nations for world-wide cooperative endeavors. We have developed an action program which embodies the ideas of the legal profession world-wide.

We have constantly set forth our great ideal that world order under the rule of law is the best and only proven route to world peace. That law is the only workable substance with which to build a peace structure for the world. We must now move from enunciating a great ideal to its specific implementation. . . . As we do this, let us ask ourselves what is the most important need to accomplish our mission. Obviously, it is to create more and more effective transnational law, more courts and similar institutions for the rendering of peaceful decisions under the rule of law. Those who seek to further world-wide cooperation, to spread social, economic and technological advances among all the world's peoples, those who seek to avoid conflict and collision by controlling threats to peace, usually urge that law is the tool whereby these things can be accomplished. Internationally, this chiefly means treaties.

History teaches that international law works well when universally accepted and thus universally adhered to. Witness the Law of Diplomatic Immunity, the Law of the Sea and the Postal Convention as irrefutable proof. To have a world ruled by law we need more treaties of universal acceptance. We need hundreds and perhaps thousands of new or updated treaties to govern and guide the ever-growing number of contacts and relations between man and man and government and government.

Since law internationally grows through voluntary acceptance by more and more nations of more and more treaties, a major need is a new mechanism which is capable of encouraging more and more nations to accept more and more international treaties.

The UN is justly praised for having generated and updated more transnational law in the past 20 years than in all of man's past history. I salute the members of the International Law Commission who are our guests here today for their magnificent contributions to the UN's law building record. The UN now stands sponsor for some 400 treaties, conventions, agreements and protocols. Yet the UN lacks an effective machinery for persuading nations to adhere to or accept its magnificent effort in the field of law.

The UN is not a law-making body. The UN and its specialized agencies draft treaties and then depend upon voluntary acceptance of their work to make this new proposed law or proposed updated law effective. Sometimes many nations accept. Sometimes very few nations accept.

Against this picture I offer a concrete proposal. My proposal consists of a practical plan by which we can help speed up and expand the law-making process internationally. I suggest that this Center create in each nation a group composed of members of the Center whose duty it will be to fill a current void in the transnational law-making process. This new group should review constantly their nation's adherence to UN treaties and study whether there are any UN treaties which its nation has not accepted but should accept to further its own vital interests. We would thus provide an impetus to action which is now lacking.

I recognize that in the vast array of UN treaties there are treaties which are inapplicable or inappropriate to particular nations. No nation can or should adhere to all 400. Some of these treaties are outmoded and need to be adapted to changed world conditions. But there are many such treaties which many nations can further their own interests by accepting. This they simply have not done either through inertia or from lack of information.

The UN bases its treaties upon world-wide knowledge and experience. UN treaties are therefore worthy of great respect and acceptance. I do not say they are perfect and remind that perfection is the utopia we in law always seek, but know in our hearts we will never quite achieve. It is good that the quest for perfection exists but its achievability must spur us on rather than discourage or deter us.

Perhaps in time the new law-making mechanism urged here as a step toward more peace through more law, can utilize the expertise of its members to draft perfecting amendments to UN treaties and draft model treaties which, after approval by the Center, it can urge upon the UN and nations.

Let me express another idea which I feel impelled to set forth as part and parcel of the program I have just proposed. When nations accept a treaty they do not give up their sovereignty. They in fact use it to acquire something of value to their people. One brake on law growth internationally is the false claim that a nation which accepts a treaty thereby gives up a part of its sovereignty. Let me again instance the Postal Convention. By adhering to that Convention, a nation secures a right for its people to send letters into some 132 nations and to receive letters from 132 nations. Absent such adherence, no such right exists. By adhering to the Law of Diplomatic Immunity, a nation secures reciprocal protection for its own diplomats. You and I could give many more such illustrations of benefits secured by nations who become parties to treaties.

Take a look at each of the 400 UN treaties I have had compiled to back up my proposal here. You have each received a copy of this compilation as you registered. Ask yourself what would the people of your nation gain or lose by accepting each treaty your nation does not now adhere to. Perhaps you can get this law-building mechanism underway yourself by using that as your yardstick and filing a personal report with the proper officials of your nation urging acceptance of some and rejection of others. There is nothing wrong with advancing the self-interest of the people of each nation through such law acceptance or rejection. That is why governments exist. But self-interests of peoples in our shrinking, interlocked, interdependent world are more and more identical regardless of the nation in which we live.

Every person has a personal stake in replacing a world ruled by force with a world ruled by law. In today's interlocked world peace is indivisible. Law building internationally is a program in which all nations can participate equally. All are therefore equally responsible for achievement of world peace through a world ruled by law. No nation can stand alone in today's interdependent world. We of the Americas are dependent upon you from Asia, Africa and Europe to help build peace. Either we work together in building a world peace structure or that structure cannot be created.

Let us replace our 24-hour military watch upon each other with a constant watch upon the law we each have. Instead of matching each other soldier for soldier, plane for plane, bomb for bomb and missile for missile, let us create a new kind of competition, a new kind of rivalry, let us match each other law for law—treaty for treaty—until all contacts and relationships in the world community are covered with law. Law which prevents disputes or law which channels disputes into law institutions for peaceful decision. Let us concentrate on creation of so much law that controls so much of mankind's interdependent, transnational contacts that disputes large enough to cause war will be guided into courthouses and away from battlefields. Thus can we render war obsolete in the "law-full" world we must have if humankind is to survive the power nations now possess.

I again remind that when used and widely accepted law works. For the good of mankind, for the good of each of us, and for the good of the billions of people who yearn for world peace with justice, let us here and now begin the greatest international law generating program man has ever known. Let us create a pride in each nation of the status of their law rather than the status of their armed might. No man, woman or child will ever lose a life or limb from a worldwide law improvement or expansion competition among nations. The human race would be the great winner of a law race.

A world law system is the imperative of our day. No group has a greater opportunity or a greater responsibility to help achieve a lasting peace than we of the law. Peace with justice is the greatest desire of the whole of humanity. We have the knowledge, the manpower and the organization to help bring this great goal into being. Let us seize our opportunity and get on with our responsibility. In such a law-creating task we will have the overwhelming—the universal—backing of all mankind.

Peace, empire, and world government

Arnold Toynbee

Professor Toynbee's answer to national sovereignty is its elimination in favor of world government. The existence of atomic weapons and of two superpowers among 123 lesser powers makes the need for world government all the more pressing if world security is to be achieved.

From Professor Toynbee's introduction to the book Major Peace Treaties of Modern History, 1648–1966, *edited by Fred L. Israel and published by Chelsea House Publishers in association with McGraw-Hill. © 1967. Reprinted by permission. Mr. Toynbee is a famed historian and the author of* A Study of History *and many other works.*

Today most people in the world are inclined to take the prevailing political dispensation for granted. It is assumed that the present partition of mankind among a number of local sovereign states that can, and do, go to war with each other is the natural order of human affairs at the political level. Yet this is not the only way in which mankind has organized itself politically since the rise of civilization about 5,000 years ago. For instance, in 800 A.D. the whole of the Western world, within its limits at that date, was united politically under the single sovereignty of Charlemagne, except for a few small states in Britain and in Northwestern Spain. And when, on Christmas Day, 800, Charlemagne assumed the title of Roman Emperor, he was deliberately reviving in the West a Roman world-state which, for more than four centuries ending about 400 A.D., had united politically the greater part of Western Europe with a ring of territories surrounding the Mediterranean basin.

In the West, these spells of political unity have been relatively short-lived. Charlemagne's unitary Western Empire did not outlast Charlemagne's own lifetime, and the Roman Empire's previous duration of four centuries in the West was short compared with its duration in the Levant, where, with its capital transplanted to Constantinople, it continued to have an effective existence till the turn of the twelfth and thirteenth centuries. The East Roman Empire's duration, again, was short compared with that of the Ancient Egyptian Empire and the Chinese Empire. The Ancient Egyptian Empire had been in existence, off and on, for about 3,000 years by the year 31 B.C., when it was absorbed into the Roman Empire. The Chinese Empire is still a going concern, and, as 1967 began it had been in existence, off and on, for 2,188 years.

These past attempts at the establishment of a world-state have had only a limited success. None of them has been either world-wide or permanent. Still, they have given peace to millions of human beings for numbers of centuries, and today their history is of more than academic interest now that the present partition of the world into a host of local sovereign states has been overtaken by the invention of the atomic weapon.

In the history of the current international system the price of local sovereignty has been a series of wars of increasing violence, culminating in the dropping of the two atomic bombs on Japan in 1945. It may be that the only alternative to self-destruction now is the establishment of some form of world government—this time on the literally world-wide scale that was never achieved by any of the would-be world-empires of the past. In the Atomic Age this cannot be achieved by conquest, for an atomic war would end, not in victory and defeat, but in mutual annihilation. In the Atomic Age world government can be established, if at all, only by mutual consent. The major political problem of our time is how we are to arrive at world government from mankind's present plight of being partitioned among about 125 local states. One essential preliminary to the solution of this formidable problem is to understand the nature and the history of the current system of international relations.

The current system of international relations orginated, on a small scale, among the medieval city-states of Northern Italy. It was extended to Transalpine Europe when the French invaded Italy in 1494. In the ensuing first bout of international warfare in the modern age of Western history, a pattern was set which had been anticipated in medieval Italy and which has been repeated, on a constantly widening geographical scale, through the time of the Second World War. Again and again, some single power has tried to unite, under its own domination, first Northern Italy, then Western and Central Europe, and finally the whole surface of the globe. In each case the power aiming at domination has been foiled.

In the first modern round of this repeatedly renewed conflict, the power that was aiming at domination was the Hapsburg dynasty, and the Hapsburgs were foiled by France. . . . France defeated the Hapsburgs' attempt to encircle and subdue it and the peace treaty of Westphalia (1648) marked the end of this attempt at empire-building.

The next round was started by the first of France's two attempts to win for itself the political supremacy in the Western world that it had prevented the Hapsburgs from winning. Each time, France was foiled in its turn; each time, by a coalition in which one power played a leading part. The moving spirit in the successful resistance to Louis XIV's attempt to unite the Western world under France's supremacy was Holland—a fragment of the Hapsburg dominions which had won its independence at the turn of the sixteenth and seventeenth centuries. . . .

France's second attempt at gaining supremacy in the Western world was made in the Revolutionary and Napoleonic wars at the turn of the nineteenth century. . . . Between them, British naval and economic power and Russia's vast spaces foiled Napoleonic France.

Until the overseas parts of the Western world grew to full stature, as they did in the post-Napoleonic age, France surpassed all other Western powers in agricultural wealth, population, and military manpower; but it was not these material resources alone that made it capable of becoming an effective unifying force in the Western world. The strongest card in France's hand, in both Louis XIV's and Napoleon's day, was the attractiveness of its culture. Peoples that resisted France's attempts to dominate them militarily and politically adopted French culture of their own accord, and indeed with enthusiasm; and the peoples that did temporarily fall under French rule or ascendancy continued to bear the impress of French culture after they had shaken off French rule. . . .

The Napoleonic regime was short-lived; yet the non-French parts of Napoleon's empire, as well as France itself, drew cultural and social profits from this regime by which they are still benefiting at the present day.

Until the invention and use of the atomic weapon at the end of the Second World War, it was assumed, as a matter of course, that it would have been a calamity if any of the powers that were successive aspirants to universal dominion had succeeded in achieving its aim, and accordingly the powers that were chiefly instrumental in foiling the aims of the ambitious empire-builders regarded themselves, and were regarded by their allies, as being benefactors of the Western society. France was given credit for having foiled the Hapsburgs; Holland and Britain were given it for having foiled France; and so were France, Britain, and the United States for having foiled Germany.

Looking back now, from the Atomic Age to the "modern" chapter of

Western history which was brought to an end by the two twentieth-century world wars, we may well wonder whether, on a long view, it would not have been better for the West, and for the world as a whole, if Napoleon had succeeded in uniting Western and Central Europe permanently under his ascendancy. If he had united that much of the world permanently, he or his successors would assuredly have succeeded in adding the rest of the world to their empire sooner or later; the French Empire, like the Roman Empire before it, would eventually have won the hearts of the peoples whom it had originally incorporated in itself by force of arms, and then mankind would have been united more or less acquiescently under a literally world-wide world government before it had been overtaken by the Atomic Age. If history had taken this turn—and it might have taken it—should we not be sleeping more soundly today than we find ourselves able to sleep now that we are haunted by the nightmare of a possible atomic third world war?

When Napoleon was foiled the world lost its chance of being united politically before the close of the pre-Atomic Age. The next and last two attempts at conquering universal dominion before the invention of the atomic weapon were Germany's. . . . Like France before it, Germany twice came near to success in its attempt to impose its rule by conquest; but, unlike Napoleon's ephemeral empire, Germany's had no prospect of lasting, for Germany failed to bring to the peoples that it momentarily conquered any gifts of the kind that had gone far toward reconciling the Germans themselves, the Italians, Belgians, and Dutch to being incorporated in Napoleonic France. . . .

In 1967 there are only two great powers—the United States and the Soviet Union—and of these two only Russia had already been a great power before the round of world wars began. The United States did not assume the role of a great power before its intervention in the First World War, though it had a great enough population and economic potential to play the part, if it had chosen, since the date of the preservation of the Union through the defeat of the Confederacy in the Civil War of 1861–1865. . . .

Of all the former great powers, France had the longest run. In spite of suffering a number of reverses, it was a great power from 1494 to 1940. None of France's competitors has measured up to France's four and a half centuries of continuous military and political potency. The Danubian Hapsburg Monarchy had been a great power for a little less than four centuries by the time of its extinction in 1918. Great Britain was a great power for about two and a half centuries, reckoning from the War of the Spanish Succession to the Second World War inclusive. Russia, which is still a great power, became one at about the same time as Great Britain. Prussia had been one for about 200 years by the time of its extinction in 1945. Holland's and Sweden's careers as great powers were only about a hundred years long. . . . Japan had been a great power for less than half a century when it lost that status in 1945. The United States has been playing the part of a great power for only half a century now.

Today it seems unlikely that any of the surviving ex-great powers will ever recover great-power status. At the same time the United States and the Soviet Union cannot count on continuing for an indefinite time to be the only two great powers on the face of the globe. . . . It is possible, though of course not certain, that in the early Atomic Age China is going to take its place side by side with the Soviet Union and the United States as one of the world's great powers.

These repeated changes in the membership of the ring of great powers have been one of the features of the modern system of international relations. Another feature of it has been the constant expansion of the geographical arena in which the power game has been played. In the Middle Ages this arena was confined to Northern and Central Italy, with Venice and Florence exerting themselves successfully to hinder Milan's attempts to achieve a pan-Italian hegemony. At the turn of the fifteenth and sixteenth centuries, which marked the beginning of the Modern Age, the arena expanded geographically from Italy to include Transalpine Europe. The Italian city-states, which had previously been the great powers within their own relatively small field, now became the prizes of victory for Transalpine great powers of the nation-state scale that contended for them on battlefields in Lombardy and in Flanders.

The turn of the eighteenth century saw a further extension of the arena to include two non-Western powers, Russia and Turkey (though Turkey's admittance into the Western system of international relations was not recognized formally until the negotiation of the Paris peace settlement of 1856, after the Crimean War). The eighteenth century saw the arena expand still further—into North America in one direction and into India in the other. Finally, in the nineteenth century, the arena became world-wide. First Eastern Asia and then Tropical Africa and Southern Africa were drawn into it. The two world wars were truly world-wide. Each of them was fought not only in Europe but all over the world as well; almost all the sovereign states that were then in existence became belligerents in each war before it ended, and in each war the outcome was eventually decided by the intervention of the United States, which is a non-European power, though not, of course, a non-Western one.

By 1967 the whole surface and whole air-envelope of the globe had been knit together into a unity for purposes of warfare. By this date any point on the earth's surface can be hit more or less accurately by a missile shot from a launching pad at any other point. By this date, too, anything that happens in any part of man's habitat may be a matter of life and death for the rest of the world. For instance, the destinies of the whole world are now involved in the war in Vietnam and in the tension along the armistice lines in the Near East and Kashmir.

There have been a number of momentous changes in the international situation since the last days of the Second World War. The first of these changes has been the invention and use of the atomic weapon. This has been different in kind from any previous "improvements" in military technique, such as the invention of gunpowder. The invention of the atomic weapon has changed the nature of war itself. War has always been wicked and destructive but, before 1945 . . . [it was not a threat] to the survival of the human race as a whole.

Since 1945, on the other hand, the cost of war, if escalated to the atomic level, has become prohibitive. It seems probable that, in a war fought with atomic weapons, there will be no victor. . . . The invention of the atomic weapon made it evident that war could no longer be used effectively as an instrument of policy. In particular, it became evident that, in the Atomic Age, the world could not be united politically by military force. In the pre-Atomic Age of Western history, each successive attempt to unite the world by conquest had been defeated. In the Atomic Age, any attempt to do this would be a symptom of suicidal mania.

The second of the momentous changes that have been sequels to the Second World War is the reduction of the number of great powers from seven to two—that is, to the number with which the competition had started at the beginning of the modern age, when the powers in the arena were the Hapsburg Monarchy and France. If the United States and the Soviet Union had not been overtaken in 1945 by the Atomic Age, they might have fought each other for the prize of supremacy, as the Hapsburgs and France had done in the sixteenth and seventeenth centuries. So far America and Russia have refrained from going to war with each other, but they have also failed to come to terms with each other. In consequence, international relations continue to be anarchic. In 1967 the United States and the Soviet Union are both facing the prospect of losing the pre-eminent power that each of them has been enjoying since the overthrow of Nazi Germany. Both powers alike are menaced by the proliferation of the possession of atomic weapons and by the possibility that China, already an atomic power, might raise itself one day to achieve parity with the present Big Two.

Meanwhile, the anarchy in the world has been aggravated by the great increase in the number of sovereign independent states that resulted from the liberation of Asian and African countries which formerly were parts of the British, French, Dutch, Italian, and American colonial empires. Since the close of the Second World War, the number of local sovereign independent states on the face of this comparatively small planet has nearly doubled. There are now about 125 of these, including such tiny entities as Andorra, San Marino, State of Vatican City, and Singapore. The increase in their number has made the world more difficult to govern. Some of these new states—e.g., India and Pakistan, or, again, the Arab states and Israel—have been at swords' points with one another from birth; and each of these new local feuds is a danger to the maintenance of world peace. Moreover, the doctrine of the equality of states, which had been recognized in 1648 in the Westphalia peace settlement, was written into the constitution of the United Nations and this doctrine puts a premium on political disruption. If, for instance, Nigeria were to break up into five separate fragments, the Nigerians would be rewarded for their political incompetence by getting five seats in the Assembly of the United Nations instead of the one seat allotted to an undisrupted Nigeria—and likewise to an undisrupted India, United States, and Soviet Union. This distribution of seats is unrealistic. It bears no relation to the real ratios of population, wealth, power, and responsibility, and it therefore threatens to bring the Assembly into disrepute. The constitution of a world government could never be built on this fantastically inequitable basis.

In the Atomic Age, the need for the establishment of some kind of world government is still more evident than it has been before. In the Atomic Age, a world government can be established by consent only, not by force, and it would be hard to induce the newly liberated Asian and African states, and even the less recently liberated Latin American states, to agree to the reduction of their voting power to the ratio to which they are properly entitled. On the other hand, there is one propitious hard fact: by 1967 the postwar power of the United States and of the Soviet Union might be a wasting asset; these two states, out of the officially sovereign 125, still hold, between them, about 90 per cent of the world's power. Since the collapse of Nazi Germany, America and Russia have been frustrating each other. If the rise of Communist China moves them to come to terms with each other and to form a partnership, they would still have it in their power to establish a world government *de facto* by acting in concert. This would not be a democratic world government, but it would be one that would ensure the survival of the human race; for America and Russia, working together, could not only eliminate the possibility of their falling into an atomic war with each other; they could also make it impossible for an atomic war to be made by any other power.

Under the political and psychological conditions prevailing in 1967, a world government is evidently going to be hard to establish. It would be hard enough for the United States and the Soviet Union to bring themselves to work together—though, by now, the vital interest of each of these two powers calls urgently for cooperation between them. It would be still harder to persuade the other 123 states of the world to reconcile themselves to seeing their sovereignties subordinated to a Russo-American directorate, even if there were a prospect that this undemocratic form of world government would be democratized progressively as time went on. Yet however difficult it might be to achieve world government, it looks in 1967 as if, in the Atomic Age, this has become a necessary condition for the survival of the human race. In the pre-Atomic Age, it was possible for mankind to survive without world government, but the cost of living in this way was a permanent state of international anarchy in which each of the spells of uneasy peace between local sovereign states ended invariably in a fresh outbreak of war between them. At the western end of the Old World, in contrast to China, this miserable state of affairs set in with the breakdown and break-up of the Roman Empire in the fifth century of the Christian Era. From the turn of the fifteenth and sixteenth centuries onward, this lamentable Western way of life has spread progressively to the rest of the world. It has partly been imposed on the non-Western majority of mankind by the West European powers' conquests of colonial empires overseas, and has partly been accepted by still independent non-Western states—e.g., by Russia and Japan—under the influence of the West's prestige.

The modern West has had many good things to give to the world in the field of science and technology, but in the field of international relations the effect of the Westernization of the world has been disastrous. It has aggravated international anarchy where this had existed before, and has imported it into regions, such as China and Peru, that had previously achieved a unified government within their own respective domains. Mankind's present major political task is to save itself from self-destruction by erecting some kind of world government in the present unpropitious circumstances. As a start, we could well be content with any arrangement—for instance, a Russo-American joint dictatorship—that would exclude the possibility of an atomic war.

Effectively enforced, law is an indispensable condition for civilized life on the world scale just as much as it is on the municipal scale. But we cannot have effectively enforced law on any geographical scale unless we have an effective government on the same scale. If there is to be an effectively enforced world law there has to be an effective world government. This is one of the lessons of modern treaties. Of the many lessons latent in such documents, this, in my judgment, is the most valuable lesson of all.

Section 2

The United Nations and order in the world

New ideas for a new world

U Thant

The U.N. Secretary-General here proposes a new dedication to the principles of the Charter, so that the common human problems of war, hunger, disease, underdevelopment, and the population explosion might be overcome by united action. It is a difficult task, but the alternative is a world of unbridled national rivalry and a drift toward war.

Saturday Review, *July 24, 1965.* © *1965. Reprinted by permission.* *U Thant is Secretary-General of the United Nations.*

Twenty years is a long time in the life of an individual, but a short one in the development of a great political institution. With our human tendency to impatience, we find it hard to accept the time lag between the formulation of an idea and its practical realization, and we are sometimes inclined to question the validity of an idea before it has had time to prove itself, or even to reject it impatiently before it has had the chance to take root and grow. Our experience of international relations in the past twenty years may sometimes tempt us to react in this way about the Charter of the United Nations.

It is a merciful fact of life that time diminishes and dims the memories of misery and horror. Time has also blunted that sense of danger and of urgency that produced the Charter. Thus we hear a good deal of talk now about the adaptation of the Charter to the modern world—talk which sometimes evades the central issue of making the Charter a working reality. There is no doubt that the world has changed in many ways since 1945, some of them unexpected, and that corresponding adjustments in the United Nations are desirable. On a previous occasion I have myself referred to the anachronistic character of certain provisions of the Charter. But defeatist thinking about the possibility or the necessity of world order merely turns a blind eye to the perils of the future because of the difficulties of the present. Should we succumb to such facile arguments we would stand convicted of gross irresponsibility by future generations. I believe, therefore, that the most important thing we can do at the twentieth anniversary of the signing of the Charter of the United Nations is to think back to the tragedies and agonies that made the Charter possible and, in resolving that humanity shall never be so afflicted again, rededicate ourselves to its aims and ideals. Having done this, we must look to the future with statesmanship as well as realism.

The danger is not, it seems to me, that the Charter will prove inadequate or unsuited to our purposes and policies. It is rather that our purposes and policies are inadequate, and in some cases inimical, to the fulfillment of the purposes and principles to which the United Nations enthusiastically subscribed twenty years ago. It is this inadequacy, which we think we can afford in relatively peaceful times, that we must guard against.

It was never realistic to suppose governments would, in a short period of time, be able to accept and act on all the practical implications of the ideals and aims to which they subscribed in signing the Charter. On the other hand, if we want some better system for peace and security than an unsteady balance of nationalistic power and aspiration, we need to work long and hard to remove the many obstacles in the way, and in that process develop a new system of relationships between states that really correspond to present needs and conditions. While working on that task we must look to the Charter as an inspiration and a goal, without any illusions as to the ease with which its objectives can be attained. If we need to assure ourselves that the goal is worth attaining, we need only turn our thoughts for a moment to the probable alternative.

I do not wish here to look back at the past twenty years either to applaud what has been done or to regret what has not been done. I do not propose to refer to our current situation except to say that it demands an urgent and serious effort by all nations to make a reality of the aims of the Charter before we revert in disunity to the helpless condition that preceded World War II. It is all too clear that the unsolved problems within the United Nations over

Article 19 and peacekeeping, combined with various ominous conflicts in the world at large, present us with a deeply disturbing situation. Despite this, I would like rather to turn to the future, with its problems and its possibilities.

In 1946 Sir Winston Churchill said of the League of Nations:

> The League of Nations did not fail because of its principles and conceptions. It failed because these principles were deserted by those states which had brought it into being. It failed because the governments of those states feared to face the facts and act while time remained. This disaster must not be repeated.

We are luckier than our fathers were in the twentieth year of the League of Nations, because we still have time to face the facts. It is, however, essential that a sense of false security should not lull us once again into the belief that somehow war can be avoided in a world where the unbridled rivalry of nations is the dominant factor of international life. That is the condition in which the drift to war almost imperceptibly gathers momentum until it becomes irresistible and inescapable. That is what we must, by a conscious and concerted effort, avoid.

Disturbing developments in various parts of the world today have, of course, direct repercussions all over the world, and for that matter on the United Nations, which is in many ways a mirror of the world. There is a danger that we may become so preoccupied with the immediate crises in Southeast Asia, in the Caribbean, in the Middle East, and elsewhere that we are likely to ignore the larger crisis that looms behind them. That wider crisis must be understood and assessed. The most serious casualty of the present conflict will be the precarious détente between East and West that has been built and nurtured so laboriously and patiently in the last ten years or so. The United Nations has contributed significantly toward that détente by serving as a catalyst, a forum, and an agency for the peaceful settlement of disputes and the relaxation of East-West tensions.

I had hoped that this détente, to be meaningful, would extend to other areas of the globe, since peace is indivisible. But we have witnessed, and are still witnessing, certain tendencies for the Cold War to intensify, and also to extend to areas that have so far been relatively immune. This trend must be arrested and reversed if humanity is to be saved from the scourge of war, the primary motivation behind the founding of the United Nations. The international community on this small planet should comprise all men and women irrespective of race and creed. As Pierre Teilhard de Chardin had observed, life should move toward a higher plane than this one on which we now live. He was undismayed by the ideological clashes men must pass through before they achieve a world community. He saw a great evolution leading toward "a common soul in this vast body"—mankind.

I believe that we are increasingly conscious of the need to harmonize our thoughts and actions toward that end. We have an increasing fear and hatred of war throughout the world, based partly upon the new destructive power of weapons and partly upon a moral revulsion against violence. The voices of peoples all over the world are raised, as never before, against war and actions likely to lead to war. We have the balance of terror between the nuclear powers, but the proliferation of nuclear weapons may end the nuclear monopoly of the major powers while greatly increasing the risks involved. We have a general agreement, in principle at least, that the domination of one nation or group of nations by another is intolerable, and that mutual aid and cooperation is the best basis for the relationship between nations. We have the possibility of raising standards of living and opportunity through international cooperation—an immense incentive to peace. We can, if we work together, provide, within a generation or so, a much higher standard of living and reasonable opportunities for all men.

We have the possibility of great advances in science, in technology, and in the unexplored realms of the human mind as well as in outer space—advances all of which will be more rapid and less risky if the skill and talent of all nations can be combined in an organized effort. Finally, we have an agreed framework, the United Nations system, within which, if we wish, we can pursue our aims and bring about an orderly development in international life. This all adds up to a considerable balance sheet of assets.

Our problems and liabilities are also considerable, and we sometimes tend to be more impressed by them than by our assets. The greatest obstacle to the realization of the Charter is the inescapable fact that power politics still operates, both overtly and covertly, in international relations. The concept of power politics, whether as the instrument of nationalism or of ideological extremism, is the natural enemy of international order as envisaged in the Charter. It is also an expensive, and potentially disastrous, anachronism. Patriotism, national pride, or ideological conviction can and must take new and more creative forms than the old concepts of political domination or material power. This is a challenge to statesmanship and political genius in all regions of the world. The basic ideas and machinery are all there; they await the national policies and actions that will put life and strength into them.

Such policies will not in the beginning be easy for governments, especially powerful ones, to adopt. The larger interests of world peace, the will or opinion of the majority of nations, or the accreditation of national prestige to international order will initially often prove hard to accept. But some governments have already found such acceptance possible without suffering disaster, and their example should encourage others.

Even if the problem of power politics were solved, we have to face other basic facts. It is now commonplace to refer to the gulf between developed and underdeveloped nations, to the population explosion, to the conservation of

policies, and have established a considerable reputation for impartiality in the international community. The diplomats and soldiers of other nations such as Yugoslavia, Ireland, India, Pakistan, Brazil, and Nigeria have made significant contributions to U.N. peacekeeping operations, too. Still other middle powers have earmarked troops for future U.N. operations, including the Netherlands, Iran, Italy and New Zealand, and the Austrian Parliament has recently voted a change of laws which will permit it to contribute troops.

Until recently, Britain, watching its empire disintegrate by stages, was on the defensive, giving only lukewarm support to U.N. police operations. The British opposed U.N. involvement in the Gaza Strip and were critical of the U.N. role in the Congo. However, they now have troops in the U.N. force in Cyprus, and have also committed logistical support to future U.N. operations. British policy has demonstrated that despite its colonial past it can be an effective contributor to U.N. peacekeeping. In this sense Britain, though one of the Big Five in the Security Council, has joined the peacekeeping nations.

The third layer of U.N. politics is made up of the eighty nations of the "Third World," the poor, relatively weak nations of Africa, Asia, and Latin America. These nations make up an important U.N. constituency. They know that they have something to gain from the U.N. both in terms of development and security. Led by Raul Prebisch, an Argentinian, the entire "Third World" group of poor nations found new unity when they unanimously endorsed the establishment of the U.N. Trade and Development Conference as a means for seeking better ways of improving their trade position with richer nations.

Understandably, the United Nations has become the center of gravity for the diplomatic life of most of the new nations. Because of their strong anti-colonial feelings, deep national pride and relative insecurity, they look to the U.N. as an organization in which they can maintain the greatest degree of national independence while having some small influence in the decision-making process. The feeling of sharing with equally underprivileged nations has great importance for them. Since U.N. peacekeeping is primarily concerned with the "Third World," there will undoubtedly be a continuing requirement to put out the brush fires and check the border disputes, racial clashes, and religious conflicts before they erupt into war.

With the exception of Korea and the recent U.N. observer role in the Dominican Republic, U.N. peacekeeping operations have been conducted in the power vacuum created by the end of the British Empire and European colonialism—the Middle East, the sub-continent, Southeast Asia, and Africa. These U.N. operations have included Palestine, Egypt at the Gaza Strip, Lebanon, the Congo, West Irian in Indonesia, Yemen, Cyprus, and Kashmir.

U.N. peacekeeping often is simply the dispatch of observers or fact-finders to a disputed area: a presence that insures a window to the world. U.N. peacekeeping forces are also sent to prevent shooting, to maintain a cease-fire, and to provide order while negotiations are being conducted. They can be sent only when a government requests a U.N. force, or at least acquiesces in the wish of a U.N. consensus that they be sent. They are politically neutral and do not fire unless fired upon. They do not have enforcement responsibilities.

Despite the fact that the primary security role for the U.N. is peacekeeping in the "Third World," and the fact that the middle powers are willing and able to assume the policing responsibility, it is nevertheless true that the U.N. is unlikely to act in the future unless both of the super-powers acquiesce in such action. All of the member nations know that both the United States and the U.S.S.R. have sufficient political power to emasculate the U.N. merely by withdrawing from the organization. Since both have the veto in the Security Council and the capability to gain the support of a blocking third of the members of the General Assembly, it is most unlikely that the U.N. can or will act when either nation is firmly opposed. . . .

This impasse will almost certainly not be broken until the United States and the U.S.S.R. reach a *modus vivendi* at least comparable to that of the period of the test ban agreement of 1963, a virtual impossibility while the bombing of North Vietnam continues. The United States' attempt to take the Vietnam war to the U.N. Security Council failed to get action not merely because the French and Soviets were opposed. Secretary General U Thant on several occasions has pointed out that the appropriate forum for Vietnam peace talks is the Geneva Conference, which includes as members both the Communist Chinese and the North Vietnamese, as the U.N. does not.

The Soviets, as co-chairman with the British, have not agreed to call up the Geneva Conference, and probably will not until they are given some substantial inducement. They are riding the crest of several diplomatic and political triumphs so that any move to ease the agony of the United States would have to be predicated on a meaningful *quid pro quo*.

Even if no United States-Soviet agreement is reached, it will still be possible for the U.N., under certain circumstances, to engage in peacekeeping operations on an *ad hoc* basis. Though their motivations may be at variance, the Soviets and the United States may support U.N. peacekeeping to thwart Communist Chinese ambitions, as in the recent India-Pakistan dispute. The Soviets are inclined, also, to go along with U.N. action supported by a large Afro-Asian consensus, as was the case in the Congo; or when the alternative courses of action are less palatable, as was the case in Cyprus. Finally, the Soviets may support U.N. involvement if they are persuaded that the alternative would be unilateral United States action.

Both the United States and the Soviets are aware that U.N. peacekeeping operations under the cloak of collective responsibility permit action without committing the vital interests of either great power. U.N. peacekeeping operations allow brush fires to be extinguished without great-power confrontation. The U.N. provides a diplomatic center where a third party—either the Secretary General, a single nation or a group of nations—can originate a proposal for action which may be acceptable to the United States and the U.S.S.R., but could not possibly have been initiated through direct Washington-Moscow channels. The U.N. is a forum where the super-powers can collaborate with minimum loss of face, and therefore less danger of adverse domestic political repercussions.

The Vietnam War and the Dominican crisis have caused Washington to begin an examination of the extent to which it can rely on unilateral military intervention. There has been growing awareness of the desirability of acting in a framework of collective security arrangements. Some policymakers have expressed hope that we could rely increasingly on regional organizations rather than the U.N., but the prognosis for the regional approach to peacekeeping is gloomy indeed. . . .

There are numerous reasons why the U.N. has been able to move forward with peacekeeping operations when regional organizations could not. For example, there is no decision more difficult for an independent national leader than to call for outside military help. The presence of foreign soldiers is such a politically sensitive matter that most nations consider the troops of their near neighbors unacceptable. The host country wants to be as certain as possible that the visiting troops come from politically disinterested governments. The U.N., with a growing number of governments earmarking troops, provides the best available source of impartial peacekeepers.

For all of its imperfection and ambiguity, the U.N. is in the peacekeeping business because a majority of the nations wants it to be. Recognizing that the U.N. can operate only in certain circumstances, and that it will probably have to rely for the most part on improvisation with voluntary troop contributions and voluntary financing, it nevertheless would be prudent for the U.S. to look for means to strengthen its policing potential.

The latest Canadian White Paper on Defense sets the highest priority for Canadian contribution to U.N. peacekeeping, stating that "Canadian forces will be trained and equipped in a way which will permit immediate and effective response to United Nations requirements," and "the combined land, sea and air forces normally stationed in Canada and at Canadian ports will be sufficiently flexible to satisfy almost any conceivable requirement for U.N. or other operations." Strong commitments for U.N. peacekeeping also have been made by the Scandinavian governments and several of the other middle powers. The United States should support this trend in all ways possible, giving more consideration to the U.N. peacekeeping nations in its own defense planning.

The United States should certainly encourage the new peacekeeping program of the British, which may soon include the availability of a British base for U.N. stockpiling and airlift. Rapidly changing British defense policy has begun to move in the direction taken by Canada. It would not be surprising some day to find the British calling on the U.N. to share the peacekeeping responsibility in Malaysia, with an arrangement similar to that in Cyprus.

The Soviets have urged the inclusion of Communist units in U.N. peacekeeping to give a better political balance. Why not? The Yugoslavs, strong supporters of U.N. peacekeeping, have made a significant contribution to the U.N. force in the Gaza Strip. Any moves which will give the Soviets a greater feeling of representation without impairing the effectiveness of U.N. peacekeeping should be supported. For example, Polish or Hungarian troops serving under the U.N. flag could perform as effectively as the soldiers of other nations.

The United States can strengthen U.N. peacekeeping by a generous gift to the U.N., and larger voluntary contributions to ongoing and future peacekeeping operations. Why should a nation that has more than 40 per cent of the world's gross national product not contribute at least that proportion to U.N. peacekeeping costs? The United States should continue to make available airlift and other logistical support to U.N. operations. It should also use the authority in the Foreign Assistance Act, so far inexplicably untapped, which provides that we can give assistance to recipient countries to participate in collective measures requested by the U.N.

The key question for the future of the U.N. is the extent to which the United States, the greatest power in the world, is willing to commit itself. If the United States decides to place greater reliance on the United Nations for the containment of brush fire disputes, Congress will find the necessary funds. Brush fires don't cost much if they are put out in time. We might have to spend as much as $200 or $300 million dollars a year, but if we helped to prevent war between India and Pakistan, Greece and Turkey, the Arabs and Israel, Malaysia and Indonesia, etc., it would be well worth it. U.N. peacekeeping can be only a small part of the world security framework, at least for the next decade, but it can become increasingly useful, particularly with strong support from the United States.

The U.N. and the Arab-Israeli war of 1967

Richard Hudson

There are many questions that will long remain unanswered about the Arab-Israeli War of 1967. Hudson here is mainly concerned with lessons for U.N. peacekeeping. He approaches the topic as both a legal and a practical problem.

The mysteries of the Arab-Israeli War of 1967 will haunt historians for years to come. The victor is clear, but these questions remain:

> Did Nasser want war, thinking he could win it? Or did he think he could get away with his blockade of the Strait of Tiran without war?
>
> Did the Soviet Union put Nasser up to his adventure, or was it dragged along reluctantly?
>
> Did Israel launch pre-emptive attacks against the Arab countries, or did it respond to Arab attacks? If Israel had held back from its lightning sweeps, could it have reopened the Gulf of Aqaba through diplomatic efforts?
>
> Would the United States, joined by some other maritime powers, have attempted to break the blockade? How would the Soviet Union have responded?
>
> If U Thant had flown to Cairo earlier, or had urged the UNEF Advisory Committee to ask for a meeting of the General Assembly, might the war have been headed off?
>
> What is the meaning of the Middle East war for the future of the U.N.?

Historians will certainly bring to light new facts bearing on many of these questions. Until they do, let me offer the following short and provisional answers based on what has been published so far and on conversations in the United Nations with diplomats and journalists of many nations—with particular emphasis on the U.N. role in the Middle East crisis. Finally, I want to ask what lessons may be learned for the U.N. from these events. . . .

First, let us look carefully at the opening chronology of events, which is very revealing: The crisis began on May 16 at 10 p.m. (Gaza local time), when Major General Rikhye, the UNEF commander, was handed a letter from General Fawzi, chief of staff of the U.A.R. armed forces, asking withdrawal of "all U.N. troops which install O.P.'s [observation posts] along our borders." The letter was delivered by Egyptian Brigadier Mokhtar, who (according to U Thant's comprehensive report of June 27) "told General Rikhye at the time that he must order the immediate withdrawal of United Nations troops from El Sahba and Sharm el Sheik on the night of 16 May since United Arab Republic armed forces must gain control of these two places that very night." Rikhye refused to comply, stating that he could act only on the instructions of the U.N. secretary general, to whom he would report immediately.

The following morning U.A.R. troops occupied El Sahba (in the Sinai near the Israel border) and advanced past the UNEF observation posts toward the Israel frontier, thus making the posts unable to perform their function. Early in the afternoon Rikhye got another message from Fawzi asking that the UNEF detachment at Sharm el Sheik, the strategic position dominating the Strait of Tiran, be withdrawn within "48 hours or so."

It was not until the day after that, May 18, at noon New York time, that the secretary general received word in answer to his queries that the U.A.R. "has decided to terminate the presence of the United Nations Emergency Force from the territory of the United Arab Republic and Gaza Strip." Later that day U Thant ordered UNEF withdrawn. In his June 27 report, he noted that the U.A.R. "had made it entirely clear to the secretary general that an appeal for reconsideration of the withdrawal decision would encounter a firm rebuff and would be considered as an attempt to impose UNEF as an 'army of occupation.' "

On May 22, as U Thant was en route to Cairo, Nasser declared the blockade of the Strait of Tiran, cutting off the Israeli port of Elath. When the secretary general later asked why this was done at that time, he got the reply that the U.A.R. had decided "some time before U Thant's departure" to resume the blockade and felt it "preferable to make the announcement before rather than after the secretary general's visit to Cairo."

Given this chronology, it seems clear that Nasser had from the first determined to oust UNEF and blockade the Strait of Tiran. He never left any leeway for bargaining on either count. But did he want war? For years Nasser had been proclaiming his objective of driving Israel into the sea, and on May 26 he declared that if war starts, "our main objective will be the destruction of

Israel." On that same date Thant reported to the Security Council that he had just been told by Nasser that the U.A.R. "would not initiate offensive action against Israel." Despite the well-known large shipments of military hardware into Egypt, most independent observers considered Israel militarily superior, in equipment, training and morale. With two defeats already chalked up against the Egyptians (one of them with Nasser in charge), the U.A.R. chief should have had no illusions about the difficulty of winning a war against Israel. It therefore seems most probable that Nasser did not want a war but rather hoped to pull off a power play that would enhance his prestige in the Arab world without war.

Nevertheless, Nasser had to know that he was *risking* war when he declared the Aqaba blockade, for Israel had long made known that it would consider this move a *casus belli.* There would seem to be three main reasons that Nasser took the risk, although it is hard to give them relative weight. . . .

First, Nasser was in personal trouble both domestically and in the Arab world. The Egyptian economy was edging toward bankruptcy; his war in the Yemen was going badly; there were reports of dissatisfaction with him in the army and elsewhere; the Arab countries had largely repudiated his leadership. If Nasser had ordered UNEF out and successfully imposed the blockade, he would once again have been the great Arab chief—in fact, he was for the days preceding the eruption of the war on June 5.

Second, Nasser may sincerely have been expecting Israel to provoke hostilities. During the U.N. debate the Arabs repeatedly declared they had information that Israel was planning an attack on Syria on May 17. On May 19 Thant reported to the Security Council:

> In recent weeks, however, reports emanating from Israel have attributed to some high officials in that state statements so threatening as to be particularly inflammatory in the sense that they could only heighten emotions and thereby increase tensions on the other side of the lines. There have been in the past few days persistent reports about troop movements and concentrations, particularly on the Israel side of the Syrian border. . . . The government of Israel very recently has assured me that there are no unusual Israel troop concentrations or movements along the Syrian line, that there will be none and that no military action will be initiated by the armed forces of Israel unless such action is first taken by the other side. Reports from UNTSO [United Nations Truce Supervision Organization] observers have confirmed the absence of troop concentrations and significant troop movements on both sides of the line.

Despite these indications that Israel probably did not plan a May 17 attack on Syria, this does not mean that Egypt and Syria did not expect one. As recently as April 7, the Israelis had bombed a Syrian village. There was a report that Soviet intelligence had warned the Arabs of an impending attack on

Syria that was to be accompanied by a coup against the Syrian government. Thus, given the rising tension and bad communication, it is quite possible that the Arabs really were expecting an Israeli attack on Syria, and that Nasser was hurriedly moving his troops to the Israel border in Sinai to be ready to open a second front.

The third reason Nasser may have been willing to risk war was that he expected strong Soviet help. The United States was bogged down in Vietnam; moreover, the Americans could not side too strongly with Israel because of their oil interests in the Arab world. So, in a showdown, Nasser may have felt he would come out all right. But if he had really wanted to have a showdown—rather than to win the smaller bluff—it seems logical that he would have found an excuse to gain the advantage of surprise, instead of leaving this to his adversaries on June 5. . . .

For his role in the crisis, U Thant came under the heaviest fire of his tenure as secretary general. President Johnson said he was "dismayed" at the secretary general's prompt withdrawal of UNEF; some delegates in the corridors spoke of "Thant's war." When Israeli Foreign Minister Abba Eban sharply condemned the secretary general's action in the General Assembly, Thant for the first time in his five and a half years in office asked to exercise his prerogative to reply to a delegate. He reminded the Assembly that Israel was on weak ground in suggesting that the U.N.'s blue berets should have stayed on in U.A.R. territory, for "Israel always and firmly refused to accept them on Israel territory." He then went on to reveal for the first time "that prior to receiving the U.A.R. request and giving my reply to it, I had raised with the permanent representative of Israel to the United Nations the possibility of stationing elements of UNEF on the Israel side of the line. I was told that the idea was completely unacceptable to Israel." . . .

Discussion of this question of withdrawal procedures is by no means of only academic or historical interest. For a while the criticism of U Thant in this regard was running so strong that it appeared it might limit his future effectiveness as secretary general. However, as more facts of the situation that had faced the secretary general came out, more observers concluded that he had had no practicable alternative to pulling UNEF out. Even more important, the principles involved could be just as crucial in determining whether or not certain future wars occur.

The central point involved, which is hardly understood at all by the public—even by much of the best informed public, is the basic difference between "peacekeeping actions" and "enforcement actions." The former are carried out under Chapter VI of the U.N. Charter; the latter under Chapter VII. When the Charter was written in 1945, in the euphoria of the United Nations victory in World War II, it was anticipated that if any further threats to world peace arose, the Security Council would act to meet them, taking enforcement action under Chapter VII. This kind of action requires unanimity of the great powers—the five permanent members of the Security Council. If another Hitler had arisen in Germany, the Security Council would have been ideally suited to take on the challenge, for that was what it was geared for. As usual, men were preparing to fight the kinds of wars they had fought in the past. But, of course, coming wars were to be different. Once the Charter worked roughly as had been planned—but only because the Soviet Union was boycotting the Security Council at the outbreak of the Korean War. Thus the Soviet veto was avoided and the U.N. launched an enforcement action.

It was when the U.N. faced violent situations but could not act under Chapter VII that "peacekeeping action" was born. The term "peacekeeping" is nowhere mentioned in the U.N. Charter but activities that were called peacekeeping fitted into Chapter VI without an undue bending of words. It can be said, however, that the framers of the Charter did not envision this kind of activity for Chapter VI, which (in Article 33) calls for disputes to be settled by "negotiation, enquiry, mediation, conciliation, arbitration, judicial settlement, resort to regional agencies or arrangements or other peaceful means of their own choice." The main point is that under Chapter VI nations cannot be forced to do anything; they can only be asked to act voluntarily to settle disputes peacefully. It was under this Chapter VI, of course, that UNEF was established.

Certain basic principles developed for peacekeeping forces: they do not take sides; they carry only small arms and fire only in self-defense; they can enter a country only with that country's permission and can stay only as long as that permission endures. It was the latter principle that Hammarskjöld sought to limit in his 1956 talk with Nasser, for the then secretary general was concerned over the possibility of the very thing that happened on May 16, 1967—that UNEF would be ordered out peremptorily, thus precipitating a conflict. It was a good try, even though it ultimately failed. When the next U.N. peacekeeping force is created, there will certainly be more attention paid to the question of whether or not there is any limitation on the right of the host country to oust the force. . . .

A peacekeeping majority: A new U.N. role?

Richard Hudson
Reinhold Niebuhr

In this brief exchange, Hudson presents a new peacekeeping proposal. Professor Niebuhr relies for his criticism on the concept of national sovereignty.

"The Ethics of War and Peace in the Nuclear Age," War/Peace Report, *February 1967.* *© 1967 by New York Friends Group, Inc. Reprinted by permission. Mr. Niebuhr is a leading theologian. Mr. Hudson is editor of* War/Peace Report.

. . . *Hudson:* Are you familiar with my proposal which would in effect make the United Nations bicameral, but in a different way? I call this idea the Peacekeeping Majority—P.K.M., for short. Initially, the P.K.M. would apply only to peacekeeping operations, but later it might be expanded to cover all important questions. There are three requirements in order for an action to be approved by a Peacekeeping Majority: first, approval by two-thirds of the members of the Security Council; second, approval by a two-thirds majority of the General Assembly, and third, inclusion in the Assembly majority sufficient nations to represent a simple majority of the population of the world. The first requirement to a large degree represents national power; the second, the sovereign equality of nation states; the third, the factor of population. The P.K.M. would eliminate the veto and make it possible for the U.N. to undertake a peacekeeping action provided a strong and balanced consensus existed in support of it. One virtue of the P.K.M. idea is that it is just complicated enough so that it would not create any clear winners or losers of power. I think it provides for a fairer distribution of power than any other scheme I have seen so far.

Niebuhr: Your idea is good as far as it goes, but there can't be world peace without a world army—a United Nations army—that would quell any defiance of the United Nations. Now, the nations are far from integrating their armies into a world army; nor is there any prospect that any nation will submit its sovereignty to a world government.

Hudson: No prospect for the immediate future, or forever?

Niebuhr: I won't say forever. Nothing is forever. I simply say there is no prospect of averting disaster in the next decades through a constitutional convention. A constitutional convention would not solve the problem of order so long as the world itself has not become integrated, as the national community has been integrated. . . .

Is the United Nations overweight? Mini-membership for mini-states

Urban Whitaker

Will 10 percent of the world's population control the General Assembly? On a one-nation, one-vote basis they could control two-thirds of the votes, and Professor Whitaker argues for a revision to restore balance and efficiency to the world organization through recognition of the wide differences in power and population among the legally sovereign nation-states.

War/Peace Report, *April 1967, © 1967 by New York Friends Group, Inc. Reprinted by permission.* *Mr. Whitaker is a professor of international relations at San Francisco State College and a member of the Commission to Study the Organization of Peace.*

What will happen when Pitcairn Island—with a population of less than 100—becomes a member of the United Nations? Impossible? Maybe. But already the Maldive Islands—with a population of less than 100,000—is a full member. And there is no minimum population requirement for a U.N. member, nor is there yet any serious discussion of such a requirement.

The problem of the mini-states is a real one. We have reached the danger point in rampant self-determination. Confidence in the United Nations has been seriously undermined. The very capacity of the organization to act responsibly and efficiently has been reduced at an alarming rate. And the worst may be yet to come. Of all the little bits and pieces of territories that have marched proudly through the flood gates of the post-war independence movement, only one, Western Samoa, has declined United Nations membership. Yet if the new mini-states have neither the inclination nor the maturity to exercise this measure of self-control, who will apply the brakes? Answer: no one. Their ex-colonial masters, under firm pressures from a continuous stream of anti-imperialist activities at the General Assembly, are not likely to halt the trend. The major powers, always competing for Assembly votes, have not been inclined in recent years to oppose new admissions. Besides, for some of the big powers, the mini-states form a more or less reliable pool of support on certain important issues.

In any case, and for whatever reasons, the trend is in full swing. Anyone who would dismiss the possibility that the Pitcairn Islanders might apply for United Nations membership ought to read the statement made in the Fourth Committee on Dec. 13, 1966, by the United Kingdom representative. It is entitled "Smaller British Colonial Territories." It reports "steady and uninterrupted progress" toward independence, and cites as primary evidence the fact that four former territories (Guyana, Botswana, Lesotho and Barbados, with a total combined population of just two million) were admitted to the United Nations during 1966. More such "progress" is promised with glowing reports of "constitutional advances" in two other territories that have "early dates" set for independence, one whose timetable is "well under way," and 21 more (including Pitcairn Island) in various degrees of "rapid and sure" progress.

In his Dag Hammarskjöld Memorial lectures in 1964, Secretary of State Rusk said that it was a "fair guess" that the United Nations membership would level off in the 1970's at about 125 to 130. But it reached 122 in 1966, and British territories alone could build the total to 146. The mini-state problem about which Rusk complained in 1964 (a two-thirds majority could be composed of members representing only 10 per cent of the world's population, and paying only 5 per cent of the U.N. budget) has already worsened, and there is no reason to believe that the membership explosion has yet run its course.

The basic problem resulting from the "open door" membership policy is that under the "one state, one vote" rule, the voting power of the mini-states has grown too large in comparison with that of the large and middle powers. This tension between large and small powers has always troubled the United Nations, although the more dramatic headline conflicts between the two superpowers have often tended to obscure the fact. Even at the founding conference in San Francisco, it was more difficult to reconcile the differences between large and small states than it was to find general agreement among the big five.

Now, as the United Nations passes its twenty-first birthday, the uneasy truce between giant and pygmy is shakier than ever. The San Francisco compromise of 1945, which sought to resolve the problem by seating all members of the organization in the General Assembly as legal equals, while recognizing special privileges in the Security Council for the five strongest powers, has fallen victim of two developments. First, the special role anticipated for the Security Council has never been realized because it depends on a degree of big power unanimity that seldom exists. Second, the General Assembly—whose *de facto* functions have expanded into the void often left by the Council's impotence—has changed so rapidly that it hardly resembles the Assembly of the 1940's and 50's.

Inevitably, the powerful few and the sovereign multitude now approach a new basic confrontation on constitutional issues. Nearly 70 per cent of the legally sovereign member states have populations smaller than that of New York City. As the membership of the General Assembly passes 120, it is increasingly apparent that its size and its composition are simply not compatible with the efficient discharge of its duties. The town meeting of the world is too big, and the *de facto* inequalities of the members are too great, to merit the confidence that the peoples of the world necessarily must place in it.

Several ways around this problem have been proposed. The easiest solution is simply to rely on the automatic corrective sometimes known as "invisible weighted voting." The tiny Maldive Islands, for example, may be the *legal* equal of the United States, but its voice carries very little *de facto* weight. This "solution" has a great deal to recommend it, particularly since it requires no formal changes in the Charter and since the *de facto* weight of a state's voice constantly changes to reflect changes in world politics. But . . . no amount of real weakness among the smaller states can eliminate the emotional discomfort of those hundreds of millions in some states who can legally be outvoted by a few hundred thousand in any one of several others.

Another solution that has often been suggested is a formally weighted voting system reflecting the enormous differences among U.N. members in population, financial contribution and experience. Besides the predictable difficulty of reaching the necessary agreement for Charter amendment (probably sufficient to kill the idea), formal weighting of votes would still fail to resolve that considerable part of the problem which is essentially physical. It takes just as much space and time to explain a vote whether it counts as a half or as a whole ballot.

Various other solutions and partial solutions have been proposed. . . . But, when all the proposals that have been made and all the reforms that have been instituted are rolled into one package, they still fall short of the minimum reorganization necessary if the General Assembly is to render full and efficient service to its members.

The time seems ripe, therefore, to propose the creation of a new category of associate membership in the United Nations. Whether such a development would offer hope for lasting relief from the pains of the severe membership crisis is not certain. The problems coming immediately to mind are substantial. But they are not insurmountable. Probably only an intensive study by the Assembly itself would bring the necessary talents to bear on the question. A good enough initial case can be made for associate membership to justify the appointment of a select committee. If the Assembly cannot get to this job (the very problem itself may block this particular road toward a solution), the secretary general could encourage initiatives to prime the pump, perhaps by asking a panel of experts to prepare a report.

Primary among the difficulties involved is the specification of criteria for associate membership. Understandably, there would be great reluctance to adopt rules that would demote such old-timers in the sovereign brotherhood as Ireland (with about a third the population of New York City) or Luxembourg (with about one twenty-fifth). In fact, the line between the demotion of any present member and the exercise of more selective discretion in handling future applications may prove to be an impregnable barrier. Any change in membership status for presently "sovereign equals" might have to be voluntary. But, with sufficient incentive, even this would not necessarily bar a significant measure of success.

Essentially, the need is to find a proper balance between each state's rights and duties of participation and its capacity to perform them. Correspondingly, as a member's resources necessitate less than full participation, the reduced role should incur significantly reduced obligations. . . .

Neither the formal category "associate member" nor a more disguised discrimination against relative impotence is new to the practical arts of international organization. Three of the specialized agencies (UNESCO, F.A.O., and WHO) have associate members, and at least three others (U.P.U., I.T.U., W.M.O.) provide for representation of territories not admitted to full membership. In each of these six instances, however, the essential element which defines associate status is the absence of statehood. . . . Perhaps the prestige of statehood is so great, and the history of *associate* membership so tied to pre-statehood status, that no member or potential member would consider such a title. The job still must be done. . . .

The United Nations Charter itself embodies a sort of gross categorization of states as *big powers* (with permanent membership and special voting privileges on the Security Council) and *others*. What is now desperately needed is some recognition of the fact that the "others" group is too big and too diverse. Japan, India, Italy and Canada, for example, are entities of a different order from Lesotho, Botswana, Maldive Islands and Trinidad-Tobago.

Is the United Nations overweight? Pitcairn Island: The ideal state

Arthur Hoppe

Humorist Arthur Hoppe maximizes the potentialities of this "miniest" of potential states.

Up Pitcairn! Throw off the yoke of British colonialism! Freedom and independence forever!

Please excuse my enthusiasm today, but Pitcairn Island out there in the South Pacific is demanding its independence from Great Britain. And if it wants to be a free country, I'm on its side.

If Russia, America, China, France and places like that can be countries, there's no reason Pitcairn can't be a country if it wants to.

Moreover, it has the ideal requisites for nationhood: a rich history (by Nordhoff and Hall); a pleasant climate; a total of two square miles of sacred soil to defend; a single, stable, thriving industry which produces a product always in demand (postage stamps); and a strategic position in world affairs—it being 5,000 miles from anywhere.

Indeed, the only conceivable objection to Pitcairn becoming a sovereign nation in the family of nations is that it only has 79 people.

This has stirred some protest. But there's definitely nothing in the old rule book which says you have to have thus-and-so many people before you can become a nation. And I think 79 is plenty.

True, Pitcairn would be unable to send an ambassador to each of the 140 or 150 (so who counts?) nations that are now in business these days. But a single roving ambassador of the Averell Harriman variety could easily deliver all the ultimatums Pitcairn is likely to deliver and still have plenty of time to sell postage stamps on the side.

Pitcairn will also, of course, need a president to lead the people selflessly and humbly and a vice president to keep telling the president how gloriously he's doing it.

A minimum of ten senators and 20 representatives will be required to pass laws in an atmosphere of harmony and dignity, plus a sergeant-at-arms to break up fist fights. And if they're going to pass laws, they'll naturally need a Supreme Court to declare them unconstitutional.

At least one admiral and two generals will be needed to attend diplomatic receptions and tell everybody how much they hate war. But an army or navy certainly doesn't seem necessary, thanks to Pitcairn's lack of territorial ambitions.

A cabinet, however, is essential in order to have cabinet crises. But it could be a small one that would fit in a corner somewhere. The postmaster general, of course, would be the key member.

But even figuring in customs guards (to prevent the smuggling in of cheap, foreign-made stamps), a regional director of urban planning (every government needs a planner), and two "high official sources who declined to be identified" (so the nation can have a newspaper), there's no question that Pitcairn can be adequately governed by 79 people.

This gives us one citizen left over. But he's absolutely essential because there's no sense setting up a government unless there's somebody to govern.

Thus we see that 79 people are sufficient to establish a nation these days; 78, no, 79, yes. And any fair-minded man must agree that Pitcairn should get to be a nation.

In fact, it will be a lovely nation. It won't go marching off to war, or pushing other people around, or threatening to blow us all up with thermonuclear bombs.

Indeed, the only question left to resolve is how come Russia, America, China and France get to be nations?

Section 3

Regional organization: Power versus order

Regionalism and world order

W. W. Rostow

Regionalism lies somewhere between the isolationist tendencies of nationalism and the as yet unachieved ideals of world organization. Rostow discusses how economic stability and growth can be enhanced through regional cooperation. Regional security, a theme mentioned but not developed here, is a prerequisite to such development.

Department of State Bulletin, *July 17, 1967. Commencement address at Middlebury College, Middlebury, Vermont, on June 12, 1967. Mr. Rostow was Special Assistant to President Johnson.*

. . . The concept of regionalism began for me in 1945 when I was a junior officer in the State Department, where I was put to work on German-Austrian economic affairs when I was not yet out of uniform. That work initially involved such issues as reparations; the provision of food and shelter and clothing to peoples of war-devastated nations; and the revival of the

German coal industry, on which the recovery of Western Europe then heavily depended.

In the midst of these urgent postwar housekeeping problems, a distinguished young French diplomat—named [Maurice] Couve de Murville—came to Washington in November 1945, after visits to Moscow and London. He argued that, because of its importance for all of Europe, the Ruhr should be detached from Germany and separately administered. I had the privilege of sitting in on his exposition of what was then French policy. His challenging proposal stirred my mind because the question he posed was real, but as an historian I instinctively felt the proposed answer would not be viable.

I concluded by deciding that the right answer was to bring about the economic revival of Europe on the basis of economic unity, which would make even a fully revived German economy part of a larger whole and which would provide to the small Austrian economy, about which I was also concerned, a market environment large enough for it to find a prosperous and orderly place.

And so, like all bureaucrats when seized with an idea, I wrote a memorandum. That bureaucratic effort has, perhaps, a very small place in the stream of American thought of that time, and happily many other bureaucrats in many other places were doing the same. But, in fact, the concept of Western European unity which gradually emerged in the succeeding months and years was the product of deep roots, powerful forces, and many men—mainly Europeans:

1. The Second World War had demonstrated to many Europeans the almost suicidal danger of Europe's continuing with its traditional rivalries.
2. The postwar power of the Soviet Union and the United States made many Western Europeans look toward unity as a way of acquiring a dignity which was no longer possible on the basis of traditional European statehood.
3. The inevitable interconnections between the United States and Western Europe were seen as better conducted between a united Western Europe and the United States than on the basis of inherently unequal bilateral relations.

Quite aside from the economic and technological advantages of a big European market, many Europeans perceived that, if Western Europe was to maintain a stature and responsibility appropriate to its tradition and capacity, unity was the right road. To the credit of our country, we decided to throw our full weight behind this movement and look to a great if not always compliant partner rather than to the superficially greater influence we might have wielded in Western Europe on a divide-and-rule basis.

The first major articulation of our support for Western European economic unity was in Secretary of State George Marshall's speech . . . 20 years and 1 week ago today.

Since that time the movement toward Western European unity has by no means been smooth or easy. The process is evidently incomplete. Nevertheless, it moves forward; and I believe it will continue to move forward as the logic of European interest and the character of the world environment in which Europe must live press in this direction.

In the last few years we have seen essentially this same logic beginning to take hold in the developing parts of the world. If I were addressing you in 1961, for example, I might have talked about our support for Western European unity and the Atlantic partnership and then referred to the common responsibilities of the Atlantic community for the nations and peoples of Asia, the Middle East, Africa, and Latin America. And at that time, representatives of those nations and regions tended to think in terms of the common interests of developing nations. But quietly, slowly, almost imperceptibly, there has been a change.

It is, I believe, one of the most important, if unnoticed, transitions in policy under President Johnson—and transitions of thought in the world community—that we are now actively supporting the building of regional institutions and regional cooperation in Latin America, Asia, and Africa as well as in Europe. And we are doing this because, despite the continuing power of nationalism, men and governments in those regions are becoming seized with the same kind of thoughts that gripped Western Europe in the late 1940's and early 1950's.

Economic unity in Latin America and Africa

For example, between the Punta del Este conference of 1961 and the meeting of Presidents in Punta del Este in 1967, the greatest change—aside from an increase in confidence in Latin America's destiny under freedom—was the rise in emphasis on the movement toward Latin American economic integration.

I have had in recent years the privilege of working with Latin Americans as closely as I was permitted to work with Western Europeans in the immediate postwar years. I have found emerging in Latin America underlying forces and thoughts quite similar to those which moved Europeans a generation earlier. Latin Americans understand the technical advantages of economic integration; they understand that they can solve more problems for themselves and acquire a position of greater strength and dignity on the world scene through economic integration; and they understand that they will be able to work as a strong partner to the United States only if they move in this direction.

As in Western Europe, the economic integration movement in Latin America is drawing to it some of the best and proudest minds and spirits in that continent.

In Africa, of course, the movement toward economic unity and cooperation is much less well developed. The nations of the region are at an earlier stage of economic and social growth. Indeed, in some cases the nations born out of colonialism have not been able to maintain their initial unity against the pull of tribal and regional differences. Nevertheless, in counterpoint, there are the first beginnings of regional spirit and organization: the Organization for African Unity; the Economic Commission for Africa; and the African Development Bank. . . .

Surge of cooperative effort in Asia

The most dramatic emergence of a new regional spirit and policy is, of course, in Asia.

In a speech at Johns Hopkins University on April 7, 1965, President Johnson said: ". . . there must be a much more massive effort to improve the life of man" in Asia; and he went on to observe that the "first step is for the countries of Southeast Asia to associate themselves in a greatly expanded cooperative effort for development."

In the 26 months since the President spoke, we have seen in Asia a quite remarkable transformation of attitudes and action.

While the war in Viet-Nam goes on, with all its suffering, the peoples of Asia have begun to define for themselves a new future. That future hinges on a conviction that we are serious about seeing it through in Viet-Nam. Prime Minister Lee Kuan Yew of Singapore has, on a number of occasions, spoken in the vein in which he was recently quoted in *Reporter* magazine. He asked of Americans: "Are your people really serious in Vietnam? If you are, we are with you." They are with us because they know that the failure of aggression from Hanoi against South Viet-Nam and Laos is essential to the security of the region and only the American commitment—along with others—can establish this foundation for the future of Asia.

But they are looking not to us but primarily to themselves to define their future and to build it. In the words of this same Asian statesman, we are "buying time" for them in Viet-Nam—time for them to do a job only they can do.

Literally for the first time in history—thousands of years of history—the governments and peoples of Asia are coming together in a spirit of cooperation to begin to map the future of the region.

The list of Asian meetings that have occurred in the past 2 years is too long to repeat here. But they have met in various groupings among themselves—without us—to consider regional programs in the fields of education, agriculture, banking, and transportation. In addition, the Mekong Committee, working on the very edge of the battlefields, is carrying forward with a new vitality; and the Asian Development Bank is in operation in Manila, led by a distinguished Japanese.

In the proportions of its initial capital stock, that Bank foreshadows the kind of cooperation that may be possible in the future: We have put in 20 percent; the Japanese, 20 percent; the other Asian nations, 40 percent; and the balance comes from many sources outside the region.

This surge of cooperative effort in the new Asia takes place against the background of remarkable momentum in South Korea, Taiwan, Thailand, Malaysia, as well as in Japan; while Indonesia moves at last to find its feet after years of stagnation or worse. . . .

Divisions in the Middle East

The one region in the non-Communist world where regional institutions and spirit have not yet begun to emerge is, of course, the Middle East. During the whole postwar period, that region has been bedeviled by multiple splits and quarrels: not only between the Arab states and Israel but also by divisions among the Arab states and between certain Arab and other Moslem states.

No one from outside a region can create a spirit of determination to face and solve problems by regional cooperation. No one outside a region can build regional institutions. But we would hope that out of the frustrations and tragedies of postwar Middle Eastern history we might see emerge a new desire to achieve dignity and stability and progress for all through regional cooperation.

I am sure we and others outside the region will be prepared to be helpful if the peoples and governments of that area themselves decide that this is the right road and if they begin to move—in their own ways—along the path already taken by Western Europe, Latin America, and Asia. . . .

We are finding, then, in regionalism, a new relationship to the world community somewhere between the overwhelming responsibility we assumed in the early postwar years—as we moved in to fill vacuums of power and to deal with war devastation—and a return to isolationism. From the beginning our objective was not to build an empire of satellites but to strengthen nations and regions so that they could become partners.

And in this we are being true to ourselves, our tradition, and our practical experience as a nation.

Regionalism is built into the Federal Constitution of this continental democracy. It is one way we have learned to share power and responsibility. We have, therefore, found it easy and natural to work with those in other parts of the world who committed themselves to building regional order and assuming regional responsibilities.

To fulfill this vision of regional partnerships will take time and patience.

Above all, it will take dogged, stubborn pride and effort by the peoples of the various regions of the world. Moreover, many problems can only be solved on a global, rather than a regional, basis.

But, in the great inherently federal task we all assumed in 1945 with the acceptance of the United Nations Charter, we have learned that regionalism has a large and hopeful place.

The record of regional architecture in the first postwar generation is on the whole good and promising; but it is evidently incomplete.

As you take stock of the tasks ahead—in your coming time of responsibility—I am reasonably confident that the development of regionalism will engage your generation as much or more than it has mine. I trust and believe this is one part of my generation's effort you will not reject and set aside—but pick up and do better.

A debate on NATO: Our view of NATO

Lyndon B. Johnson

President Johnson concludes that NATO has been successful in its goal of bringing security to the North Atlantic Community. As a living organization, he feels it should adjust and adapt to the changing world but without sacrificing its might and its strength of purpose.

The Atlantic Community Quarterly, *Summer 1966. Address before the Foreign Service Institute at the Department of State, Washington, D.C., on March 23, 1966.*

I speak of a structure that some of you have helped to build: the North Atlantic Treaty Organization.

Let me make clear in the beginning that we do not believe there is any righteousness in standing pat. If an organization is alive and vital, if it is to have meaning for all time as well as for any particular time, it must grow and respond and yield to change. Like our Constitution, which makes the law of the land, the North Atlantic Treaty is more than just a legal document. It is the foundation of a living institution. That institution is NATO, the organization created to give meaning and reality to the Alliance commitments.

The crowded months which immediately preceded and followed the conclusion of the North Atlantic Treaty 17 years ago had produced an atmosphere of crisis. It was a crisis that was born of deep fear: fear for Europe's economic and political vitality, fear of Communist aggression, fear of Communist subversion.

Some say that new circumstances in the world today call for the dismantling of this great organization. Of course NATO should adapt to the changing needs of the times, but we believe just as firmly that such change must be wrought by the member nations working with one another within the Alliance. Consultation, not isolation, is the route to reform. We must not forget either in success or abundance the lessons that we have learned in danger and in isolation: that whatever the issue that we share, we have one common danger—division; and one common safety—unity.

What is our view of NATO today? We see it not as an alliance to make war but as an alliance to keep peace. Through an era as turbulent as man has ever known, and under the constant threat of ultimate destruction, NATO has insured the security of the North Atlantic Community. It has reinforced stability elsewhere throughout the world.

While NATO rests on the reality that we must fight together if war should come to the Atlantic area, it rests also on the reality that war will not come if we act together during peace. It was the Foreign Minister of France who, in 1949, insisted that to be truly secure, Europe needed not only help in resisting attack but help in preventing attack. "Liberation," he said, "is not enough."

The success of NATO has been measured by many yardsticks. The most significant to me is the most obvious: War has been deterred. Through the common organization, we have welded the military contributions of each of the 15 Allies into a very effective instrument. So convincing was this instrument that potential aggressors took stock and counted as too high the price of satisfying their ambitions. It has been proved true that "one sword keeps another in the sheath."

War has been deterred not only because of our integrated military power but because of the political unity of purpose to which that power has been directed and bent. It is difficult to overstate the importance of the bonds of culture, of political institutions, traditions, and values which form the bedrock of the Atlantic Community. There is here a political integrity and an identity of interests that transcends personalities and issues of the moment. . . .

For our part, the United States of America is determined to join with 13 of her other Allies to preserve and to strengthen the deterrent strength of NATO. We will urge that those principles of joint and common preparation be extended wherever they can be usefully applied in the Atlantic Alliance.

We are hopeful that no member of the treaty will long remain withdrawn from the mutual affairs and obligations of the Atlantic. A place of respect and responsibility will await any Ally who decides to return to the common task, for the world is still full of peril for those who prize and cherish liberty—peril and opportunity.

These bountiful lands that are washed by the Atlantic, this half-billion people that are unmatched in arms and industry, this cradle of common values and splendid visions, this measureless storehouse of wealth, can enrich the life of an entire planet.

It is this strength—of ideas as well as strength of arms, of peaceful purpose as well as power—that offers such hope for the reconciliation of Western Europe with the people of Eastern Europe. To surrender that strength now by isolation from one another would be to dim the promise of that day when the men and women of all Europe shall again move freely among each other.

It is not a question of wealth alone. It is a question of heart and mind. It is a willingness to leave forever those national rivalries which so often led to the useless squandering of lives and treasure in war.

It is a question of the deeper spirit of unity of which NATO is but a symbol. That unity was never better expressed than when, at the conclusion of the North Atlantic Treaty in 1949, a great French leader declared that: "Nations are more and more convinced that their fates are closely bound together—that their salvation and their welfare must rest upon the progressive application of human solidarity."

And it is to the preservation of human solidarity that all of our efforts today should be directed. . . .

A debate on NATO: A problem of alliance

General Lauris Norstad

General Norstad suggests six problem areas and their possible solutions in the interest of collective security for all.

Atlantic Community Quarterly, *Spring 1966. Excerpts of an address before the Life Insurance Association of America, New York, December 9, 1965. General Norstad is former Commander of NATO.*

Recognizing that some aspects of [the] problem are inherently so complex, so technical, that even those who have lived with it for years have difficulty understanding it, let me offer a short summary:

1. Europe feels that the nuclear forces and weapons essential for its safety must be available under all reasonable circumstances, and that Europeans should exercise proper influence or control over the use of this capability. Since neither we nor our Allies have taken any effective initiatives in this field for several years, let us get on with the business of developing one that has a reasonable chance of being accepted on both sides of the Atlantic.
2. Europe's nuclear needs in the NATO defense plan can only be supplied by the three producing nations—the United States, Britain and France. Whatever we and the other two agree to put into the common nuclear pot, under the NATO compact, should in an emergency be available in the common interest, unimpaired by a last-minute restriction by one or another of the nuclear powers.
3. Command and control over weapons committed to NATO can be exercised by an executive group, subject to guidelines laid down by the Alliance as a whole and open to *all* powers whenever their interest may become directly and critically involved. It should consist of the Standing Group countries, the United States, the United Kingdom and France, plus the

Federal Republic of Germany. This body should be established whether or not France chooses to participate at this time.

4. Since at the outset of hostilities or in anticipation of such an event only heads of governments could in fact take the all-controlling decision for or against nuclear action, the Presidents, appropriate Prime Ministers and Chancellors should form the executive committee.

5. In the interest of prompt decision, the committee, and through it the Alliance, should be governed by the rule of the majority. A majority decision would not bind, at least initially, a nation positively dissenting.

6. The distribution of nuclear weapons, critical materials and nuclear techniques should not be materially broader than is now the case. However, to insure maximum effectiveness of the resources committed to, or required by, the Alliance, a far wider exchange of technical and tactical information—non-nuclear—relating to the development, production and use of delivery systems, including missiles, should be encouraged.

The Alliance provides today, as it has for more than 15 years, the main foundation stone supporting our foreign policy, West and East. It has withstood every external assault, but now shows signs of internal erosion. It has become the very embodiment of the principle of collective security and, if it weakens, we risk losing "this last, best hope of earth," for achieving lasting peace with freedom.

Our Allies who have watched the deterioration without fruitful counteraction ask for new initiatives and the effective leadership that only the United States can provide. In our own interest and in theirs, we must respond.

A debate on NATO: The Soviet view of NATO

L. I. Brezhnev

This Soviet leader makes no attempt to hide his fear of a rearmed West Germany and his contempt for NATO. The alliance to him is contrary to European national interests of security and peace.

U.S. Senate, House, Subcommittee on National Security and International Operations of the Committee on Government Operations, 90th Congress, 1st Session, 1967. U.S. Government Printing Office, 1967. A speech by Mr. Brezhnev, who is chairman of the Communist party of the USSR, before the Conference of Communist and Workers Parties of Europe, April 24, 1967.

American and West German imperialism: The main threat to European peace

It might be asked: Why do we sharply pose the question of military danger in Europe today? Is the threat so serious? Yes, comrades, there are grounds for this. We do not want to exaggerate the danger of war, but neither do we wish to underestimate it.

Where and in what do we see the threat to European security today?

We answer: The threat to peace in Europe is borne by the aggressive forces of American and West German imperialism. What is the increasingly close partnership of these forces built upon? For American imperialism, collusion with the ruling circles of the Federal German Republic is the chief means, convenient for the United States and in essence not very expensive, of preserving its military-strategic positions in Europe. And this gives the United States significant levers for pressuring the policy and economics of the West European countries. As far as West German politicians are concerned, in their calculations partnership with the United States opens up for them real opportunities for implementing revanchist plans.

The aggressive policy of German imperialism has brought vast calamities to many European countries. This is well-known not only by the peoples of the Soviet Union but also by the peoples of Poland, Yugoslavia, Czechoslovakia, France, Britain, Belgium, Holland, Norway, Denmark, and other European states.

The Soviet people have not forgotten and never will forget that 20 million Soviet citizens gave their lives in the name of the victory over fascism. We had to develop vast efforts to heal the wounds of war, to restore thousands of destroyed towns and villages. . . .

The foundations of Europe's postwar structure were defined by the Potsdam Agreement. Its main demand is for eradication of militarism and Nazism so that Germany shall never again threaten its neighbors and world peace. This demand has force now and in the future. . . .

Facts show that the military threat which today stems from German imperialism is an indisputable reality. In the past 10 years the German Federal Republic has created one of the largest armies in West Europe, numbering almost half a million troops, and a sufficient quantity of command cadres to enable numerous armed forces to be mobilized in a short period, as was done on the eve of World War II. . . .

The military presence of the United States in Europe encourages West German militarism and increases the threat to peace in Europe. Hundreds of thousands of U.S. troops on European soil, U.S. military bases, U.S. aircraft carriers and atomic submarines patrolling the seas around the continent, U.S. bombers flying in European skies with their nuclear loads—all this creates a constant threat to the security of the peoples of Europe.

The basic instrument of U.S. policy in Europe has been and still is the NATO bloc. From the beginning, this pact has been maintained on the artificially fabricated myth of "the danger of Communist aggression," of the "threat from the East." The peace-loving policy of the Soviet Union and other Socialist countries, the entire course of events in Europe and throughout the world, have destroyed this myth. All can now see that "the hand of Moscow," with which imperialist propaganda has slanderously frightened the peoples, has been holding and still firmly holds the banner of peace, peaceful coexistence, and friendship among peoples. . . .

In this situation, the peoples of the NATO member countries and their governments face with particular acuteness the question: In whose name does this bloc exist, and what price is being paid for participation in it?

During the period of NATO's existence, the European states belonging to this bloc have spent over 300 billion dollars on military preparations. These expenses strike painfully at the interests of the working people, slow down economic developments, and retard the progress of science and culture. . . .

We do not hide the fact that the buildup of military efforts by the NATO countries forces the Soviet Union and the other Socialist countries to raise their level of military preparedness and to devote considerable sums to defense needs.

U.S. influence on politics, economic developments and the armed forces of several West European countries, the penetration of "Americanism" into every pore of social, scientific, and cultural life, becomes increasingly intolerable to all who cherish national dignity and the interests of peace.

The West European peoples are not willing to put up forever with using large areas of their territory to quarter U.S. expeditionary forces. Even certain monopolistic circles, making an effort to compete with their rivals across the ocean, find the military, economic, and political presence of the United States in West Europe, now extending into the third decade, a burden. The solution of European problems without the interference of the power across the ocean, by the efforts and common sense of the Europeans themselves—this demand finds ever more supporters throughout Europe.

In the past few years, plans for the so-called "modernization" of NATO have been urgently proposed, artificial arguments have been raked up to save this "holy alliance" of U.S. and European reaction at any price. This even went as far as to assert that NATO is capable of playing a positive role in developing contacts between West and East. It is difficult to conceive a more absurd argument! . . .

Experience shows that the process of expanding political, trade, economic, and cultural relations between the European Socialist and capitalist countries proceeds faster when our Western partners put their national interests first and act directly contrary to the recommendations of the NATO Council, ignoring the discriminatory measures it has introduced in relations with the Socialist countries. . . .

The way to security in Europe

For several countries, including those of northern Europe, neutrality could be an alternative to participation in military-political groupings of powers. The CPSU thinks that much depends on the initiative of the neutral states and on their good services in the cause of strengthening European peace. The Soviet Union would be ready to welcome initiatives serving this end.

Overcoming the division of the world and Europe into military blocs or alliances is part of the general struggle of the peoples to limit and completely end the arms race, to check militarism, and to clean the political atmosphere in Europe and throughout the world. From this point of view, there would be considerable significance in partial measures to reduce military tension in Europe, from the establishment of nuclear-free zones in separate regions of the continent to the liquidation of foreign military bases. . . .

The Warsaw Pact in evolution

Thomas W. Wolfe

Wolfe might well have entitled this selection "The Problem of the Other Alliance," for the Warsaw Pact is evolving as surely as its counterpart towards an emphasis on national interests rather than the bloc interests defined by its senior member. By attempting to counterbalance NATO, Moscow has inadvertently released a "national interest genie," strongly evident in recent Rumanian and Czech behavior.

This article originally appeared in The World Today *(May 1966), the monthly journal published by the Royal Institute of International Affairs, London. Reprinted by permission. Colonel Wolfe is senior staff member of the Rand Corporation (Washington office) and a member of the faculty of the Sino-Soviet Institute, George Washington University. He is the author of* Soviet Strategy at the Crossroads *and other works.*

A good deal of attention has been given recently to the changing pattern of relationships within NATO, one conspicuous symptom of which has been the efforts of France to convert the NATO alliance into a much more loosely knit association than hitherto. At the same time, there has been comparatively little awareness of developments affecting NATO's counterpart to the East: the Warsaw Pact military alliance, which embraces the Soviet Union and six of her East European neighbours. The fact is, however, that during the past five years or so a number of important changes have been taking place in both the character and potential of the Warsaw alliance. Before discussing these developments and some of their political and military implications, it may be useful to recall briefly the main lines of Soviet policy towards the Warsaw Pact military alliance during the earlier years of its history.

At its inception in May 1955, the Warsaw Pact appeared to be mainly a Soviet political-propaganda answer to the inclusion of West Germany in NATO rather than a serious effort to integrate the military activities of the Eastern bloc countries on a multilateral basis. The Soviet Union already had bilateral military arrangements with the various Pact countries, and her own military forces—both those garrisoning East Europe and those deployed behind the borders of the Soviet Union herself—were clearly counted upon to carry the burden of any military undertakings in Europe in which the Soviet Union might become involved.

Although the territory of East Europe was important to Soviet security for geographic and strategic reasons, the actual contributions expected of the other Pact armed forces to military operations in the European theatre—whether defensive or offensive—were apparently of secondary importance in Soviet eyes. The development of command arrangements for conducting modern theatre warfare on a joint basis received little attention; no joint exercises were held, and the Joint Command of the Warsaw Pact, headed by a Soviet officer, remained largely a paper organization with even less real work on its hands than the Political Consultative Committee, the Pact's policy organ. The latter apparently functioned less as a genuine policy-making body than as a forum for presentation of the Soviet policy line of the moment. Soviet propaganda treatment of the Warsaw Pact and the rare meetings of its formal organs, together with failure to flesh out these bodies in the first years of the Pact's existence, all tended to support the view that its symbolic political role initially carried far more weight in Soviet thinking than its cooperative military aspects. . . .

Changes in Soviet policy

In any case, changes in the Soviet conception of the role of the Warsaw Pact forces began gradually to appear towards the end of the 1950s, and by the summer of 1961 had become unmistakably evident. In this period, the Soviet Union embarked upon a series of moves, the general effect of which over the next few years was to upgrade the Warsaw Pact publicly in terms of the common defence of the Communist camp. Specifically, Soviet policy served to enhance the importance of the military contribution of the other Pact countries in overall Soviet planning; to extend the mission of the East European Pact forces from primary emphasis on air defence to a more active joint role in defensive and offensive theatre operations; and to promote joint training and re-equipment of the Pact forces commensurate with their apparently enlarged responsibilities.

The first joint Warsaw Pact manœuvres were held in October 1961, when Soviet, East German, Polish, and Czechoslovak forces participated in a major field exercise. Nine joint exercises involving various combinations of Pact forces have been reported to date, the latest being the widely publicized 'October Storm' manœuvres in East Germany in October 1965. . . .

Along with joint exercises, which presented such novel departures from tradition as the mingling of troops from various East European countries on each other's soil, went a programme for re-equipment of the East European forces and further standardization of their arms. Beginning in the early 1960s, the programme focused mainly on the ground forces and their supporting tactical air strength, which had received lower priority than air defence forces in the preceding years. . . .

During this process of modernization, the numerical strength of the East European Armed Forces remained relatively stable, totalling about 900,000–1,000,000 men. These forces are organized in some sixty divisions, of which about half are near combat strength, according to various Western accounts. Poland, with ground forces of about fifteen divisions and the largest air force in East Europe (about 1,000 aircraft), has emerged with the strongest national armed forces among the non-Soviet Pact members, followed by Czechoslovakia with an army of fourteen divisions and an air force exceeded only by that of Poland. The East German armed forces, while smaller than those of the other Pact countries, are among the best equipped and have often received new items of ground armament and aircraft from the Soviet Union before the others. Only four of the East European Pact members have naval forces. All of these are small, with Poland in the lead.

For the most part, the East European forces have been trained and equipped for conventional warfare. By contrast, the Soviet forces deployed in East Europe—which consist of twenty divisions in East Germany, two in Poland, and four in Hungary, plus sizeable tactical air elements and tactical missile units—possess both conventional and nuclear capabilities. This discrepancy between the essentially conventional posture of the East European forces and the nuclear-oriented posture and doctrine of the Soviet theatre forces began to change somewhat about two years ago, however, when the Soviet Union started furnishing potential nuclear-delivery systems to the East European countries in the form of tactical missiles with ranges of up to about 150 miles. Nuclear warheads for these missiles presumably were kept in Soviet custody and probably remain there today, and the missiles themselves are of little value without such warheads; nevertheless, missile acquisition by the other Pact armed forces marked a significant step towards possible nuclear sharing at some future date.

By the time Khrushchev's leadership came to an end in the autumn of 1964, it was clear from developments of the preceding four or five years that substantial changes had taken place, not only in the Soviet Union's policy towards the Warsaw Pact military alliance, but in the role the Pact forces themselves were capable of playing. . . .

Post-Khrushchev developments

Under Khrushchev's successors since October 1964, the main lines of Soviet policy towards the Warsaw Pact have remained essentially unchanged. The new regime has continued to stress more thorough integration of East European forces into Soviet operational plans by means of joint training and manœuvres, and it is going ahead with re-equipment and modernization of the Pact forces. At the same time, however, there have been some signs that the policy of greater reliance on East European forces, which was intended to improve bloc unity and cohesion, may be having the unintended effect of encouraging challenges to Soviet dominance and of giving the East European countries more leverage to influence Pact affairs.

Among the major problems of Soviet Warsaw Pact policy inherited from Khrushchev was that of nuclear access and control within the alliance. This problem again came to the fore in January 1965 when the seventh meeting of the Political Consultative Committee was convened in Warsaw—reportedly at the initiative of East Germany's Ulbricht—to consider measures to counter NATO plans for a multilateral nuclear force. Should such plans be implemented, it was declared, the Warsaw Treaty States would be 'compelled to take the defence measures necessary to ensure their security'.

While similar warnings had been sounded before, the situation was now somewhat different. Having already provided the East European forces with potential means of nuclear delivery in the form of tactical missiles and advanced fighter-bomber aircraft, the Soviet Union now faced the question as to whether she was also prepared to take the next step of furnishing nuclear warheads to her allies. Presumably, in considering new defence measures, the Warsaw meeting in January took up the knotty problem of East European access to nuclear weapons. Apart from subsequent Soviet reference to the existence of 'joint nuclear forces', however, there has been no clarifying comment on present procedures for nuclear access and control within the Warsaw alliance.

In the absence of evidence on this question, one can only surmise that the Russians have strong reservations about giving up the substance of their nuclear monopoly within the alliance, although pressures for sharing could build up in the future. One source of such pressure might be the possible reduction of Soviet troops in East Europe. Another factor that might conceivably lead the East European countries to press for nuclear weapons of their own is the possibility that under some nuclear-age circumstances the Soviet commitment to the defence of East Europe might come to be doubted, or—to put it in an idiom more well known in the West—the credibility of the Soviet deterrent might come to be questioned by the Soviet Union's Warsaw Pact allies.

Aside from the nuclear question, several other developments in Warsaw Pact affairs under the new Soviet regime deserve mention. One of these concerns the problem of getting the various Pact members to pull their proper weight within the alliance in return for closer integration and greater military responsibility. Some of the Pact members, most notably Rumania, have displayed considerable reluctance to accept the burdens entailed by larger Pact commitments. In the case of Bulgaria, an abortive conspiracy which took place in April 1965 was apparently inspired by a nationalist-minded faction of army and Party officials who hoped to orientate Bulgarian policy in a more independent direction, perhaps on the Rumanian model. Such a movement in Bulgaria, long considered the most conformist of the Soviet Union's Warsaw Pact allies, did not speak well for the solidity of the alliance's southern flank.

Perhaps partly as a hedge against soft spots in the southern sector of the alliance, a trend has emerged towards conferring privileged status on the northern members of the Pact. This has taken the form of referring in public media to the northern quartet—Poland, the G.D.R., Czechoslovakia, and the Soviet Union—as the 'first strategic echelon' of the Pact. Both military and political considerations seem to account for this emergent regional differentiation within the Warsaw Pact. The territory of the three East European members of the northern quartet lies directly in line with what in war-time would be the main axis of a central European campaign. These countries are also the most immediately affected by the German question. In Soviet eyes, their adherence to Moscow's interests may seem more certain than that of other Pact members by virtue of their concern over the so-called 'German threat'. The G.D.R. and Poland, however, may well differ on the terms of any future settlement of the German problem.

On the whole, the management of Soviet relations with other Warsaw Pact members has not grown notably smoother since Khrushchev's departure. The Soviet Party chief, Leonid Brezhnev, let fall a revealing remark in September 1965 which seemed to suggest that the Soviet leaders were getting a bigger dose of coalition politics than they would like. Commenting on the need to strengthen bloc unity in the realm of defence, Brezhnev said: 'The current situation places on the agenda the further improvement of the Warsaw Pact organization . . . We are all prepared to work diligently to find the best solution.' Two weeks later, referring to a series of talks with East European leaders, Brezhnev disclosed that the talks had dealt among other things with the need for establishing within the Warsaw Pact organization 'a permanent and operative mechanism for considering urgent problems'.

These acknowledgements that the Warsaw Pact faces urgent problems calling for reorganization suggests that the Soviet regime is under pressure from East European leaders, perhaps for adoption of new forms of decision-making in areas of policy and strategy that once were the sole prerogative of the Soviet Union. While it would be stretching things to say that this foreshadows the development within the Warsaw alliance of an open policy debate of the kind that takes place in the NATO forum, it does seem warranted to surmise that the East European members of the Warsaw Pact have begun to press for a more influential voice in matters affecting their own interests, such as the choice of alliance strategy, the sharing of military and economic burdens, and ultimately foreign policy issues bearing on the question of war and peace.

From the Soviet viewpoint, Warsaw Pact developments of the past few years are not necessarily to be regarded as largely unrewarding. Despite the difficulties that have arisen, the Pact continues to perform a significant function, not only as the basic treaty obligation binding the East European States to the Soviet Union, but also as an important multilateral institution tying the several countries of the bloc together. As a cohesive factor, the Pact may still prove more successful than such institutions as Comecon, at least so long as the ruling regimes in East Europe remain persuaded that their ultimate security rests on the protection afforded by Soviet military power and influence.

Furthermore, the Soviet Union may find it possible to turn a policy of greater military co-operation with the other Warsaw Pact countries to her own advantage in the area of disarmament negotiations and European security arrangements. Specifically, if convinced that the Pact countries can pull their own weight in a joint military alliance under Soviet guidance and that they are reliable, the Soviet Union may be able to contemplate some withdrawal from East Europe of her own forces, using this prospect as leverage for reciprocal reduction or withdrawal of NATO forces. This approach, long adumbrated by various Soviet bloc proposals for collective security measures in Europe, would fit logically into a Soviet foreign policy aimed at promoting the dissolution of NATO when its treaty comes up for renewal a few years hence.

Summing up, one may say that the main trends at work within the Warsaw Pact alliance seem to pull in two directions: towards closer military integration and interdependence on the one hand, and towards the assertion of separate national interests and a new balance of decision-making power among the Pact's members on the other. Though it would be unrealistic to expect the Soviet Union to surrender her dominant role in Pact affairs, the evidence suggests that the Warsaw Pact may be evolving into a more conventional sort of alliance, where decisions will be subject in greater degree than hitherto to the interplay of coalition politics.

Is the European idea dying?

Raymond Aron

Professor Aron points out the weakness of the European unification attempt via economic cooperation. The nationalistic tendencies of Gaullist France are as strong in this as in the military sphere, and the troubles of both attempts lie in the failure of either to provide sufficient security to its member states.

The Atlantic Community Quarterly, *Spring 1967. A summary of a series of articles from* Le Figaro *(Paris), November–December, 1966. Reprinted by permission of the author. Professor Aron is the author of numerous books and articles on international relations that have been translated and widely read throughout the world.*

Perhaps the question is superfluous. Have not the Six agreed on a common agricultural policy? Will not the last customs barriers within the Common Market fall on January 1, 1968? Despite the cold war between Paris and Washington, despite Franco-German disagreements over the Atlantic Alliance and despite the Franco-Russian rapprochement, the work of economic unification based upon the Schuman Plan goes on and seems to be coming to a head. M. Jean Monnet is not admitted into the establishment of the Fifth Republic but his idea has become reality.

On the economic level, the Common Market is both a failure and a success. It is a success as a free trade area. Intra-Community trade had increased annually by 8.4 per cent between 1952 and 1958; it increased annually by 13.5 per cent from 1958 to 1964. Extra-Community trade increased respectively during the two periods by 7.5 and 10 per cent. Imports from other members of the Community represented 34 per cent of the total imports of the Six in 1952, 36 per cent in 1958 and 40 per cent in 1964. For exports the figures were 37 per cent, 38 and 40 per cent.

Progress of intra-Community trade has been particularly marked in the case of France; the percentage of French exports to the other Five has grown in the same three years from 18.5 to 22.2 and 39 per cent, imports from 16 to 27 to 36 per cent.

In other words, intra-Community trade has developed faster than external trade since before 1958, when the Common Market entered into effect, and the trend is still accelerating. However, some other countries are even closer to the Six than its members are to each other. Switzerland takes 60 per cent of its imports from the Six.

It is less easy to determine the influence of the Common Market on the economic growth of the Six. Industrial production grew faster from 1952 to 1958 than from 1958 to 1964 in the Federal Republic (9 and 8.3 per cent respectively), and in France (7.8 and 5.8 per cent), less quickly in Italy (7.8 and 9.6 per cent), the Netherlands (5.6 and 8 per cent), Belgium (2.5 and 6.6 per cent), and Luxembourg (1.8 and 3.6 per cent).

It would be unwise to conclude that certain countries have derived more profit than others from the Common Market. The differences, considerable in industrial production, are less marked on national products. Moreover, the conditions of industrial growth were not the same during the 60's. The Common Market probably contributed to a high rate of growth in the national product of the Six countries (7 per cent in the Federal Republic, 6.1 in Italy, 5.4 in France and 5.2 in the Netherlands).

Perhaps the principal benefit the Six have derived from the Common Market has been lack of synchronization of circumstances. While Italy and France were forced to combat inflation with restrictive policies, the Federal Republic was passing through rapid expansion. By buying goods from Italy and France, the Federal Republic kept up their production and helped them re-establish commercial equilibrium. In 1966, the situation reversed; Italy and France can give the same assistance to West Germany.

No true European unity

The success of the Common Market, undeniable as it is, is nevertheless doubly limited even on the economic plane. Trade liberalization has proceeded faster than harmonization of legislation. Despite everything, there is no sign whatever of an irresistible or irreversible evolution from the Common Market to a true European unity comparable to a national unity. There is no fatality of federalism.

The Treaty of Rome would have begun the progressive creation of a kind of economic government of the Common Market if the governments of the Six had had the will. In its absence the Economic Community continues and prospers—but not without the risk of losing both its soul and its faith, of degenerating into a combination of free trade at the base and anonymous bureaucracy at the top.

The second reservation about the economic success of the Common Market is even more serious. Surprisingly at first sight but understandably on reflection, the attempt at European unification has encouraged a certain "Americanization" of all the economies of the Continent, and especially that of France. This "Americanization" is in certain respects, beneficial. The high rates of growth of all the European economies since the Second World War have been due largely to introduction of technology, and especially the technology of management, by American companies. We would prefer to make our own computers that business needs, but it is better to buy them from IBM than not to have them at all.

Certainly direct investment by American companies in Europe has grown rapidly since the Common Market and certainly the Market itself was one of the causes of this influx of trans-Atlantic capital. The Common Market constituted a great actual and potential outlet. During the 50's it had the highest rates of growth of any of the developed nations after Japan and was destined to be enclosed within an external tariff wall. The American companies were attracted by the prospects of this vast market and worried by the external tariff. From January, 1958 until August, 1964, according to American statistics, the value of direct American investment in France increased by 167 per cent. The increase was even greater in Germany, about the same in Italy.

Briefly, the Common Market is tending to become a commercial unity, not an economic one and still less a technical one. And the political failure is obviously complete.

The political failure

Since 1947, the European idea has become a driving force of history, one of the inspirations of Western policy. The first organization of European cooperation was born at the same time as the Marshall Plan. Like all ideas of historic importance, the European idea has different interpretations.

During the Cold War, Europe represented both an ill-defined geographic entity and an inherited civilization. The East was separated from this Europe by the Iron Curtain but belonged in the aspirations of its people. Yet, because of the Iron Curtain, the Western fragment of the Old Continent became Europe par excellence—that is to say by the union of will and tradition.

The division of non-Communist Europe into two parts—the true Europe of the Six, and the other countries, dates from 1950. At that date the quarrel between "Europeans" began. The French negotiators demanded acceptance of the principle of supranationality before any participation in the negotiations. Britain decided to stay out of the undertaking which she tried vainly to join 10 years later and from which, despite the hesitant goodwill of Mr. Wilson, she still risks being excluded.

Those in France responsible for this exclusion were not hostile to the British or to Anglo-Saxons in general. Robert Schuman and Jean Monnet were convinced that only experience could convert the British to "Europe," but also that it could not be built without an institutional system which, in fashionable terms, implied surrenders or transfers of sovereignty. Thus the "European Party," of which Jean Monnet was the symbol, seemed to be defined by the concepts of a Little Europe (reduced to six nations) and integrated (provided with an Executive). The M.R.P. Ministers, even Maurice Schumann, brought back by circumstances to the role of spokesmen for de Gaulle, left the government when the President turned his scorn in a press conference on the doctrine of so-called supranationality.

In 1960 the positions have been more or less reversed. The "Europeans" who had not been too displeased by the British rebuff of 1950 but who had been more or less hostile to the European Free Trade area, rallied in 1962 to the British candidacy, some because they had given up hope of a supranational Europe, others because they believed that the British had become converted, but both, probably, because the policy of Gaullist France worried them. . . .

European community is growing

The Common Market goes on and candidates for admission or association are still knocking on its doors. I repeat, its success is undeniable, but limited. The European Community is weaving indissoluble ties between its member States, maintaining a climate of competition and promoting a high rate of growth. It is still far from any semblance of a "national economic unit," even further from providing itself a government.

The "European Party" imagined an alternative evolution from economics to politics: the Six would be led by the experiment of economic cooperation between them to try the same experiment in other fields. Why should not a common diplomacy emerge from the Common Market? Here again, and even more so, the response of events has been negative.

The policies of France and of the Federal Republic within the Atlantic Alliance have been irreconcilable. The governmental team in Bonn, especially after the departure of Chancellor Adenauer, gave first priority to ensuring the security of Berlin and of Germany by the American presence; de Gaulle was primarily preoccupied with "American hegemony." If Washington's diplomacy had been less clumsy and French diplomacy less subtle, the Federal Republic might have avoided its present crisis, or at least the crisis might have been less severe.

The key to the quarrel of these last years—the relationship between the

European Community and the Atlantic Alliance—has been outdated in its turn, as the key of the previous quarrel had been outdated since 1960. What is henceforth in question is the relationship between the two parts of Europe or, if you will, a Europe from the Atlantic to the Urals. Is that Europe, certainly geographically defined, a theme for speech-making or an objective for action?

The Europe of nations

Whether success or failure, the experiment of the Common Market in these past years has confirmed that there is no inevitable transition from economic cooperation, even with partially supranational institutions, to political integration. Everything depends on the will of governments. Such elements of sovereignty as the Six have transferred to the Commission in Brussels, or, more precisely, exercise henceforth in common with it, do not involve the formation of a new State and do not imply a common diplomacy. The Europe of the Six was born in the shadow of the Atlantic Alliance and it will continue to live there, even if France has pulled out of NATO. This would probably remain true even if France denounced the Atlantic Treaty, which shows both the solidity and the limits of what has been accomplished. . . .

French and American diplomacy have had at least one thing in common—minimum regard for the effect in Germany. The one has sought an agreement, wholly meaningless in practice, on the nonproliferation of atomic weapons, the other an agreement between the two atomic powers of the Continent which would confirm its reestablished equilibrium and territorial status quo. . . .

Opposing systems can live in peace

In terms of centuries it is possible, even probable, that nations weigh heavier in the balance of history than ideologies. As Stalin said, National Socialism passes, the German people remain. In political terms, of years or decades, systems count and determine at least in part the foreign policies of nations. The Soviet systems and the systems of Western Europe can live in peace but they cannot collectively constitute a community comparable to that which the Europeans wished to build within the Six and which, if they have the resolve, they may still create tomorrow with the British and other members of EFTA.

Between advocates of European unity and visionaries of Europe from the Atlantic to the Urals there is therefore not only a difference as to what it would be opportune to do *hic et nunc*, there is also a radical conflict of philosophy.

Europe in the past has never been a political unit; she has lived and almost died in conflicts between sovereign states. General de Gaulle conceives of no international order other than that of equilibrium between countries jealous of their independence and with no ties other than those of changing interests. Evocation of a "reassembled Europe" which would impose peace in Asia sounds like the oratory of a speech after an official dinner. Nations, "these cold monsters," will not reassemble except under orders from a master, and if the nations of Europe ever submit to a master he will not be in Paris.

The fundamental conflict between the Europeans of yesterday and of today is reflected in different approaches. The Europeans of yesterday, accepting the fact that partition was bound to last for years, wished to offer the Germans of the Federal Republic what might be called a welcoming structure. In the impossibility of realizing the national ambition to reunify their country, the Germans would become Europeans, treated as equals by their partners. Militarily, equality of rights would imply access to atomic weapons which is, for many reasons, forbidden to the Federal Republic, but within the European Community their political and moral unity was otherwise recognized.

It is not refused them today. Unfortunately the Common Market is only an administration without a soul. Between a neutral France, or one half allied with the Soviet Union, and a Federal Republic which cannot detach itself from the United States, there is hardly anything left but economic solidarity. If the Federal Republic one day decides to follow on its own a policy of "opening to the East" it will have no need of intermediaries in Paris. The men of the Kremlin today prefer Paris to Bonn but there is nothing to prevent a different choice tomorrow.

It is time, a close associate of the General tells me, for the Germans to remember that they lost the war. That is the language the Germans used to the French at the end of the last century and the French to the Germans after 1919 and before 1933. Perhaps it is the only language some men understand, men formed by a long tradition.

I still hope that the youth of Europe will understand another language.

The prospects for a Latin American common market

Robert W. Bradbury

As in Europe, economic cooperation in Latin America has been divided into a Common Market and a Free Trade Association. The problem of combining these into a single strong unit is discussed by Professor Bradbury. Again, sovereignty and nationalism are the main barriers.

Economic Leaflets (*University of Florida*), *May 1967. Reprinted by permission. Mr. Bradbury is a professor of economics at the University of Florida.*

On April 12 to 14, 1967, the presidents of the countries of Latin America (with the exception of Cuba and Bolivia) and the President of the United States met at Punta del Este, Uruguay, for a summit meeting in order to revitalize the Alliance for Progress and to make other significant changes in the "inter-American system." In order to extend the scope of the Latin American market, one of the significant agreements was that which pledged a continuing effort to establish a Latin American Common Market. This agreement was signed by all of the Latin American presidents who participated in the meeting with the exception of President Arosemena of Ecuador.

The proposal of a common market was not a new idea but one which had been studied since shortly after World War II. Prior to World War II, Latin America had been predominately an exporter of agricultural products and other raw materials and an importer of manufactured goods. This does not mean that there was no manufacturing within Latin America, as important industrial complexes already existed in the vicinity of Mexico City, Mexico; Sao Paulo, Brazil; and Buenos Aires, Argentina. These major centers plus centers of lesser importance in other Latin American countries supplied a rather wide range of consumer goods, but the general observation that the Latin American countries were not highly industrialized when regarded in relation to other more advanced industrial areas of the world is obviously true.

During the war years of 1941 to 1945, there were many new industries established in Latin America because of the shortage of supplies available from the United States and from the other belligerent nations. These new industries were not always well established and were still operating at high cost and consequent uneconomic competitive advantage at the end of the conflict. They continued in existence largely because of various protective devices, i.e., high tariffs, import permits, import quotas, and exchange controls.

In order to help to create a viable economy in Latin America, the United Nations established the Economic Commission for Latin America (ECLA). ECLA was located in Santiago, Chile.

The most influential economist in ECLA was the Argentine, Raul Prebisch, who influenced the economic thinking of a large majority of the economists in Latin America, particularly those employed in governmental development and planning. Dr. Prebisch's main contention was that the Latin American countries, as exporters of raw materials, would continue at a disadvantage relative to the developed countries under the present economic conditions. In his opinion, the Latin Americans would have to give more and more of their raw materials in return for the manufactured goods which were imported from abroad because the demand for raw materials (and particularly for foodstuffs such as sugar and coffee) was inelastic while the demand for imported manufactured goods was highly elastic.

According to Dr. Prebisch, the solution to this dilemma of an unfavorable trend in terms of trade was to industrialize to the extent that the Latin American countries would no longer be dependent on foreign sources for the major portion of their manufactured consumer goods. It was thought that domestically produced consumer goods would in the near future substitute for the imported consumer goods. The demand for imports would thereby be lessened and the Latin American countries might then find it possible to use the proceeds of their exports to buy capital equipment.

Dr. Prebisch believed that one important stimulus to economic development was a widening of the market so that firms of the most efficient size could be established. Thus an integrated market of most or all of the countries would permit economies of scale and, therefore, a great increase in industrialization.

As a result of the studies made at Santiago, Chile, committees representing the various countries were appointed during the 1950's to try to form a common market for Latin America. It proved to be impossible to get a majority of the countries together at any one time, but in 1960, eight nations met in Montevideo, Uruguay, to discuss the formation of a common market. These eight included the three countries with the greatest industrial development and, therefore, with the greatest interest in the establishment of a common market. These three were Mexico, Brazil, and Argentina. In addition, three others with certain established industries, Uruguay, Chile, and Peru, attended and were quite enthusiastic, while the remaining two, Paraguay and Bolivia, were industrially underdeveloped by any criteria.

The discussions led to the rejection of a common market but to the establishment of the Latin American Free Trade Area (LAFTA). Some of the countries felt that establishing a common external tariff would involve an impairment of their national sovereignty. While the countries agreed to a gradual reduction in tariffs among themselves, this reduction was to take place only over a period of twelve years.

The reductions of the intra-regional tariff barriers were to be accomplished by two different devices. First, each year the representatives of the countries would meet and agree bilaterally to a reduction of 8 percent on their intra-regional trade. Second, every three years they were to meet and agree to a multi-lateral reduction of 25 percent.

The agreement included many escape clauses and, for each reduction, it was required that agreement be reached at these periodic meetings. Bolivia and Paraguay argued that they should be given special dispensations because of their underdevelopment, and special escape clauses were therefore included for their protection. In spite of this, Bolivia did not join LAFTA at that time, but the other seven signed the agreement in 1960. By 1961, the seven had ratified and LAFTA started operations. Since then Ecuador and Bolivia have joined under the same escape clauses as did Paraguay, and Colombia and Venezuela have become members.

These eleven countries, which comprise the bulk of the population and of the gross national product (GNP) of Latin America, have been cooperating for almost six years. Their intra-regional trade, however, constituted less than 10 percent of their total international trade at the time that LAFTA was initiated. This intra-regional trade has increased by about 100 percent during the life of LAFTA but still constitutes only a small fraction of their total international trade.

During the first three years, many substantial tariff reductions were granted on a bilateral basis. However, the organization ran into difficulties when unanimous agreement on the multilateral agreements was attempted. The Chase Manhattan Bank in its publication, *World Business*, estimates that the regional tariffs have been reduced to about 50 percent of the level applicable to nonregional imports. Thus it would seem that LAFTA has been reaching its goal and would at this rate eliminate tariff barriers in the twelve years specified.

The tariff reductions made so far, however, have generally affected items which are not produced by the countries granting the concessions. Thus there have been no domestic producers who might oppose the tariff concessions. When the attempt is made to generalize these bilateral agreements, opposition appears. Almost 60 percent of the intra-regional trade is accounted for by trade between Argentina and Brazil, and the major bilateral concessions were between these two countries. Thus an erroneous feeling of success may be conveyed by viewing the results on a percentage basis which obscures specific detail.

The many uses of escape clauses and the long discussions involved in obtaining the multilateral reductions have contributed to a sense of discouragement among the members regarding the future of LAFTA. To try to revitalize LAFTA, President Frei of Chile asked four leading Latin American economists, Felipe Herrera, Raul Prebisch, Jose A. Mayobre, and Carlos Sanz De Santamaria to serve as a committee to recommend changes in LAFTA. These four gentlemen met and recommended certain changes which were largely in line with the successful development of another experiment in economic integration that had taken place in Central America.

The Central American Common Market (CACM) was established at almost the same time as was LAFTA. CACM was composed of the five republics; Guatemala, El Salvador, Honduras, Nicaragua, and Costa Rica. Panama was not included, but indicated in August of 1966 a desire to join. The writer believes that the successful integration of CACM, which contributed materially to an increase of intra-regional trade of approximately 400 percent in the Common Market area, can be traced to the following four factors.

First, the five countries of Central America had been part of a federation during their first 15 years of independence. Thus, even after their separation into unaffiliated, independent countries, a tradition of cooperation continued. For this reason, the spirit of nationalism and the possible consequence of mutual suspicion is not as pronounced politically as among some of the countries of LAFTA. . . .

Second, it is easier to form an economic union of countries that are in the same stage of economic development and with approximately equal gross national product per capita. These conditions are met by the countries of CACM but not by the countries of LAFTA. . . .

The third factor affecting the potential for economic integration has great importance. Monetary stability is conducive to the development of intra-regional trade and in this respect CACM has an outstanding record. The five countries have exchange rates that are stable in the international money markets. . . .

On the other hand, some of the countries of LAFTA have experienced extreme inflation, which hinders intra-regional monetary stability. Chile, Uruguay, Argentina, and Brazil have all endured extreme and continuing inflation. Paraguay and Bolivia had an inflationary period during the early 50's but in recent years these countries have been successful in stabilizing their currency. The price rise in Brazil has been as much as 89 percent in one year, and even last year was 41 percent. . . .

Fourth, ease of transportation is another essential for the continued growth of a large integrated market economy. While Central America is not outstanding from the standpoint of transportation, the Inter-American Highway does connect the capital cities of the five republics by paved roads. Therefore, goods manufactured in one country can be delivered by truck to another country with little delay.

On the other hand, between some of the LAFTA countries the movement of goods can be slow and very costly. From Ecuador to Argentina the only effective route is by water by way of the Panama Canal, which places Buenos Aires at a much greater distance from Ecuador than from the major ports of the United States or Europe.

The four economists who were engaged in the effort to revitalize LAFTA recommended that a sincere attempt should be made to establish a Latin American Common Market with a common external tariff; that CACM be permitted to join as a unit; and that those countries of Latin America that were outside the two groups be urged to join the common market. The economists recognized that a willingness to cooperate must be fostered among the Latin American nations and that outstanding political difficulties must be resolved. They also recognized that inflation was a drawback and urged the nations suffering from chronic inflation to try to stabilize their currency. The necessity of improving the transportation systems between the countries was also given due weight. . . .

The Latin American Common Market would evolve from a merger of the Latin American Free Trade Association and the Central American Common Market. Because of the recent lack of success of LAFTA, it was felt that it would be unwise merely to adopt minor proposals whose only purpose would be to strengthen the present organization. It was considered far more judicious to make a more dramatic proposal for the common market. The new common market would involve much more cooperation and would require the adoption of a uniform tariff against nonmember imports. To be worked out in the next three years will be agreements to permit the free movement of labor and capital among the member countries and the coordination of monetary and fiscal policies. Of vital importance will be the elimination of the high rate of inflation now existing in some of the Latin American countries.

It is the hope of the founders that there will be a gradual reduction in the feeling of nationalism and an accompanying growth in the spirit of cooperation not only at the level of economic interchange but also in the realm of political cooperation. It is hoped that Latin America will cooperate in other fields such as the interchange of technological advances, including improvements in agricultural technology, and that the new common market may follow the lead of Central America in many other cooperative adventures such as the Joint Tariff Commission and the Council for University Cooperation. . . .

A danger in developing a common external tariff is that the Latin American countries may be tempted to adopt a high tariff towards goods which are produced outside of the common market. Such a program, while it might give an initial stimulation to any industries within the market, might potentially lead to long-run stagnation. It is hoped that the external tariff will be relatively low and subject to later reductions.

Within the recent success of the Kennedy round of GATT negotiations in Europe (which may lead to an estimated reduction of 35 percent in trade barriers) as an incentive, it is to be hoped that this pattern may eventually be followed by Latin America. Latin America must continue to depend on the outside world for much of its heavy machinery and equipment and as a source of quite a few raw materials which are needed in their developing industries and which are not found within the confines of the common market.

The development of a common market in Latin America, while it will reduce the imports into Latin America of some products from the United States, will lead to greater trade between the two continents rather than less. Our exports to the European Common Market have expanded very rapidly in spite of the close economic integration of that area. As a region becomes more prosperous, demands increase and a larger amount of imported goods are purchased.

The United States will watch with interest the negotiations that will occur during the next three years looking toward the start of a common market by 1970. Many problems, obviously, must be overcome. While the leaders of the cooperating countries pledged themselves to work toward a common market, national interests within the countries may present many stumbling blocks. Moreover, the smaller and less industrialized nations will ask for special dispensations, and yet, if too many special concessions are granted, a true common market will not come into being. True statesmanship will be required in order to eliminate some of the political frictions that exist between the nations. It will be necessary for individual businessmen to face the unhappy fact that certain special advantages must be relinquished in order to promote the general good.

We in the United States wish the Latin American Common Market every success in this formative period, knowing full well that a strong, prosperous, viable economy in Latin America will foster in the long run closer ties, economic and political, between nations and groups of nations which are more nearly equal in size and in economic condition.

The struggle for Arab unity

Abbas Kelidar

Regionalism in the Middle East is based principally on a common nationalism and thus should be easily obtainable. Race, religion, and the presence of a common enemy are strong roots for unity, but Professor Kelidar points out that these are not enough to overcome conflicting national interests; not even a common defeat has been able to provide the final impetus for coalition.

This article originally appeared in The World Today *(July 1967), the monthly journal published by the Royal Institute of International Affairs, London. Reprinted by permission. Mr. Kelidar is a lecturer in the Department of Economic and Political Studies, School of Oriental and African Studies, London University.*

Most ideologues of Arab nationalism seem to speak in terms of having a mission for the Arab peoples. This is no more than the express intention of all nationalists to liberate, unite, and reconstruct the Arab world and revive its cultural traditions. It means that they will conduct a campaign to end Western influence and domination, to assemble a nation of all the Arabs, and to adopt revolutionary action against all evils, intellectual, economic, social, and political. They reject evolutionary processes of change because their society is not healthy enough to produce such change. Revolution in this context means an intellectual and moral change which requires a change in the social system of values. However, most observers of the Arab nationalist scene seem to take these ideas at their face value, never doubting their foundation in historical and social reality; or else they question the expression of Arab nationalist sentiment and unionist aims, whether made at the official or the popular level. It may be more profitable to the understanding of Arab politics to focus attention not so much on the theme of the establishment of an independent and united Arab State—though recent developments in the Middle East have made this once more a burning issue—but on the failure to achieve such a political objective.

There is no doubt that Arabism as a belief constitutes a great source of social power; but when it is advocated by different leaders, expressing divergent interests, this power is dissipated. There is also no doubt that the Arabs have not been able to agree on the leadership of this movement and in recent history the orientations of the leadership have changed many times, reflecting the interests of local ruling groups in the separate nation-States. The adoption of the Arab nationalist cause by Egypt in 1956 and her subsequent union with Syria two years later gave President Nasir unquestionable command over the Arab revolutionary movement. But the emergence of a revolutionary regime under General Qasim in July 1958 revived Iraqi claims to the leadership of Arabism after they had been in abeyance under Nuri al-Sa'id since 1945. With Syria's secession from the union with Egypt in 1961, and the elimination of Qasim in 1963, the issue of pan-Arab leadership became more of a contest between the so-called 'revolutionaries' and 'reactionaries', the 'revolutionaries' comprising such States as Egypt, Iraq, Syria, Algeria, and the Republic of Yemen, led by Nasir, while the 'reactionaries' consisted of Jordan, Saudi Arabia, Tunisia, and Morocco, with no accepted leader.

Revolutionary socialism

In recent years, however, the concept of Arab unity has been accompanied by the idea of revolutionary socialism, which has tended to overshadow nationalist hostility to the West. Anti-colonialism has remained the rallying-cry, but ever since 1958 there has been a shift of emphasis in the radical political currents in the Arab world, and this was given a strong impetus by the rise of the United Arab Republic and the Republic of Iraq. The appearance of these two republics on the Arab political scene led to the identification of the opponents of Arab unity as the 'reactionaries', i.e. the hereditary monarchs, oligarchic politicians, and wealthy landowners and businessmen who had found it easier to protect their political and economic interests by keeping the Arab world divided. Their alleged reliance and co-operation with the Western Powers was held to be simply a facet of their reactionary outlook. At first sight, the division in the Arab world looks like a contest between the monarchies, with their accepted and traditional basis of legitimacy, and the newly established republics, seeking a fresh formula to legitimize their rule by responding to the political aspirations of the masses in their own territory and further afield. But on closer examination it is clear that the division is really a struggle for the leadership of the Arab world by the contending parties. Furthermore, this division is not as clear-cut as many people seem to think, nor has it any real ideological basis. The differences between the 'revolutionaries' and the 'reactionaries', no matter how real they may have been, have had to give way from time to time to political exigencies. The support and active cooperation offered to Egypt, Syria, and Jordan by the other Arab States, regardless of their previous political identification, was highlighted in the Arab-Israeli war. . . .

The establishment of the U.A.R. was seen as the finest achievement of the movement for radical nationalism and revolutionary socialism. A tumultuous wave of enthusiasm greeted the union in the two countries concerned and in the rest of the Arab world. It was regarded as the turning-point in the history of the movement; the initiative had passed to the revolutionary nationalists who expected the peoples of the other Arab States to rise against their oppressors and join the union. Iraq and Jordan were quick to protect themselves with a federation of their own, but the Iraqi revolution in July 1958 soon brought this to an end. It also blurred the distinction that had been developing between 'reactionaries' and 'revolutionaries'. . . .

Egyptian withdrawal

In September 1961 the union between Egypt and Syria collapsed. Egypt's explanation for Syria's secession was simple. The union had failed because it was stabbed in the back by the Syrian wealthy class, the 'reactionaries,' who had been affected by the programme of socialist legislation which Nasir had decreed in July 1961. These reactionaries, with the help of the Western Powers and the Arab monarchs, had bribed and subverted a clique of officers in the Syrian army to carry out a *coup* to restore the old regime and to repeal the socialist reforms. However, the Syrian secession brought to an end all the anomalies under which the U.A.R. leadership had suffered. Egypt contracted out of active Arab politics, and instead declared an ideological war on all the conservative 'reactionary' regimes in the area. She withdrew behind the barricades of socialist reconstruction at home. Egyptian troops were withdrawn from Kuwait, since it was no longer possible to co-operate with 'reactionary' Jordan and Saudi Arabia, or with 'secessionist' Syria. The revolutionary regime of Qasim in Iraq was also explained away in ideological terms: he was a 'deviationist'. . . .

By the end of 1963, the Arab world was witnessing the collapse of any semblance of solidarity in either the reactionary or the revolutionary camp. Syria was quarrelling with Egypt and Iraq; Egypt and Saudi Arabia were feuding over the Yemen; Algeria was fighting with Morocco; and Morocco was irritated by Tunisia's recognition of Mauritania. Egypt and Syria found it ideologically convenient to be hostile to 'reactionary' Jordan, Morocco, and Saudi Arabia. None the less the general lines of division had become clear. The revolutionary States were pitted against the conservative and moderate regimes: Egypt, Algeria, Iraq, Syria, and the Republic of the Yemen against the others. But of all the feuding parties, the rivalry between Egypt and Syria for the leadership of the revolutionary movement was the most intense. . . .

Throughout 1966, and until the war broke out between the Arabs and the Israelis in June of this year, the main dividing line between the 'revolutionaries' and the 'reactionaries' has been that between the supporters of King Faysal's Islamic alliance and of President Nasir's pan-Arabism. In December 1966 Nasir launched his bitterest attack on the 'reactionary elements' in the Arab world. . . . In a review of the discussions on united Arab action over the previous three years, he claimed that Egypt had been ready to let bygones be bygones but that King Faysal had made a deal with the Americans and deposed his brother, and that King Hussain had seized the opportunity to obtain funds from the summit conferences and from King Faysal. Faysal, in Nasir's words, had launched the Anglo-American-inspired Islamic alliance while Hussain wagged his tail. He concluded by saying that the Arabs could have no confidence in Faysal, Hussain, or Bourguiba. Egypt, on the other hand, was not immune from criticism. By maintaining her troops in the Yemen, she laid herself open to the charge of conducting a fratricidal war—a charge which Hussain and Faysal lost no time in making. 'Revolutionary' Syria taunted the Egyptian leadership for turning a blind eye to the Arabs' main enemy, Israel. Egypt was condemned by 'reactionaries' and 'revolutionaries' alike for her continued acceptance of the U.N. emergency force on her border with Israel.

Nasir, under great pressure from his rivals and critics, had to act. In 1963 he had called for an Arab summit meeting to contain the Syrians, who were clamouring for war with Israel over the Jordan waters, by committing them to a general unified Arab policy. At the time, this was seen as a clear indication that he was not prepared to be dragged into war with Israel provoked by the Syrians. By 1967, however, conditions in the Arab world had changed. Though Nasir was still at war with the supporters of King Faysal's Islamic alliance and committed to protect the Republican regime in the Yemen, Syria had produced a new regime in February 1966, more radical than the one that had been in power since March 1963. This regime manifested a more militant attitude towards Israel and gave active support and encouragement to Palestinian commandos operating inside Israel and on her borders with Jordan. It also advocated radical notions of nationalism and socialism, and made some friendly overtures to the Egyptian leadership by focusing attention on the danger from King Hussain, who was thought to have supported an attempted *coup* by some Syrian officers in September 1966. Nasir, with Iraq and Algeria engrossed in their own internal problems, was left with only Syria and Sallal of the Yemen—both of them insecure—in his revolutionary camp. Thus in November 1966, relations between Syria and Egypt were brought closer than they had been since the Syrian secession in September 1961. A defence pact was signed and diplomatic relations resumed. . . .

The question that now has to be asked is: did Nasir want war with Israel in May 1967, when he shunned it in November 1966, or was he trying to make a grand gesture of strength in order to restore his command over the Arab leadership? In spite of his decision to close the Strait of Tiran to Israeli shipping, all the evidence would indicate that he was aiming at the latter policy rather than the former. Indeed, a case could be made that in fact what he wanted was nothing more than the maintenance of the *status quo*. By stating that Egypt would attack Israel only if Syria was attacked, he would have discouraged Israel and protected Syria, and at the same time restored his leadership of the Arab revolutionary movement and his reputation as the champion of the Arab cause in Palestine. But this was not to be.

Future of the Arab leadership

The other question that has to be asked is: what is to become of this leadership following the disastrous defeat of the Arab armies? President Nasir has secured his position by acceding to the popular demands in Egypt and other Arab countries protesting against his attempted resignation on 9 June. However, in the final analysis the security of his position must depend on the attitude of the remnants of his army. King Hussain, who tried to insure the safety of his throne by signing a defence pact with Egypt, has enhanced his reputation as a courageous man but has lost the west bank of the Jordan. The Syrians are too insecure to last long. President 'Arif of Iraq does not have the aptitude to be a popular leader. King Faysal, who has come out of the war unscathed, suffers from several handicaps if he is to assume the mantle of pan-Arab leadership, the least of these being his position as a traditional ruler of a relatively backward country.

This leaves President Houari Boumedienne of Algeria, but it is very doubtful if the Arab world could be led from North Africa. Nevertheless, President Nasir in his abortive resignation speech declared that there was a need for 'a unified voice on the part of the entire Arab nation, that is a safeguard for which there is no substitute in these conditions'. The Arabs, in their anger and grief at what has befallen them, are seeking to hold a summit conference, the purpose of which, as *al-Ahram* put it, is 'to work out a plan to erase the effects of the present setback and to adopt a unified stand on forthcoming conspiracies'.

There is no doubt about the genuineness of the Arab desire for unity in the face of the defeat they have suffered, but whether Arab emotion can be translated into concerted political action remains to be seen. Judging by past experience this seems doubtful. The obvious differences in their political orientations have kept them divided, and the diversity of political institutions and forms of government, and the differences in levels of economic and social development among the various States, further complicate the issue. The one element which remains identifiable to all Arabs, in spite of the differences between their rulers, is Islam. An Arab anywhere in Morocco, the Yemen, or Iraq accepts Arabism more readily if it is equated or linked with Islam, and this applies with equal validity to the Egyptian, who has always been conscious of being both an Egyptian and a Muslim. This may favour King Faysal's assumption of the pan-Arab leadership, but the other differences among the Arab States are bound to throw up rivals.

Section 4

The progress of international trade, investment, and cooperation

The next steps in trade liberalization

Lester B. Pearson

Former Prime Minister Pearson decries the dangers of increased trade between rich nations while poor nations get both less trade and less aid. His thesis is that continuation of this trend will be political, economic, and humanistic folly.

Atlantic Community Quarterly, *Summer 1967. Excerpts of an address delivered to the XXIst Congress of The International Chamber of Commerce, Montreal, May 15, 1967. Mr. Pearson is former Prime Minister of Canada.*

What is particularly striking in this ever changing era is not only the nature but the rapidity of change. And we must face the prospect that the pace will accelerate.

The changing world has brought great opportunities but also great challenges. Unquestionably the most crucial is the task of achieving conditions that will ensure peace and enable men to devote their many talents to the task of development rather than destruction.

The post-war years have been a period of dynamic developments in world trade, in growth, composition and direction. It has increased by unprecedented amounts. Equally important, its character has changed.

Exports of manufactured goods have grown at nearly triple the rate of primary products and double that of industrial materials. Among the more important long-run factors affecting the flow of world trade since the war have been a wide range of technological developments and the initiative of businessmen in applying them. These have fundamentally altered methods of producing and distributing goods and the means of communicating with one another.

Another important factor has been the multilateral trade and payments system and the substantial reduction of tariffs and other restrictions to trade which it has brought about. Indeed this multilateral trade and payments system is one of the major achievements of postwar international economic co-operation.

But all is not clear sailing because now, more and more, trade discussions have to deal with a variety of new and complicated barriers and new techniques of negotiation are needed. There is a growing appreciation that certain whole sectors or industries must be approached on a broad international front. Generally, these industries are characterized by high levels of capital investment, advanced technology, large-scale production and, not infrequently, widely dispersed international operations. Unfortunately, another frequent characteristic of these industries is that non-tariff as well as tariff barriers can and do impede international trade in the products they produce. By dealing with these industries as a whole, it may be possible to negotiate balanced bargains covering both tariff and non-tariff barriers.

Less aid and less trade

The concern of the developed countries for their own growth and stability should lead, and in some cases has led, them to agree to remove trade barriers, affecting products of low-income countries without full reciprocity. The need for this is shown by the fact that the share of these countries in world trade has been falling at the very time that the flow of aid funds has levelled off; and indeed threatens to be reduced. Less aid and less trade could be a catastrophic combination for the developing countries—indeed for us all. It would simply mean that while we may be conquering outer space, we are losing the war on this planet against poverty, hunger and disease. These have been the constant enemies of man since the beginning of time.

Despite all of our boasted technological triumphs, they maintain their tyranny over two-thirds of the world's population. In the next ten years starvation alone could claim as many lives as all the battle casualties of history.

This confronts us with a new kind of challenge for a new kind of enterprise based on constructive compassion and enlightened self-interest. This is not a struggle of man against man, but of man joining with man in united action against a mounting threat to the stability and security of all mankind. If this threat were joined to the increasing threat of a major war, well, I would not want to be my grandchildren.

Poverty, hunger and disease are not new. Man has struggled against them since the very beginnings of life on this planet. What is new about today's struggle is that for the first time in human history we have the capacity to win, if we have the will and the persistence to do so. Yet we are losing—and at a time when we must win if life is to flourish on this planet.

Today the miracles of modern science and technology have indeed given the world the space-time dimensions of a single community. But we have yet to make the immense adjustments in our own social and political attitudes and behavior patterns which would be essential if we are not to be destroyed by our scientific and technical genius.

It is evident today that every nation can best serve its own highest interests by serving the universal interests of humanity. For as no individual can be an island in his own community, neither can any nation be an island in today's world.

Income and access to markets

During the last decade the peoples of the advanced free democratic countries increased their per capita annual income by some $330. This increase is twice as much as total per capita income of people in most countries of the developing world. So what kind of private enterprise can be expected in that world?

Access by the developing countries to the markets of the more prosperous countries must be made easier to help them strengthen their agriculture and establish their industrial capacities. It is clear that only greater export earnings will provide these countries with the funds required for these purposes. There is little logic in encouraging the industrialization of these countries through aid, and at the same time imposing restraints on imports of the products that they can produce on a competitive basis. So further progress in the reduction of barriers to trade must be on a worldwide basis, with special consideration for the underdeveloped world. This progress could be prejudiced by the establishment of new regional trading groups.

While movements toward economic integration can also have important and beneficial political advantages, discriminatory, inward-looking groups are today no answer to the problems of either the developed or the underdeveloped world, whether formed on a European, North American or any other basis.

Unless the dismantling of internal tariffs proceeds simultaneously with the reduction of external tariffs, discriminatory trading arrangements could bring about a substantial distortion of the international trading system. Such a development would be wasteful and uneconomic.

Even more serious, however, is the danger of political frictions which would arise from a significant distortion of traditional trade patterns and ties, frictions which would intensify if other countries entered into special trading arrangements devised largely as measures of defence and retaliation.

If Britain and other members of EFTA join the European Common Market, therefore, it is all the more important to make further progress on the multilateral front as perhaps the best means of easing adjustments to new trading patterns.

Trade with the USSR

George W. Ball

Change and security are strongly evident in this speech by Ambassador Ball. Changes are inevitable within the Soviet society, and the U.S. should anticipate and account for these in policy. Security is fragile if the basis is a "balance of terror at a progressively higher level of cost and destructiveness." Relaxed trade restrictions might be one avenue to take advantage of the change and to reduce the fragile nature of security.

Address before the National Industrial Conference Board's Third Annual Public Affairs Conference in New York, April 20, 1967. Reprinted by permission. Mr. Ball was chairman of Lehman Brothers International, Ltd., former Undersecretary of State, and former American Ambassador to the United Nations.

. . .We are at the beginning of 1967, and that means it is now slightly more than 21 years since the end of the Second World War. This figure has a special significance, since in 1939, just 21 years after the end of the First World War, the world was again plunged into catastrophic conflict. . . .

The year 1967 is certainly not like 1939. . . . In France, the catch-word of the day was, "il faut en finir"—get it over with—reflecting the sinking sense of an unsettled world poised on the brink. In Britain, in that tense August, a harassed Prime Minister Neville Chamberlain remarked wearily to a friend, "Every time Hitler occupies a country he sends me another message." . . .

We have lived with the fear of a renewal of those troubles for two decades now, but today that fear has begun to recede. An uneasy tolerance has been achieved and men have begun to think hopefully about a future in which we might develop arrangements for living, and even working, with an evolving Soviet Union—arrangements that could give a new and ultimately a constructive meaning to coexistence. . . .

Since 1945, when the Second World War ended, the United States has behaved in an adult manner. We did not—as in the twenties—retire under the sheets and pull the bed clothes over our head. We did not turn our back on history and comfort ourselves with the fatuous cliches of isolationism. We recognized what America was—the strongest and most competent nation in the free world—and we came to the hard but inescapable conclusion that American power was essential to prevent the Red Army from overrunning the whole of Western Europe as the Wehrmacht nearly succeeded in doing two decades ago. . . .

This precarious balance with the Soviet Union has prevented war, but it has not brought a secure peace. Both sides remain armed to the teeth. Massive military forces still confront one another on opposite sides of the Iron Curtain. . . . So we can hardly say that we live with the Soviet Union in a state of peace—more a state of suspended belligerency. . . . Let us stop, therefore, being complacent. A balance of terror at a progressively higher level of cost and destructiveness is a fragile basis for security and we should never forget it.

But if euphoria is not a proper mood, neither is pessimism, since the world is changing and not necessarily for the worse. The most significant changes are probably those in the internal politics and economics of the Soviet Union and the Communist world, and they in turn are closely related to the emergence of the Soviet Union as a modern industrial nation. This has happened—almost unnoticed—in the last twenty years. After the War the Soviet national income was smaller than Britain's, but today it is three times greater, about $300 billion. In the last seventeen years average per capita income has risen sevenfold—which, of course, does not mean that the Soviet citizen is that much better off or that the national increment has all, or even in large part, been available for consumer goods.

It is a fact of history that—except for the twelve-year Nazi interlude in Germany—no modern industrial society has been ruled by a dictatorship. One can certainly argue—though there is nothing absolute about this as Hitlerism and Stalinism show—that modern technology unleashes forces and creates conditions that, for their sustenance, require a degree of political freedom and a relatively open society.

Such forces are at work in the Soviet Union today. Their net effect is to stimulate a kind of Marxism-in-reverse; a series of material changes as impersonal as Marx ever envisioned are eating away at the theory of the Soviet state.

First, secrecy has become a wasting asset. Not only are the requirements of an intricate industrial society compelling a freer exchange of ideas and a greater interplay with the outside world, but, with space full of satellites and electronic detection apparatus at a high point of effectiveness, secrecy as a technical matter is becoming progressively less efficient.

Second, the Soviet citizen is beginning to show his mettle as a clamorous consumer. He is asking the hard question: Are the tangible and visible benefits of fifty years of socialism to be limited to the possession of a one-room apartment in Moscow? And the presidium in turn must face the problem of providing incentives—consumer goods that can be bought by the workers—including collective farmers. Otherwise, why should they produce? The Soviet Government has quite clearly gotten the word. There must be incentives—and so it is increasing the production of that most seductive of all incentives—the automobile. But do the Soviets appreciate the full implications of what they are doing? For the automobile, as we Americans know better than anyone, is no ordinary item of consumer goods; it is an ideology on four wheels with a vast revolutionary potential, and once the Soviet people begin to move about under their own power, they will never be the same again. They will insist on roads and snack bars and filling stations and motels—and all the other service apparatus that a motorized society requires. Obviously such things cannot be conjured up without a sharp impact on the allocation of resources—and this means increased pressure to limit the drain to the military sector.

Third, the development of a complex industrial society requires competent engineers and managers who necessarily measure success in terms of productivity and economic pragmatism and who cannot help but be impatient when Communist theology gets in the way. . . .

Slowly and painfully they are making the point clear that the centralized methods of a Party-directed state are quite inadequate for the management of a large industrial society. Even the most sophisticated computers and linear programming will never enable Soviet economic managers to solve the problems of the allocation and control of resources solely by central planning. In order to measure performance and need, they have had falteringly to move toward a kind of socialist market mechanism with a pricing system to relate supply and demand.

Such accommodations to reality cannot help but undercut Marxist economic theory, while Russia's East European neighbors conduct ever more daring experiments in the *avant-garde* economics of the West. Yugoslavia has recently decided to restore private ownership of retail trade, which it abolished nineteen years ago. On a small scale Moscow has decided to encourage privately owned village handicraft industries to combat rural unemployment caused by an inefficient collective agriculture. The management of Soviet agriculture has now been put on a profit basis. . . .

The meaning of these changes in the Soviet economy—which, by themselves, have great importance—is heightened by the interplay of forces in the tangled politics of the Communist world. Russia has formidable problems within the Warsaw Pact but her most intense preoccupation at the moment is the bellicosity of Red China and the turmoil in that huge and ancient land. There is reason for them to be worried for China and the Soviet Union are intimate—and historically unfriendly—neighbors. Their common frontier is a thousand miles longer than our frontier with Canada and substantial parts of it are in dispute. Can one imagine our own anxiety if we lived next to a billion people, who daily denounced the United States in strident terms and were caught up in the swirling forces of a vast internal convulsion?

These then are elements that make for change—the diminished efficiency of secrecy, the growing hostility of a China touched by the sun, a lessening fear of the West, the imperatives of industrial economics, and a swelling demand for one Fiat in every garage. Hopefully over the next few years these elements can combine to make possible a greater East-West understanding. Certainly the leaders of the Soviet Union do not want their country blown up any more than we wish the destruction of ours. And if we are sensible and mature and sufficiently flexible, the time may come when rationality will triumph over fear and suspicion, ideological ambitions, and the lust for power. . . .

We are not helpless and we should not immobilize ourselves in dealing with the obsolete orthodoxy of Moscow by an almost equally rigid attachment to an obsolete orthodoxy on our on side. Slowly and with considerable hesitation we have found some areas of common interest with the Soviet Union: the Limited Test Ban Treaty of July 1963, the Consular Treaty which was ratified last month, our sale of wheat to Moscow announced in the autumn of 1963, and the Administration's bill to remove discriminatory obstacles to East-West trade, now pending with the Congress.

These limited agreements are, it seems to me, sound policy. They dispose of specific problems that it is in our national interest to solve, while at the same time contributing to an atmosphere of cooperation that is basic to any enduring peace. Thus they can serve—or so we may reasonably hope—to help create the conditions that will bring the Russians and East European peoples back into a single family of nations, back toward the Western mainstream and away from a dangerous and irrelevant Eastern despotism. . . .

Though some advocates of new and bigger East-West agreements exaggerate their significance as panaceas, the opponents of such measures go far to the other extreme, denouncing any and all diplomatic contact with the Forces of Evil as a "sellout" of the native virtues. This attitude reflects, to my mind, a shocking lack of confidence in the strength of our free society. If we really believe that liberty is a benign but hardy bacteria then why should we seek to protect the closed societies from its infection? And a part of the question is: why should we make it so difficult to trade with them in non-strategic goods?

This point is one of particular importance, since I discovered, in dealing with representatives of the Soviet Union over an extended period, that they are particularly sensitive to being discriminated against in trading relations. . . . They feel they should be entitled to the same treatment in commercial matters as is accorded other nations. Under existing law, however, anything we import from the Soviet Union—or, for that matter, from most of Eastern Europe—is subject to the Smoot-Hawley Tariff, which was the highest in our history. In other words, Soviet exports to America get no benefit from any of the tariff reductions that have occurred since the Reciprocal Trade Agreements Act was first passed back in 1934.

I urge you, therefore, to support the President's efforts to obtain passage of this new legislation. It would simply authorize him, in his discretion, to extend most-favored-nation treatment to the Eastern European countries when, in his judgment, it was in the interest of the United States to do so. Certainly the volume of our trade with the Soviet Union is never likely to be very great since there is not much that they have to sell that we would wish to buy. No one is proposing to extend them long-term credits. But the passage of this legislation would remove one very serious impediment to easier relations across the Iron Curtain. And, in my judgment, we have nothing to lose and something substantial to gain by getting rid of this quite unnecessary abrasive element. For a modest amount of useful trade is possible between us, and it is high time that we got over the quite silly idea that we do people a great favor and get nothing in return if we engage in a little old-fashioned buying and selling.

If we behave sensibly, carefully trying to find limited areas of common interest and to remove irritants in our relations we should be able to make slow progress toward a more stable world on one major condition—that the West stays politically cohesive and economically strong. No amount of military might can secure the peace and freedom of the Atlantic world unless the member nations keep in economic good health. . . .

International investment: Sound business? Multinational corporations and nation states

George W. Ball

Looking beyond the free exchange of goods, Ambassador Ball here speaks of the free movement of "all of the factors of production." The flow of capital is extremely important in the development of industrial capacity, but it threatens "national integrity," especially in smaller countries. It threatens national economic planning because the board controlling the capital may meet 5,000 miles away. The dilemma is one of world business being hampered by national interests and vice versa. Ball proposes the establishment of truly international corporations.

Address before the British National Committee of the International Chamber of Commerce, London, England, on October 18, 1967. Reprinted by permission. Mr. Ball was chairman of Lehman Brothers International, Ltd., former Undersecretary of State, and former American Ambassador to the United Nations.

. . . I propose . . . to say a few words about how we as businessmen and bankers and financiers are facing the problem of efficiently utilizing resources —without always appreciating the larger meaning of what we are doing— . . . and then to glance forward toward the possibilities and problems that will confront us in the years ahead.

You industrialists of the postwar period have broadened and deepened your conception of your own function. You have recognized in action, if not always in words, that the political boundaries of nation-states are too narrow and constrictive to define the scope and activities of modern business.

As might be expected this realization has found some reflection . . . in political action. Six countries in Europe have frontally attacked the stifling restrictions imposed on commerce by the archaic limits of nation-states that are organized on a scale inadequate for the modern age. They have created a thriving common market. Next summer for the first time goods will move with full freedom throughout Western Europe to serve the needs of nearly two hundred million people. Nor is this the end of the process, . . . [for] I have no doubt whatever that within a few months or years, the European Community will be expanded to include Great Britain. . . .

The importance of common markets and free trade areas rests not only on their economic value but also on the seeds of political unity they carry with them. Yet they by no means provide the full answer to the imperatives of world efficiency; nor should we look for only one answer.

International trade is, of course, as old as time, but internationalized production is less familiar. You in the United Kingdom are old hands at making your living in world markets and exporting capital to produce goods abroad but this has not always been true of America. Except for the extractive industries most enterprises in my own country have, until recent times, concentrated their activities on producing primarily for the national market and exporting their surpluses to other national markets—and many still do. That, however, is an old-fashioned concept. It is no longer good enough, since it does not satisfy the urgent need of modern man to use the world's resources in the most efficient manner. That can be achieved only when all the factors necessary for the production and use of goods—capital, labor, raw materials and plant facilities—are freely mobilized and deployed according to the most efficient pattern —and that in turn will be possible only when national boundaries no longer play a critical role in defining economic horizons.

It is a fact of great importance, therefore, that at a time when politicians have been moving to create regional rather than national markets, businessmen have been making quiet progress on an even larger scale, as more and more great industrial enterprises in your country and mine and the other industrial centers of the world have begun to cast their plans and design their activities on the operating assumption of a total world economy.

In this development—as is so often the case in history—commerce has been in advance of politics. In a thoroughly pragmatic spirit it has improvised the fictions that it needed to shake free from strangling political impediments. To make possible the global activities of modern business it has extended the fiction of the corporation—that artificial person that lawyers invented so that entrepreneurs could do business with limited liability and could thus mobilize capital from diverse financial sources. Originally the corporation was conceived as a privilege granted by the state to serve its own political purposes, but over the years the widespread acceptance of the institution has enabled business to roam the world with substantial freedom from political interference, producing and selling its goods in a multiplicity of national markets, and creating corporate offspring having various nationalities in unlimited numbers.

Today we are beginning to perceive the great potential of this emancipated corporate person. For at least a half century a handful of great companies . . . have brought, produced and sold goods around the world. But since the

Second World War their number has multiplied many fold. Today a large and rapidly expanding roster of companies are engaged in transforming the raw materials produced in one group of countries with the labor and plant facilities in another to manufacture goods it can sell in third markets—and, with the benefit of instant communications, quick transport, computers and modern managerial techniques, are redeploying resources and altering the pattern on a month to month basis in response to shifting costs, prices and availabilities. . . .

By and large, those companies that have achieved a global vision of their operations tend to opt for a world in which not only goods but all of the factors of production can move with maximum freedom, while, at least in my own country, other industries—some of great size and importance such as steel and textiles—that have confined their production largely or entirely to the United States, anxiously demand protection whenever a substantial volume of imports begins to cross our national boundaries. . . . [However,] at long last, my own countrymen have become too much engaged in the world ever again to turn their backs on it. Yet there will be trouble at various points on the globe as business continues to expand its horizons; conflict will increase between the world corporation, which is a modern concept evolved to meet the requirements of a modern age, and the nation-state, which is badly adapted to the needs of our present complex world. . . .

Even in economically advanced countries such as those of Western Europe we sometimes hear the shrilly expressed concern that local enterprises are being menaced by the superior size and resources of the world companies. This phenomenon is a complex one, reflecting, as it does, not only honest business anxiety but a kind of neo-mercantilism that is beginning to show itself in all too many places. On the Continent it stems in considerable part from concern and envy and frustration because the measures taken to liberate the movement of goods have not yet been accompanied by an adequate modernization of the structure of enterprise. They have not yet produced the industrial concentration across national boundaries that is essential if European industry is to stand on its own feet, unafraid of competition from direct investment by great corporations from across the seas.

The problem is perhaps even more agitated in Canada, where our friends to the North are deeply worried about how they can maintain their national integrity while living next door to an economy fourteen times their own, and yet not jeopardize the flow of our investment capital on which their prosperity depends.

We see comparable phenomena in the new countries, the developing countries. Hypersensitive to anything that suggests colonialism, they fear that their economies may fall under foreign domination, and, therefore, impose obstacles and restrictions on the entrance of foreign firms. Thus they discourage the inflow of capital they so desperately need.

Yet, though the anxieties of local business cannot be ignored, I doubt that this is the most serious danger to world-wide corporate enterprise. A greater menace may come from the actions of governments addicted to a regime of planning, who see in the world corporation a foreign instrumentality that may frustrate their grand economic designs. The basis for their concern is easy to understand, especially in countries where a great world company may be the largest employer of labor or consumer of raw materials.

As it appears to local political leaders, the problem is something like this: how can a national government make an economic plan with any confidence if a Board of Directors meeting 5,000 miles away can alter a pattern of purchasing or production that will have a major impact on the country's economic life for reasons that may be thoroughly sound with reference to the world economy but quite irrelevant to the economy of the country in question? . . .

On more than one occasion [my own government] has sought to enforce its domestic legislation abroad by trying to extend its writ to the actions of foreign subsidiaries of American companies. Some of you may have had personal experiences with this unfortunate tendency, but I hope and expect that it will prove a diminishing problem. More and more in my country there is a growing realization that we cannot use world corporations based in America as vehicles to export . . . our own prejudices whether with respect to trading with China or other Communist countries or controlling monopolies or restrictive practices—without diminishing the utility of the corporate institution itself. And, if we are going to be consistent in our encouragement of the world economy and the world company that inhabits it, we shall have to change our ways.

Not that this would solve or even touch the fundamental problem, for it is in the nature of things that the world company should frequently tread on hostile ground. After all, it is a new concept and one that has not yet fully found its own rationale. Implicit in its operations is a troubling question of political philosophy not yet fully resolved: it is the central question of the legitimacy of power. On the one hand, the shareholders of corporations have a right to expect a reasonable rate of return on capital and a chance to earn income in relation to entrepreneurial risks. But, at the same time, a foreign government is quite validly concerned with the ability of corporate managements to influence the employment and indeed the prosperity of the country. The dilemma arises because neither the people nor the government of the country in question play a part in selecting the directors or the management of world corporations, and, since it is only through national legislation that managements can be made in any way responsible to them, there is bound to be frustration when the managements of world companies are effectively out of reach of such legislation. . . .

In an almost perfect world the obvious solution would be to modernize our political structures—to evolve units larger than nation-states and better suited to the present day, but that is going to take a long time. Meanwhile, many company managements— . . . sensitive to the problem if not always to the full range of considerations that produce it—have developed corporate diplomacy to a high level of sophistication. Not only do they take great pains to ease the pressures on national governments but many seek to attach a kind of national coloration to their local subsidiaries.

Such schemes take a variety of forms. For example, world corporations may associate themselves with local partners in each country, sometimes taking only minority interests in their national subsidiaries. In other cases they may leave the effective control of the national subsidiaries to local managers with only a minimum of direction from the parent company.

All of you know the arguments for and against each such approach. Some of you can no doubt affirm from your own experience that a particular scheme works well; others that it works badly. But, over the long pull, it seems clear to me that local ownership interests in national subsidiaries necessarily impede the fulfillment of the world corporation's full potential as the best means yet devised for using world resources according to the criterion of profit which is an objective standard of efficiency. For the obvious drawback of local interests is that they necessarily think in national and not in world terms, and thus are likely to impress their narrowly focused views on vital policies with respect to prices, to dividends, to employment, to the use of plant facilities in one country rather than another—even to the source of raw materials.

In other words, once the central management of a world company is restricted by the divergent interests of national partners, it loses its ability to pursue the true logic of the world economy. And this leads me to suggest that we might do well to approach the problem at a different level not by nationalizing local subsidiaries but by internationalizing the parent. Only in this way can we preserve the full economic promise of the world corporation as an institutional instrument of the highest order. . . .

The essence of this suggestion is that those artificial persons, which I have referred to as world corporations, should become quite literally citizens of the world. What this implies is the establishment by treaty of an International Companies Law, administered by a supranational body, including representatives drawn from various countries, who would not only exercise normal domiciliary supervision but would also enforce such regulations as an anti-monopoly law and guarantees with regard to uncompensated expropriation. An International Companies Law could well place limitations, for example, on the restrictions that nation-states might be permitted to impose on companies established under its sanction. The operative standard defining those limitations would be the freedom needed to preserve and protect the central principle of assuring the most efficient use of world resources.

Obviously such an international company would have a central base of operations. It would not be like Mohammed's Coffin suspended in the air, since it is clearly necessary that there be a single profit center. And its operations in its home country would, of course, be subject to local law to the extent that the organic treaty did not contain overriding regulations.

I recognize, of course, that a company will not become effectively a citizen of the world merely by a legal laying on of hands. It requires something more than an International Companies Law to validate its passport; the company must in fact become international. This means among other things that share ownership in the parent must be widely dispersed so that the company cannot be regarded as the exclusive instrument of a particular nation. Of course, in view of the underdeveloped state of most national capital markets even in economically advanced countries, this is not likely to occur very soon. But, over the long pull, as savings are effectively mobilized for investment in more and more countries, companies should assume an increasingly international character, while we might, at the same time, expect a gradual internationalizing of Boards of Directors and parent company managements.

I offer these suggestions in tentative and speculative terms, recognizing that these are not the only means through which a solution may be sought. . . .

But if this seems extravagant to you, let me be quite clear on one point. I am not talking tonight about world government or anything resembling it. I have lived far too long on the exposed steppes of diplomacy and practical politics to believe in such an apocalyptic development within foreseeable time. Nonetheless what I am suggesting necessarily has its political implications. For freeing commerce from national interference through the creation of new world instrumentalities would inevitably, over time, help to stimulate mankind to close the gap between the archaic political structure of the world and the visions of commerce which vault beyond confining national boundaries to exploit the full promise of the world economy.

International investment: Exploitation? Does the U.S. exploit the developing nations?

David S. French

Is all profit on foreign investment exploitation? Is it a sufficient reply to the charge of exploitation to argue that the economy is better off than it would have been without this foreign investment? French dismisses both as simplistic responses to a complex problem. There is "exploitation," but more because of what Pearson described as diminishing concern for developing economies and increasing concern for sound business approaches described by Ball. There is too much concern for profit and too little concern for humanity.

Reprinted from Commonweal, *May 19, 1967. © 1967, by permission. Mr. French, a Ph.D. candidate at Harvard, was assistant program economist for the American aid mission to Ethiopia.*

When President Julius Nyerere set about nationalizing banks and industries in Tanzania earlier this year, he explained his action as an attempt to free Tanzania from the influence of those foreign "parasites" who had historically been "exploiters of Africa." Something of the same spirit has characterized Congolese spokesmen in justifying their seizure of Union Minière assets in the Congo (Kinshasa). And from his position in exile, Kwame Nkrumah continues to condemn what he considers to be the West's predatory economic behavior throughout the African continent.

Charges of Western economic exploitation are not confined to Africa, but these recent events point up dramatically the need to arrive at some common understanding of what constitutes genuinely "exploitative" economic relationships between developed and developing nations. This need is particularly acute in the United States, which is most vulnerable to such accusations, if only because of the extent of its economic penetration abroad: at the end of 1965, America's direct foreign investments totalled $20 billion in all areas outside of

Canada and Europe. And these investments have proved unusually profitable; over the two years 1964–65, American annual earnings on investment averaged 23 percent in Africa, 36 percent in Asia, and 13 percent in Latin America, as opposed to slightly more than 9 percent in Europe and Canada.

Such investments, moreover, are far from an unqualified boon to the balance-of-payments positions of recipient nations. Over the last six years, American transfers of investment capital abroad were $2 billion less than American income on these investments. For many developing states, this characteristic capital outflow constitutes a serious economic problem. In India, for example, foreign exchange losses on private capital account were nearly three times gross foreign investment over the critical period 1948–61. These data are not the whole story, of course; but they are taken seriously by those who hold to "parasite" theories of international economic activities.

The question remains, is all this really "exploitation"? To provide an answer in terms which can be accepted by all participants in the debate, it is necessary first to escape the conceptual fetters of both Marxism and doctrinaire capitalism. Accordingly, I reject here the simplistic labor theory of value adopted by Kwame Nkrumah, who argues that all Western profits on investment, whether repatriated or reinvested, amount to pillaging the developing nations involved. I also contend that lapses into Western international economic theory will be largely without meaning. Except in the most limited of senses, it is not a sufficient response to a charge of exploitation to argue that the natives are better off than would have been the case in the absence of foreign capital or trade. Simply because Ghana has a comparative advantage in cocoa exports to the United States does not in itself prove that the relationship is not an exploitative one.

These are caveats which we must accept if we are to communicate in any meaningful way with the developing world. At best, any insistence on the necessarily benign workings of a "free" world market lays us open to a charge of hypocrisy. At worst, posturings about the God-given economic right (of others) to be poor ring in foreign ears like racist polemic. After all, we have not expected our own people to observe the full impact of the market mechanism: one has only to mention American agriculture and textile production to realize this. The difference is simply that nobody in the southern hemisphere has the vote here, while agriculturalists and industrialists in America have not only this but congressional lobbies as well. This is a historical fact—it does not mean that the world economic order is "natural," or "equitable," or "benign." It is precisely the accuracy of these labels that we must reassess.

Let me then propose a working definition of "exploitation." I believe that we could reasonably call the relationship between the United States and the developing world exploitative if two conditions were met. First, we would need to show that the nature of the world's present—and arbitrary—economic order, including the institutions which sustain it, is such as to work toward a permanent widening of the division between rich and poor nations, as well as toward generally chaotic economic conditions in developing states. Second, we would have to demonstrate that the United States is in a systematic way working to preserve this economic order. This approach may have less esthetic purity than pronouncements on comparative advantage or surplus value, but it provides a definitional area of debate within which critics of greatly differing political persuasions could operate.

It is undeniably the case that income in developing nations is now increasing far less rapidly than in developed states. In part, this follows from financial, institutional, and skills barriers within the developing world. At least as important, however, are economic conditions over which poorer nations have little control. Most of these states, for example, are dependent on exports of primary products, which amount to about eight times the value of manufactured exports throughout the developing world. Trade in primary goods is subject to great annual fluctuations: since 1959, to note an extreme case, year-to-year changes in the unit value of cocoa have averaged 15 percent. As a result of these tendencies, from 1948 to 1963 annual export fluctuations of 25 percent or more occurred in developing countries on the average of once every five years, twice as often as for developed states.

Nor is there a readily apparent way out, as developing nations are discouraged from expanding exports other than in primary products by prohibitively high effective tariffs imposed by developed states. As a result, poor nations are chronically beset by shortages of foreign exchange required for development projects. As Sidney Dell, now in the New York offices of the U.N. Conference on Trade and Development (UNCTAD), has noted, "this in turn compels them to beg continually for economic aid in order to secure the funds that they believe would be theirs by right in an equitable world trading system, instead of coming to them at the whim and fancy—and under the political pressures—of the richer nations of the world." It is not just what Americans like to call "unsound economic policies," then, that restrain the growth of the developing world; the structure of the international economy is a weight of at least equal significance.

Along lines dictated by the developed nations, this economic structure has been codified in such instruments as the General Agreement on Tariffs and Trade and the Charter of the International Monetary Fund, which inhibit fundamental attacks on problems of the developing world. According to the current ground rules, no general system of tariff preferences for goods of developing states would be possible, nor would tariff reductions on a basis of non-reciprocity from these states be likely. Even proposals for reform have tended to institutionalize problems more serious than those to be solved: when the World Bank published a study on supplementary financial measures in 1965, it included in the mandate of the administering agency effective veto power over development policies of the nations affected. Given the predilections of the World Bank family, which would probably control such a scheme, it is clear that access to this facility would be in direct proportion to the fiscal conservatism and devotion to private enterprise of participating countries.

Essentially, the nature of the world economy offers little but despair to developing nations, and there is no relief in sight. In full recognition that the developing world is economically prostrate, capitalist nations have but two suggestions. Developing countries can grant concessions sufficient to attract massive private capital, thereby turning critical development decisions over to foreign investors. Or for marginal needs which cannot be met privately, there is foreign aid—with all its political ramifications. This is what Nkrumah has described with some accuracy as the "sugared water of aid . . . the stop-gap between avid hunger and the hoped-for greater nourishment that never comes."

Complacency and opposition

The developed nations' complacency in the face of all this is truly monumental. Consider the analysis of current world economic conditions by the World Bank, which generally speaks for the United States in international economic affairs. Admitting that the volume of export earnings will be critical to developing-nation progress, the bank says only that this "depends to a considerable extent upon the level of production in the industrial countries, on which the developing countries must rely for 80 percent of their export sales as well as virtually all of their net inflows of capital."

What is good for the rich is good for the poor, the Bank announces; and what is best for the rich? "The continued swift growth of the industrial countries, as well as some replenishment of their stocks of primary materials, which will depend in part on *the state of international tension*, may well increase their demand for imports from the developing countries at a higher rate than last year." (My italics.) In the face of unrelieved deterioration in the relative economic position of the developing world, the Bank offers only the hope of a bigger, better, and more expensive Vietnam war.

The situation above does not reflect simply a lack of initiative on the part of the developed nations. Rather, these nations—and particularly the United States—have actively opposed virtually every proposal by UNCTAD or the developing states to correct these conditions. The American attitude was made painfully clear at the 1964 UNCTAD meeting in Geneva. At the conclusion of this session, a series of general principles was adopted to govern international trade relations. General Principle One reads in full: "Economic relations between countries, including trade relations, shall be based on respect for the principle of sovereign equality of states, self-determination of peoples, and non-intervention in the internal affairs of other countries." 113 nations voted for the adoption of this principle; one—the United States—voted against. Of 15 such principles adopted, the United States voted against or abstained from voting on 11; in four of these cases, America's was the only negative vote.

A more recent case was the United States' sabotage of the 1966 Cocoa Conference, held in New York during May and June. America alone refused to agree to an area of compromise in which all other participating states, developed or developing, had concurred; and the conference ended in anger. The delegate of Ghana suggested that the American cocoa industry, which wants "a commodity produced by cheap sweated labor," had influenced the United States position. The Brazilian representative also regretted that the United States had "not been able to negotiate on the basis accepted by all the other countries," and the delegate of Cameroon interpreted the outcome as showing that one "of the most prosperous states did not subscribe to the idea of finding effective remedies to under-development." Utterly isolated, the United States delegate maintained that the negotiations had been "fruitful."

In addition, the United States has worked consistently to weaken or scuttle such proposals as those for preferential tariffs on produce of developing nations, for international monetary reform aimed directly at needs of the developing world, and for concessionary finance in quantities sufficient to allow a real attack on problems of development. And we have acted with some condescension in rejecting these and other initiatives. Discussing last November a United Nations resolution designed to increase the proportion of resources received by developing nations from exploitation of their natural resources, the United States delegate explained his abstention from voting as a function of doubt over whether the resolution really served the interests of developing nations. These nations, who like to believe they can themselves determine their interests, evidently felt otherwise; the final vote was 104 to 0, with the United States and a handful of Western nations abstaining.

A recurrent theme in this summary is American isolation in international economic debate. Although sometimes joined by a few Western allies, the United States not infrequently stands completely alone. This point has been illustrated above; it is underscored by a further look at United Nations action on key economic issues at the last session of the General Assembly. One resolution on external financing of economic development was approved 99 to 0; the United States and four other nations abstained. Another measure on the flow of external resources to developing nations was passed 98 to 0; the United States and ten other nations abstained. And on a vote reaffirming the urgency of concluding an international cocoa agreement, which has come to take on considerable symbolic significance as a measure of willingness to attack basic problems of world trade, the United States alone abstained; the resolution was adopted by a vote of 110 to 0. For most of these measures, American participation would be necessary for success, and American abstention constituted an effective veto of actions proposed.

It may be said that it is foolish to expect America to act against what it sees to be its economic interests; and this is correct, although irrelevant. It may also be said that America is acting as a bastion of "objective" behavior in international economic affairs; and while this is at least open to debate, it is also irrelevant. No rich nation can long argue to an audience of the poor the rationality of a system which ceaselessly works to widen the disparity between them: as Frantz Fanon has noted in a parallel context, "For the native, objectivity is always directed against him." The tone of debate today when, say, African and American clash in international forums is reminiscent of the arrival of the first New Dealers in Hoover's Washington. Learned Hand anticipated the present confrontation in 1934: "The Filii Aurorae . . . are so conceited, so insensitive, so arrogant. But on the whole the Old Tories are intellectually so moribund . . . so stupid and emit such dreary, hollow sounds." In the 1930's, America gladly improvised in the face of an intolerable economic situation, even when this conflicted with economic orthodoxy. In the 1960's, the heirs of the New Deal have themselves become the dreary spokesmen for an orthodoxy which is as clearly unequal to a new economic situation.

The evidence is persuasive that the United States is working to preserve an international economic order which systematically works to the disadvantage of developing nations; and by my earlier definition, this constitutes a form of "exploitation" of these nations. Americans need to recognize this fact; most of the developing world has already done so. And it is a problem of some urgency; as Frantz Fanon has warned, "the question which is looming on the horizon is the need for a redistribution of wealth. Humanity must reply to this question, or be shaken to pieces by it." So far, there has been only a negative reply from the United States.

Joint development of the seas: International cooperation for development of the oceans

Hubert H. Humphrey

Oceans are the connecting link between nations and continents, and Humphrey describes how international cooperation can provide food, scientific data, economic development, and, ultimately, greater security and peace for all. The brief note that follows this article is an example of such cooperation.

Department of State Bulletin, *August 21, 1967. Address before the State of Maine Conference on Oceanography at Bowdoin College, Brunswick, Maine, July 29, 1967.*

. . . One year ago Congress enacted and the President approved unprecedented legislation which established as the policy of the United States the development of a coordinated, comprehensive, and long-range national program in marine science for the benefit of mankind. We have moved rapidly during the past year to respond to this challenging mandate:

> We have established a truly unified program.
> We have begun to establish national goals.
> And we have selected major oceanic programs requiring immediate priority attention.

I have the privilege to serve as Chairman of the National Council on Marine Resources and Engineering Development, which was established last year to bring together the Cabinet-level officials responsible for marine science policies.

We have quickly realized that oceanography is in a state of transition. No longer is it a purely scientific pursuit; it must now serve very concrete national and international needs.

Our new oceanography faces many challenges:

1. The challenge of using vast food reserves of the sea to help end the tragic cycle of famine and despair which haunts much of the world today.
2. The challenge of pollution and erosion on our seashores, bays, estuaries, and Great Lakes, which threaten the health of our people and destroy the resources of the sea.
3. The challenge of understanding the effects of the oceans on the weather so that we may improve the long-term forecasting of storms and sea conditions, protect life and property in coastal areas, and improve the prediction of rainfall in the interior.
4. The challenge of gathering the mineral wealth of the ocean floor.
5. Finally, the challenge of international understanding and cooperation in marine affairs.

The oceans provide important opportunities for peaceful international cooperation and development.

They wash the coasts of many nations, from East to West. The phenomena of the oceans are universal; also, many nations are intensifying their use of the sea's resources.

Therefore, it is essential that we work with all countries, including the Soviet Union, bilaterally and through international organizations in exploring, understanding, and using the seas and their resources.

During the past several months the President and I have discussed cooperative marine science with many leading government officials in Western Europe, Asia, and Latin America. Without exception they are as enthusiastic as we are about the unlimited potential for working together for the benefit of all.

We can work with the advanced nations to jointly explore and develop ocean resources; we can assist the less developed countries to promote coastal development, open new waterways, and strengthen food economies; and we can work with all nations to establish a framework of laws which will encourage an accelerated use of the oceans and their resources by all nations.

In brief, through cooperative international efforts we can foster economic development; help raise the level of scientific competence; promote regional cooperation; and strengthen the bonds of understanding throughout the world.

At the top of our list of priorities, we must help tap the abundant unused food potential which the oceans hold.

We have heard repeated warnings about the stark misery of hunger, the ravages of malnutrition, and the threats of political upheaval and social strife posed by food shortages. We know that more than one-half the world's population is hungry—more than 1½ billion people. Yet the world's food supply stretches thinner and thinner in the face of a spiraling population.

The oceans can help alleviate this problem, and we are determined that they will.

We have embarked on an intensified, long-range program to exploit the oceans as a source of food to help feed the undernourished people of the world—a program which includes

1. Multiplying fivefold the present use of food resources from the oceans.
2. Developing more effective regulatory policies to maximize the worldwide fishing yields and improve fishing efficiency.
3. Encouraging expanded participation by private enterprise in harvesting the oceans' food resources.

To fulfill this pledge, we are vigorously developing technologies for the production of fish protein concentrate and for mapping the living resources of the sea.

We call on the other advanced nations of the world to join with us, through the agencies of the United Nations and bilaterally, in this humanitarian endeavor of unprecedented scope.

The dimensions of world hunger are too great to be solved by any one country alone. Only through a cooperative sharing of the burden by all people and nations can our very survival on this planet be insured.

We also anticipate developments in other areas of marine technology which will provide new opportunities for strengthening maritime ties and contributing to a peaceful and stable world. We are, for example, examining the international aspects of mining in the deep oceans, and deployment of unmanned ocean stations for collecting environmental data of benefit to many nations.

Accurate navigation is fundamental to the advancement of these oceanic endeavors. . . .

I am pleased to announce another step in our effort to strengthen worldwide navigational aids for civilian use. This step, which will couple the technological achievements of our space program to our endeavors in the ocean, is doubly rewarding for me since I also serve as Chairman of the Space Council.

This week the President approved a recommendation that the Navy's Navigation Satellite System be made available for use by our civilian ships and that commercial manufacture of the required shipboard receivers be encouraged. This recommendation was developed by the Department of the Navy in support of initiatives of the Marine Sciences Council to strengthen worldwide navigational aids for civilian use.

Our all-weather satellite system has been in use since 1964 by the Navy and has enabled fleet units to pinpoint their positions anywhere on the earth. The same degree of navigational accuracy will now be available to our nonmilitary ships.

For the past year there has been an increasing interest in this system in the oceanographic community, among offshore oil exploration companies, and among other segments of U.S. industry which require extremely accurate navigation or positioning. These users will be direct beneficiaries of this new dividend from our military research and development programs.

The system includes a ground station complex of four tracking stations; satellites in polar orbits; shipboard receivers and associated computers.

There is, of course, no commitment by the Navy to maintain the system indefinitely for nonmilitary use. However, recognizing the need for strengthening our worldwide navigational capabilities, the Marine Sciences Council has requested the Department of Transportation to prepare a recommended plan for meeting future nonmilitary navigational requirements, with consideration given to the role of land-based radio systems and navigation satellites.

Internationally, the United Nations Committee on the Peaceful Uses of Outer Space is considering the need for a navigation services satellite system, and several other nations have expressed interest in developing their own capabilities in this field. We anticipate that there will be requests for purchase of U.S. receivers from our close allies, and the policy and procedures for responding to these requests are currently under consideration.

The fabric of peace must be woven to stretch unbroken from the outermost reaches of our solar system to the bottom of the oceans.

During the past year we have made a good beginning at the United Nations toward preventing warlike activities in outer space and creating conditions favorable to cooperation among nations for the exploration and use of outer space.

Now let us turn to the task of further insuring the cooperative and productive use of the oceans. They tie the nations of the world together. They have from time immemorial been bonds of culture and commerce. In the words of Longfellow, the sea "divides and yet unites mankind."

Joint development of the seas: U.S. offers India oceanographic research vessel

Department of State Bulletin, *July 3, 1967.*

The Department of State and the National Science Foundation on June 8 announced that the President has approved a proposal to transfer the RV *Anton Bruun,* an oceanographic research vessel owned and operated by the National Science Foundation, to the Government of India. The arrival of Indian representatives to survey the ship and conduct technical discussions with NSF relating to the proposed transfer is expected in the near future. The transfer itself would take place later this year.

The *Bruun,* formerly the Presidential yacht *Williamsburg,* was built in 1930 and has in recent years been operated as a biological oceanographic research ship. During 1963–1964 she participated in the International Indian Ocean Expedition, in which 13 nations including the United States and India cooperated in the first comprehensive study of the Indian Ocean. The *Anton Bruun* will be used by the Indian Government for scientific research in oceanography.

The *Bruun* carries the name of Dr. Anton Bruun, a Danish oceanographer who, until his death in 1961, was one of the world's most distinguished marine biologists and proponents of international cooperation in science. Dr. Bruun was the first chairman of the Intergovernmental Oceanographic Commission, which sponsored the International Indian Ocean Expedition.

Joint development of the seas: North Sea gas: A case study in international cooperation

A. Denis Clift

A very difficult point in international law is related to the development of undersea natural resources. Clift here develops a case study on how the problem of ownership of natural gas under the North Sea was resolved—an especially difficult problem because the entire sea is continental shelf.

This article originally appeared in The World Today *(April 1967), the monthly journal of the Royal Institute of International Affairs, London. Reprinted by permission. Mr. Clift, a former U.S. naval officer, was from 1963 to 1966 editor of the U.S. Naval Institute Proceedings.*

The North Sea, which has long served the nations of Europe and the world as a fishery, maritime highway, and battlefield has now been found to have a new dimension of value. Deep in the sedimentary rock of its sea bed vast quantities of natural gas (and limited quantities of oil) have been discovered—methane gas of such high quality that much of it is fit for use without any refinement. . . .

In 1942 the first international agreement concerning sea-bed mineral rights was entered into by Great Britain and Venezuela, dividing such rights in the Gulf of Paria between Venezuela and Trinidad. On 28 September 1945, President Truman issued a proclamation in which he stated that 'the Government of the United States regards the natural resources of the subsoil and sea bed of the continental shelf beneath the high seas but contiguous to the coasts of the United States as appertaining to the United States subject to its jurisdiction and control,' and concluded, 'the character as high seas of the waters above the continental shelf and the right to their free and unimpeded navigation are in no way thus affected.' Other nations were quick to issue proclamations of their own, and by 1951 the United Nations had published the texts of forty-one national claims to various rights on the world's continental shelves.

The need to reach international agreement on national rights to off-shore mineral resources and continental shelves was recognized by the International Law Commission (established in 1947 by resolution of the United Nations General Assembly) which had undertaken as part of its work the codification of the law of the sea. The report of the eighth session of the Commission in 1956 recommended the summoning of an international conference. . . .

At its eleventh session, the General Assembly acted favourably on the International Law Commission's report, passing a resolution asking the Secretary-General to convoke the conference. On 24 February 1958 the U.N. Conference on the Law of the Sea opened at Geneva with eighty-six nations represented. As the members of the International Law Commission had foreseen, the conference was unable to reach agreement on a single, universally acceptable breadth of the territorial sea, but it was able to move ahead in less politically controversial areas and adopted four important conventions: on the territorial sea and the contiguous zone; on the high seas; on fishing and conservation of the living resources of the high seas; and on the continental shelf. It was this fourth convention that was to have such profound effect on subsequent activities in the North Sea area.

Three articles in the convention are of special significance for the discussion that follows. Article 1 states that 'For the purpose of these articles, the term "continental shelf" is used as referring (*a*) to the sea bed and subsoil of the submarine areas adjacent to the coast but outside the area of the territorial sea, to a depth of 200 metres or, beyond that limit, to where the depth of the superjacent waters admits of the exploitation of the natural resources of the said areas . . .' Article 2 states that '1. The coastal State exercises over the continental shelf sovereign rights for the purpose of exploring it and exploiting its natural resources. 2. The rights referred to in paragraph 1 of this article are exclusive in the sense that if the coastal State does not explore the continental shelf or exploit its natural resources, no one may undertake these activities, or make a claim to the continental shelf, without the express consent of the coastal State.' And Article 6 states that '1. Where the same continental shelf is adjacent to the territories of two or more States whose coasts are opposite each other, the boundary of the continental shelf appertaining to such States shall be determined by agreement between them. In the absence of agreement, and unless another boundary line is justified by special circumstances, *the boundary is the median line, every point of which is equidistant from the nearest points of the baselines from which the breadth of the territorial sea is measured.*' (Italics mine.) Article 6, paragraph 2, uses almost identical wording to define the situation for two adjacent States rather than for States with coasts opposite each other.

The convention seemed of relatively little significance to the nations bordering the North Sea until 1959 when the Shell-Esso oil group which had been prospecting for oil in the Netherlands since the end of the Second World War discovered an enormous natural gas field in Groningen province. Almost overnight the Netherlands switched from being a 'gas-consumer' to a 'gas-producer' nation with enough natural gas both for its own needs and for export for the foreseeable future. And almost overnight the world's major international oil companies became extremely interested in the sea bed of the North Sea. During the next three to four years (1959–63) geophysical surveys undertaken by these companies revealed that the North Sea bed appeared to have considerable promise as a reservoir of gas and oil. As the entire North Sea (with the exception of a deep, narrow trough off the Norwegian coast) is less than 200 metres deep, it was realized that the entire sea would come under the terms of the convention on the continental shelf.

In June 1964 the convention entered into force, with Great Britain having just provided the last of the required minimum number of twenty-two ratifications. The median line/equidistance principle set forth in Article 6 was to serve as the basis for bilateral negotiations to divide the sea-bed rights among the coastal nations. The total area of the North Sea continental shelf is approximately 513,000 square kilometres, and its division according to the median line/equidistance principle yielded the following results: Great Britain—240,000 square kilometres, Norway—131,000 square kilometres, the Netherlands—62,000 square kilometres, Denmark—54,000 square kilometres, West Germany—22,000 square kilometres, and Belgium—4,000 square kilometres. . . .

By mid-1964 then, international co-operation had opened the way for national exploration and exploitation, and Great Britain, now holding rights to approximately half of the North Sea for this purpose, was in the forefront of the exploitation. At much the same time that she ratified the convention, she passed the Continental Shelf Act, 1964 and published regulations for petroleum production on the continental shelf, giving the Ministry of Power responsibility for licensing of petroleum production from the North Sea. . . .

The then Minister of Power, Mr Frederick Erroll, set out five main criteria governing the awarding of licences . . . By 17 September 1964 the Minister was able to announce that there had been a total of thirty-one applications (involving sixty-one different organizations) for some 400 of the 1,305 available blocks, that competition had been intense for blocks in a 10,000-square mile area between the east coast of the English Midlands and the Dogger Bank, and that already twenty-two of the applicants had accepted the blocks for which the Ministry was prepared to grant licences to them.

It is important to note the three essential factors bearing on the race that had developed for gas and oil in the British sector of the North Sea: first, the existence of appropriate international and national law; second, the recent discovery of gas in the Netherlands and the undertaking of surveys which had indicated the likelihood of gas and oil under the North Sea; and third, the development of the technology required to construct and operate the mammoth off-shore drilling rigs and platforms required for North Sea operations. It has only been within the last decade that 10,000–20,000-ton rigs able to operate in 100–300-foot depths of water have been built and put into operation at the world's major off-shore oil production areas. . . .

. . . [By] December 1966, the Minister of Power was able to state in a speech . . . that enough natural gas had been found in the British sector of the North Sea to supply one-fifth of Britain's gas consumption by the end of 1967. By February [1967] he was able to make the dramatically revised estimate that 'enough natural gas has been found in the North Sea to supply twice the amount of gas Britain is consuming at present and probably more.' . . .

For a variety of reasons, other North Sea countries have not moved as quickly as Great Britain in the exploitation of the sea-bed resources. While some survey work has been conducted off the Belgian coast, the Belgian sector is generally considered to lie south of the oil and gas deposits. Off-shore drilling has not yet started in the Netherlands' sector, primarily because, under existing Dutch law, the oil companies have been unwilling to risk their time and money: exclusive production rights are not granted to a company during the exploration stage; the company that finds oil has no guarantee that it will be granted a concession to produce it; and the conditions under which production is to take place cannot be agreed upon before a commercial quantity of oil or gas has been discovered. However, as the Dutch have discovered more gas ashore than they can at present use themselves, theirs is not too pressing a problem. More liberal proposals are now under consideration. . . .

The operations of the oil and gas companies are, of course, only a part of the increasing tempo of activity in the North Sea. Navigational and fisheries problems exist, and are further intensified by the appearance of the off-shore drilling rigs. But again, international co-operation—this time in part in the form of the North Sea Hydrographic Commission—marks the continuing efforts by the coastal nations to make the most efficient and productive use possible of their sea. No recent development in the area has been more dramatic or important, however, than the discovery of commercial quantities of natural gas. And it has been the existence of adequate international law, codified by the U.N. Conference on the International Law of the Sea, that has allowed and is allowing for the exploitation of this valuable resource in an orderly, efficient manner.

Section 5

The many faces of foreign aid

A dialogue on the foreign aid crisis: The haves and have nots

B. K. Nehru

The thesis of Ambassador Nehru's speech is that trade and aid are two parts of the same whole needed for development. Before trade can reach a level of sustained and self-perpetuating growth, aid must help develop wide diffusion of property ownership and purchasing power. The crisis is that the gap between the haves and have nots is widening and that the momentum toward liberalization of trade and aid is being diminished. He calls for a more meaningful dialogue between the two economic worlds.

Vital Speeches of the Day, *December 16, 1966. Address to the National Trade Convention, New York, November 1, 1966. Mr. Nehru is India's Ambassador to the United States.*

. . . Today I have chosen for my theme the somewhat enigmatic title of "The Interrupted Dialogue". In developing it, it will be my attempt to put across two very simple theses: firstly, that the dialogue between the rich and the poor countries of the world, in the entirety of its gamut and in any meaningful sense, is threatening to come to a standstill. It is, secondly, my theme that since international relations as such can never remain frozen but can only take a turn either for the better or for the worse, this interrupted dialogue in economic cooperation has serious portents for the political stability of the world in which we live unless those of you in the affluent part of it decide, early and consciously, to do something about moving the dialogue forward.

In this dialogue between the two worlds of this one globe, the main areas of relationship are clearly trade and aid. Trade has primacy over aid in that trade represents the normal and continuing relationship between nations and aid is an extraordinary form of the transfer of resources across international borders which, from the point of view of both the aid-givers and the aid-recipients, needs to be self-liquidating within a definite period of time. But trade cannot grow without aid because it is self-evident that a sustained growth in the international exchange of goods and services depends ultimately on the widest possible diffusion of property and purchasing power, the creation of which is the proper function of aid. . . .

The year 1958 . . . represented something of a landmark in the history of aid. The urgent and large-scale requirements for balance of payments support thrown up by the Second Five Year Plan of my own country drew substantial funds for development in the United States and Great Britain as well as in the then new sources of Germany, Canada and Japan. The succeeding years saw the admission into the United Nations of a large number of former French, British and Belgian colonies, most of them in Africa, and the independence of many other African countries was scheduled to take place during the next few years. The ex-colonial powers felt the need and the responsibility to put their former colonies on their feet. The United States encouraged and sustained them in this concern with the successful idealism that had been generated by the Marshall Plan, the results of which had demonstrated the value and function of international aid. The exigencies of the cold war lent a further edge to these efforts. This, then, was the beginning of the dialogue. . . .

[A] contemplation of the basic inequalities in the conditions of the rich and poor countries—nearly a decade after the dialogue began—can by itself give us an idea of what has happened or rather of what has failed to happen. Out of the 3.3 billion people who inhabit the globe 2.1 billion or nearly two-thirds live in the poor or in the very poor countries. Their average per capita income is $85 a year or the princely figure of 23 cents a day and, currently, their incomes grow at around $2 per annum. On the other hand, there are 1.2 billion people in the middle income and rich countries with a per capita income of $1750 per annum. The average citizen in the richest among them, the United States, enjoys a per capita income of nearly $3,500 and adds to it at the rate of $235 per year. . . . If these trends continue, the situation at the end of the century will be that per capita incomes in the richest and in the poorest countries will be $4500 and $170 respectively. The process of tearing the world asunder into two parts will by then have gone so far as to make any kind of meaningful relationship among them a virtual impossibility. . . .

In the developing countries, rising expectations have been matched by rising efforts, above all, in the willingness and ability to achieve tangible results in economic development. Currently, three-quarters to four-fifths of investment in the poorer countries is being financed from their own savings; there has been a vast expansion in education, especially in the enrollment of primary school children; a great offensive has been launched, and has been successful, in eradicating malaria and other diseases which have been the traditional enemies of mankind; organized efforts for population control, with the full backing of governments, are under way in a number of developing countries; in the last ten years, the number of miles of roads in Africa, in Latin America and in Asia has more than doubled and the same rate of increase has occurred in the carriage of railway freight; industrial production, mining and the installation of electric power have all doubled in the developing world in the last decade. These facts . . . show . . . the practical success they have shown in translating their expectations into reality by relying to the maximum extent on their own self-help. They also show that in most developing countries, the basic ground work for sustained growth is being surely and steadily laid and a definite potential for future development has become widespread and visible.

Why then are absolute levels of living still so low and the annual rates of growth so dismally poor in relation to what they need to be? I shall answer this question in the words of Mr. George D. Woods, the President of the World Bank, who sums up the situation by pointing out that

> it is a matter of high irony that development, instead of proceeding at the faster pace of which it undoubtedly is capable, is threatened by a serious loss of momentum. The effort is faced by a crucial finance gap—the difference between the capital available and the capacity of the developing countries to use increasing amount of capital effectively and productively.

What has been the capital available and what relation does it bear to the wealth of the capital-exporting countries of the world? . . . The rich countries have got a great deal richer in the past five years; the combined annual national income of the developed countries who are members of the OECD has, for instance, increased by $250 billion. . . . The unfortunate fact, however, is that no part of this vast new wealth has been shared with the poor countries. The level of official capital flows from the developed countries of the Western world to the poorer nations and to multilateral aid-giving institutions has remained static, and is, in net terms, around $6 billion a year. On a conservative estimate, this level of $6 billion is less than two-thirds of the aid flows that the poor countries need and can effectively absorb. With the boom in the incomes of the richer countries, and the levelling off of aid, the ratio of these capital flows to the combined national income of the developed world has steadily declined. What is significant is that it has declined by as much as a fourth—from 8/10ths of 1 per cent in 1961 to 6/10th of 1 per cent in 1965. This is indeed a far cry from the minimum net amount of one per cent of national incomes which the developed countries, in their own best judgement, have adopted as the target for aid in the United Nations Decade of Development.

A further contradiction in the aid picture arises from the fact that while every developing country looks for certainty and continuity in aid commitments in order that it may undertake its programmes of development within the framework of well laid-out plans that can promise tangible results within definite time-horizons, there is on the part of the developed countries a refusal to provide commitments of aid for periods of more than a year. The consequences of this dichotomy are two-fold: firstly, development cannot proceed rationally if it has to jog along in an atmosphere of uncertainty in regard to levels and terms of aid; secondly, and even more importantly, short-term commitments of aid lead on the part of the developed countries to a preoccupation with the question of the so-called leverage that should go with economic aid. Long-term assurances of aid could properly coincide with the long-term interests of the aid-giving countries, which can be no less, but at the same time, no more than the increased prosperity of the poorer world. By the same token, short-term commitments lead to efforts to obtain short-term political advantages from the aid-receiving countries. It seems to me to be unwisdom of a high order for aid-giving countries to seek to influence the political behaviour of the poor countries by promises of aid or by threats to withhold it. . . .

It is . . . true that the interests in the developed world who are involved in, and stand to benefit by, an expansion of foreign trade have failed to appreciate the developments on the aid front or to understand fully how closely they affect the growth of world trade.

There are a number of reasons why aid and trade are closely interlinked. Firstly, there is the fact of the indivisibility of prosperity. Selling involves buying and you cannot hope for a steady growth of world trade unless there is a concomitant increase in the purchasing power of the world as a whole. In other words, prosperity cannot grow unless it is shared.

Secondly, since two-thirds of the world consists of the peoples in the poor countries, the growing markets of today and tomorrow lie with them. The problem of increasing world purchasing power becomes, therefore, in effect, the problem of increasing the levels of living, and of the demand for goods and services, in the poor countries.

Thirdly, just as the poor countries have to be in a position to buy what the rich countries are already in a position to sell to them, the poor countries in turn need to reach the position of being able to sell to the rich to the extent that they need to buy from them. If they are to do this, they should first be able to produce the goods which they can sell and the production of goods needs the investment of capital.

Fourthly, the need for the diversification of investment in the world through the export of capital to the less developed countries is also necessary from the point of view of achieving a sound economic functionalism in an international sense. The developing countries are rich in resources and in manpower. They can and they do produce many manufactured goods in a very economic way and unless their comparative advantages and resource endowments are fully exploited, the productive apparatus of the world as a whole is not being used to the optimum.

Finally, during any period of economic development, aid and trade have an area of overlap between them in the sense that to the extent that the developing countries are not allowed to earn the most from their exports, a correspondingly increased flow of aid becomes necessary to help them balance their external payments. . . .

The essential question in the trade relationship of our two worlds is to what extent and at what speed we are proceeding towards a truly economic complementarity. . . . The answers to this question are again far from encouraging. High import duties on products of interest to developing countries appear to have become the normal feature of the tariff structure of the industrialized countries. Quota restrictions on the imports from the poorer countries are a more pernicious form of discrimination, . . . despite the fact that such restrictions are considered immoral not only by GATT but by your own country in its dealings with the rest of the world. Added to these, are heavy excise duties within developed countries which are designed to restrict the demand for imports from the developing countries. . . . The poorer nations of the world have in effect had no bargaining power, politically or economically, to change this system, the only purpose of which is to protect the strong against the weak. . . .

What is more, tariff structures in the developed world also discriminate in favour of raw materials and primary products and against the export of processed and even semi-processed goods from the developing to the developed countries. . . . What this amounts to in essence is that the developed countries should continue to enjoy the entire value that is added in the processing of raw materials, and that the poorer countries should be inhibited from industrializing themselves and should continue to carry on their existence as the world's hewers of wood and drawers of water. If I seem to sound too harsh, I need give you only one random example which is that a developing country can export raw cocoa bean to the European Economic Community paying a duty of only 5 per cent, while if it were presumptuous enough to make cocoa powder or cocoa butter out of the beans, exports of these simple processed items would be rewarded with a duty of 136 per cent! . . .

The simple fact seems to be that at this point of history there are two worlds on one earth; and the dialogue between them is being carried on, in terms that cannot in all conscience, be described as meaningful. . . .

A dialogue in the foreign aid crisis: A fair deal?

Tun Tan Siew Sin

The minister from Malaysia shows how, despite strong internal efforts, the economy of Malaysia has been hampered by tariffs, quotas, and discriminatory freight rates imposed by the advanced states. He questions the sincerity and fairness of their encouragement for development.

Address before the Far East America Council, New York, on October 4, 1967. Text made available by the Embassy of Malaysia, Washington, D.C. The author is Minister of Finance, Malaysia.

. . . As you might know, our nation of ten years and of just under 10 million people occupies only a corner of South East Asia and is hence one of its youngest and smallest nations. It is one of the smallest, both in terms of population and area, and more to the point, it is one of the poorest, if not the poorest in terms of what is commonly known as natural resources, i.e. resources other than human resources. . . .

In spite of these handicaps, Malaysia has achieved an average growth rate of 5.8% per annum in the 1960's, even though we have been independent for only 10 years. Our per capita income is about US$320 per annum, which is one of the highest in Asia. Our external reserves which stood at US$615 million when we won independence 10 years ago, now stand at about US$800 million, and this is sufficient to pay for 8½ months' imports at the current level. If I am not mistaken, we are perhaps the only developing country among those which gained their independence in the post-war period which has actually increased its external reserves since independence. Our cost of living has remained stable for the last 15 years. . . .

To put it very briefly, we have achieved growth without inflation and this is regarded as a phenomenon even in the highly industrialised world. We even have a full-fledged democratic system of government, based largely on the British Parliamentary system, and that system seems to have worked with us. . . .

In spite of all this, we are in financial and economic trouble. In fact, we are in really serious financial difficulties through no fault of our own. Our most important export commodity, viz. rubber, which used to account for 30% of our gross national product and 56% of our export earnings and which accounts for about 30% of our total labour force, has reached its lowest level in 18 years, i.e. US 15 cents per lb. Between 1960 and 1966, Malaysian natural rubber production increased by about 27%. In 1967, production is expected to rise by a further 7% to reach the million ton mark for the first time. Yet during this period earnings from rubber exports declined as a result of steadily falling prices. Between 1960 and 1966, the unit value of Malaysia's exports of rubber fell by about 38% from an average of US 35 cents a lb. to an average of US 21 cents a lb. In 1960 we exported just over US$667 million worth of rubber; by 1966, although the export volume was nearly 19% higher, export proceeds were 27% lower. For 1967, it is expected that the export volume would probably rise by about 7%, but owing to the prevailing price level, export earnings from this commodity are expected to be about 9% lower.

A comparable situation for the industrial countries would be the complete reversal of the present upward trend for the prices of manufactured goods which we largely import from them. If the selling price of rubber had kept pace with that of such manufactured goods we would be very well off indeed. In fact, had the export prices of rubber which prevailed in 1960 been maintained throughout the sixties, Malaysia's increased export volume during this period would have reaped an additional sum of about US$1,807 million in foreign exchange during these 7 years, which is about 57% of our estimated G.N.P. for 1967. . . . Under such circumstances, we would not only not need any aid from anyone, we would be able to give aid to other developing countries and even a little to some of the highly industrialised countries as well. . . .

In the case of natural rubber, we were told that it was inferior to synthetic rubber in certain properties and we, therefore, set about in earnest to improve the quality of our natural rubber so that it could match synthetic rubber in all respects. Thanks to our research scientists, we can now produce special rubbers tailored to meet the most rigorous demands of consumers. As a result, we have come up against another difficulty because a number of such technically superior natural rubbers are classified as manufactured goods on entry into some developed countries and thus attract import duties which really hurt.

If we manage to survive these obstacles, in spite of the heavy odds, our troubles are still not over. If the exports of the developing countries, whether of primary commodities or manufactured goods, begin to show signs of becoming lucrative, the tightly organised, world-wide, and all-powerful shipping cartels, euphemistically known as "shipping conferences," all too often raise their freight rates to the limit which the market can stand and thus skim off the cream resulting from our sweat and toil. There is no justice or logic in the determination of such freight rates. Quite often a commodity transported over a shorter distance is charged more than the same commodity transported over a much longer distance. For example, the current freight rate for rubber from Singapore to the United Kingdom is between US$31–27 per long ton, whereas the same bulk can be exported from Djakarta to London at a lower freight rate of US $27–21 per long ton.

It seems to us that the determination of these rates is largely based on the ability of the so-called conferences to extract the maximum without fear of retaliation. Where the victim does not possess the power to retaliate, the maximum is charged. Where he does, the shipping conferences are more circumspect and thus we have the anomaly of the same article being charged less when carried over a longer distance.

Last, but by no means least, the developing countries are advised to industrialise. So long as they are only partially successful, no great harm results. If, however, they become really successful, then the fun begins. Crippling quotas or import duties or a combination of both are imposed against their goods which attempt to seek entry into the industrial countries. We, therefore, get the paradoxical situation where it is not worthwhile for a developing country to be really successful in this field because that would be the surest way to trouble. If, on the other hand, it is only partially successful, then it might enlist the pity of the industrial countries and thus attract a certain amount of aid.

One is, therefore, increasingly driven to the conclusion that the only real hope for the developing countries is for them to realise that they must largely rely on themselves, if they wish to prosper. This is reasonable enough, because nations, like individuals, have to learn to be self-reliant and, as the old saying goes, God helps those who help themselves. At the same time, we in the developing world would like to make it clear that we do not desire aid as such. We do not desire aid which weakens rather than strengthens, what we require most of all is fair terms of trade. What we require most of all is a square deal. . . .

Aid and the World Bank: The crisis in foreign aid

Escott Reid

Professor Reid is concerned that the crisis of aid, which he enumerates, be resolved by multilateral as well as bilateral effort. The biggest obstacle to the sustained effort needed in "the international war on poverty" is overcoming domestic political obstacles. He shows how the World Bank, as one of many agencies, might assist in the effort.

This article originally appeared in The World Today *(August 1966), the monthly journal published by the Royal Institute of International Affairs, London. Reprinted by permission. Mr. Reid is the principal of Glendon College, York University, Toronto. He was Canadian High Commissioner in India from 1952 to 1957; Ambassador to Germany from 1958 to 1962; and director of the World Bank's operations in South Asia and the Middle East from 1962 to 1965.*

There exists today in all countries a widespread uneasy feeling among those concerned with the problems of the economic development of poor countries that the world has reached some kind of crisis in the relations between rich and poor countries, an uneasy feeling that, if we cannot together resolve this crisis in a reasonably sensible way within a reasonable time, most of the poor of the world—and two out of three men, women, and children in the world are poor—will be left without much reason to believe in the possibility of a much better life for themselves and for their children. The consequences of this would be profound. The problem of the economic development of poor countries is one of the two great problems of the last third of the twentieth century, the other being the problem of relations between the Western world and China.

There are perhaps five main reasons for the present feeling of crisis. First, the yearly rate of economic growth of the poor countries has been slowing down in the last fifteen years. It was about 5 per cent a year in the first half of the 1950s but by the second half of the 1950s it had slowed to 4½ per cent, and in the first four years of the 1960s to 4 per cent. Secondly, while the rate of economic growth of poor countries has been slowing down, their rate of population growth has been speeding up. Therefore, the rate of growth in income per person has been shrinking. Thirdly, the amount of financial resources moving from the rich countries to the poor countries has been levelling off. The gross flow now is about the same as it was in 1961. The rich countries have got a great deal richer in the past five years; the combined gross national products of the rich members of the World Bank, expressed in terms of 1963 dollars, have probably gone up by about $250,000 m. a year. The rich countries have not shared any of this vast new wealth with the poor countries. Fourthly, not only has the population of the poor countries been exploding but their international debt has also been exploding. In 1964 the poor countries had to spend four times as much as in 1956 to service their outstanding international debt, to pay amortization charges, interest, and dividends. If present trends continue they will, in about fifteen years' time, be paying the rich countries as much as the rich are lending or investing or giving to them. As George Woods, the President of the World Bank, has put it: 'To go on doing what the capital exporting countries are now doing will, in the not too long run, amount to doing nothing at all.'

The fifth main reason for the feeling of crisis about the problem of assistance to developing countries is that in many rich countries public support of, or even acquiescence in, government aid to poor countries seems to be weakening. Some leaders of public opinion in rich countries are displaying a mounting impatience with what they consider to be the ingratitude of the poor for the favours they have received, or with what they consider to be their inefficiency and corruption or the way they waste their resources on fighting and preparations for fighting. Other leaders in rich countries consider that their own expenditures on fighting and preparations for fighting are far more important than finding money to promote the economic development of poor countries. Others in rich countries seem to believe that the struggle against poverty in poor countries is virtually hopeless and that there is little use in pouring good money after bad.

The President of the World Bank, in his article in *Foreign Affairs*, January 1966, has painted a sombre picture of what is likely to happen if these present trends persist. The World Bank, he said, has 80 underdeveloped member countries with a total population of about 1,500 million. In 40 of these with a total population of about 750 million, real income *per capita* is rising by only 1 per cent a year or less; the average *per capita* income of this lagging group is $120 a year. At a 1 per cent growth rate, income levels will hardly reach $170 a year by the year 2000 in terms of dollars with the purchasing power of today's dollars. In some of the countries income levels will be much lower. On the other hand, if *per capita* income in the United States continues to grow at the current rate, it will rise from its present level of $3,000 a year to $4,500 a year by the year 2000. One way of putting this is to say that the gap between these 40 poor nations and the United States will have increased from under $3,000 in 1965 to about $4,300 in the year 2000. The gap between the poorest and the richest would have widened by about 50 per cent.

If this situation were to exist in the year 2000 it would be intolerable, not so much because the gap between the richest and the poorest in the world was so wide but because the gap between the income of the poorest at the end of this century and their income today was so narrow. What would be intolerable would be that in a third of a century there had been so little improvement in the conditions of the poor; that the average income of the half-starved people of the poorest countries would have gone up by only $4 a month in a world where the wealthy out of their increasing wealth could have afforded to give vast sums to help the poor speed up their economic development, and where rich and poor and middle-income countries out of their increasing wisdom and experience should have been able to create an effective partnership in economic development.

What can we do to ensure that this kind of intolerable situation does not exist at the end of this century? . . .

We know that, if aid is to be decisive, the rich countries must pour into the poor countries a much greater flow of materials and skills. They must provide more of their aid on easy terms. They must open their markets much wider to the goods of the poor countries. They must have patience for a long pull, patience not for a decade of development but for a generation of development, patience not till 1970 but till 1999. . . .

Amount of aid required

What order of magnitude of aid is required? The net official flow of long-term capital from the rich members of the World Bank to the poor members is now about $6,000 m. a year, or less than six-tenths of 1 per cent of the combined gross national products of these rich countries. I have no hesitation in saying that the flow should be increased immediately by at least 50 per cent, that is, to $9,000 m. or $10,000 m. a year. This is the minimum figure suggested by the conservative economists of the conservative, tough-minded World Bank. The President, in his article in *Foreign Affairs*, said:

> A preliminary study made by the World Bank staff, utilizing available data and their own experienced judgment, suggests that the developing countries could put to constructive use, over the next five years, some $3 to $4 billion more each year than is currently being made available to them.

Most of this additional aid should, in my opinion, be provided without interest or at a low interest rate. At least $500 m. of the additional aid should be given by governments to the International Development Association, the agency of the World Bank which grants soft loans for hard projects in deserving poor countries. IDA now receives $250 m. a year from governments; it should receive at least $750 m. a year.

We must not delude ourselves that this kind of increase in aid from $6,000 m. a year to $9,000 m. or $10,000 m. will be sufficient for long. My own guess is that we should think in terms of a tripling of net aid over the next ten years. Our target for 1976 from the rich members of the World Bank should therefore be about $20,000 m. a year at 1963 value, which would probably be about 1 per cent of the combined gross national products of the rich members of the World Bank. World Bank experts have estimated the combined gross national products in 1963 as $1,038,000 m. In 1976 at a 5 per cent annual growth rate this would have increased to about $1,950,000 m. in terms of 1963 dollars.

I hope that in ten years' time about 90 per cent of this net flow of about $20,000 m. a year from the rich to the poor countries of the World Bank will be administered or at least co-ordinated by the World Bank. And, as I have said in my essay on the future of the World Bank, I hope that by 1970 governments will have agreed to add to international liquidity each year by an appropriately sized contribution to IDA of credit created by the International Monetary Fund, and that by the mid-1970s this Fund contribution plus substantially increased contributions from governments will provide IDA with resources of $1,500 m. to $2,000 m. a year.

Need for partnership

I am convinced that if the international war against poverty is to have a reasonable chance of success the rich nations of the world must mount a massive effort over a long period. I am equally convinced that there is not the slightest chance of this, unless the poor countries and the international aid agencies do much more then they are now doing to help the leaders of these rich countries find a way around the domestic political obstacles to mounting this kind of effort. The partnership against poverty must be strengthened. We must return to the grand design of the founders of the United Nations, whereby the Economic and Social Council was to be the leader of a galaxy of U.N. specialized agencies, which were to help the nations of the world undertake a world-wide, co-ordinated, massive, and sustained offensive against the economic and social causes of international tension and war. . . .

Role of the World Bank

Each of the U.N. agencies has its special task to perform. Here I want to say something about the special task which the World Bank could become capable of assuming on behalf of the two-thirds of the world outside Eastern Europe, the Soviet Union, and China. It seems to me clear that if a country wants massive aid over a long period from the rich members of the World Bank it must accept the political reality that its chances of getting that aid will be greatly increased if it requests the World Bank to make searching investigations into its economic policies, programmes, projects, and performance and if these investigations are followed by reasonable improvements in its policies, programmes, projects, and performance. This will also increase the chances that the aid will be well used and that the country's whole programme of economic development will be improved and its rate of economic growth speeded up. Poor countries need wise unpalatable advice on what they should do to speed up their economic development. They need to take this advice. The experience of the World Bank has indicated that it is easier for an international institution rather than a national government to give such advice and for poor countries to take the advice of an international agency rather than that of a national government. . . .

If, before aid givers and aid receivers were to commit themselves to a big project, they were to secure such an assessment by the World Bank, they would protect themselves against pressures from special interests with special objectives: pressures from salesmen for fertilizers, salesmen for pesticides, salesmen for nuclear power plants, for example; pressures from single-minded enthusiasts for fertilizers, pesticides, and nuclear power plants, for example. There would be less danger that pressures in the giving country from the exporters concerned added to pressures in the receiving country from the advocates of prestige projects would lead to a waste of the scarce resources available. Such waste on a large scale has taken place in the last fifteen years, notably by the building of steel plants in under-developed countries. In some poor countries such as India, steel plants, if efficiently managed, will yield high real rates of economic return. They can be good investments. They will speed up the whole process of economic growth. But there are at least half a dozen poor countries whose pace of economic advance has been slowed down in the past fifteen years because they built steel plants instead of investing their limited resources in projects of higher economic priority. A great Western European statesman was talking to me some years ago about the economic development programme of a poor country whose President had just been visiting him. He said: 'This country has a very sensible development programme.' He paused: 'No steel plant.' His simplification was the simplification of a political realist. For that country at that time to have included a steel plant in its development programme would have been to demonstrate that it was not serious in its efforts to raise the standards of living of its people

Agreement by aid givers and aid receivers on a joint approach to the World Bank with a request for an expert assessment of a big project of economic development before they commit themselves to it would protect the taxpayers of giving countries against their aid not doing as much good as it should to the economic development of poor countries. Most important of all, the precedents established in making the best use of international aid would help the leaders of the poor countries to make a wiser use of all their resources for development, whether these resources are derived from foreign aid or domestic resources, from private foreign investors, from taxes, from the profits of publicly owned enterprises, or from domestic savings. And it is only if they make a wise use of all their resources that the poor countries can lift themselves out of their poverty. . . .

A particular responsibility rests on the political leaders of rich countries. It is essential that they make clear that they realize the weight of the tragic burden borne by the political leaders of the poor countries, who know that, if their country is to lift itself out of its poverty, they must hold down increases in consumption by the poor; they must put off doing much to reduce inequalities and inequities among regions and among groups within regions; they must sacrifice today's goods for tomorrow's hopes. Out of their poverty, out of their very scarce resources of materials and skills, the poor countries, if they are to succeed, have to squeeze a greater proportion for economic development. They have to be willing to postpone indefinitely the prestige projects, such as big dams, steel plants, nuclear power plants, international airlines, or new capital cities, if these yield a low real rate of economic return. They have to concentrate on projects which have a quick and a high yield, most of them, at least for the time being, in agriculture. Most of them have to curb their population growth. They have to be willing to change many of their traditional patterns of life and thought which constitute impediments to rapid economic growth. They have to be willing to participate to the full in outside expert investigations into their domestic economic affairs and to consider sympathetically the conclusions of those investigations. They have to accord to the appropriate international agency three basic rights: the right to be informed, the right to warn, and the right to encourage. This can be bitter medicine for proud poor countries and it is only proud countries which are worth helping. . . .

During the three years I was with the World Bank, I became deeply involved in discussions with poor countries about loans and studies and consultants and advice. During those years I found myself thinking of a statement by the great Indian poet and philosopher, Rabindranath Tagore. He was contending that in India in the past the use of wealth had been subject to what he called 'the strong pressure of social will.' 'The donor,' he wrote, 'had to give with humility'; the Sanskrit saying *Sraddhaya deyang*, 'give with reverence,' is significant. Those of us in the rich countries who are called upon to give advice and money to the poor countries can usefully meditate on this saying.

U.S. aid in give and take: Charting the future course of U.S. foreign aid in South Asia

Raymond A. Hare

Speaking for the State Department, Mr. Hare explains the purpose of a specific U.S. aid program. The objectives are the stability of the governments concerned and a stable power balance—an attempt to satisfy the national interests of both parties.

"Charting the Future Course of U.S. Foreign Aid in the Near East and South-east Asia," Department of State Bulletin, *April 25, 1966. Statement made before the House Committee on Foreign Affairs on March 22, 1966. Mr. Hare is Assistant Secretary for Near Eastern and South Asian Affairs.*

. . . In compliance with the desires of the Congress and the President we have carefully reexamined our requirements in the area and the extent to which the individual nations are making genuine efforts on their behalf. The program proposals have been modified to meet new circumstances, to emphasize and accelerate self-help, and to focus attention on agriculture, health, and education. As they now stand, they are designed as the minimum consistent with the achievement of our objectives in . . . South Asia.

There has been no basic change during the past year in the great significance of the area to us or in the nature of the problems with which we must grapple. Most of the states of the area are underdeveloped, subject to internal stresses and strains, threatened by domestic disruptive forces and, in some cases, by external power. They very much want for themselves true national independence and the modernization that will meet the reasonable expectations of their people. Their basic objectives are generally, but not necessarily always, consistent with ours. . . .

South Asia is the heartland of non-Communist mainland Asia. The will and determination of the peoples of this region to withstand the pressures from Communist China will, in the long run, bear decisively on the question of whether Communist China can be contained and brought to respect the dictates of international law and society. We should not let this view of the importance of the region be obscured.

The war last fall between India and Pakistan was a tragic experience for us as well as for the belligerents, but, like many tragedies, this one has been followed by constructive action. The participants seem now to have a new and sober appreciation of the fact that peace on the subcontinent is essential if their universally felt aspirations for national security and a better life are to be achieved. . . .

[W]e have concluded that future aid to India and Pakistan must be related rather directly to progress toward securing the peace between them, since without peace economic development is not possible, and without economic development stability is uncertain. . . .

We trust that a continuing process of reconciliation will permit the flow of free-world aid resources to build up once again to the level required to provide the critical margin between stagnation and progress.

Our future economic aid to the subcontinent, as to other recipients, will continue to be clearly contingent on the readiness of the recipients to undertake those measures of self-help which experience has shown are necessary if our assistance is to achieve its agreed objectives. We have had encouraging signs that a large measure of underlying agreement has developed amongst us as to what these measures should include. . . . While drought and war set back the economy in 1965–66, the Indian Government appears determined to do the necessary trimming and to make the necessary policy adjustments to attract more foreign private capital and improve its general economic performance. With our help, coupled with that of others, India should be able to make substantial economic progress and maintain an influential stake for free-world interests in the Asian struggle against Chinese communism. . . .

India and Pakistan have many essential assets, but they do not have the necessary capital. We would hope that our help, friendship, and encouragement may serve to assist them in promoting their objectives of economic self-sufficiency and internal and external stability. We would hope that this would also contribute to a more stable power balance in Asia. That is our objective. . . .

U.S. aid in give and take: America's global giveaway

Otto E. Passman

To Congressman Passman, foreign aid is a "dismal failure" and encourages socialism to expand control of the governments of the people we are trying to help.

Excerpts from an address entitled "Socialism or Americanism?" delivered before the annual convention of the Association of American Physicians and Surgeons, Houston, Texas, October 5, 1967. Text was made available by Mr. Passman, who is a congressman from Louisiana and chairman of the Foreign Operations Subcommittee on Appropriations.

. . . Now, my friends, may I discuss another matter of deep concern to me and of great importance to the American people—and that is the rate by which we have been giving away our wealth to foreign nations. Important to you because the cost of foreign aid for fiscal 1968 will be an average of 146 dollars for each of the 70 million working Americans.

This Nation became great building a world reputation based on trade. Giving away our wealth to secure friends is a new concept in foreign policy, and it has contributed to bringing about a world of confusion and turmoil with America actually having fewer friends now than when we started the program. Foreign aid dollar diplomacy has been about our only foreign policy since the end of World War II. Our foreign aid program has been a dismal failure.

The foreign aid program is so wasteful and handled in such a slipshod manner that the Administration must bluff, flatter and flim-flam members of Congress and the press to keep the global giveaway program going. The facts are conclusive that the foreign aid program—which has cost our country *152 billion dollars* since the end of World War II, when you include the interest on what we have borrowed to give away,—is beyond the realm of reason.

U.S. aid encourages the development of socialism by leaders anxious to maintain power over all facets of life in their countries. U.S. aid frequently gets no farther than the ruling class of a country. Usually, the United States gets no recognition for the good our aid is said to accomplish.

Under the law by which the AID Agency operates, funds are obtained on an "illustrative" basis. Congress does not actually know to what projects or to what countries the money will go. Therefore, without violating the law, the Agency can testify for funds for a hospital in Brazil, but spend the money for a summer resort in Morocco.

I doubt that any program in the history of mankind has had as many paid lobbyists as the foreign aid program. It would take many pages, if not a book, to list the names of all individuals who are lobbying for, or are recipients of, the aid program.

The foreign aid program was created and is being continued because of the scares and claims of the one-worlders, liberals, schemers, dreamers and personnel in our State Department and embassies in 100 countries of the world.

The foreign aid program has created a very serious threat to the U.S. dollar and to our gold reserves. It is mainly responsible for our dangerous balance-of-payments situation [as well as other problems].

Foreign aid creates foreign competition; it is mainly responsible for our ever increasing non-competitive position in world markets.

The program this year alone will dissipate your wealth and resources in 100 countries and 5 territories of the world at a cost of over *9 billion dollars*, not including the interest on what we have borrowed to give away, hidden in 16 places in the voluminous budget. This does not include the cost of the Vietnam War—it is foreign aid and assistance only. This is the correct figure, and I challenge any bureaucrat to successfully refute it.

All nations, large and small, old and new, earn convertible currencies from their exports. But, when nations are credited free with foreign aid dollars with which they may purchase our goods, the invoices are sent to the U.S. Treasury for payment—from the taxpayer's till—not to the governments which receive our goods and services. In normal practice, when the United States sells a nation goods, the U.S. receives something in return: dollars, gold or goods. Under the foreign aid program, however, it is usually a one-way deal; the goods go out, the U.S. Treasury pays the bills, and the United States receives very little of a tangible nature in return. Since the nation gets free what it would normally spend its earnings for, it can use the dollars it earns from its exports to buy our gold.

So great has been the outpouring of America's wealth to foreign nations that many of the recipients have accumulated dollars far in excess of their needs for commerce. Therefore, they demand gold in exchange for the dollars they earned from their exports—or we gave them—and in the past 13 years, they have reduced our gold reserves from twenty-three and one-half billion dollars to thirteen billion dollars. While depleting our gold stockpile—which is the source of strength of the dollar—and increasing theirs, so-called "free-world" foreign nations have also increased their short-term U.S. dollar claims to thirty-one billion dollars (from ten and one-half billion dollars 13 years previously). For these dollars, those countries can demand gold, and if such a demand should come, the United States could not meet it. It is clearly within the power of those countries to control the monetary system of our country.

The United States is the only country in the world that is giving away its wealth. We are borrowing money to give away, when our public debt exceeds by 37 billions of dollars the combined public debt of all other nations of the world. Our generosity and overspending at home and abroad are forcing us out of many world markets. The foreign aid program is not good for our country because it destroys our world markets and our monetary system, and it places a public debt upon the heads of unborn generations.

Wasteful and wild federal spending—the dissipation of your wealth, if you please—urgently needs to be curtailed, not only in aid to foreign countries, but also excessive spending for unnecessary programs in our own country. There are those in the highest places in government who parade as conservatives but indeed perform as liberals. My friends, a liberal is an individual with high-pressure feeling, low-pressure thinking, and a constant urge to give away that which belongs to somebody else. . . .

U.S. aid in give and take: A giving of oneself: A peace corpsman looks back

Efrem Sigel

In this report, one of the early Corpsmen looks back with mixed emotions—feeling good about his own experience but a little concerned about "official overstatements" of the value of the program.

Peace Corps volunteers arrive in the tropics loaded down with many sorts of equipment, not all of it physical. In addition to cameras, tape recorders, spray deodorants, and insect repellent, they carry with them a whole train of mental baggage: a set of attitudes and expectations about their new environment. The notion of romantic encounter is recurrent. After five months in an upcountry town in the Ivory Coast, one volunteer despaired of ever finding the elemental, sensual, somewhat evil Africa he found in Conrad's novels. In his isolated post, the values, if not the pace of life, were unfailingly bourgeois. "L'Afrique," he wrote me resignedly, "c'est le Brooklyn." . . .

Before departing for the Ivory Coast as a teacher in 1964, I was as subject to these fantasies as anyone else. I insisted on spending part of my clothing allowance on a pair of heavy leather camping boots, imagining they would prove invaluable on long treks through the jungle. Once overseas, I realized the boots would have made odd apparel in a classroom or in the restaurants of nearby Abidjan, and they stayed on the bottom shelf of my closet for two years.

For me, as for most others, my Peace Corps career began on the campus. In a senior-year mood of "anything is worth a thought," I filled out the questionnaire and took the test and promptly forgot about it until a day in April when I received a bulky envelope in the mail marked "Invitation to Training." At the time, I was cramming for a final examination in English history, but my eyes kept wandering to the brochures for French-speaking Africa that the Peace Corps had sent me. They had pictures of happy African children and were written in pseudo-realistic public-relations prose. A typical passage went something like this: "The days will be long and hot. The people may be unfriendly. You won't be paid anything. You probably won't accomplish much either. But . . ." There was always a but. Already I had two images: Kurtz paddling his lonely canoe up the river, and Churchill enumerating all the obstacles to victory and pledging a fight to the finish. I told myself: "It may be tough, but *I* won't surrender either."

Obviously no two Peace Corps volunteers give exactly the same reasons for joining, but there is an astonishing similarity in their backgrounds and experience. By almost every criterion, they are a highly distinct and unrepresentative group. Of the forty-two individuals in the Ivory Coast when I was there, all but six were between twenty-one and twenty-three when they entered the Peace Corps, all but three were recent college graduates with degrees in the liberal arts, and the overwhelming majority—this is a personal impression—came from middle-middle and upper-middle-class families. Such apparent uniformity is not limited to the Ivory Coast project. These are characteristics that hold for Peace Corps volunteers in general. . . .

The experience and education of all applicants disposed them to be internationalist and humanitarian, naturally oriented toward service and good works. . . . Whatever the initial motivation, however, a volunteer's ideas and attitudes change overseas. . . . From all the evidence, we were great idealists before reaching our assignments and great cynics afterward.

Not all of the change was due to disappointment. A good deal of it, I think, was simply growing up. Much of what we felt was the disillusionment of young men on any first job at suddenly finding that however extraordinary their ideas or talents may seem to them, the world in which they live is quite ordinary. On the other hand, there *is* one set of conditions peculiar to the Peace Corps that quickly teaches one the limits of professional idealism—the difficulty of communication. The market lady who saw me coming and mentally added ten francs to the price of a pineapple would have been quite immune to any suggestion of the noble sacrifice I was making. Telling my pupils of the rigors of Peace Corps training would not have pricked them into studying furiously. And of course if I had waved my altruistic credentials at my French colleagues, they either would have snickered at this new confirmation of American gullibility or recited a litany on the hopelessness of any effort in Africa.

Living with the people

The difficulties experienced by some volunteers are more deep-seated. . . . [For example, a] girl working in the *foyer feminin* program—women's adult education—was given a part of the building that contained the women's center for her own quarters. In the middle of the year an Ivorian co-worker moved into the same building, installing, in African fashion, several cousins and relatives, while other casual visitors dropped in from time to time. The family tracked mud in the volunteer's kitchen, borrowed her dishes, stole her soap powder, took water from her filter, and stored beer in her refrigerator. Though the co-worker had the equivalent of a sixth-grade education, she insisted on running the center her own way. She ignored the part of the syllabus that dealt with hygiene and baby care—the only lessons that were of practical value—in order to concentrate on reading. For reading class she took the so-called advanced class, those who could recognize letters and words, and left the others to the volunteer, who could take little consolation from the fact that she was ostensibly fulfilling two of the precepts of Peace Corps orthodoxy: living with the people and working with a host-country counterpart. . . . It is no coincidence that the girls in the *foyer feminin* project who enjoyed their work most were those who were alone in a center and could run the program the way they wanted. . . .

The spirit that the volunteers brought to their work varied so widely that one sometimes could hardly believe that two Peace Corspsmen had been in the same country. In the last report on his work, a teacher in the Ivory Coast wrote: "And finally there is the observable fact that most students are incredibly spoiled, show no gratitude for their *completely free* education, and have no concept of human or civic responsibility." But another teacher in a different town wrote:

> Students are serious and will work for an interesting teacher. This bosh from the French teachers that they willingly sabotage exams to spite a teacher is not to be believed. . . . Pressure at the school is such that students' free study time is not sufficient. They study clandestinely at night (after lights-out) with small lamps that strain the eyes, or even with candles. They get up early, sometimes as early as 4 A.M., to go over the lessons, and if your class is not interesting they will use it to get their math done in.

My own conclusions about the diligence of Ivory Coast students fall somewhat short of this encomium, but I could never accuse them of lacking all notion of "human or civic responsibility."

Fulfilling the contract

There are admittedly also great variations in the intellectual quality of students and in the general school atmosphere from one institution to another, but it was not experience so much as the mental predispositions that each brought to his work that made the difference between these two reports. Cases where a volunteer fails to meet the minimum demands of his job are rare, especially in an area like teaching that has well-defined working hours. Much more common is the teacher who does a conscientious day-to-day job of teaching but does not extend himself in any other direction. I asked a Peace Corps evaluator how he went about judging the effectiveness of volunteers in out-of-the-class activities. "It's easy," he replied. "I just ask him, 'What are you doing in the community?' Most of the time the answer is 'Nothing.' " . . .

One explanation of such behavior is that volunteers are lazy. A more balanced conclusion, however, would try to match volunteers' behavior against the conditions in which they live. As with their attitudes toward their counterparts, volunteers' feelings about job or extra-curricular activities usually grow out of their firsthand experiences. This was certainly true of my own efforts to lead a Red Cross club. On Thursday mornings in the Ivory Coast there is no school, and I well remember the concentration of will it took me to get out of bed and up to the local hospital by 8:30 to meet the few devoted members of the club. My reluctance had something to do with the knowledge that my colleagues were all sleeping late, or with my desire to get to Abidjan later and do some shopping. Mostly, however, the reluctance came from a private input-output equation that went whirring through my head, an equation that always seemed to crank out the same answer: Don't bother, it doesn't pay. And there were good reasons to listen. The president of the club would show up half an hour late with a report on his friends: "Atakpa has to work for his uncle; Jean can't come. All the girls had to go to school to serve a punishment." Already the forces of voluntarism had thinned considerably.

At home, before going to the hospital, I had prepared some materials for a lesson on infant feeding: pictures of porridge, of oranges, vegetable puree, and eggs that I slapped professionally against a felt blackboard. I had in mind making a talk to assembled expectant mothers in the prenatal clinic. But I had fallen victim to the inertia of the world I was in. Who could confront the impassivity of those African women and find even a twinge of any inspiration to teach?

One day, however, I pedaled resignedly up to the hospital, the felt board under one arm, pictures and displays in a manila envelope.

"I'm ready to give my course," I announced to the head midwife, who had become a friend. The waiting room was crowded with silent women holding bottles; they had come to give urine specimens for the prenatal checkup. The midwife, an educated woman, smiled noncommittally. "I'll talk in French, of course; all I need is someone to interpret," I continued.

"Well, there are many languages," she said.

"If you translate into Dioula and Appolo, won't that do?"

"Some are Abouré, some are Agni. They won't understand." Her unspoken question was: What would it all accomplish, beyond satisfying my own need to make a gesture? I saw that I was really debating with myself and losing. "Well," I said, shamefaced, abashed at my own lack of resolution, "why don't we put it off, then?" "Putting it off," of course, meant dropping the whole idea. I backed out quickly and disappeared.

Crisis of commitment

. . . I once asked the director of the French volunteers in the Ivory Coast, young men working in agriculture and rural construction, whether he was satisfied with his program. He called it a success, which prompted me to ask what he meant by the word. "Oh, a ten per cent rate of efficiency. If ten per cent of the people we reach respond, then we're doing magnificently."

Apart from the inevitable slackers, the volunteer who fails does not lack good intentions. He is probably cursed with a too reasonable turn of mind: he cannot stop asking himself what good any particular action would serve. This is the genuine crisis of commitment for Peace Corps volunteers. I doubt if its resolution lies in choosing those individuals who will persevere at any cost—there are too few of them. If there is an answer, it is to make the volunteer's job easier, not harder—to give him a task where he will have a stake in commitment, and where the commitment flows more or less naturally from the importance of what he is doing. A job that is a treadmill of frustration cannot stimulate enthusiasm. . . .

Glyn Roberts, who studied long-term volunteer programs in Africa for

UNESCO, made a similar point after extensive travel and observation. On the basis of seven months in Africa interviewing headmasters, officials, and volunteers of several nations, he wrote in the Peace Corps *Volunteer*, "I am more than ever convinced that it is the project which makes the volunteer." And he went on to say, "Most of the volunteer 'failures,' from what I can gather, have never had a fighting chance. And many of the 'successful' volunteers admit candidly that it is the job which is good and they were just lucky to find it."

In addition to the quality of the effort put forth, a factor that separates volunteers is the level of their intellectual curiosity, their interest in the host country. The Peace Corps talks a great deal about culture shock, which is simply the feeling of alienation that one has from living in a foreign country and being unable to understand the behavior of people. A frequently cited example in the Ivory Coast is the first visit to the post office. The volunteer walks briskly to the counter and demands his stamps. Nothing happens. Only after waiting ten minutes does he realize that it is necessary to wish a very cordial good morning to the clerk before any transaction can take place. An important but little explored corollary of culture shock is culture ennui: the volunteer thinks he understands the foreign culture but tells himself that it is uninteresting. The customs are slightly primitive, the people a little dull and simple, and the diversions silly. Once the volunteer slips into this frame of mind, it becomes extremely difficult for him to generate any enthusiasm for helping people. He may teach irregular verbs or demonstrate baby care from a sense of duty, but he is bound to find it painful and unrewarding.

In Africa in general there seems to be a high incidence of boredom among teachers. They are working in a western-oriented school system and are cut off from more traditional and informal African life. . . . Girls who worked in the mobile *foyer* program often had a different experience, however. They visited several villages a week to give the women courses in child raising, nutrition, and disease prevention. In the course of these visits they had extensive contact with village notables—the chief and elders—as well as the chance to observe the current of everyday life in a small African community. Not all the girls benefited equally from this exposure, but those who went at it with the proper mixture of élan and toughness learned a tremendous amount. . . . It . . . serves as an example of how the right kind of job automatically projects volunteers into the workings of a foreign culture.

Unwelcome hyperbole

"Would you do it again?" the volunteers are asked on questionnaires at the end of their Peace Corps service. Nine out of ten say "Yes." "We learned a lot" is the common theme. But there is all the difference in the world between young Americans learning "a lot" and official claims that the work of the

Peace Corps is laying the foundation for a new world community. Jack Vaughn, the Peace Corps director, quoted with approval a Dominican official who sobbed that the Dominican Republic might have been spared its revolution and bloodshed if the Peace Corps had only sent four hundred volunteers as requested. Warren Wiggins, the deputy director, suggested in a speech that the Peace Corps was concretely involved in "nation-building." . . . He gave the example of Malawi, an African country where "two-thirds of the high-school teachers with degrees are volunteers." Charles Peters, director of the Evaluation Division, argued, . . . "We have a cause—the struggle for world peace." . . .

Helping a country sidestep revolution, building a new nation, promoting world peace—these are large achievements. Few activities of the Peace Corps seem to merit such grandiose description. In the Dominican Republic, volunteers in urban-development projects are organizing neighborhood clinics or helping to obtain piped water for a *barrio;* those in rural-community development are setting up agrarian leagues and advising on local school construction. This is important work, the kind that, if carried out on a large scale, might begin bearing fruit in eight or ten years. But it is hard to see how five times as many volunteers would have affected either the rebels who tried to take over the government in 1965 or the unyielding military junta that resisted them. Peace Corps teachers in Malawi may be working in classrooms in large numbers, but African officials there and elsewhere are not about to turn over the task of charting national policy to young American volunteers. Malawi, in fact, is one of the few countries where volunteer activities have drawn an official reprimand: President Hastings Banda complained in a speech that volunteers were trying too hard to live like the people, when as teachers their job was to take a more professional, more aloof attitude. Instead, here were Americans living in huts, dressing sloppily, sleeping with local girls, and, worst of all, getting mixed up in local politics.

It is with good reason that volunteers are impatient with official overstatements of their work. In the first years of the Peace Corps, a comic dialogue developed between volunteers and staff that went something like this: "We didn't accomplish anything." "Of course you did. You were just too close to the situation to appreciate what you had done." According to official theory, the staff member who visited from time to time had a better idea of what was accomplished than those on the spot, while those who stayed in Washington had the best idea of all. Fortunately this logic has fallen somewhat into disrepute, and much of the shifting emphasis in Peace Corps programming and operations has in fact come from listening closely to what volunteers have said.

Those who listen closely cannot fail to observe that the difficulties cited most frequently on the questionnaires given to corpsmen at the end of their tour of duty were "frustrating work experience" and "lack of activity of nationals in helping themselves." From my own experience, I would say that it is the second problem, the one of host-country attitudes, that shapes the views of volunteers about their own contributions, whether or not they are conscious of it. As in the case of Japan or China, the initial stimulus to development may come from outside—in the shattering influence of a technologically more developed society. But the drive itself depends on a local leadership disciplined enough to forgo its own pleasures in order to promote advancement. This is the consideration that should inform all programs of assistance, whether monetary, technical, or human.

A balance sheet of Soviet foreign aid

Marshall I. Goldman

Both the successes and the failures of Soviet attempts in foreign aid are presented by Professor Goldman. The "other" aid program is also undergoing an intensive review.

Reprinted by special permission from Foreign Affairs *(January 1965). Copyright by the Council on Foreign Relations, Inc., New York. Mr. Goldman is an economist and an associate of the Russian Research Center at Harvard University.*

Amid the various anniversaries of the last year, one seems to have passed unnoticed. It was just ten years ago that the Soviet Union embarked on its program of economic aid to neutralist countries. Beginning with a grain elevator and highway program in Kabul, Afghanistan, and the Bhilai Steel Mill in India, Soviet promises of aid mounted rapidly until they reached a peak of more than $1 billion in the year 1960. In terms of gross national product, this was as much as the United States was providing at the time. Subsequently, however, in late 1961, promises of Soviet aid diminished and remained insignificant until late 1963.

The ten-year mark is an appropriate point at which to evaluate the program of Soviet aid which in that period has totaled $3.5 billion. Heretofore, Soviet successes in foreign aid have usually been so breathtaking that they have not only overshadowed the much less dramatic American projects, they have also eclipsed Soviet shortcomings. The coming of age of the program reveals, however, that the Soviets have also had their failures. To their surprise, they have encountered almost all of the problems which have frustrated us, plus some that we have been spared.

The Russians have a knack for the spectacular. What success they have had in foreign aid has come from concentrating on certain key projects which are often industrial in nature. These major impact projects not only excite the imagination but often have productive and visible results. The workmanship and administrative efficiency that go into completing these showpieces are good, indeed often better than are found in the U.S.S.R. itself. The steel plant at Bhilai is one of the largest and most successful in all of the underdeveloped world. The decision to build it came after West Germany and Great Britain had also agreed to build steel mills for India. Resolved to win the competition, the Russians not only shamed the West Germans into offering a lower interest rate, but completed their plan much faster and built their mill more cheaply than either the English or Germans did. Although the German and British plants are technically more complex, most Indians agree that the Soviets have outperformed their competitors.

The success of the Soviets at Aswan is even more impressive. World opinion was dubious when they assumed the financial and physical burden of building this dam immediately after the Americans and the World Bank had refused to do so. On the upper Nile, 100-degree heat was regarded as the norm and the granite to be moved defied the finest drills in the world. Nevertheless, the Russians helped excavate more than ten million cubic yards of dirt and rock so that the first stage of the dam could be completed on schedule. Ultimately the dam will have a water storage capacity double that of the combined resources of the Grand Coulee Dam in Washington and the Kuibyshev Dam in the U.S.S.R. . . .

The major Soviet triumphs at Aswan and Bhilai, along with several other projects, have helped to create the general impression that the Soviets are more adept at handling foreign aid than we in the United States. A close look at American and Russian aid projects in Africa, however, reveals that just as we have had our successes which no one seems to have heard about, the Russians have had their failures which have gone unnoticed. Moreover, as more and more of their programs are completed, the shortcomings become more and more evident. The Russians are beginning to learn only too well that foreign aid can pose a variety of challenges.

Some of them are by no means unique to the Soviet Union. To begin with, economic aid to underdeveloped countries, whether from the U.S.S.R. or the

U.S., is inherently difficult to render. Most developing countries do not as yet have the resources to implement complicated foreign aid schemes easily. They lack qualified manpower, supporting equipment and sufficient supplies. Since there are few if any qualified subcontractors, the donor must be prepared to undertake the most elementary production and construction tasks on its own. This makes it difficult to adhere to schedules and standards.

The tropical climate in most developing countries further complicates the process and jeopardizes even simple operations. Proper maintenance is a problem even in temperate zones, but in Africa and Asia it is a major challenge. Thus Russian-built roads wash away in the rains of Indonesia and Russian equipment rusts on the docks of Guinea, Ghana, India and Indonesia. Even when machinery has been installed, heat and humidity accelerate the normal process of deterioration and hamper repair work. In the 100-degree sun of Mali, a useless Soviet crane, its hoist separated from the cab, sits impotent at the portal of the Russian-financed stadium; apparently there are no suitable repair facilities nearby and it is too enervating to attempt to make repairs manually. Similarly, after only a week's work, two Soviet bulldozers lie disabled outside the Russian-financed coke oven in Helwan, Egypt. Nearby, one of the plant's two boilers, only two months old, is completely scorched; the other is still operating, but it too is partially burnt. Even the successful Soviet operations at Aswan and Bhilai have been affected. In the frantic drive to complete the first stage of the Aswan Dam before the onset of the spring rains, safety measures were discarded. It was necessary to remove large quantities of dynamited rock before it could be determined that all the charges had been properly detonated. As a result, more than 220 lives were lost. Even at Bhilai there have been blemishes on the impressive record. The 40,000 Indians mobilized to build the mill refused to accept the fact that only about 7,000 could be retained after the completion of construction. This led to a hunger strike and the slogan: "We built the plant—now you are throwing us out." The plant is still plagued by jurisdictional strikes among the unions. . . .

The Russians may have been so busy re-assessing their successes and failures of the last decade that perhaps they have failed to notice the anniversary of their first aid program. Clearly they have learned much. They seem to be moving away from economically useless stadiums and hotels and wherever possible encouraging projects which have more economic rationality, including some that are financed on purely commercial terms. There may also be fewer large loans in the immediate future. One of the criticisms of Khrushchev was that he sometimes overcommitted his country. Nonetheless, the new Soviet leaders cannot abandon their program and most likely would not if they could. But surely one of the most painful lessons for all the Russian officials must have been the discovery that mistakes in foreign aid are not an American monopoly.

How poor nations give to the rich

Walter F. Mondale

The "brain drain" is the paradox described by Senator Mondale. Too many of the best foreign students fail to return to help in the development of their homelands.

Saturday Review, *March 11, 1967.* *Mr. Mondale is a senator from Minnesota.*

There is nothing, quite literally, that the industrialized nations of the world can do for their less affluent neighbors that is more important than helping them develop the special knowledge and skills they so desperately need. The ideal and obvious way of accomplishing this purpose is to provide specialized training. So the United States Government has made it possible for thousands of students from Asia and Africa to receive high-quality education in this country.

One hundred thousand foreign students are in the United States today, about three-quarters from developing nations. Tens of thousands of other top professionals come here under exchange programs in medicine, science, and other priority fields. We have opened the doors of our colleges and universities to them, for the knowledge and professional skills they seek are indispensable to the progress of their homelands.

But before they can contribute to this progress, they must return home. And large numbers do not. Estimates of the number of Asian students who fail to go back range as high as 90 per cent. Thousands remain here as doctors, scientists, engineers, or teachers in our universities. And the percentage from other continents, though not so large, is still highly sobering.

Far from always bringing progress to poor nations, we are, in many cases, helping drain them of their most precious resource—human talent. And this brain drain is one of the prime reasons why the gap between the rich and the poor of the world is not narrowing, but growing wider every day.

There are, of course, many brain drains. . . . There is the migration of scientists from Britain to America. Our nation was built by a brain drain from Europe. And many centuries ago, there was a brain drain to Rome from the outlying provinces.

But the brain drain from developing countries is particularly urgent. It compromises our commitment to development by depriving new nations of high-level manpower indispensable to their progress. It runs directly counter to the education and training we provide in our foreign aid. It is, in the words of Assistant Secretary of State Charles Frankel, "one of the steady, trying, troublesome diplomatic issues confronted by [our] government . . . one of the most important problems faced not just by the Department of State, but more important, by the United States and by mankind as a whole."

The brain drain is serious among scientists. The National Science Foundation estimates that, between 1956 and 1963, 2,858 scientists and engineers from South America and 4,114 from Asia moved permanently to the United States. Charles V. Kidd of the Office of Science and Technology calls this loss a "national catastrophe" to developing countries, since they have so few to build a base for scientific and technological progress.

The brain drain is severe and growing among doctors and health specialists. Dr. G. Halsey Hunt, executive director of the Educational Council for Foreign Medical Graduates, reports that 10,974 of the 41,102 residents and interns serving in American hospitals are graduates of foreign medical schools. About 8,000 of these come from developing countries. Nigeria, with one-fiftieth as many doctors per person as we have, graduated nineteen physicians in 1963 from its one medical school; in the same year, sixteen Nigerian doctors were working in American hospitals. The Philippines graduates 1,010 doctors a year, and provides us 2,108 residents and interns.

According to Dr. Kelly M. West of the University of Oklahoma, "We would have to build and operate about twelve medical schools to produce the manpower being derived through immigration. The dollar value per year of this 'foreign aid' to the United States approximately equals the total cost of all of our medical aid, private and public, to foreign nations."

The brain drain is acute among foreign students. In the July 1966 issue of *Foreign Affairs*, Cornell President James A. Perkins cites an estimate that more than 90 per cent of the Asian students who come here never return home. Incomplete Immigration and Naturalization Service statistics indicate that about 30 per cent of Asians entering on student "F-visas" adjust their status to permanent resident. We don't know the exact figures, but we do know that the nonreturn of students from Asia is of massive proportions—particularly severe for countries such as Taiwan, Korea, and Iran.

The record of government programs is far better. Of those that our Agency for International Development (AID) brings to this country for education and training, more than 99 per cent return, as they are in fact required to do. Yet while some 16,493 Asians, Africans, and Latin Americans were receiving such training from 1962 to 1964, 8,151 *other* students from the same areas adjusted their status to permanent resident. Only half as many, perhaps, but for each man that left, a developing country lost an educational investment of many years, while the AID training averaged but nine months. Thus, the brain drain among students cancels out, several times over, one important phase of our foreign assistance program.

Under other circumstances we might rejoice that our Statue of Liberty has today become a beacon attracting men of high talent from all over the world. Should we wish simply to siphon off the world's best-trained people for our own benefit, we would consider the brain drain an unmixed blessing. But in today's world it is barely a mixed blessing. We may gain in the short run, but it threatens one of the vital long-run objectives of American foreign policy. For as Secretary of Defense McNamara said in his speech in Montreal last year, world security—and American security—depends on development in the less developed countries: development at sufficient speed to satisfy at least a portion of their rising aspirations.

Since the brain drain threatens development, it is ultimately a threat to the security of this country. So we must develop a comprehensive program to meet this threat.

Such a program must be selective, focusing on those nations and occupations where the problem is most acute. Some countries, which lose 50 to 95 per cent of their students who go abroad, could probably not put all of them to effective use, though they might benefit from a much higher rate of return. Other countries may not face a substantial brain drain. And certain professional skills—for example, that of atomic physicist—may not be in demand in some developing states.

A brain drain program must respect the spirit of the 1965 immigration law ending the discriminatory "national origins" quota system, legislation that I was proud to co-sponsor. It must also take account of very serious American manpower shortages in a number of fields. A brain drain program must be humane, placing value on the uniting of families, and providing refuge to men cut off from their homelands for political reasons. It must be coordinated with our allies, for we do not wish to reduce the drain to our land only to increase it in equal measure to Canada and Western Europe.

But there are, in my view, at least five areas where action is clearly called for.

First of all, we need more research on the magnitude and causes of the brain drain. Dr. Perkins writes that 90 per cent of Asian students do not return; INS figures indicate about 30 per cent. The true figure may lie somewhere in between, but we need to know where, and in what countries, and—more difficult—for what reasons. Nor are our statistics much better for doctors or other professional groups. . . .

But, though more research is needed, the knowledge we now have is sufficient to provide the basis for positive action. This suggests a second urgent step on our part—a substantial expansion of educational opportunities for Americans in areas like medicine where we are seriously dependent on manpower from developing countries.

The present medical situation is a national disgrace. The growing shortage of American health personnel has been evident for many years. That we should, in the face of such clear evidence, need doctors from countries where thousands die daily of disease to relieve our shortage of medical manpower is inexcusable. And our dependence has increased—in 1951, only 9 per cent of our hospital residents were foreign; by 1964, this proportion had risen to 24 per cent. . . .

As a third part of a brain drain program, we should encourage our colleges and universities to make their programs for foreign students more relevant to the needs of their homelands. In opening their doors to these students, our colleges and universities perform a national and international service of the first order. But they face a difficult paradox—the better their foreign students adjust to university life, the longer they extend their studies; and the more successful they are academically, the more likely they may be to want to stay permanently in the United States.

To resolve this paradox, we must devise programs for foreign students which orient them toward the needs of the developing nations to which we hope they will return. For this purpose, I would urge that the Congress authorize funds for pilot grants to educational institutions, to support special curriculums to relate particular fields of study to problems faced by developing countries, and special counseling to help students maintain contact with their homelands and shape educational programs which prepare them for rewarding careers there. Such programs should concentrate particularly on foreign students not sponsored by the federal government, since it is among these students that the brain drain is most acute.

As a fourth step, we must give far more attention to helping developing countries make effective use of the skilled people they do have. These countries thirst for skilled, professional manpower, yet often do not provide good opportunities for those already there. This is, of course, why many leave. . . .

And as one American university dean has put it, it is difficult to advise an Indian engineer to return home if "there is a high risk that he will be a clerk-typist for the next ten years." Many underdeveloped countries lack effective economic and social institutions to attract the right man to the right job, to award posts on the basis of potential and capabilities rather than personal connections, and to allow a bright young man to advance as fast as his abilities merit.

The responsibility for meeting this problem rests primarily with the countries affected. We have learned through hard experience that self-help is the crucial factor in the progress of developing nations. Without it, any aid program is futile. But in countries that are serious about self-help, our aid can supply a vital ingredient to development, by providing needed capital and concentrating attention on fundamental problems. . . .

Improved placement is, of course, only part of the answer. Another part may lie in promoting diversity and pluralism in developing countries, so that individuals can establish their own businesses or schools or cooperatives, and develop and test their talents in the crucible of experience. Another need is to remove some of the deep-rooted frustrations of professional life in developing countries—low salaries, lack of adequate facilities, limited opportunities for advancement, and insufficient recognition of the value of professional work. None of these can be accomplished overnight. But it is surely time to give this problem the priority it deserves.

Finally, we should consider negotiating bilateral agreements with developing countries severely hurt by the brain drain, to modify the effect of our visa and immigration policies. This is an area where we must tread with extreme care. . . .

Because of the severity of these problems, together with the importance of maintaining the general provisions of our immigration law, we should explore the possibility of bilateral agreements with certain developing countries to deal with brain drain problems as they arise in each national case. Such agreements might require that students from particular countries return home for two years before becoming eligible to immigrate to America, as those on the exchange program must now do. And these agreements might establish a mechanism for considering the needs of a developing country in our immigration policy, as well as our own needs. Any such bilateral agreement should definitely require that the developing country take specific steps to improve opportunities for talented individuals.

Such agreements, of course, would involve some limits on the freedom of the individual who wishes to come to our shores. Yet no one is advocating today an open immigration policy; the question rather is whom we shall accept, and who shall be kept out. Since we have determined, as one basic principle, to place high priority on our need for skilled people, we should likewise find some way to consider another principle, the needs of countries whose development is a goal of our national policy.

In other words, what is needed is some way to strike a balance, in immigration policy as in the other areas I have discussed. For our people do need doctors, as our economy thirsts for more scientists and engineers. We prize the presence of foreign students on our campuses. We profit from the contribution of immigrants from all continents to our national life. Yet if we would build a world where our children can live in peace and freedom, development of poor nations must likewise receive high priority in our national policies. And if we continue to neglect the brain drain, the gap between rich and poor will grow wider still, and hopes for lasting peace will vanish for our century.

Such a disaster we must do all in our power to avert.

Chapter Five

Peace in whose time?

Security and *peace* are words that are often found together. The problem is that the priority of security too often precedes and prevents the attainment of the goal of peace. In 1967 wars were raging in Cyprus, in the Middle East, and in Vietnam. All the participants in these wars had peace as a goal, but in reality the security of all the individual nations involved was always of prior concern.

Throughout the readings there is a constant recurrence of the theme that the vital national interest of security must be obtained and protected by the full use of national power even, if necessary, at the expense of international order. However, national security exists not in a vacuum but within national and international environments. The constantly changing nature of these brings inevitable alterations in the conditions affecting security. Such alterations—particularly the development of new and suicidal weaponry—as the readings on international law and disarmament have reminded us, indicate that perhaps security and peace are no longer necessarily mutually exclusive.

Even if we mean by peace merely the avoidance or absence of war, we find that it is still a difficult goal to attain. Our discussions of regional and world organizations have illustrated the weaknesses of multilateral defense agreements and peace-keeping efforts. Lichtheim's essay attempts to evaluate the suggestion of a Russo-American enforced peace. The idea is based on the assumption that the national interest of the military-industrial giants includes a tranquil and stabilized community of nations. Given their monopoly of economic and military power, equal political power is assumed to follow, thus providing a complete base for the assurances of a peaceful world.

Such a "realpolitik" solution to the "crisis of stability" may be an effective short-run solution, but the long-run question of a stability based on order rather than power remains an urgent question, for the power of China, India, and other nations is certainly not a static quantity. The movement toward a world order acceptable to all must be one based on the "human factor," as U Thant puts it in his own plea for order. Larson calls this factor the "world revolution for human rights." It is a long-range drive to promote the social and economic progress which will bring about a condition of security that can be personally felt. Such a state of personal security would be superior to mere national security because it would be acquired mutually rather than at the expense of the security of others.

How can "peace on earth" ever be achieved? International politics remains a politics of open and unstructured conflict, unlike the structured and controlled conflict typical of stable domestic politics. In an attempt to utilize U Thant's "human factor," a number of politicians, scientists, educators, and religious leaders were recently invited to a "peace convocation" in Santa Barbara, California. The purpose of this conference was the development of nonsectarian, nonpolitical human response to the papal encyclical of Pope John XXIII. Hundreds of conferees from around the world came in search of peace and security through human understanding. A variety of the participants, representing the leading points of view, discuss the encyclical in some detail.

Pleas for peace and for recognition of the needs of humanity over and above the needs of nations are insufficient. There is a need for clear recognition of the fact that each nation-state continues to seek its own security by means of its own choosing and according to its own power. This realism must be complemented by concrete proposals which allow states to see how their mutual security interests are best served by an orderly process for the handling and settling of disputes and for the development of all peoples. Peaceful coexistence is only a dream now, a dream requiring a new international empathy for it to become a realizable vision.

On November 22, 1963, John F. Kennedy was on his way to deliver a speech entitled "America's Goal: Peace on Earth." We have asked: Peace in whose time? Young people today are restless because this goal remains so elusive. The power of bigger and more explosive nuclear weapons in underground silos and on nuclear submarines has brought us no nearer to security. Even President Kennedy could only promise restraint and wisdom in the use of power, and there was no mention in his speech of order. Are "security in a world of change" and "peace on earth, goodwill toward men" to continue as mutually incompatible elements among the slogans of mankind?

Section 1

Avoiding future wars

Pax Russo-Americana?

George Lichtheim

Is the mutual threat of Red China sufficient to cause the two superpowers to form a coalition to preserve peace? Although he is not sure, Mr. Lichtheim feels that its consideration at high levels merits a closer look. It is conceivable to him that the Soviet Union would admit the possibility of war between Communist nations while making peace with the West. He feels that largely because of Vietnam the West is not yet ready to reciprocate.

 The author is a free-lance British writer on world affairs.

The London weekly *Spectator*, the intellectual organ of British Conservatism (a respectable creed, not to be confused with the demagogic nonsense that elsewhere goes under the same label), some months ago headlined an editorial "Towards a Pax Russo-Americana."[1] Admittedly, this was last January,

[1] This article originally appeared in April 1966. All references by the author to previous months are either to 1966 or 1965.

during the bombing pause in Vietnam and in the midst of the Indo-Pakistani peace conference at the Tashkent "summit." But the heart of the argument is not affected by the subsequent escalation of the war in Southeast Asia. It remains as true today as it was three months ago that "the basic force for order in the focal areas of instability in the world today must be [the] further development of the emergent Pax Russo-Americana." To state this is not of course to say that it is actually going to happen. Political reality does not always evolve along lines that seem rational to the observer. The two German wars of this century can serve as evidence that great nations are quite capable of embarking upon self-defeating and suicidal courses. Yet it is significant that the custodians of Britain's imperial tradition should view present realities in a mood very different from the temper prevalent during the 1950's. Twenty years after the outbreak of the Cold War signalized the breakdown of the 1945 peace settlement in Europe, a significant section of British opinion has come around to the belief that a Soviet-American partnership is not merely desirable, but actually at the point of being established.

This clearsightedness is the more admirable in that it goes with a dispassionate appraisal of Britain's shrinking role in a world in which the wartime alliance of equals with the United States is no more than memory.

> In the interests of peace, we can only welcome the emergence of the Pax Russo-Americana. . . . But we cannot ignore the fact that as America turns her back on the struggle against Russia in Europe to devote her energies to the struggle with Russia against China in Asia, the status of Britain degenerates from principal ally to something like displaced person. To be precise, we are wanted, but no longer needed.

It takes a degree of stoicism on the part of a Tory journal to deliver this kind of judgment, but then the British have in recent years had plenty of opportunity to practice this mood. For the rest, the more intellectual Tories share with De Gaulle (whom they publicly oppose and privately admire) a conviction that great conflicts between nations or empires are something more substantial than disputes over what is comically known as "ideology." Sir Alec Douglas-Home, speaking before the Economic Club at the Waldorf-Astoria in New York not long ago, delivered himself of a fairly traditional appraisal when he remarked that the Sino-Soviet split had been brought about by China's growing appetite for Siberia—"a much more tempting target . . . than the impoverished and overcrowded Indian subcontinent." This may be a bit too simple: a clash between totalitarian states by definition involves the totality of their rival structures (party leadership included), not just territorial control. But it is a safe guess that there are men high up in the Soviet administration who share the outlook of Britain's last Tory Prime Minister. The Russian military leaders, at any rate (like their colleagues elsewhere), must privately regard all the fuss over the correct interpretation of Lenin as so much eyewash. They are probably mistaken so far as Mao Tse-tung and his colleagues are concerned, for there is reason to believe that the present leadership in Peking is genuinely addicted to the doctrines it proclaims in public. But mistaken or not, this kind of military realism undoubtedly plays its part in shaping Soviet attitudes toward the mounting Chinese threat.

What, then, is the role of Maoism as a doctrine in the recent aggravation of the Sino-Soviet dispute? The question would be easier to answer if the Peking regime had not repeatedly displayed a strain of shortsighted cynical empiricism quite irrelevant to its long-term strategy and highly embarrassing to its sympathizers abroad. By now the list is fairly lengthy. It includes the 1962 military assault on India over a trivial border dispute; last September's unprincipled intervention on the side of Pakistan (a far more conservative regime than India's) during the brief flare-up between the two successor-states of the former Indian Empire; adventurous bluster against Delhi at the expense of the Indian Communist party, leaving that party (even its pro-Chinese left wing) in a highly vulnerable position; long years of cynical backing for Sukarno's demagogic anti-Westernism in Indonesia, followed first by an abortive attempt to get rid of him, and then by silence while some 300,000 Indonesian Communists were slaughtered by the army and the Moslems in the greatest disaster ever to befall a Communist party in Asia since Chiang Kai-shek's notorious massacres in 1927; hasty support for the Boumedienne regime in Algeria on the morrow of *its* successful anti-Communist coup, followed once more by embarrassed silence when Algiers showed no desire to reciprocate; pointless intrigues in half a dozen African states; the grotesque and extremely damaging (for Peking) quarrel with Castro; and last but not least, the continued propaganda barrage against real or alleged Soviet peace moves in Hanoi, coupled with reckless advice to the North Vietnamese to fight to the last drop of (their own) blood.

Against this background of bluster and failure, it is not surprising that Moscow has succeeded in swinging the greater part of the world Communist movement back into its own orbit. Peking has indeed left its supporters in the movement high and dry. On top of this, the combination of doctrinal intransigence with cynical "realism" has by now made most of the Afro-Asian world wary of China, dissipated much naive goodwill, and paradoxically played into the hands of those Soviet diplomats who really believe that a Russo-American *cordon sanitaire* around China is a matter of urgency.

This provisional balance sheet, it must be supposed, is sufficiently obvious to have caused some concern among the party leaders in Peking, who after all are quite familiar with Asian realities, even if not very good at interpreting Western thought processes. Why, then, do Mao and his colleagues persist in a course which by now has resulted in their isolation within the Communist movement, not to mention the non-committed world? Psychological factors may account for obstinacy on the part of aging men never too well informed about the world beyond their borders. But in the main, Peking's commitment to its peculiar strategy must be seen in the context of Maoism as a political movement.

It is a mistake to regard Mao and his followers as Leninists concerned to preserve the purity of the original doctrine. They are no longer even Stalinists, for Stalin never renounced the long-term perspective of a seizure of power by some, at least, of the West European Communist parties. However "Eurasian" his own cast of mind (not to mention his political methods), he remained to the end a prisoner of the Leninist doctrine that a "proletarian revolution" in the advanced industrial-capitalist countries was an ultimate inevitability. The originality of the Chinese Communists lies in the fact that they are no longer bound by Lenin and Stalin (not to mention Marx, who has simply been promoted to the vacant place of Confucius). The proletarian revolution, and with it the international working-class movement, has been written off and replaced by a strategy based on the antagonism of the have-not countries against the haves: more precisely, on the revolt of the world's agrarian hinterland against the metropolitan centers. It is ludicrous to call this Marxism, or even Leninism (itself a fusion of German Marxism with Russian Populism). The Maoist mentality goes back to Bakunin, the prophet of revolt against industrial civilization. But it is Bakuninism minus the anarchist hostility to the state, for to the Maoists (as to their unsuccessful Nationalist precursors), the state is the great engine of popular education and national regeneration. If "the people" remains the ultimate source of authority, the state is the concrete embodiment of that revolution-from-above which is to make China great and respected: provided, of course, that the state continues to be identical with the party, whose superior wisdom is transmitted to the lower echelons of the bureaucracy, and thence to the people as a whole.

There is some logic in this position. Given the tasks facing the regime, in a country far more backward economically than the Russia of 1917, the fusion of Communist totalitarianism with traditional Chinese nationalism was a relatively simple matter. So was the commitment to breakneck modernization and the near-total militarization of public life. What prevents the rest of Asia (not to mention Africa and Latin America) from taking Maoism more seriously as a "model" is the evident failure of the industrialization drive: the "great leap forward" was not, after all, a success. The fashionable comparison with India is spurious, for China's real rivalry is with the USSR and with Japan. India may suffer from catastrophic famines and industrial mismanagement: Japan does not. As for the USSR, it has successfully industrialized itself on a "socialist" basis and can now claim to be America's only rival. Thus China finds itself blocked, and it is this failure that accounts for the political fury of Maoism.

To escape from the impasse in which it finds itself, the regime must rely on the total mobilization of its only major asset, the Chinese people, while beyond the borders of China it can count on support only from those who are similarly situated: either because they have failed to modernize themselves, or have no desire to try, or because the political context is such that it is plausible to hold "Western imperialism" responsible for the prevalence of misery and exploitation. There is no lack of such regions, or of students and vagrants ready to take to the hills. Yet the quarrel with Castro shows that Peking tends to lose out in the competition with Moscow wherever the revolution carries the "socialist" label. It is a political necessity for *every* modernizing regime in this age to call itself "socialist," and the only question that remains is under which of the competing international flags the country in question prefers to set sail. So far, Moscow is ahead in the competition, its only rival being Gaullist France, with Labour Britain nowhere, and the United States universally regarded as the rich man's friend and the scourge of the poor and homeless.

It is, of course, most unfair that America should be viewed in this light, especially when one considers that U.S. food shipments, however inadequate, currently represent the slim margin between ordinary famine in India and wholesale catastrophe. But fairness has little to do with the matter. India may be dependent on U.S. food surpluses, but in itself this is more likely to rouse resentment than to promote gratitude. Indian nationalism has for years been kept going by the hope of achieving a degree of economic self-sufficiency permitting India to play an independent role on the world stage—possibly a foolish aim, but nationalist movements are alike in valuing prestige above all else. As matters stand, Delhi is back to the starting line, with repeated monsoon failures threatening to make the country wholly dependent for years on the United States, and with political trouble brewing in the countryside at the same time. However much the pro-Chinese wing of the Indian Communist party may have been weakened by Peking's recent behavior, it probably retains sufficient strength to rouse sections of the peasantry to revolt in those parts of the country where food shortages can plausibly be blamed on Indira Gandhi's Congress party and its local following of landowners and grain merchants.

If the policy-makers in Washington were capable of lifting their eyes from the Vietnamese bog, they might perceive the outline of coming troubles on a scale large enough to inspire Toynbeean rhetoric about the convulsions in prospect for the 1970's. China, at least, seems to have solved its food problem, to the extent of guaranteeing a bare minimum for everyone, or almost everyone. India has not, and it does not look like it will make significant progress in the coming decade. This is the other side of the coin when viewed from Peking. It makes up for some recent political setbacks and for the relative failure to speed the rate of China's industrialization. The latter, incidentally, if it were ever to gather speed and transform the country's archaic structure, could only lead to the dissolution of the primitive consensus which is the social basis of Maoism. An industrial China would infallibly reproduce some of the tensions now racking the Soviet Union. At the very least, it would set the technicians against the regime, and the urban workers against the peasants: in short, it would induce what old-fashioned Marxists used to call "class conflict." Mao is right in asserting that at present this is not a problem, the reason being quite simply that Chinese society is still backward enough to afford a large measure of primitive egalitarianism. At the risk of sounding paradoxical, one might say that if Chinese Communism ever became a real economic success at home, China would at last make the acquaintance of capitalism, or something like it: at any rate, enough of it to give its Marxists something to do. If the regime lasts long enough, this may turn out to have been its chief contribution to the country's social development: one of those ironies of history that are so much easier to perceive if one assumes with Hegel that nations, like individuals, seldom know what they are actually up to.

No heretical thoughts of this kind are likely to trouble the mental slumber of China's present rulers. Their intellectual sophistication has hardly advanced to the stage of such self-questioning. In any case, they have no choice. Nationalism and pseudo-Leninism propel them in the same direction, and if they had any doubts as to the overriding importance of industrial-*cum*-military strength, these uncertainties would have been settled for them by the consistent hostility of the U.S. government: an antagonism antedating the Vietnamese conflict.

That the United States and China are on a collision course has by now become a conviction so solidly implanted in the rest of the world, from Europe via the Middle East and India to Japan, that one can hardly blame Mao and his colleagues for treating it as an axiom. They are, of course, to blame for having evolved a self-fulfilling prophecy which has the effect of closing all other options, but then an almost similar degree of fatalism has lately been manifested by others, including the British. One reason why the idea of a "Pax Russo-Americana" has become popular in Britain is quite simply the growth of a conviction that large-scale "trouble" with China is to be expected at some time in the 1970's. Similar considerations doubtless underlie recent French moves, including De Gaulle's intervention in Hanoi and his forthcoming visit to Moscow in June.

It has not escaped the attention of the Europeans that U.S. involvement in Southeast Asia is increasingly rationalized on grounds having little to do with the entanglement in South Vietnam. The emphasis has shifted toward long-range considerations which would not be markedly affected if some sort of settlement could be patched up between Hanoi and Saigon, or even if Hanoi moved away from Peking to the extent of acquiescing in an American military "presence" in the South. The stakes are getting bigger, and even another Geneva conference would hardly affect the growing conviction on all sides that Washington and Peking are simply maneuvering for position with an eye to the coming showdown.

As to the probable date of that confrontation (to employ a fashionable synonym: the old-fashioned term "war" being unpopular, and probably illegal as well under the UN Charter), no more than guesswork is possible, but a small amount of light has recently been shed. At the NATO conference in Paris last December, Mr. McNamara tried to make the Europeans' flesh creep with forecasts of China's growing nuclear capacity in the coming decade. Other hints were dropped in Washington and London on the occasion of last January's visit to the United States by leading British personalities. Both before and after Mr. Denis Healey and Mr. Michael Stewart, respectively in charge of Defense and Foreign Affairs, had met Messrs. Rusk and McNamara, the British press was filled with officially inspired speculation about Britain's role "East of Suez" after 1970: clearly an important date. On January 26, the London *Times* felt able to report a significant difference of opinion between the U.S. State and Defense Departments on this subject: Mr. McNamara, it appeared, was prepared to accept "a partial rundown of British forces in Western Europe" by way of filling what was described as "the gap in the American defense perimeter, a gap that stretches from the Persian Gulf to the Gulf of Siam"; he also appeared to be undisturbed by hints that Britain might have to give up Singapore and Aden, and fall back upon less costly bases in Australia. Mr. Rusk, on the other hand, in the opinion of the paper's Washington correspondent (from whom the British Embassy keeps few of its secrets), "wants Britain to stay where she is. He would welcome a British contingent in Vietnam . . . but would be happier if she stood ready to defend the former imperial territories in Africa, while the United States took care of China." These high-level geopolitical discussions caused some consternation among Mr. Harold Wilson's followers when reports of them filtered back to London, but the British Cabinet showed itself ready to accept the logic of the situation. At any rate Mr. Healey soon took off for Australia, to see what could be done about a replacement for Singapore, and on his return the Cabinet voted in favor of buying American aircraft rather than developing Britain's naval carrier-based forces: apparently on the grounds that time mattered and that the early 1970's were likely to be a danger period (also, perhaps, because the alternative to purchasing American aircraft was Anglo-French co-production of a rival plane—a project strongly backed by the Conservative Opposition).

As usual in the case of the Labour Government, the pro-American school defeated the pro-Europeans, whose chief exponent, Mr. Roy Jenkins, was moved from the Air Ministry to the politically less exposed Home Office. On February 18, the New York *Times*, with a perspicacity rare for that journal, noted: "The British are asking the United States to join in financing a substitute base in Western Australia to be ready in 1970" (again the magic date) "to receive some of the F-111's that Defense Minister Denis Healey has come to Washington to purchase. But the Johnson Administration—unwilling to be left alone in Southeast Asia so long as the Vietnam war continues—is urging the British to hold on in Singapore whatever the cost."

Whatever the cost to the British taxpayer, that is. That cost is almost certain to include the devaluation of sterling and a consequent rise in the domestic price level. As an editorial in the *Spectator* on February 11 put it with uncommon frankness: " . . . we cannot continue to afford well over 300 million pounds a year in military spending overseas, most of it 'East of Suez,' and at the same time avoid devaluation. In plain English, either East of Suez or the pound will have to go."

A fortnight later, the official Defense White Paper made it clear that the Cabinet was determined to preserve at least the semblance of a British role "East of Suez"—while limiting the total defense budget in 1970 to a figure insufficient to provide an independent British carrier-based force. As Mr. Christopher Mayhew (who resigned from the Government in protest, along with a bevy of admirals) correctly pointed out, this decision not merely sacrificed the navy (for which he happened to be responsible), but also reduced Britain to an auxiliary of the U.S. in the Far East. On these grounds, he recommended complete withdrawal from the region, and a further reduction of the defense budget, in the interest of economy (and of saving the pound, though this was only implied). His colleagues plainly believe that in a financial emergency the U.S. Treasury will bail them out. But how often can this performance be repeated?

Against this somber background, the deepening American involvement in Vietnam begins to make sense, if not politically, then at least militarily. For as long as one of General Gavin's "enclaves" can be held (and before long this may become the unstated aim of the policy-makers), it is at least possible to find an excuse for holding on to bases like Camranh, now rapidly being built up as a major naval fortress far exceeding in size and importance what it was under the French. One does not hear much being said about Camranh, but the significance of its swelling size is unmistakable. As the Manchester *Guardian* remarked on January 27, " . . . even in this country, let alone in Hanoi, it does not much look as though the Americans are going to withdraw from Vietnam in the foreseeable future, peace or no peace; too much has been invested, politically and even economically. The building of the base at Camranh, for instance, is no short-term project."

Indeed it is not. Hence there was no ground for surprise when last February's Senatorial hearings in Washington extracted both from Mr. Rusk and from General Maxwell Taylor the admission that the "independence" of South Vietnam (its independence from the North, that is) remained the prime objective of American policy. So much for the offer of "unconditional" negotiations. Any process of negotiation which threatened to compromise the "independence" of Saigon would clearly translate itself before long into a "dependence" on the Vietcong sufficient to rule out an American armed presence in the South. Clearly, this is what the war is currently about. Those American critics of the official policy who dislike its consequences while accepting, or not challenging, its presuppositions have lately taken to arguing that conceivably even the Vietcong might in the end compromise on this issue, even if Hanoi (not to mention Peking) did not. The war is after all being fought largely by Southerners, and a peace conference might give them a chance to assert themselves. This kind of reasoning, whether realistic or not, inevitably leads one into the trackless bog of Southeast Asian politics. Whatever the local complications, it is now fairly clear that the only settlement acceptable to both Peking and Hanoi is one that rules out an American armed presence; while the only outcome acceptable to Washington is one that perpetuates it.

The public rhetoric to which office-holders in a democracy are necessarily committed is not a safe guide to such topics. Consider the embarrassment of having to affirm officially that U.S. retention of the base at Camranh is no longer negotiable. The public can hardly be expected to understand these niceties, after having been told for so long that the war is about abstractions like "freedom" and "honor." On the other hand, one must be fair to the policy-makers: just because they obviously cannot "win" the war, it does not follow that they are irrational in trying not to lose it. They can after all argue that if Vietnam can be partitioned once more (whatever the legal formula), the essential minimal "presence" in the South can perhaps be saved. What is more, they may be right (though by now even this modest aim is beginning to look a bit utopian).

The unspoken presumption behind all this is the need to go on with the "containment" of China, and the near-certainty of large-scale trouble with the rulers of that country in the 1970's, when it is supposed they will have a nuclear establishment big enough to represent a threat to Japan and Australia, if not (as yet) to the United States. On this subject there now appears to be a consensus among the experts sufficient to warrant the statement that China can afford the minimum outlay necessary to qualify as a serious nuclear power, i.e., one equipped with something more than primitive plutonium bombs. In the case of France, a relative newcomer to the club, the equivalent expenditure was reckoned by the London *Economist* (January 15) to amount to a capital outlay of 1,000 million pounds, or about three billion dollars: not an excessive sum for either a modern European country or—at the other extreme—a very large and determined Asian one like China. (On the other hand, the cost is probably just too high for India in its present condition, not to mention such recent disasters to Delhi's plans as the death of its leading nuclear physicist, Dr. Homi Bhabba, buried in the snows of Mont Blanc amid the wreckage of an Air India jet.)

What, then, are the distant prospects of a tacit alliance between the United States and the Soviet Union—an alliance in whose actual present existence the Chinese, but few other people, affect to believe? (Castro plainly does not, for which one can hardly blame him.) It is probably a misfortune that this subject generally tends to be discussed in terms appropriate to what is known as "a deal." In reality, more than that is required, though deals cannot be ruled out (they are more likely, however, to emerge at the close rather than at the beginning). What is required, after all, is a reorientation of long-range Soviet strategy, hitherto mesmerized by the conflict with the United States, and a corresponding change of attitude on the part of the American government and public: not to mention America's allies, among whom the West Germans, at any rate, have every reason to regard such a prospect with the direst of forebodings.

It is easy to see that the two super-powers have something in common. Above all, they both have a great deal to lose, and in this sense they share an interest in avoiding a major conflict anywhere in the world that might oblige them to intervene on opposing sides. This community of interest in the avoidance of catastrophe underlay the Cuban confrontation of October 1962. It has been made manifest once more by the limited extent of Soviet intervention in Vietnam, though thanks to Washington's elephantine subtlety this particular issue continues to be posed in such terms ("resistance to Communist aggression") that Moscow cannot well use its break with Peking as an excuse for withdrawing from Hanoi. When even the French are fed up with American intervention on the side of the Saigon regime, the Russians would have to deny their entire revolutionary faith, and lose their hold over the "third world" (not to mention their own supporters in Asia) if they did not uphold the North.

There is deadlock here, but it is a deadlock which no longer pits Communists against anti-Communists in the manner of the 1950's. Since the United States and China represent extreme positions in this conflict, it is becoming possible for the Russians, the Indians, the French, and various minor countries, to appear as moderators: and this without prejudice to Moscow's continued leadership of most of the Communist bloc. This is a welcome change from the old uncomplicated Dulles pattern, when extremists on both sides had the more or less willing support of almost everyone in Europe and Asia. All this is gone, as India's and Pakistan's recent acceptance of Soviet mediation in their private quarrel showed. Communism is no longer the *only* issue that matters (except to the Washington policy-makers). The Russians themselves are beginning to realize that a conflict between Communist states is possible, while conversely it is not inconceivable that peace—genuine peace—may be made with the West. This mental change is the biggest event of the past few years. Its continuance is bound to condition the chances of a genuine East-West settlement.

It does not follow that the West can do nothing but sit and wait. It, too, has to alter its collective mental orientation: away from the crusading faith of anti-Communism and toward a pragmatic (blessed word) acceptance of the world as being necessarily made up of pro-Western, Communist, and neutral regimes, with the Communist bloc increasingly polarized between the belligerent faith of Peking and the conservative mood of Moscow. Does this represent a return to ordinary "power politics"? Taken literally, the question is meaningless: politics is about power and about nothing else. There is no such thing as a particular brand of politics concerned with power, as distinct from a nobler and more idealistic kind. Insofar as the absurd term "power politics" is meant to describe a state of affairs where nations are concerned with the defense of their interests, and not with the promotion of world-revolutionary upheavals, it does indeed appear that the world outside China is slowly reverting to this traditional pattern, if only because the spread of nuclear weapons cuts across the issue of world revolution: no country, whatever its regime, can afford to disregard *that* kind of threat. In this sense, there is now a tendency to return to the kind of pattern of relationships that was formerly considered normal.

China is the great exception. But it is just this fact which tends to promote the cooling of revolutionary and crusading ardors in both Washington and Moscow. Their cooling, not their disappearance. Nor need there be an abandonment of national beliefs and traditions. It is as foolish to expect the Russians to give up Leninism and the cult of the October Revolution as it is to expect Americans not to celebrate the Fourth of July. What may be expected to change is the practical relevance of these quasi-religious obeisances. Their polarity reflects the simple circumstance that, politically speaking, there is no such thing as One World. When this has been acknowledged by both sides, it will be time to consider the means for bridging the gap dividing the rest of the international community from China.

Vietnam and the real nature of the world revolution

Arthur Larson

Professor Larson's thesis is basically that the tragedy of Vietnam is doomed to be repeated unless two cardinal mistakes are rectified: (1) the failure to work through the United Nations and (2) the failure to recognize that the nature of the current world revolution is distinct from the nationalist revolution in Vietnam. The "revolution of human rights" is on center stage and he calls for U.S. support and understanding of it. Peace will come only when human rights are secured by all. (Editors' note: Recent events in Czechoslovakia, France and the ghettos of America illustrate that no regime or ideology is immune from this drive for human rights.)

"The Real Nature of the World Revolution," Saturday Review, *June 3, 1967.* *Professor Larson is director of the Rule of Law Research Center at Duke University.*

I happened to look out the window of my fortieth-floor office one day and noticed, several floors above me, a window-washer recklessly moving about on his scaffolding without using a safety belt. I repeatedly shouted suggestions at him on how to avoid the danger he was risking and he repeatedly ignored my suggestions. A little later I saw him falling headlong past my open window and as he went by he uttered these words: "Now please let us not rehash past mistakes; I am only interested in what you would do *now* if you were in my position."

This is a parable, of course, and not a true story, as the reader will have gathered from the length of the speech made by the descending window-washer. The point of the parable is simply to sum up how some of us feel when, in the course of the continuing Vietnam debate, we are told that no comment is legitimate except that which presents a viable alternative proposal on what to do right now. I have been presenting alternatives for five years, in books, booklets, symposia, speeches, and articles—several of them in these pages. But to limit current discussion to immediate alternatives ignores the fact that there are two principal reasons—not just one—for the great debate on Vietnam. The obvious reason for the debate is to find the best way to bring the war to a satisfactory end. But the second reason, perhaps even more important in the long run, is to learn how to avoid making a similar mistake in the future.

If it is off limits to discuss the mistakes of the past, or indeed if it is insisted that no mistakes were made, then we may find the agony of Vietnam repeated in other parts of the world for years to come. The dictum that those who ignore history are condemned to repeat its mistakes was never more apt than here.

Two cardinal mistakes stand out above the many that could be cited. The first . . . [is] the refusal to handle the Vietnam problem through United Nations channels from the moment Secretary Rusk and President Kennedy in 1961 announced that it was a threat to the peace, in spite of the requirement of Article 37 of the United Nations Charter that, when other methods have failed, threats to the peace "shall" be referred to the Security Council.

The second cardinal mistake was a fundamental misunderstanding of the nature of the current world revolution and the relation of the Vietnam conflict to it. The American action in Vietnam is based on the theory that the revolutionary situation there is the prototype of the revolutionary situation in much of the rest of the world. From this follows the conclusion that Vietnam is a testing ground of a global struggle, and that what happens in Vietnam will determine what happens in perhaps dozens of other countries. The true fact is that the revolutionary situation in Vietnam is unique. The word "unique" is deliberately chosen here with full recognition of its etymology: there is only one of it.

To demonstrate why this is so, it is necessary to begin by identifying three "world revolutions." These three, classified by their primary motivations, are the revolutions of communism, nationalism, and human rights. The theme of this article is that, of these three revolutions, except in two or three places, the only one that has *independent* contemporary revolutionary vitality is human rights.

As to the first, the communist world revolution, it never did have, and certainly does not have now, a coherent independent motivation. The communist revolution is essentially a parasitic movement. It attaches itself and attempts to ride to success on whatever might be the most promising true revolutionary or other force operating at the moment. In its original Marxist version, the communist revolution was to take place first in the most advanced industrial societies, utilizing the force of the discontent of downtrodden industrial workers due to a combination of overproduction and maldistribution. (It is significant that, with the various translations of *The Communist Manifesto* at the time, it never occurred to anyone to translate it into Russian.) Lenin, and more recently Khrushchev and his successors, tried to show how communism could flourish in the least advanced countries by identifying communism with the force of world-wide anticolonialism. This attempt failed, principally because the United Nations took over the role of patron of the decolonialization process. Under Stalin, communism was a sort of adjunct to the primary force of Russian nationalist expansionism.

The second world revolution has been that of nationalism, with the goal of national political independence. It is this development that in a few years has been principally responsible for the addition of seventy new nation-states to the membership of the United Nations. The swiftness of this process has made it easy to overlook the fact that, with only a couple of exceptions, the world nationalist revolution has been completed. It has been completed in Asia, except, as we shall see, for what is going on in Vietnam. It has been completed in Africa, except in Angola and Mozambique, with Rhodesia in a somewhat unclassifiable position. It was completed in Latin America long ago for the most part, with a few recent additions.

The mistake that has been made by the United States, and in this it has been joined by the Chinese Communists, is to assume that in most of these countries there still remains something resembling the original quantum of revolutionary force, needing only a few manipulations by a handful of sinister communist agents to turn it into a second revolution comparable to the first. What this overlooks is that in all these countries there is now an indigenous Establishment. Their own leaders, frequently those who rose to power as a result of the original revolution, now control almost all physical, administrative, and political force in the country. They control the army, the police, perhaps even an air force. They do not want a second revolution, thank you. When the Chinese Communists, who were once conspicuous in many of these countries, began to be suspected of interest in promoting such a second revolution, they were thrown out in one country after another, with Indonesia and Ghana being the most conspicuous examples.

The breathtakingly rapid completion of the liberation-from-colonialism revolution has also caught the Russians with their slogans down. "Wars of national liberation" was to be the rubric under which global revolution should proceed. But national liberation, in any reasonable sense of the term, is now mostly an accomplished fact. The slogan now has to be tortured into covering somehow the idea of replacing one home-grown regime with another. That may or may not be some kind of "liberation," but it is certainly not "national" liberation. Except—once more—in Vietnam, where what might appear to be a home-grown regime in Saigon is actually a military group that fought on the side of the French against the forces of national independence.

In a revolutionary situation only two kinds of force count. One is sheer military force. Failing this, there must be an overwhelming if intangible surge of mass will and emotion so great that eventually even military power recedes before it. Such a force was the passion for political freedom and national independence. But if that force has spent itself in achieving its goal of an indigenous government, and if that indigenous government also has a virtual monopoly on military and police power, what force remains that can possibly compete with these and upon which can be built within a few years another revolution upon a revolution?

Indeed, when these two sources of force—intangible revolutionary fervor and physical power—have themselves come into competition after independence, it has invariably been the latter that has won out. No one could have embodied more fully the charisma and power attendant upon the leadership of a nationalistic revolution than Nkrumah and Sukarno. Yet when this source of power, which had prevailed against the colonial masters, was pitted against the indigenous Establishment it went down in defeat. It is quite possible that something of the same sort is now being acted out in the People's Republic of China. Mao is apparently trying to rekindle the original revolutionary fires, but even with all his prestige and posters and booklets he is learning the same lesson of the unpopularity of a second-run revolution.

We are now ready to appraise the relevance of all this to the Vietnam question. The situation in Vietnam was unique because it was the one place in the world where the nationalistic revolution had not been allowed to complete itself. The pristine force of nationalism was and is still in full play. All the most potent components of a successful nationalistic revolution were present in more than usual abundance. There was the charismatic leader, Ho Chi Minh. There was a high level of nationalistic fervor, developed over a long history and most recently under the stimulus of Japanese and French imperialism. There was a clear objective: a unified and independent nation. There were well-developed military power, seasoned and disciplined fighters, considerable stocks of weapons, and no lack of confidence and morale. They had for all practical purposes defeated the French in 1954, after inflicting 172,000 casualties. The completion of the revolution of national independence seemed to be within reach.

At this point the United States cuts into the story. By the time the major American military effort was undertaken there was no other place, except the Portuguese territories in Africa, where the force of nationalism had not run its course. There was, therefore, no other place where this unique threat of combined communism and nationalism could come into play. The central theme of American involvement, "If we can't stop the communists here we can't stop them anywhere," will have to go down in history as the most tragic misjudgment of our times.

But to say that the world revolution of nationalism has largely run its course is not to say that the age of revolution is over. Far from it. There remains the unfinished revolution of human rights. This is the real world revolution of today and tomorrow. The future of the United States—and of any other country—will turn on how well it learns to understand this revolution and to find the right relation to it.

The first thing we must understand is the most obvious. The successful completion of a nationalist revolution (and certainly of a communist revolution) is not by the same token the successful completion of a human rights revolution. Sometimes there is a high degree of coincidence between the two. For example, the American Revolution resulted in both political freedom for the American colonies and enhanced personal freedom for individual Americans, through the Constitution and the Bill of Rights. But Americans should not for this reason confuse the two revolutionary achievements in other settings. In Latin America the basic revolution of political independence goes back 150 years for a number of republics, to the revolt of the Spanish-American colonies under Simon Bolivar from 1810 to 1824. And yet, because of the failure to overcome the gulf between the aristocratic elite and the impoverished masses, the unsatisfied demand for human rights in Latin America is still one of the most explosive forces in the world today.

The driving energy of the human rights movement takes different forms in different parts of the world. In Latin America, as just noted, it is seen in the struggle of the impoverished many against the privileged few. In the newly developing countries of Africa and Asia it is the gigantic task of raising living standards in spite of economic, educational, managerial, and almost every other kind of backwardness. In the Eastern European countries and Russia it is the change of their economies from state-demand to consumer-demand economies, with the inevitable wrenchings away from socialist dogmas and toward market incentives and private enterprise practices. In the United States it is the racial revolution.

Although the manifestations of the human rights drive take these varied forms, and although the danger of violence also varies widely from area to area because of the varying speed of response to these demands, there can be only one American policy as to them all. The United States must be found on the side of human rights. To be found on the other side, for any reason, is to invite eventual defeat.

This should be a congenial enough role for Americans, if they have not forgotten their traditions as a people. These traditions stood us in good stead during the world revolution of national independence. We took our stand firmly alongside the colonies aspiring to nationhood, sometimes to the intense annoyance of our oldest friends, such as the British, the French, and the Dutch. We are finding it harder to adopt as forthright a posture in the world revolution of human rights. There are several reasons for this, of which three may be mentioned: diplomatic ineptitude, economic shortsightedness, and blind anticommunism.

In spite of the efforts of succeeding administrations, we still cannot seem to get our diplomatic representatives abroad to concentrate on "tuning in with" the right people—"right" in the sense of getting us on the right side of the human rights story. It is so much easier to hobnob with the titled, the wealthy, the beautiful people than to get next to the discontented students, the intellectuals, the young struggling professionals, the reformist politicians, the labor leaders, not to mention the workers and the peasants. As for economic shortsightedness: Central to the whole job in the newly developing countries is the provision of vast amounts of capital, technical assistance, managerial and skills training, and all the other ingredients of economic development and nation-building. We cannot begin to do this total job for all countries at once but we can do much better than we have been doing. Merely quantitatively, we could well afford to double our investment immediately in view of what is ultimately at stake.

As for blind anticommunism: Communism, as noted earlier, so far as its revolutionary potential is concerned is a parasitic movement. It would now like to attach itself to the world human rights revolution and borrow its force from this immensely potent source of social change. The only way to prevent this is to get there first ourselves if possible. But if we do not get there first—that is, if we see some communists already busily working on that side—let us never again, as we did in the Dominican crisis, thereupon automatically take up our position on the opposite side. Rather, we should consult our own traditions and interests, and if these place us on the human rights side of the struggle we should—always within the limits imposed by the rule against interference in internal affairs—crowd the communists out and by our support of the movement remind the world once more who the true sponsors of individual rights and freedom are.

It was said earlier that the Vietnam pattern could not repeat itself elsewhere in today's world—in the sense of displaying the merger of nationalism and communism as revolutionary forces. If, however, as a result of our own ineptitude and miserliness and indiscriminate anticommunism the revolutionary potential of unsatisfied human rights reaches an intensity comparable to that of the nationalistic fervor that produced the anticolonial revolutions, and if the United States takes up its stand on the side of entrenched privilege while the communists are left a clear field to ally themselves with the vast majority of the population, the Vietnam pattern could be reproduced elsewhere, with the human rights drive substituted for the independence drive. The danger of this is probably more imminent in Latin America than anywhere else. The Castro revolution is the prime example of this combination.

Never in history has the basic pattern of world revolution changed so many times so swiftly. It is asking quite a lot of our leaders and spokesmen to throw away speeches only twenty years old on "Communism as the Great Fountainhead of World Revolution" and speeches only ten years old on "Nationalism as the Great Fountainhead of World Revolution," but that is what they are going to have to do if they are not to be one or even two revolutions behind the times.

Peace: The human factor

U Thant

Are human rights as important as national sovereignty? Thant tries to show that a pax Russo-Americana in combination with a recognition of the human rights factor is the realistic hope for the security of the human race.

These are the conclusions of an address delivered to the Fourth Friends World Conference, Greensboro, N.C., July 30, 1967. U Thant is Secretary-General of the United Nations.

I believe that both in Viet-Nam and in the Middle East there will be no solution to the problem if the human factor is ignored, and the problem will become susceptible of solution only if the interest of human beings involved is kept in mind. . . . There is imperative need for making a fresh search for peace in the Middle East so that the rights of all countries in the area may be respected, because the various countries are inhabited by human beings, and their rights as nationals of Member States are as important as the sovereign rights of the States themselves. If this simple fact were accepted it would become easier to agree upon solutions which would produce a durable peace in the Middle East and put an end to the cycle of threats and counterthreats leading to actual armed conflict which has three times during the last 20 years produced so much suffering for the unfortunate people involved.

Another regrettable aspect of both the war in Viet-Nam and the conflict in the Middle East is the effect that they have had on the relations between the two super-Powers. It seems to me that, if these conflicts can be resolved, there may be a resumption of the *détente* between East and West which was developing until the recent escalation of the Viet-Nam conflict. There are a number of global problems for which solutions cannot be found except on the basis of a closer cooperation between the two super-Powers. This is also true of such problems as disarmament, the conclusion of a treaty for the non-proliferation of nuclear weapons, and the ending of the arms race between the two super-Powers. It seems to me that the super-Powers already recognize that they have a common interest in solving these problems but they seem to be very wary about making any positive approach for reasons which are well known.

I realize, of course, that a *détente* between the two super-Powers cannot by itself bring about peaceful conditions over the rest of the world. However, it is an indispensable first step and I believe that it would immediately produce a congenial climate for cooperation in the United Nations itself. . . .

Let us remind ourselves that the Charter of the United Nations speaks in the name of "We the peoples of the United Nations," as distinct from the Covenant of the League of Nations, which opened with the words "The High Contracting Parties." Although the Charter was signed by the representatives of Member Governments and their aim was to establish an intergovernmental organization, they themselves intended that it should be the people of the United Nations who are speaking in the Charter, it is their will that must be felt and their interest that must be protected.

The peace that we have to seek in order to save succeeding generations from the scourge of war must therefore be a peace that will envelop the whole of humanity. The promotion of "social progress and better standards of life in larger freedom" is another goal of the Charter that belongs equally to all of mankind. In the absence of a realization that the human race is one and indivisible there can be neither lasting peace, nor effective international co-operation for any purpose. By the same token, I believe that real and effective international cooperation can be achieved, if there is an awareness at all levels that no man can save himself or his country or his people unless he consciously identifies himself with, and deliberately works for, the whole of mankind.

Section 2

Peace on earth

Pacem in Terris: Excerpts from the encyclical letter of Pope John XXIII

The theme of the encyclical is to seek nation by nation "social progress, order, security and peace" through recognition of the "human rights revolution."

Interdependence between political communities

Recent progress of science and technology has profoundly affected human beings and influenced men to work together and live as one family. . . . The social progress, order, security and peace of each country are necessarily connected with the social progress, order, security and peace of all other countries.

At the present day no political Community is able to pursue its own interests and develop itself in isolation, because the degree of its prosperity and development is a reflection and a component part of the degree of prosperity and development of all the other political Communities.

Insufficiency of modern states to ensure the universal common good

The unity of the human family has always existed, because its members were human beings all equal by virtue of their natural dignity. Hence there will always exist the objective need to promote, in sufficient measure, the *universal* common good, that is, the common good of the entire human family.

As a result of the far-reaching changes which have taken place in the relations between the human family, the universal common good gives rise to problems which are complex, very grave and extremely urgent, especially as regards security and world peace. On the other hand, the public authorities of the individual political Communities—placed as they are on a footing of equality one with the other—no matter how much they multiply their meetings or sharpen their wits in efforts to draw up new juridical instruments, they are no longer capable of facing the task of finding an adequate solution to the problems mentioned above. And this is not due to a lack of good-will or of a spirit of enterprise, but because of a structural defect which hinders them.

It can be said, therefore, that at this historical moment the present system of organization and the way its principle of authority operates on a world basis no longer correspond to the objective requirements of the universal common good.

Connection between the common good and political authority

There exists an intrinsic connection between the common good on the one hand and the structure and function of public authority on the other. The moral order, which needs public authority in order to promote the common good in human society, requires also that the authority be effective in attaining that end. This demands that the organs through which the authority is formed, becomes operative and pursues its ends, must be composed and act in such a manner as to be capable of bringing to realization the new meaning which the common good is taking on in the historical evolution of the human family.

Today the universal common good poses problems of world-wide dimensions, which cannot be adequately tackled or solved except by the efforts of public authorities endowed with a wideness of powers, structure and means of the same proportions: that is, of public authorities which are in a position to operate in an effective manner on a world-wide basis. The moral order itself, therefore, demands that such a form of public authority be established.

The universal common good and personal rights

Like the common good of individual political Communities, so too the universal common good cannot be determined except by having regard to the human person. Therefore, the public authority of the world Community, too, must have as its fundamental objective the recognition, respect, safeguarding and promotion of the rights of the human person.

The principle of subsidiarity

The public authority of the world Community is not intended to limit the sphere of action of the public authority of the individual political Community, much less to take its place. On the contrary, its purpose is to create, on a world basis, an environment in which the public authorities of each political Community, its citizens and intermediate associations, can carry out their tasks, fulfil their duties and exercise their rights with greater security.

Modern developments

An act of the highest importance performed by the United Nations Organization was the Universal Declaration of Human Rights, approved in the General Assembly of December 10, 1948. In the preamble of that Declaration, the recognition and respect of those rights and respective liberties is proclaimed as an ideal to be pursued by all peoples and all countries. Some objections and reservations were raised regarding certain points in the Declaration. There is no doubt however, that the document represents an important step on the path towards the juridical-political organization of the world Community. For in it, in most solemn form, the dignity of a person is acknowledged to all human beings; and as a consequence there is proclaimed, as a fundamental right, the right of free movement in search for truth and in the attainment of moral good and of justice, and also the right to a dignified life, while other rights connected with those mentioned are likewise proclaimed.

It is our earnest wish that the United Nations Organization—in its structure and in its means—may become ever more equal to the magnitude and nobility of its tasks, and that the day may come when every human being will find therein an effective safeguard for the rights which derive directly from his dignity as a person, and which are therefore universal, inviolable and inalienable rights. This is all the more to be hoped for since all human beings, as they take an ever more active part in the public life of their own political Communities, are showing an increasing interest in the affairs of all peoples, and are becoming more consciously aware that they are living members of a world Community.

The encyclical of Pope John XXIII

John Cogley

This analysis of the encyclical calls "humane communication" the source of permanent and indispensable peace. Four basic and "natural" human rights are discussed as roots for communication. The problems of peaceful coexistence and disarmament are basically the problems of human trust and understanding.

On Coexistence (*Santa Barbara, Calif.: Center for the Study of Democratic Institutions), copyright 1965 by the Fund for the Republic, Inc. Reprinted by permission. Mr. Cogley is staff director of the Center's Study of the American Character.*

Coexistence has always struck me as a propaganda word that says either too much or too little to make political sense. But the word, for all its ambiguity, expresses a genuine concern—it is shorthand, really, for the hope that the cold war can be brought to an end; that both the Communist and the Western worlds will develop along their characteristic lines, without either fearing the other or being interfered with by the other; that the fundamental differences between them will be blurred with the passing of time; that they will enter a stage of collaboration, rather than of rivalry, in improving the lot of mankind; and, finally, that the threat of the nuclear holocaust will be removed if only because the major nuclear powers will no longer have anything to fear from one another. Taken in this sense, *Pacem in Terris* also seems to be devoted to coexistence as an immediate goal for the achievement of peace on earth. But though Pope John was not so rude as to say "We will bury you," he did end his encyclical with a prayer that God would "banish from the earth of men whatever might endanger peace, may He transform them into witnesses of truth, justice and brotherly love! . . . By virtue of His action, may all people of the earth become as brothers, and may the most longed-for peace blossom forth and reign always between them!" In his own way, then, Pope John was as apocalyptic as Nikita Khrushchev was when he spoke of burying the West. For the Pope, too, coexistence was a prelude to a peaceful conquest. How to reconcile coexistence with the ultimate goals and beliefs of both men, then, is a problem that transcends the boring propaganda uses of the word.

Pacem in Terris largely avoids condemnations and anathemas. Like its author, it is eminently positive, optimistic, and "open." And in the final analysis the major contribution of the encyclical may be the spirit in which it was written. . . . the fact that its author somehow managed to set a tone of reasonableness and create the kind of atmosphere in which humane communication becomes possible and the idea of permanent peace among men is seen not only as desirable and credible but as wholly indispensable, even in a divided world. . . .

Of its nature a papal encyclical is a didactic document. *Pacem in Terris* is no exception. It is not merely a series of pious exhortations but the outline of a total philosophy of social life and of politics. . . . There are no hidden premises in the encyclical. It is patently the work of a Christian believer, specifically a Roman Catholic Pontiff. By the same token, it is also unmistakably the work of one who accepts the philosophy of natural law. Pope John of course knew how to distinguish between theology and natural law and presumed others did too, though the two are frequently intermingled in his encyclical. . . .

Because the document is also directed to "all men of good will"—which would include millions who accepted the Pope as merely one more moral leader in a pluralistic world—the major content of the encyclical is based not so much on the theological teachings of the Christian Gospel and the Roman Catholic Church as on philosophic doctrine. . . .

The encyclical enumerates a number of specific human rights that are derived from man's nature. They include religious liberty, the right to marry or to embrace the monastic life, an *a priori* parental right in deciding the education of children, "free initiative" in the economic order as well as "the right to work," the right to private property "even of productive goods," the "right of assembly and association," and the right to establish "a great variety of . . . intermediate groups and societies [between the individual and the state] in order to guarantee for the human person a sufficient sphere of freedom and responsibility." In addition to these "rights," any one of which could be a bone of contention in the modern world, the encyclical affirms "the right to freedom of movement and of residence within the confines of [one's] own country: and, when there are just reasons for it, the right to emigrate to other countries and take up residence there." And how much general agreement would there be on this point?

Practically every one of these "rights," in fact, is already a cause of dissension and disagreement in the present divided world. . . . Nor is there any sound reason for believing that all political and ideological camps could agree on the proposition that men in their social relations should "act chiefly on [their] own responsibility and initiative" without "being moved by force or pressure brought to bear on [them] externally." Indeed, if there were significant agreement on such questions as these, many of the reasons for the cold war would no longer exist. . . .

Pacem in Terris supports governmental intervention in the economic sphere, after the manner of what is generally called "the welfare state." This made the encyclical unpalatable to certain laissez-faire diehards in the West. A more serious limitation on its value as a guide to coexistence, though, is its forthright declaration:

> *For this principle must always be retained: that State activity in the economic field, no matter what its breadth or depth may be, ought not to be exercised in such a way as to curtail an individual's freedom of personal initiative. Rather it should work to expand that freedom as much as possible by the effective protection of the essential personal rights of each and every individual.*

Like another statement quickly following, namely, that "it is in keeping with the innate demands of human nature that the State should take a form which embodies the threefold division of powers," this preference would not appear to be shared equally by all parties to coexistence.

The third section of the encyclical, "Relations between States," comes to grips with some of the more immediate problems connected with coexistence. . . . Again he excoriated racism and, from an affirmation that all men are created equal in dignity, he derived the "consequent recognition of the principle that all States are by nature equal in dignity"—vested with the right to existence, to self-development, to the means fitting to its attainment, and *to be the one primarily responsible for this self-development.* He then emphasized the need to recognize the national sensitivities of others and to discard the broadcasting of propaganda which impairs "the reputation of this people and that."

Here is the first clear-cut practical and hopeful guide to coexistence to be found in the encyclical. If it were taken seriously, it would mean that, in the interests of peace, governmental campaigns of scurrility would end and officially sponsored hate-mongering would be eliminated from the world scene. This would not necessarily mean that black would have to be called white. Pope John's own example of sticking to his principles without stressing the failings of his "enemies" could be followed by governmental leaders, official broadcasters, and private propagandists.

Of course no government frankly acknowledges that it is engaged in vicious propaganda policies: it merely underwrites a program of presenting *true* "information" to counter the false propaganda of others. But the fact is that peoples do have strange and distorted views of one another, and the libels simply do not come out of nowhere. Eliminating hate-producing propaganda, then, could be a useful step toward genuine coexistence. In addition, the Pope's proposal suggests that imaginative cultural exchanges should be increased to make up for some of the mischief of the past.

The Pope's practical advice regarding respect for reputations is immediately followed by an exhortation to settle the inevitable disputes between states not by force, deception, or trickery but "by a mutual assessment of the reasons on both sides of the disputes, by a mature and objective investigation of the situation, and by an equitable reconciliation of differences of opinion." . . .

To expect such high-minded conduct from "political communities" (to use Pope John's designation) may verge on naïveté, as many have said. But the Pope was no political innocent, though he was a moralist. . . . In any case, in his fervent appeal for the exercise of reason for the settlement of political arguments, the Pope was being faithful to his natural law doctrine and to his role as a spokesman for the moral forces in the world. Here, clearly, he presented another guide to coexistence.

It was in the section on disarmament that Pope John made his most forthright bid for a state of coexistence between antagonistic political forces. The arms race, it is evident, struck him as unreasonable, wasteful, and possibly fatally dangerous. He condemned the race itself rather than any party in the race. The frantic search for equity of armaments, he said, has resulted not only in burdening the richest nations with a hopeless contest but, as a consequence of the waste of wealth, has stood in the way of the progress of less fortunate peoples. The Pope believed that both sides were honestly operating in accordance with the deterrence theory and that neither side had any truly serious intentions of destroying the other. ". . . it is difficult to believe that anyone would deliberately take the responsibility for the appalling destruction and sorrow that war would bring in its train." Still, he insisted, the mere existence of these monstrous instruments of mass destruction is a threat; war could be set off "by some uncontrollable and unexpected chance." The very testing of modern weapons could have "fatal consequences for life on earth." So, in the traditional terms of natural law, "right reason and humanity urgently demand that the arms race should cease."

The Pope did not involve himself in the technicalities of disarmament but simply stated that disarmament must eventually be thorough and universal and must *proceed from inner conviction.* The peace of the world, he said, cannot be interminably based on equality of arms. The present emphasis on parity, the going principle, is self-defeating; it must be replaced by a new principle of international life: *"mutual trust alone."*

A number of reasons were offered for this seemingly idealistic advice. One, reason itself declares that the relations between states can no longer be based on force or the threat of force, any more than relations between individuals—the arms-race is suicidal. Two, there is really no one left who does not want to see war abolished, since no one stands to gain from it. Three, the benefits of an arms-free world would be enormous. Its advantages would be felt by individuals, families, nations, all mankind. A fourth reason is cited later by the Pope, speaking as a moralist: *"It is hardly possible to imagine that in the atomic era war could be used as an instrument of justice."* . . .

There are principles enunciated in the final section that have much to do with providing a guide to coexistence. For one, the Pope warns against a too easy jump from principle to application. . . . In this, Pope John was appealing for careful prudence in political matters and a sensitive weighing of all the factors that must be taken into account in making wise (and incidentally moral) political judgments. He was in fact warning Catholics against the "crusade mentality" that can be expected to produce not the hopeful spirit of coexistence but the fanatical spirit of the holy war.

Secondly, John XXIII asked the faithful to distinguish carefully between "error" and "the person who errs." The former is always an abstraction; the latter is a human being, with a claim on all the human rights and dignity so eloquently outlined in the earlier parts of the encyclical. Honest meetings between human beings can never do real violence to the truth. The confrontation of individuals, whatever their philosophic differences, can in fact result in surprising practical agreements, for the service of the common good is not dependent on perfect philosophic or theological accord between those who are moved to join together to make a better world. . . .

[Thirdly,] the Pope seemed to be telling the faithful that not even the Communist movement can be judged simply by citing the principles that gave rise to it. As a tangible political entity and social force in the world, after almost fifty years, the Communist movement has an existence of its own that may have been derived from but is not simply identifiable with its philosophical presuppositions. Catholic-Communist collaboration in practical matters, then, the Pope seemed to be saying, is not forever unthinkable, even though the two views of life are utterly incompatible.

But while Pope John's "opening to the left" was unmistakable, he hedged it in by certain safeguards. He insisted, for example, that such collaboration must always be "in accordance with the principles of the natural law, with the social doctrine of the Church, and with the directives of ecclesiastical authority."

John XXIII was no more "pro-Communist" than his predecessors or his successor. A convinced Communist, inevitably, would find the main lines of *Pacem in Terris* no more congenial than he would find the intellectual orientation of any other theistic, profoundly Christian, and pro-natural law document. What is significant, though, is that the Johannine version of theism, Christianity, and natural law, in the interests of world peace and mankind's needs, provided for a mode of genuine coexistence between the Communist and the Christian world.

It is only fair to the encyclical and to the Pope who signed it that it be taken *in toto*. And when it is, it will be evident that in itself it is not enough. It needs to be supplemented by equally reasoned, equally forthright statements on the requirements for peace from other schools of thought, religious and anti-religious. Then, when all have spoken *ex corde* and candidly about their separate visions of "*pacem in terris*," will we finally know, whether, intellectually, peace is really possible, or indeed whether even long-range coexistence is possible.

The problem of pluralism remains. John XXIII showed that his philosophy is compatible with it. Differences need not result in disaster, even differences as profound as those between Catholicism and communism. Now we must hear from others. . . .

Pacem in Terris: The response of a communist

N. N. Inozemtsev

The editor of Pravda gives a response again revealing that the ultimate Soviet goal is "the victory of communism." He challenges the West to "peaceful economic competition" so men will have a choice of system and social order. He attacks American intervention in "legitimate struggles," but he does not mention Soviet support. He concludes by almost calling for a pax Russo-Americana.

On Coexistence (*Santa Barbara, Calif.: Center for the Study of Democratic Institutions*), *copyright 1965 by the Fund for the Republic, Inc. These are comments delivered at the* Pacem in Terris *Convocation in February 1965. Mr. Inozemtsev is deputy chief editor of* Pravda.

The existence of a threat common to all of mankind as well as the existence of a common objective—that of preventing the catastrophe—provides a basis for rallying very differing forces in the struggle against a threat of war, despite the differences that may exist among them on political, religious, or other grounds. The Soviet people are prepared to adopt a most positive attitude toward any initiative tending to safeguard peace and promote understanding, whatever the origin of such an initiative: the United Nations, the church, public organizations, etc.

One of the foremost tasks of this conference is the search for ways to promote mutual understanding and trust among states. In order to accomplish this, it is necessary for all of us to have a clear idea of the aims and views of each other. We have never tried to conceal that we believe the socialist system to be a higher form of the social and economic structure of society than capitalism, and that we strive to achieve the victory of communism. This attitude of ours is, however, a testimony to our deepest concern for peace, not of a desire for a new world war.

In the constitutive manifesto of the International Brotherhood of Workers, Karl Marx, the name with which our ideology is closely associated, wrote that in the field of foreign policy the task of the working class is to ". . . secure that common laws of morals and justice which should be followed by the individuals in their mutual relationships also become supreme laws in the relations among nations." The Soviet Union and the other socialist countries, the Communist Party of the Soviet Union and the other Marxist-Leninist parties, consider the struggle for peace as their paramount task. The Soviet Union takes a firm and consistent position that there is and can be no justification for unleashing a new world war which, taking into account the destructive nature of modern weapons, would become a catastrophe for all people. It is our deep conviction that prevention of a new world war and the elimination of wars from the life of society represent a real, feasible task.

Wars are not an ill fate hanging over humanity as an inevitable atonement for its sins, as some religious figures insist. They are not a manifestation of "animal instincts" and "irrational destructive emotions" organically inherent in the people, as is alleged by some philosophers. They are not the result of the "psychological inferiority" of some people and the "superiority" of others, as racists claim. In the Marxist view the basis for conflicts resulting in wars, the basis for cataclysms undermining normal international relations, is found in deep social factors, and as changes occur in the arrangement of class forces, connected with the development of social progress, more favorable conditions for peace are created.

Achievements of the scientific and technological revolution, its effect on industry and agriculture, on means of transport and communication, on the field of international economic relations, have toppled many barriers that once stood in the way of contact among peoples, and have brought about new and more favorable conditions for the development of economic, cultural, and other ties. Thus, ours is not just an epoch of sinister dangers looming over mankind in connection with the creation of unheard-of means of destruction and extermination but an era of radiant hopes and possibilities.

Ideological opponents of communism assert that "war and socialist revolutions are synonymous notions," that "Communists advocate armed violence everywhere at all times," and that "Communists believe that every means is justified for the sake of the triumph of revolution."

But there is nothing more alien to the spirit of Marxism than the doctrine of the export of revolution and "revolutionary wars." Socialist and national liberation revolutions result from the most acute class antagonisms of the capitalist society, as an expression of the impact of internal forces and the struggle of the people in each of the countries. Revolution cannot be brought about artificially; it cannot be brought on bayonet tips. The main and by far the most complicated task of the socialist revolution is that of construction, not destruction. Only the successful accomplishment of this task and the higher productivity of labor can lead to a better life for people (after all, that is why people make revolution) and guarantee victory for a new system. That is why the Soviet Union devotes paramount attention to the problems of peaceful economic competition with capitalism, for the people will then have the opportunity to judge the merits or deficiencies of every system and choose the social order of their liking.

Marxists resolutely oppose the export of revolution. But they also oppose the export of counterrevolution, of forceful interference into the domestic affairs of any nation in order to support a regime that the country itself abhors. America's Declaration of Independence declared that every people has the right to alter or abolish any form of government, "organizing its powers in such form, as to them shall seem most likely to effect their Safety and Happiness." These principles have become universally recognized in international law. Their violation is the source of dangerous tension in international relations, as has been vividly demonstrated by foreign intervention in the Congo and, of course, the international crisis connected with U.S. intervention in South Vietnam. The Soviet government has come out strongly in favor of the cessation of military provocations directed against the Democratic Republic of Vietnam, Laos, and Cambodia, in favor of the right of the peoples of Indochina to decide their own matters for themselves.

The struggle for freedom and independence is a legitimate struggle. One can accept or not the national liberation struggle, but it is a real factor of present-day life, and there can be no real policy while the historic necessity of such struggle is denied.

The Communist Party of the Soviet Union and the Soviet government have been directed in their foreign policy and their relations with capitalist countries by the principles of peaceful coexistence. The doctrine of peaceful coexistence is a Leninist doctrine. Its essence is still unchanged. It lies in recognizing as an objective reality the fact of simultaneous existence on the earth of countries with different social systems that can and must live in peace.

The general course of the foreign policy of the Soviet Union is that of safeguarding peaceful conditions for building socialism and communism, of strengthening unity and solidarity among the socialist countries, of supporting the revolutionary liberation movements, of all-out widening of solidarity and cooperation with independent Asian, African, and Latin-American states, of consolidating the principles of peaceful coexistence with capitalist states, of saving mankind from a world war.

Peaceful coexistence, says the program of our Party, provides for the rejection of war as a means of solving disputes between states and for solution of disputes by way of negotiations; equality of rights, mutual understanding and trust between states, respect for the interests of one another; non-intervention into internal affairs and recognition that every people has the right to solve independently all questions within its own country; strict respect for the sovereignty and territorial integrity of all countries; the development of economic and cultural cooperation on the basis of full equality and mutual benefit. In our view these principles contain important criteria for the scope of peaceful coexistence among states with different systems and for the correlation between peaceful coexistence and ideological struggle.

The Soviet Union has not concealed its intention to win the economic competition with the capitalist world, but this does not at all mean abandoning economic cooperation. The principle of peaceful coexistence provides for the development of normal economic and political relations between states of different social systems and the development of various forms of international cooperation.

Soviet foreign policy categorically rejects the dictatorial methods to which certain bourgeois governments frequently resort or seek to resort. At the same time it is always prepared to consider constructive proposals of the Western powers and to achieve mutually acceptable solutions. Soviet foreign policy never renounces reasonable compromise as long as that compromise takes into account the opinions and legitimate interests of the contracting parties and promotes the peaceful settlement of major issues.

At present, the most concrete tasks in the struggle for peace are, to our mind, as follows:

> . . . The elimination of the hotbeds of danger such as Vietnam, the Caribbean basin, the Congo, which have developed as a result of the military intervention of certain powers and their attempts to interfere in the internal affairs of peoples.
>
> . . . The solution through negotiation, with consideration of the interests of all countries concerned, of outstanding issues associated with the consequences of World War II; first and foremost, the problem of a German peace treaty and the recognition of currently existing national borders.
>
> . . . The reduction of the danger of nuclear conflict through the prevention of further proliferation of nuclear weapons and the barring of the so-

called "NATO multilateral nuclear forces," which would open up access to nuclear weapons to the West German revenge-seekers; the banning of underground tests; and the creation of atom-free zones in different regions of the globe.

. . . The slowing-down of the arms race, particularly through the reduction of military budgets; the liquidation of foreign military bases on alien territory; the adoption of effective measures aimed at banning the use of nuclear weapons and at carrying out disarmament.

. . . The further relaxation of international tensions, the strengthening of trust between states, the establishment of international relations based not on dictate and threat, not on violence and arbitrariness, but on the equality and self-determination of all nations and on respect for their sovereignty. Effective measures in this direction could be the recognition by all states of the principle of peaceful adjustment of all territorial questions and the creation of a system of means to avert sudden attack.

The complexity and the controversial nature of the international situation call for concrete actions designed to improve the international climate. The solution of this task can and must be promoted by normalizing the activities of the United Nations, the international organization whose effectiveness we are all interested in developing; by the further expansion of world trade and economic ties between nations; and by further cooperation in the fields of culture, science, and technology. Peaceful coexistence is a common, universal principle. It is of particular significance in the relationships between the Soviet Union—the first country where the socialist revolution emerged victorious—and the United States of America—the main country of modern capitalism.

Throughout the entire history of this relationship there have been neither wars nor major disputes. During the years of such grave trial as the Second World War, the United States and the Soviet Union were allies in the struggle against Hitlerite Germany. The Soviet people have a feeling of profound respect and sincere friendliness for the American people and their democratic traditions. We believe that there are real possibilities today of ensuring that this relationship is built on the foundations of peace and friendly cooperation. To ensure progress, which is in our mutual interests, it is necessary that both sides exert their best efforts.

Vice-President Humphrey has noted that all states, great and small, are interested in peace. It should be added that all people, whatever their other views and convictions may be, are interested in the prevention of world war. The clarifying and comparing of different viewpoints, the joint search for ways of solving the most pressing international problems, the creation of a fitting international climate—these make up a complex but lofty task which accords with the most vital needs of mankind.

Pacem in Terris: The response of an American

George F. Kennan

Unlike the Communist response, this response is that of a private citizen talking about his own feelings. He suggests that before casting stones, the Soviet Union show more concern for "the true civil liberties" of the people under their control. On the other hand, he sees little hope for achieving the ideals of the encyclical in the environment of suspicion and fear that permeates the West. Basic Western policy should be altered to create more flexibility of response. His plea is that both sides develop new faith in humanity based on the mutual interest of survival.

On Coexistence (*Santa Barbara, Calif.: Center for the Study of Democratic Institutions*), *copyright 1965 by the Fund for the Republic, Inc. These are comments delivered at the* Pacem in Terris *Convocation in February 1965. Mr. Kennan is former U.S. Ambassador to the USSR and to Yugoslavia.*

Let me . . . say, by way of preface, that I can speak here only to the Western position in the questions at hand. By doing so, I would not wish to imply that there has not been at times in the past, or is not today, serious fault in the Soviet and Communist position as well. The Communist governments of the Soviet Union and Eastern Europe will have to search their own consciences and render their own accounting on those many points—particularly the denial of true civil liberties to the peoples under their control, the resistance to adequate inspection in the case of disarmament arrangements, the oversuspiciousness, and the steady poisoning of international understanding by propagandistic distortion—where many of us would feel they had done a disservice to the future of Europe. My own loyalties and obligations of conscience relate to the West, of whose culture I am a child and where I bear the responsibilities of citizenship; and it is to Western concepts and policies that I wish primarily to speak.

For several years, now, the Western coalition has pursued a European policy marked, as I see it, by the following characteristics:

1. The assumption of a strong Soviet desire to attack, or at least to intimidate by superior military force, the western half of the continent with a view to obtaining a commanding influence over its peoples and governments.
2. A belief that the Soviet government could be deterred from acting on this desire only by a Western defense policy relying heavily on nuclear weapons and including, as a primary component, the military power of a heavily rearmed Western Germany.
3. Pressure for German unification, by procedures which apparently envisage a unilateral retirement of Soviet forces from Eastern Germany in the face of a continued Western military presence in the ensuing united Germany, plus a full-pledged association of that united Germany with the Atlantic Pact.
4. The cultivation, not everywhere but in some instances, of a species of "little-Europism," in the form of efforts to organize the European community for peaceful purposes within the framework of the western half of the continent alone, through institutions closely related to the Western military alliance and thus involving a heavy reliance on the United States, and so conceived that they would, if fully realized, serve to impede rather than to facilitate the ultimate overcoming of the division of the continent.

It is evident that the results of a policy embracing these elements have been sterile and unsatisfactory. No general agreement has been reached on European problems, and no perceptible progress has been made in that direction. German unification has been brought no nearer. The dangerous uncertainty surrounding the position of Berlin has been prolonged and intensified. Grievous disunity has emerged within the Western community over the problems of economic unification and those of control and possible use of nuclear weapons by members of the Western coalition, in peace as in war.

None of this is surprising. Such a policy is replete with inner contradictions. Its military objectives—notably the inclusion of a united Germany, as a major component, in a Western defense system based primarily on nuclear weaponry—are in obvious conflict with its major political objective, which is the military and political retirement of the Soviet Union from Central Europe; for no Russian government, Communist or otherwise, could afford to retire in the face of such a demand. The difficulties encountered in the control of nuclear weaponry within the Western coalition reflect merely the contradictions inherent from the start in the cultivation of weapons suicidal in their implications, indiscriminate and politically incoherent in their conceivable effects. Schemes for economic and political unification in the western half of the continent alone are in contradiction not only with the divided and uncertain state of the Germany they are supposed to include, but also with that heavy and unnatural dependence on the United States which the prevailing political and military approaches imply. Britain is placed in a difficult position by the confusion between Atlantic and continental principles of economic and political unification. France, animated now by a natural and basically sound desire to see Europe the main architect and guarantor of its own future, is frustrated by the difficulty of realizing this concept within the framework of a divided Europe, where the western part has been taught to look for its defense mainly to the American nuclear capability.

The elimination of these contradictions and the reshaping of Western policy on a more hopeful basis would not alone suffice to assure to Europe a future of greater security and promise. For this, a reciprocation on the Communist side would be essential too; and relations between the Soviet Union and the United States would probably have to be less disturbed by developments outside of Europe than is the case at this present sad and dangerous moment. But without the elimination of these contradictions and without such a re-shaping of Western policy, I must confess that I can see little hope for an advance of European life along the lines indicated in the late Pope John's encyclical; for such advances in the human spirit cannot take place in an atmosphere of pervasive suspicion and fear—particularly fear addressed to the inconceivable disasters of a war conducted with nuclear weapons.

I turn with some reluctance to the question of what would be required to make possible this change in Western policy; for the answers, as I see them, cut deeply into established assumptions and attitudes, and the mere suggestion of them will no doubt again encounter incredulity and rejection in many quarters. But our troubles are not trivial ones, and the cures cannot be other than drastic.

As the first of these essential changes I would name a basic review of our position with relation to nuclear weapons and their place in our defenses. I recognize with appreciation the changes that have been introduced into American policy, in this connection, in recent years. I consider them a step in the right direction, and commend the insight and courage that inspired them. But I believe we could go further.

I see no reason why a primary reliance on nuclear weapons should be considered permanently essential to the defense of my own country or of Western Europe. I fail to see why we could not at least explore and discuss seriously the various proposals that have been brought forward over the years by the Polish government, looking to a restriction of the place of nuclear weapons in Europe's defenses. I think we could usefully re-examine our acceptance of the principle of "first use" in the employment of any and all weapons of mass destruction, and thus place ourselves in a position where we could proceed more effectively towards the eventual elimination of these weapons, and above all their delivery systems, from national arsenals. Without such a change I can see no possibility of halting the present trend towards the proliferation of control over such weapons to a point where all hope of preventing their eventual use, somewhere and at some time, would have to be abandoned.

In the case of Germany, I should think there could be evolved a general Western policy less heavily geared to the domestic-political compulsions that bear on West German governments. Everyone would understand it if West German political parties could accept such a policy only under protest and with the reservation of their own position. We should not, I think, leave the rearmament of Western Germany effectively open-ended, as it must today appear to be in the eyes of people in the East. Greater reassurance could be given to Poland and to others on the question of Germany's eastern borders, if not as a unilateral concession then at least hypothetically, as one component in a possible accommodation of East-West differences. And if, as it appears, there is to be no military disengagement in Germany in this present historical period, then one must learn to accept with better grace at least the provisional existence of a separate East German political entity, avoiding, if you will, the recognition of it as a final solution for the problem of the relation of that area to the rest of Germany, but promoting closer contacts with it and a more intimate association of its people with peoples to the west. It is not unreasonable to hope that there could be created in this way an atmosphere in which the Berlin Wall would become redundant even in the eyes of its creators, and the natural forces pressing for uniformity in the development of all modern societies could have a chance to diminish contrasts and to alter in this way the terms of the very problem of unification itself.

Finally, I should like to plead for a basic revision of assumptions concerning Soviet intentions, both hypothetical and actual. Western policy is apparently based on an assessment of these intentions which has not changed appreciably from the days of the Berlin blockade and the Korean War, and which, even then, probably embraced serious elements of misinterpretation. The assumptions commonly made with respect to Soviet military intentions (assumptions reflected in the very word "deterrence") are ones that can be reconciled neither with Communist doctrine (which does not envisage the bringing of socialism to peoples exclusively or primarily on the bayonets of foreign armies), nor with the moral commitments the Soviet leaders have assumed to their own people, nor with the present state of relations between Moscow and the Communist countries of Eastern Europe. They impute to the Soviet leaders a total inhumanity not plausible even in nature, and out of accord with those humane ideals which we must recognize as lying, together with other elements less admirable in the eyes of some of us, at the origins of all European Marxism.

I should like, therefore, to end these observations with a plea for something resembling a new act of faith in the ultimate humanity and sobriety of the people on the other side; and I would like to address this plea to our Communist contemporaries as well as to ourselves. History reveals that the penalties for over-cynicism in the estimation of the motives of others can be no smaller, on occasions, than the penalties for naïveté. In the case at hand, I suspect they may be even greater. For in the predication of only the worst motives on the adversary's part there lies, today, no hope at all: only a continued exacerbation of mutual tensions and the indefinite proliferation of nuclear weaponry. Our sole hope lies in the possibility that the adversary, too, has learned something from the sterility of past conflict; that he, too, sees—if only through the dim lens of ideological prejudice, suspicion, and accumulated resentment—the identity of fate that binds us all; that some reliance can be placed, in the adjustment of mutual differences, on his readiness to abstain, voluntarily and in self-interest, from the wildest and most senseless acts of physical destruction.

If this possibility fails us, we have little to fall back on. Let us make it our purpose therefore to nurture it, to give it the chance to bear fruit, to assure that it is not destroyed by fear, by suspicion, or by the reaction of others to what we ourselves do. The act of faith that this requires is something we must learn to see not only as the assumption of new risks to ourselves but as perhaps the only means whereby wholly intolerable risks could be avoided. Only in this way do we have a hope of approaching that state of mutual trust in international affairs which, in the words of the encyclical, "is something which reason requires, . . . is eminently desirable in itself, and . . . will prove to be the source of many benefits."

Pacem in Terris: The response of an African

Alex Quaison-Sackey

Mr. Quaison-Sackey pulls forth from the encyclical ideas of love and tolerance as requirements for both peaceful coexistence and world cooperation. The instrument for these is the United Nations.

To Live as Men: An Anatomy of Peace (*Santa Barbara, Calif.: Center for the Study of Democratic Institutions*), *copyright 1965 by the Fund for the Republic, Inc. Reprinted by permission. Mr. Quaison-Sackey addressed the* Pacem in Terris *Convocation in February 1965. He was the Representative of Ghana to the United Nations and President of the United Nations General Assembly.*

. . . The great encyclical of Pope John XXIII . . . is a guiding beacon in a world anxiously searching for concord and understanding. . . . Through the medium of *Pacem in Terris* he has stirred the consciences of all men, whether or not they are Catholics, or whatever their faith. . . .

The message of Pope John contained in *Pacem in Terris* is clear and loud. It deals with every field of human relations, human rights, economic, social, and cultural cooperation, elimination of ignorance, disease, and poverty, and peace and harmony among men:

> We feel it Our duty to beseech men, especially those who have the responsibility of public affairs, to spare no labor in order to ensure that world events follow a reasonable and humane course. . . . Nevertheless, unfortunately, the law of fear still reigns among peoples. . . . There is reason to hope, however, that by meeting and negotiating, men may come to discover . . . that one of the most profound requirements of their common nature is this: that between them and their respective peoples it is not fear which should reign but love, a love that tends to express itself in collaboration.

Pacem in Terris is both a plea for peaceful coexistence and an assertion that it is possible for people of different ideologies to live together in peace. Pope John did not look at the world with his eyes blinded by the clash of controversial issues. . . . He saw men as struggling for a happier life on this earth. And above all, he saw men poised on the edge of a precipice, retreating from it toward darkness, and crying desperately to be shown the light. He has told us what we can do. In his unfailing wisdom, his clear mind never ceased to heed the message of his heart: that love is the saving grace of humanity, the only justification of society, the redeeming weapon against hatred and exploitation. Pope John saw love and understanding as the mechanism of a coherent international community.

We in the United Nations immediately understood the message of this good man. . . . The principle of peaceful coexistence . . . is in accord with the purposes of the United Nations. In this great international assembly, we have year after year worked to achieve peaceful coexistence, because we would like to think that the days of war are over, since there could be no victor in a nuclear holocaust that would destroy all nations. Tolerance has therefore become an imperative if we want to survive and to save succeeding generations from the scourge of nuclear war. . . .

Pope John showed us the way and it is up to us, the humble servants of anguished humanity, to find the means to proceed even further. We must not be dissuaded by the inevitable obstacles which are bound to be encountered in such a tremendous task. . . .

The world today is centered around the United Nations. It is the only world body established for the preservation of peace in which every race on this earth is represented. We are members of a great organization. The United Nations reflects the hopes and realities, the needs and aspirations, of the modern world. What started as an ideal has become so concrete a part of our international relations that the mere idea of living in a society without the United Nations is inconceivable to me. . . .

Perhaps what we need in this moment of uncertainty is a powerful reminder of the testament left to posterity by a man of greatness and saintliness. Perhaps the lofty inspiration of the good Pope John XXIII will make us realize the value of true, undivided cooperation to make this world a better place for all.

Section 3

Goodwill toward men

The watchmen on the wall

John F. Kennedy

From the text of the speech to have been delivered before the Dallas Citizens Council on November 22, 1963, the day of President Kennedy's assassination.

We in this country, in this generation, are—by destiny rather than choice—the watchmen on the walls of world freedom. We ask, therefore, that we may be worthy of our power and responsibility—that we may exercise our strength with wisdom and restraint—and that we may achieve in our time and for all time the ancient vision of peace on earth, goodwill toward men. That must always be our goal—and the righteousness of our cause must always underlie our strength. For as was written long ago: "Except the Lord keep the city, the watchman waketh but in vain."

Recommended further readings

Chapter One:

The law of change

Charles O. Lerche, "The Crisis in American World Leadership," *Journal of Politics*, May 1966.

Nationalism

J. B. Priestly, "Wrong Ism," *New Statesman*, February 25, 1966.

Arthur P. Whitaker, "Varieties of Nationalism in Latin America," *Orbis*, Winter 1967.

Marvin H. Zim, "Pakistan Feels the Pains of Division," *The Reporter*, January 12, 1967.

Sovereignty

Ann Weill-Tuckerman, "The Malaise of Sovereignty," *Nation*, June 28, 1965.

Power bases

J. W. Fulbright, "Fatal Arrogance of Power," *The New York Times Magazine*, May 15, 1966.

Eugene Skolnikoff, "The New Imperatives: Science and Technology," *Atlantic Community Quarterly*, Summer 1967.

National interests

Julian Amery,"East of Suez up for Grabs," *The Reporter*, December 1, 1966.

Ideology

Alfred G. Meyer, "The Functions of Ideology in the Soviet System," *Soviet Studies*, January 1966.

Imperialism

Henry Fairlie, "A Cheer for American Imperialism," *The New York Times Magazine*, July 11, 1965.

George Martelli, "Portugal's African Provinces," *The Reporter*, December 29, 1966.

Chapter Two:

Foreign policy

Norman Cousins, "The Four Centers of U.S. Foreign Policy," *Saturday Review*, July 2, 1966.

Maurice Couve de Murville, "France and Her Destiny," *Atlantic Community Quarterly*, Summer 1966.

Arthur S. Lall, "Change and Continuity in India's Foreign Policy," *Orbis*, Spring 1966.

Diplomacy

Zbigniew Brzezinski, "The Framework of East-West Reconciliation," *Foreign Affairs*, January 1968.

Charles Burton Marshall, "Notes on Conferencemanship," *The New Republic*, February 16, 1963.

Richard Lowenthal, "Germany's Role in East-West Relations," *The World Today*, June 1967.

Chapter Three:

The arms race

Neville Brown, "Towards the Super-Power Deadlock," *The World Today*, September 1966.

James R. Schlesinger, "The Strategic Consequences of Nuclear Proliferation," *The Reporter*, October 20, 1966.

Arms control and disarmament

William C. Foster, "U.S. Proposed Seven Point Program for Disarmament at Geneva," *Department of State Bulletin*, February 21, 1966.

Geoffrey Kemp, "Arms Sales and Arms Control in the Developing Countries," *The World Today*, September 1966.

Alvin Z. Rubinstein, "Political Barriers to Disarmament," *Orbis*, Spring 1965.

Contemporary war

Anthony Harrigan, "Conflict in the Modern World," *Contemporary Review*, January 1966.

Bernard Lewis, "The Arab-Israeli War: The Consequences of Defeat," *Foreign Affairs*, January 1968.

Chapter Four:

World law and government

Eilene Galloway, "International Regulation of Outer Space Activities," *Bulletin of the Atomic Scientists*, February 1965.

John Somerville, "World Authority: Realities and Illusions," *Ethic*, October 1965.

Earl Warren, "World Peace through Law," *Vital Speeches of the Day*, April 15, 1966.

The United Nations

Arthur Goldberg, "The U.N.—A Progress Report," *Department of State Bulletin*, May 9, 1966.

Richard C. Hottelet, "The Same Mandate, A Different World," *Saturday Review*, July 24, 1965.

Regional organization

Dennis Austin and Ronald Nagel, "The Organization of African Unity," *The World Today*, December 1966.

Bernard K. Gordon, "Regionalism and Instability in Southeast Asia," *Orbis*, Summer 1966.

Trade and cooperation

Lord Hailsham, "Imperatives of International Cooperation," *Bulletin of the Atomic Scientists*, December 1962.

John F. O'Connor, "Winning the Battle of the Dollar," *Atlantic Community Quarterly*, Summer 1966.

Alexander B. Trowbridge, "Harmonizing East-West Trade with U.S. National Interests," *Department of State Bulletin*, January 19, 1966.

Chapter Five:

Avoiding future wars

N. N. Inozemstev, "The Alternative to War," *Vital Speeches*, May 1, 1965.

Arthur Larson, "Can Science Prevent War?" *Saturday Review*, February 20, 1965.

Peace on earth

Luis A. Ferre, "Peace—the Modern Approach," *Vital Speeches of the Day*, May 15, 1966.

John F. Wharton, "The Causes of Peace," *Saturday Review*, July 2, 1966.

List of Authors